a Walking Guide to

OREGON'S ANCIENT FORESTS

a Walking Guide to

OREGON'S ANCIENT FORESTS

Wendell Wood

OREGON
NATURAL
RESOURCES
COUNCIL

Portland, Oregon 1991

Acknowledgments

Of course, many people and organizations gave generously of their time and knowledge in helping create the *Walking Guide*. I especially wish to thank Laurie Gerloff, Diane Valantine, Tim Lillebo, Russ Jolley, Michael Donnelly, Marc Prevost, Dave Willis, Dick Hentze, Pat Loveland, Steve Walti, Judy Johnson, Chris Fischer, Mike Anderson, Ric Bailey, Dave Corkran, Barbara Ullian, Eleanor Pugh, Loren Hughes, L. J. Aurbach, Art Dingell, Tom Giesen, Ken Glasgow, Don Tryon, Rick Brown, Scott Greacen and James Monteith.

ONRC received early financial support for this project from the Mountaineers (based in Seattle) and Mazamas (Portland). We deeply appreciate their faith in our idea and their commitment to its success.

I also want to thank Powell's Books (Portland) for their valuable donation of USGS topographic quad maps, enabling us to confirm map references for the book and expand ONRC's map library. We urge our readers to consider Powell's when purchasing their own maps and other outdoor travel items.

Finally, I wish to thank those who contributed their photographs for publication in the *Walking Guide*. I am proud to feature my own pictures with the offerings of some of my favorite photographers: Diane Kelsay, Gary Braasch, Phillip Renault, John Bauguess, Bob Harvey, Frank Isaacs, Michael Williams, Sandy Lonsdale, Ed Meyerowitz, Eric Forsman, Ray Fillon, Chris Maser, Chuck Swanson and Don DeFazio.

Thanks to all of you, and many others, especially those who came before us and kept the big trees standing.

Dedication

To my wife Kathy, who has tolerated my tireless passions and endless obsessions and has made it possible for me to be involved in a wide range of natural history and conservation pursuits through these last (and our first) 18 years together.

The last two years of weekends and holidays have been devoted almost exclusively to the search for Oregon's most magnificent ancient forest groves in research for this book. The breakneck pace at which we often travelled from one place to the next is not the way the reader (or any sane person) would seek to spend their vacation or to fully enjoy the ancient forest groves, trails, wildflowers, waterfalls and other places of beauty described herein. Yet the descriptions contained in these pages are, in too many cases, still a race against time. The question remains: will our society and nation come to appreciate the irreplaceable values of North America's and the world's only remaining temperate rain forests, before most of these last cathedrals are forever gone?

With you, Kathy, many of these places now deserve to be revisited, while others are still to be discovered—this time at a slower, more loving and reflective, leisurely pace.

Sandy Lonsdale

Foreword

Growing up on Upper Klamath Lake in southern Oregon, I naturally thought the whole world was covered with big trees. The "yellow-belly" ponderosa pine forests of south-central Oregon seemed to go on forever. They symbolized everything I loved about the Northwest: wildness, vastness, and lifeforms of stunning beauty. Little did I know how quickly they could disappear.

The huge old snag on the edge of the woods behind our house was home to a pair of bald eagles who raised young almost every year. Small metal placards on fenceposts along fire roads in the forest depicted weasel-like furbearers called fishers, and implored the observer to not shoot or trap them, because they preyed on porcupines and consequently protected trees. While deer hunting with my father in the Sycan River Canyon on a blustery fall morning, I got cold and discovered thermal cover—I had simply walked under a canopy of old growth trees which insulated the deep forest, creating noticeably warmer temperatures. Wildlife habitat was becoming something personal to me. Little did I realize that these small, everyday occurrences—and many others—were outward expressions of ancient forests.

The once-Great Oregon Forest used to harbor monster old growth trees from the beaches of the Pacific Ocean east across the Coast Range and Cascades to the edge of the high desert, and throughout the Blue Mountains of northeast Oregon. Native Americans and (later) white settlers found a landscape dominated by perhaps the most magnificent forest in the world. Conifers of almost every genus reach their largest sizes here, a result of several unique factors including genetic isolation, climate and soils. These Northwest temperate forests contain more biomass than tropical rainforests, and are among the most biologically diverse ecosystems in North America. Unfortunately, most of them are gone.

Like many of my fellow Oregonians, I didn't notice what was happening to our forests until I left the Northwest, in my case to attend college. My visits home were sobering, as I realized what had been and how little was left. As a budding wildlife biologist, I found myself keenly drawn into the ancient forest debate from the world of science, but I quickly discovered that politics had more impact on land and resource decisions than did scientific facts. This was a deeply disturbing experience, one that many have experienced in their academic pursuits.

After beginning a graduate program at Oregon State University on furbearers and associated old growth forest habitat, I soon left school to become a full-time conservationist. I began my employment with the Oregon Natural Resources Council in 1974, two years after it was founded. What attracted me to ONRC (then called the Oregon Wilderness Coalition) was the sense of commitment I felt from its founders and (then-small) cadre of volunteers to fighting the tough battles over the most difficult issues in the region: timber and dams. The citizens who built ONRC seemed acutely conscious of the necessity not to lose the last of the big old trees and free-flowing rivers which were—and are—threatened by incredibly powerful and insidious forces. In many other organizations, many people seemed willing to duck those two issues in order to achieve success on easier-won battles. I knew, and ONRC certainly knew, that Oregon would cease to be Oregon without its ancient forests and wild rivers.

As we have become more and more aware how important North American temperate ancient forests are, and how quickly they have dwindled, an amazing coincidence has occurred. The Oregon economy has changed. Not only is it in transition, but it *has already* transformed itself in many ways. We need to continue to diversify, but the trends are increasingly obvious. Employment in the timber industry is dwindling, due to automation, log exports and overcutting. Over 25,000 wood products workers have lost their jobs in the last decade; the timber industry now employs only 5% of Oregon's workforce, a far cry from its dominant role of yesteryear. In contrast, the potential for jobs in the commercial, sport and Native American fishing industries is immense, and tourism is Oregon's fastest growing industry. Secondary wood product manufacturing ("value-added"), outdoor recreation, construction, high technology and many service industries are all growing. Oregon's economic advantage, its competitive edge, is its natural assets: the ancient forests, free-flowing rivers, uncluttered coast, open space and way of life which attracts the kind of sustainable economy we need. All of a sudden, it is *economically* necessary to protect our old growth forests, as well as biologically critical that we do so.

Besides the new economic climate, another need and opportunity challenges us— the trans-national linkage first with British Columbia and then the rest of the Pacific Rim. *The Word for World is Forest*, the title of an Ursula K. LeGuin book, says it best. The conservation community in the Pacific Northwest has created or embraced every workable proposal to assist timber-dependent communities with economic transition programs, and have participated in economic diversification efforts which are now bearing fruit. But we must do more to promote regional and international policies and protected area programs, to encourage ecosystem research, and to view this unparalleled forest as the vast diverse global community it is.

The *Walking Guide* is an educational document, not a lobbying book. However, it is important the reader understand the public policies which have resulted in most of these last ancient trees having been cut, and what plans the Oregon conservation community has for these areas. (It is indeed ironic that decisions about something so tangible and honest—land—are made by a process so superficial and inherently unreal—politics.) Consequently, areas which are publicly proposed for classification for Wilderness, Research Natural Areas, National Parks and other legislative and administrative designations are noted. Because the only places on Earth that have even a remote chance of permanent protection are those shielded by legislative allocation, American conservationists have relied on the National Wilderness System, National Wild and Scenic Rivers System, Oregon Scenic Waterways System and similar federal and state legislation to accomplish that end. The ancient forest saga can be no different, which is why there will inevitably and repeatedly be bills introduced into Congress and the Oregon Legislature to protect these and other irreplaceable natural treasures.

It is not the purpose of this book to ask people to act in any certain way or take a particular position, but it is necessary for the public to know how specific debates over public lands have been and will probably always be framed. For those who choose to become involved with natural resources policy issues, we do hope the information this book (and other ONRC publications and activities) provides will contribute to the soundness of the decision.

Over the years ONRC has attracted hundreds of extremely talented individuals, who serve as volunteers, staff, or even members of the Council's Board of Directors. I must confess I never thought a native southern Californian would actually write the book about which several of us had long fantasized: a citizens' guidebook to Oregon's most accessible ancient forest groves. But he did.

Most people in Oregon's conservation community know or have heard of Wendell Wood. One of Oregon's most active leading conservation professionals, Wendell spent years working as a full-time, unpaid volunteer, and served as ONRC's Board President for several of them. Today, on the staff as our Conservation Coordinator, he has his hands on almost everything ONRC touches, and his virtuosity is renowned. Also a former biologist, Wendell finds himself more likely on the phone and/or riding his desk then in the woods. But, for the past three years, he and his wife Kathy have dedicated most of their weekends and vacations researching this book. We are all in their debt for the tremendous effort and outstanding results.

The *Walking Guide* is intended to help you discover for yourself just what's at stake. Obviously, the Council hopes to enlist your interest as a citizen in securing lasting protection for these groves, but first go and experience their awe and majesty for yourself.

For our part, the Oregon Natural Resources Council minces no words. The chainsaws should be silenced in these last ancient forest groves. There are lots of places to log, but not here. These islands of life are part of and fundamental to the Oregon we know and love, and we will defend them.

James Monteith
Portland, 1990

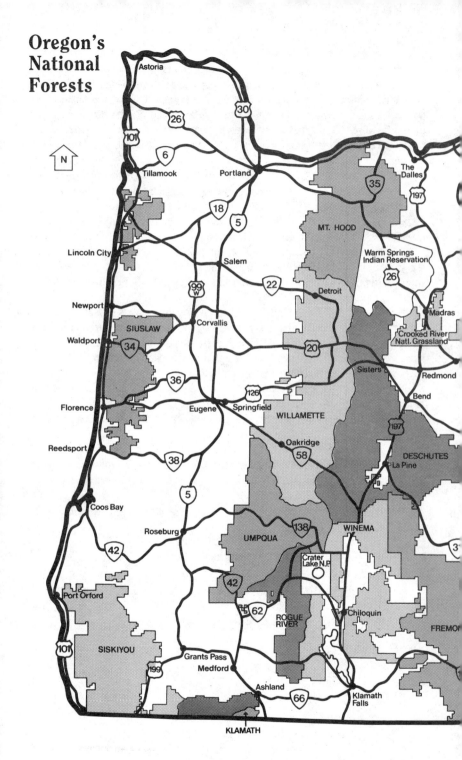

Oregon's National Forests

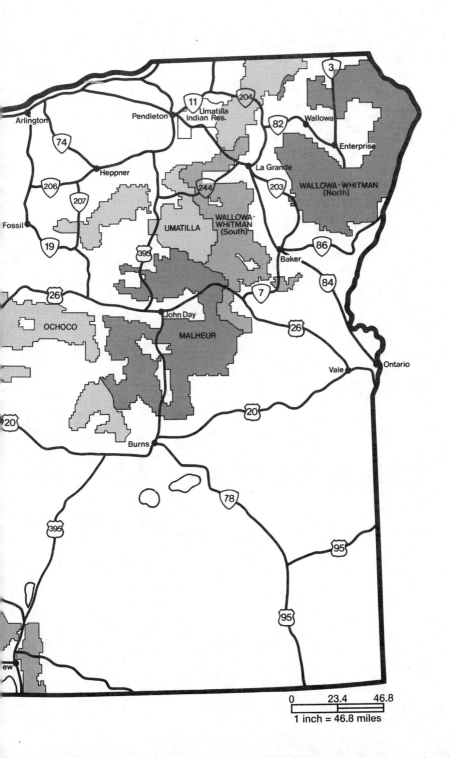

0   23.4   46.8
1 inch = 46.8 miles

On the cover: A western red-cedar reaches for the sky. (Photo by Phillip Renault)

Contents

Acknowledgments iv

Dedication v

Foreword vii

State of Oregon Map x

Preface xxi

Introduction 1

   How To Use This Guide 3
   About Maps 4
   The Ancient Forest Ecosystem 4
   Have a Safe Trip 9

Deschutes National Forest 11

  1. Metolius Breaks Wilderness (proposed) 11
  2. Jefferson Lake Trail, Candle Creek 14
  3. Metolius River Trail 15
  4. Black Butte 16
  5. McKenzie Pass Ski Tour 16
  6. Cultus River, Benchmark Butte 17
  7. Crane Prairie Osprey Management Area 18
  8. Browns Mountain, Deschutes River 20
  9. Rosary Lakes Trail, Maiden Peak Wilderness (proposed) 21
 10. Crescent Lake, Diamond Peak Wilderness 21
 11. Davis Lake 23
 12. Upper Deschutes River Floats 23
 13. Upper Deschutes River, Pringle Falls Research Natural Area 25
 14. Oregon's Biggest Ponderosa Pine 26
 15. Benham Falls 28
 16. Pine Mountain 29

Fremont National Forest 31

  1. Buck Creek, Yamsay Mountain Wilderness (proposed) 31
  2. Fremont Point 32
  3. Dead Horse Rim Wilderness (proposed) 34
     West Side of Dead Horse Rim, Wagon Wheel Flat 34
     South Side of Dead Horse Rim, Augur Creek 36

    East Side of Dead Horse Rim, Tamarack Creek 37
  4. Gearhart Mountain Wilderness 39
  5. Coleman Rim Wilderness (proposed) 39
    West Side, Top of the Rim 40
    East Side, Below the Rim 42
  6. Cottonwood Meadows Lake 43
  7. Crane Mountain Wilderness (proposed) 45

Klamath National Forest **47**
  1. Cow Creek Trail 47

Malheur National Forest **51**
  1. Magone Lake, Nipple Butte Wilderness (proposed) 51
  2. Murderers Creek Wilderness (proposed) 53
  3. Strawberry Mountain Wilderness 54
  4. Myrtle Park Meadows 55
  5. Myrtle-Silvies Wilderness (proposed) 55
  6. Malheur River Canyon Wilderness (proposed) 56
  7. North Fork Malheur River Wilderness (proposed) 58
  8. Monument Rock Wilderness 59
  9. Spring Creek and Glacier Mountain Wilderness (proposed) 60
 10. Reynolds Creek, Wildcat Backcountry (proposed) 61

Mount Hood National Forest **63**
  1. North Lake 63
  2. Herman Creek Ancient Cedar Grove 64
  3. Wauna Viewpoint Trail 65
  4. Larch Mountain Unit, Multnomah Basin Additions to
    Columbia Wilderness (proposed) 66
  5. Wahtum Lake, Columbia Wilderness 67
  6. Lost Lake 69
  7. Eagle Creek, Salmon-Huckleberry Wilderness 70
  8. Salmon River Trail 71
  9. Roaring River Wilderness (proposed) 72
 10. Clackamas River Trail 73
 11. Memaloose Lake 74
 12. Riverside Trail 75
 13. Big Bottom 75
 14. Bagby Hot Springs, Bull-of-the-Woods Wilderness 76
 15. Elk Lake, Bull-of-the-Woods Wilderness 77
 16. Boulder Creek to Boulder Lake 78
 17. White River 79
 18. Barlow Pass 81

19. Bennett Ridge Connector Cross-Country Ski Tour 81
20. Badger Creek Wilderness................................... 83

Ochoco National Forest 85

1. Mill Creek Wilderness and Green Mountain 85
2. Ochoco Summit and Bandit Springs Rest Area 86
3. Lookout Mountain Wilderness (proposed)..................... 87
4. North Fork Crooked River 89

Rogue River National Forest 91

1. Miller Lake 91
2. Middle Fork Applegate River Trail 92
3. Red Buttes Wilderness 93
4. Applegate Wilderness (proposed) 95
5. Seven Mile Ridge, Red Mountain Special Interest Area 95
6. City of Ashland Watershed.................................. 97
7. Muir Creek.. 98
8. Union Creek... 99
9. Upper Rogue River Trail and Scenic Drive 100
10. Red Blanket Creek, Sky Lakes Wilderness 102
11. King Spruce Trail, Sky Lakes Wilderness 103
12. South Fork Rogue River Trail 104
13. Rye Spring 105
14. Fish Lake 106
15. Big Draw 107

Siskiyou National Forest 109

1. World's Largest Port-Orford-Cedar 109
2. Johnson Creek Trail 110
3. Coquille River Falls Research Natural Area................. 111
4. Lobster Creek Botanical Area 112
5. Lower Rogue River Trail 113
6. Pine Grove Trail.. 114
7. Illinois River Trail 115
8. Upper Briggs Creek 116
9. Onion Creek Trail 117
10. Eightdollar Mountain Botanical Area....................... 118
11. Babyfoot Lake, Kalmiopsis Wilderness 119
12. Sucker Creek, Red Buttes Wilderness 121
13. Page Mountain Ancient Forest Grove 122
14. Oregon's Ancient Redwoods 123
15. Redwood Tree Nature Trail 125

Siuslaw National Forest 127
  1. Cascade Head 127
  2. Gordey Creek... 129
  3. Drift Creek.. 130
  4. Drift Creek Wilderness 131
  5. Marys Peak Watershed.................................. 133
  6. Cape Creek 135
  7. Gwynn Creek.. 135
  8. Cummins Creek Wilderness............................. 136
  9. Kentucky Falls.. 138
  10. Wassen Creek Wilderness (proposed) 140

Umatilla National Forest 143
  1. Walla Walla Watershed Wilderness (proposed) 143
  2. Grande Ronde Canyon Wilderness (proposed) 146
  3. North Fork Umatilla Wilderness 147
  4. South Fork Umatilla River, Hellhole Wilderness (proposed) 148
  5. Bear Creek Trail, Hellhole Wilderness (proposed).............. 149
  6. Umatilla Ancient Forest Auto Tours,
    Bridge Creek Wildlife Management Area 150
  7. South Fork Desolation Creek............................ 152

Umpqua National Forest 155
  1. Brice Creek 155
  2. Fairview Peak Wilderness (proposed) 156
  3. Canton Creek Roadless Area 157
  4. North Umpqua River Trail, Upper Segments 158
  5. Pine Bench, Boulder Creek Wilderness 160
  6. President Taft Grove 161
  7. Twin Lakes, Calf Creek Wilderness (proposed) 162
  8. Yellow Jacket Glade Loop Trail........................ 163
  9. Incense-Cedar Grove 164
  10. Camp Comfort.. 165
  11. Fish Lake 166
  12. Acker Divide Trail 166
  13. Triangle Lake, Cripple Camp.......................... 167
  14. Cougar Butte Trail 168
  15. Upper Cow Creek Trail 169

Wallowa-Whitman National Forest (North Half)............ 171
  1. Hells Canyon National Recreation Area 172
  2. Thomason Meadows, Chesnimnus Creek 174
  3. Minam River, Eagle Cap Wilderness 176

4. Baker Canyon, Huckleberry Mountain Additions to
   Eagle Cap Wilderness (proposed) 177
5. Catherine Creek Additions to Eagle Cap Wilderness (proposed) 179
6. Eagle Creek 179
7. Imnaha River 180
8. Lake Fork Additions to Hells Canyon Wilderness (proposed) 182

Wallowa-Whitman National Forest (South Half) 185

1. Mount Emily Lookout and Wilderness (proposed) 185
2. La Grande Watershed.................................... 188
3. Dutch Flat Creek Additions to the Elkhorns Unit,
   North Fork John Day Wilderness (proposed) 189
4. Rock Creek Additions to the Elkhorns Unit,
   North Fork John Day Wilderness (proposed) 190
5. North Fork Burnt River 192
6. Bull Run Creek Additions to
   Monument Rock Wilderness (proposed) 193

Willamette National Forest 195

1. Opal Creek Additions to
   Bull-of-the-Woods Wilderness (proposed)..................... 196
2. Breitenbush Spotted Owl Trail............................. 197
3. Pamelia Lake Trail, Mount Jefferson Wilderness 199
4. Gordon Peak Trail 201
5. Middle Santiam Wilderness and Pyramid Creek 202
6. Pyramids Unit, Old Cascades Wilderness (proposed) 203
7. House Rock Loop 204
8. Millennium Grove, Gordon Lakes Unit,
   Old Cascades Wilderness (proposed)........................ 205
9. Echo Mountain - Iron Mountain Unit,
   Old Cascades Wilderness (proposed)........................ 206
10. Hackleman Creek Ancient Forest Grove 208
11. Browder Ridge Unit, Old Cascades Wilderness (proposed)........ 208
12. Fish Lake 210
13. Upper McKenzie River Trail (North)........................ 210
14. Upper McKenzie River Trail (South)........................ 212
15. Lost Lake 213
16. Hash Brown Loop Ski Tour 214
17. H.J. Andrews Experimental Forest 215
18. Delta Grove 216
19. Lost Creek Grove....................................... 217
20. French Pete Creek, Three Sisters Wilderness 217

21. Towering Trees Ancient Forest Grove 220
22. Fall Creek Corridor 221
23. Hardesty Mountain Wilderness (proposed) 222
24. Larison Creek and Larison Rock Trails 223
25. Warm Springs 224
26. Shale Ridge Trail 225
27. Lillian Falls, Waldo Wilderness 226
28. Mount Ray - Fuji Mountain Additions to
    Waldo Wilderness (proposed) 227
29. Gold Lake Bog Engelmann Spruce 229

Winema National Forest **231**
1. Jackson Creek, Yamsay Mountain Wilderness (proposed) 231
2. Blue Jay Springs Research Natural Area 233
3. Sycan River Gorge 234
4. Malone Springs and Pelican Butte Additions to
   Sky Lakes Wilderness (proposed) 235
5. Lake of the Woods 237
6. Brown Mountain Wilderness (proposed) 238

Bureau of Land Management Forestlands **241**
Salem District BLM **242**
1. Valley of the Giants 242
2. Crabtree Valley 243
Eugene District BLM **244**
3. Mohawk Research Natural Area and
   McGowen Creek Outdoor Education Area 244
Coos Bay District BLM **246**
4. Wassen Lake 246
5. Cherry Creek Research Natural Area and Vaughns Creek 247
Roseburg District BLM **248**
6. North Umpqua River Trail, Tioga Segment 248
7. Wolf Creek Falls 249
Medford District BLM **250**
8. London Peak 250
9. Chinquapin Mountain Grove, Pacific Crest Trail 251
10. Hobart Bluff Grove, Pacific Crest Trail 252
11. Soda Mountain Wilderness (proposed) 253
    Northwest Access,
        Scotch Creek Headwaters and Pilot Rock 254
    North Central Access,
        Dutch Oven and Camp Creeks (cross-country) 255

Lakeview District BLM 256
12. Surveyor Campground 256
13. Abert Rim Wilderness Study Area 257
Prineville District BLM 259
14. North Fork Wilderness Study Area 259

National Parks & Monuments 263
1. Crater Lake National Park 263
2. Oregon Caves National Monument 265

State & County Forestlands 267
1. City of Astoria, Urban Forest City Park (proposed) 267
2. Tongue Point 269
3. Tillamook Head 270
4. Ecola State Park 271
5. Oswald West State Park (North) 271
6. Oswald West State Park (South) 273
7. Cape Meares State Park 273
8. Munson Creek Falls County Park 274
9. Cape Lookout State Park 275
10. Van Duzer State Park 275
11. Oxbow Park, Sandy River Gorge 276
12. Silver Falls State Park 277
13. Cascadia State Park 278
14. Gold and Silver Falls State Park 278
15. Humbug Mountain State Park 279

Broadleaf Forests 281
1. Sauvie Island Wildlife Management Area 281
2. Willamette Mission State Park 284
3. Luckiamute River 287
4. William L. Finley National Wildlife Refuge 289
5. Middle Fork Willamette River Old Growth Riparian Area 290
6. Whitehorse County Park 291

Checklist: Oregon's Trees 293

About the Author 295

About ONRC 297

Selected Agency Addresses & Phone Numbers 299

Suggested Reading 305

Index to Walks 313

Preface

As an "expatriated" Californian, I came to Oregon in 1976 to teach high school biology in Myrtle Creek, south of Roseburg. My parents had moved to California from the Northwest in the 1930's, shortly after they were married. At that time, Oregon's southern sister was no less beautiful (or spoiled) than perhaps Oregon is today. Growing up in the 1960's I lived in Ventura County for a few years along an "arroyo," a canyon with an intermittent seasonal stream that was shaded by grand old oaks and held bathtub-like sandstone pools containing dragonfly nymphs and "toe bugs," minnows, turtles, crayfish and other wild delights. I never viewed it as the small "wilderness" it was, but rather more of a playground: a place to build dams of round boulders, to go on afternoon hikes with my dog, and where I ran my first trap line— for a few hapless skunks and opossums whose less than prime pelts later adorned my bedroom walls.

In southern California, where nobody's natural history memory could recall anything much before "orange groves," even most of these had already begun to disappear. Then, as now, a new lane on the freeway was the only true measure of progress, and new shopping centers and housing tracts (the latter, sometimes complete with bomb shelters and swimming pools) were the norm.

With the coming of the next housing tract came a new sewer. Like so many new developments we have all suddenly discovered unexpectedly in our lives, I never even knew of its planned construction. But one summer day the bulldozers and backhoes suddenly showed up in my arroyo. The swath they left with the ditch they dug was as wide as a two lane road, and it followed the exact contours along the edge of the stream as my narrow trail had, now disemboweled, when it still existed just days before. Many of the ancient oak trees that hugged the bank were also overturned. Once the initial deed was done, a few horse enthusiasts began riding along the bulldozer road under which the pipe was buried.

One kid drove his father's car several miles along its length, but in crossing one major side channel, got the car stuck with both bumpers wedged tightly between uncompromising bedrock. Though the irony never struck me at the time, my little black dog was later to die in that new lane on the freeway, just over the hill where she ran beyond the now ditched and scarred arroyo.

That winter it rained—and I (and perhaps also the sewer builders) had my first real lesson in soil erosion. As my favorite crawdad holes were filled with mud, sections of the white, six-foot wide concrete sewer pipe once again revealed itself in numerous places along the arroyo where only a few months before it had been buried. That spring the workers returned, this time to cover the swath, not with dirt but with a permanent broad grey scar. From the root wads of the fallen oaks high on the now undercut banks, clear to the edges of the muddy water, a mantle of boulders and concrete were permanently applied. Finally, nature lay conquered.

Many of my teenage summers were spent in the Sierras, near Mono Lake, east of Yosemite. Though my father had taken me on my first camping trip at age six, our central purpose was always to catch fish from a boat we anchored on Lake Crawley. The lake was really a reservoir that had been named for a priest after the reservoir's source, the Owens River, was properly dammed. Father Crawley, I was later to learn, had years before won the farmers' and ranchers' trust and confidence, in the end only to have sold them out, persuading the local folks to sell their water rights to the City of Los Angeles. Our Velveeta cheese balls, covering golden-barbed treble hooks, lay beneath the boat on the flooded earth that was once their farms.

It wasn't until my middle teens that I struck a path up a mountain one day, and fully discovered the wonder, beauty and exhilaration of the Sierra Nevada wilderness. After that day, I never cared if I ever again caught another fish in the slack water reservoir they called Crawley Lake. Smaller but wilder brook and golden trout (which hit flies instead of processed cheese) awaited me in the higher lakes. I now walked cross-country along gentle ridges or on trails adorned with firs and pines, and surrounded by glaciated, snow-covered granite peaks—getting there was most of the fun.

One night in the Sierras to the north, on a camping trip at Donner Lake, the ranger who ran the campfire program happened to mention he had majored in wildlife biology at some place called "Humboldt" in Arcata, California. I got ahold of a catalog, applied and was accepted. Those next four years, probably more than any other life experience, profoundly affected and forever initiated, developed and reinforced my awaking awareness of the natural world and the possible consequences of its destruction.

Early on I read what Aldo Leopold had written: "A thing is right when it tends to preserve the integrity, stability and beauty of the biotic community. It is wrong when it tends otherwise." With this I agreed. I received but needed no more convincing.

In college I made friends with people with whom I truly shared a mutual interest in and a love of the outdoors; bought a totally unsafe raft and took my first ride on a wild river; celebrated Earth Day and protested the invasion of Cambodia; fell in love with both my wife and northern California's ancient redwoods; became active in conservation politics (helping organize and staff the Northcoast Environmental Center in its early years); published a field study on muskrats; and obtained degrees in both Wildlife Management and Biology.

As I reflect on the battles that rage today over Oregon's old growth forests, I often think of similar battles that raged before, during and after my stay at Humboldt in the effort to create and expand Redwood National Park, and the many people who dedicated years of their lives to save California's coastal Sequoias—one of the grandest of all lifeforms on the face of this Earth.

Today, all of that original forest that was not saved over a decade and a half ago (in that all-too-small and in some places damaged park) is gone. Yet unbelievably, even with the redwoods, the timber industry's greatest myth was widely believed and perpetuated, that it was just good forest management to cut the ancient redwoods down, to create new "thrifty" stands, for if we don't, the industry argued, "they are all going to fall over and rot anyway." "But when?" a few people courageously questioned, "in another 2000 years?"

Today, we have heard much about Brazil and other third world countries, where we disapprovingly point at supposedly uncaring and uneducated people who are destroying their tropical rainforests at alarming rates. But what also of North America's last temperate rainforests? In this vein, David Brower so aptly expressed, "We are not just borrowing from future generations, we are stealing from them...What is more, these forests may hold answers to questions that we still have not thought to ask." How can the other industrialized nations expect the underdeveloped countries to protect their forests (and thus the entire global environment) when we still persist in systematically liquidating our forests at home?

About 15% of the Amazon Forest has been logged. Virtually 90 percent of the Pacific Northwest's most productive forestlands are already committed to permanent timber production. No society in the history of civilization has ever not cut down all their native forests. If in the end we choose to significantly protect what still remains of North America's temperate rainforest, we will be among the first nations to have ever done so.

I am convinced that someday we will stop logging our ancient forests, and as we or future generations walk through the splendid cathedrals left to stand, all will wonder how it could have been that the destruction of a such a magnificent, timeless resource continued for so long.

Although our learning of the significance of ecosystem destruction has come late, recent nationwide polls reflect a rapidly increasing national consciousness which favors retention of our wilderness as well as recognition of the need to protect our global environment. I am encouraged that public concern will be heard in time, and that Congress will reaffirm, that our planet's survival depends, in part, on ending the carnage in Northwest forests; that these ancient forests belong to all Americans; and that it is reasonable, both ecologically and economically, to strongly advocate and pursue protection for all of the world's remaining ancient forests, temperate and tropical.

Wendell Wood
Eugene, 1990

Michael Williams

Introduction

The ancient forests which once blanketed the Pacific Northwest are nearly gone. Most has been logged; only ten percent of the Great Oregon Forest is left. What remains is an unfathomable treasure of intricate lifeforms and biological diversity, as well as an economic base upon which the Northwest economy can diversify and flourish.

The *Walking Guide* contains only examples of Oregon's ancient forests, but with 206 entries (some of which are multiple entries) it does provide an impressive range of forest types. As you sample these places, you'll also get a feel for the extensive overcutting of our forests.

Oregon is a word almost synonymous with forest. With over half the state's 60 million acres classified as forestland, how could so little land remain undisturbed? Haven't we been following sound management practices in the State of Oregon, a place whose past and future are inextricably interwoven with its forests? Unfortunately, almost any way one looks at the problem, the answer is no.

Oregon's thirty million acres of forest varies greatly in ecotype and ownership. Over 20 million acres are publicly owned, but these are generally higher elevation and less productive tree-growing lands. The most fertile forests are lower-elevation private lands. The majority of these high-site lands were purchased (or claimed) by the timber industry during the past century, and have been used almost exclusively for industrial purposes (read clearcutting).

Oregon's public forestlands are owned by the people and managed through a variety of federal, state and local agencies. Best known is the US Forest Service, which is part of the Department of Agriculture. Oregon contains all or portions of fifteen national forests, with thirteen supervisor's offices based here; they cover about fifteen million acres, or a quarter of the state. The Bureau of Land Management (BLM), along with the National Park Service and US Fish and Wildlife Service, are within the Department of Interior. All include significant forestlands; BLM manages over two million acres of important forests in western Oregon, which includes most of the famous "O&C" lands (revested railroad grant lands). State and county forests are scattered throughout the state. What all these forests have in common is that they have been overcut—most of the old growth and roadless areas are gone, and roads penetrate most of the landscape.

Virtually all of Oregon's private lands have been "managed" to some degree, and consequently very little old growth forest remains. Almost all of the ancient forests which still survive are found on public lands, even though most of the old growth has been liquidated there as well.

The actual figures for how much ancient forest still exists are difficult to pinpoint. This is due to differences in definitions, inadequate inventories by the Forest Service and BLM, and to some extent the dynamic nature of forests and the man-made landscape patterns which now result from roads and logging. ONRC

1

estimates that somewhere between four and six million acres of ancient forest might still stand in Oregon, on all ownerships, but we are fast approaching the lower numbers. Because of the intensity and the extensiveness of logging and roadbuilding, Oregon's forests have become highly fragmented. The net result of this structural deterioration is the "unravelling" of these ecosystems as they begin to break down functionally.

Although over two million acres of Oregon's federal lands have been designated as Wilderness by Congress, most of these areas are high-elevation lands affectionately known as "rock and ice." According to Forest Service, BLM and university biologists and other scientists, less than 300,000 acres of the ancient forest has been protected in Wilderness, Research Natural Areas, National Parks or State Parks in Oregon. Almost all our remaining older forests are in jeopardy.

The mainstay of the Northwest wood products industry has been old growth, but this will soon no longer be true. The Pacific Northwest is currently undergoing the transition to a second growth economy. A more diversified economic structure will place more emphasis on sport and commercial fisheries, tourism, outdoor recreation, retirement industries, agriculture, technology, and timber at a sustainable (lower) level. In order to provide a sustainable log supply for the future timber industry, greater emphasis must be placed on small woodlots and other private lands which can be managed sensitively for timber production. Some of our tax, raw material and log export laws must be changed to remove the irresistible incentives for massive timber liquidations by this boom and bust industry that time has once again shown was never really sustainable.

Without the availability of older forests and their uniquely associated characteristics, greater economic and biological declines will result. Not only will we continue to lose much of our forest's plant and animal species diversity, but with basic nutrient cycles broken, the forest's past and present productivity could be seriously degraded or even lost as well.

We can continue on our current path towards ancient forests liquidation, as some would have us do, or we can begin encouraging fundamental changes now. The latter would create a smoother transition to a diversified and truly sustainable economy—where citizens of Oregon, and visitors from around the world, would still know and enjoy (and reap profits from) the remaining magnificent ancient forests of the Pacific Northwest.

There are many issues of forest policy which the reader may wish to pursue, and we encourage such involvement. Developments in planning (for example, the famous Thomas Report, which demonstrated that an absolute minimum level of ancient forest protection for northern spotted owl populations alone would require millions of acres protected from logging and roadbuilding in what are called Habitat Conservation Areas), in court (injunctions to stop cutting old growth forests, roadless areas and more) and in Congress (ancient forest legislation, lowered budgets for old growth liquidation in the budget and appropriations processess, and site-specific bills) all beckon the activist.

How To Use This Guide

Almost all of Oregon's remaining ancient forests are found on public lands. For the most part, "public lands" here refers to federal lands, where the largest and most numerous old growth groves still remain. Consequently, the bulk of this *Walking Guide* focuses on Oregon's National Forests and Bureau of Land Management forestlands. One entry each in Oregon's only National Park (Crater Lake) and one of only two Park Service-managed National Monuments (Oregon Caves) are included. But there do exist significant remnant stands of ancient forest on state and county lands, and a chapter is dedicated to them. (In two instances, for purposes of proximity, state-owned ancient forest entries are included in National Forest chapters: La Pine State Recreation Area in the Deschutes National Forest chapter, and Bridge Creek Wildlife Management Area in the Umatilla National Forest chapter.) Finally, the least-known old growth forests, deciduous trees, are of great interest, and some notable examples are included in the final chapter.

A Walking Guide to Oregon's Ancient Forests is intended for use by all citizens, not just those willing to undergo strenuous expeditions deep into the wilderness. Although there are outstanding groves of ancient trees awaiting those hardy explorers, this *Walking Guide* focuses on the most accessible and easy-to-locate stands, almost all of which can be reached by anyone with a regular passenger car, the willingness to walk short distances, and the ability to read road maps and follow trail directions. (A few are accessible by wheelchair-bound and other physically limited citizens as well.)

Each chapter begins with an overview/locator map, and then proceeds with individual entries noted on the map. Each entry includes a brief description, location and name of the correlating topographic map(s), followed by a more detailed description of the area's resources and specific instructions how to find the ancient forest grove(s) of note. You will need a State of Oregon highway map, as well as recreation maps for each National Forest you want to visit. The statewide Bureau of Land Management map is essential for that chapter. Site-specific maps are included for the few entries that require them.

These entries have been field-checked by the author and those who have contributed to the book. Special note has been made of those situations of which the reader should be aware, such as especially dangerous roads or places one might easily get stuck. But it is Oregon Natural Resource Council's hope that you will participate in the evolution of this *Walking Guide*, and we welcome your comments. Undoubtedly, there are errors or less-than-clear directions, and we need to know about them. It is likely that some of these stands may be cut (we hope not, but...), or might be affected by "natural" events, like windthrow. You may wish to nominate new places for inclusion in future editions. Please inform us of such observations and suggestions. After all, these are your forests, and the more accurate and comprehensive this *Walking Guide* is, the more likely they will be there tomorrow.

About Maps

Why did we not include site-specific maps for each entry? This question was hotly debated by the many people who spent more than two years working on the *Walking Guide*, most of whom are familiar with guidebooks of many kinds. For several reasons, it was decided that entry-specific maps would not add to the book's utility, but would increase costs significantly. First, you need a National Forest (and even highway) recreation map to find the general area of each entry anyway. It seemed redundant to include that information on hundreds of maps in the book when Forest Service recreation maps would do the job, probably at higher quality than we could afford to produce.

Secondly, many of the entries are on trails already on those same National Forest recreation maps. When they are not, instructions to locate them are quite specific in the text. In those cases where there may be confusion, site-specific maps are included. Lastly, including maps for over 200 entries would have vastly (and needlessly) increased the size and expense of a handbook already much larger than originally envisioned. If it becomes obvious those additional maps would greatly enhance the *Walking Guide*, they will be included in the second edition.

There are many different and quite detailed maps available from government agencies, especially on-the-ground managers. Forest Service Ranger Districts and BLM Resource Areas often create their own maps and these can be very handy. In particular, ask for transportation and fireman's maps. Get to know your local ranger station staff. They can be very helpful, and will often provide you special resource or other maps. Others like the Forest Service's "Forest Trails of the Columbia Gorge," the State Parks Division's Willamette River Recreation maps, and various Pacific Crest Trail maps are also available.

For instructions on obtaining these as well as other maps (including United States Geological Survey topographic maps), see **Selected Agency Addresses & Phone Numbers** beginning on page 299.

The Ancient Forest Ecosystem

Oregon's ancient forests represent a forest ecosystem that has developed over centuries, principally devoid of major catastrophic disturbances. Primarily because of their high timber values, these types of forests are increasingly rare.

Throughout much of western, central and northeast Oregon, coniferous forests dominated vast expanses before white settlement, despite periodic wildfires. While these forests represented a valuable resource, they were initially seen as a hindrance to early agricultural development. (Indeed, they were so extensive and awesome that, according to occasional entries in early settlers' diaries, sometimes people cut trees simply for light.) Consequently, their elimination began with the arrival of the first settlers, but has been accelerated since World War

II. Today, less than 10% of Oregon's forests are in an old growth condition. Almost all the remaining ancient forests are found on public lands. Even in the National Forests and Bureau of Land Management forestlands in the Pacific Northwest, no more than 15% of the public land area (counting small and fragmented parcels) still contains old growth forests.

The northern spotted owl is threatened due to widespread destruction of its ancient forest habitat. (Photo by Eric Forsman, Oregon Department of Fish and Wildlife)

From the Sitka spruce rain forest along the coast, through the diverse mixed-evergreen forests of southwest Oregon and northern California, and the wide ranging Douglas fir/hemlock association of the Coast Range and western Cascades, to the arid ponderosa pine and mixed-conifer forest in the east, less than 300,000 acres of Oregon's remaining low-elevation ancient forest is protected from logging as part of National and State Parks, Wilderness Areas, or Research Natural Areas. Most of our National Forests and Bureau of Land Management (BLM) lands are heavily roaded, and clearcutting is still the dominant use on these public forestlands.

Ancient forests, which typically begin exhibiting old growth characteristics at about 200 years, were first best described in a 1981 research publication, *Ecological Characteristics of Old Growth Douglas-Fir Forests:*

> Trees typically vary in species and size; dominated specimens are truly impressive. The multi-layer canopy produces a heavily filtered light, and the feeling of shade is accentuated by shafts of sunlight on clear days. Numerous logs, often large and in various stages of decay, litter the forest floor, creating some travel routes for wildlife. Standing dead trees, snags and rotting stubs are common. It is quiet; few birds or mammals are seen of heard except perhaps the melody of a winter wren, the faint songs of golden-crowed kinglets in the tree canopies, or a chickadee(scolding at your presence).But don't be fooled by the lack of what you don't readily see or hear, as these forests are teeming with life. Current research provides compelling evidence that the old growth stage is one of the two most diverse stages in forest succession. Mature and old growth forests in western Oregon, for example, provide primary habitat for 137 species of vertebrates, including 82 species of birds, 38 mammals and 17 reptiles and amphibians. More than one-third do not find primary habitat outside this forest type, and

at least 45 species will not occur in intensively managed, short-rotation plantations that do not contain abundant snags, broken top trees and fallen logs. Hundreds of invertebrate species also inhabit the ancient forest. A single grove may support over 155 species in the canopy alone.

Ancient forest ecosystems are dynamic and self-perpetuating. Existing old growth trees will survive for centuries longer if we permit them to, and other trees will take their place if we don't convert all our forests to single species, even-aged tree farms. Trees that do die provide important nesting and feeding habitat essential to dozens of bird and mammal species, whose habitat requirements are not met in managed forests. Down logs provide additional wildlife benefits and are one of the most important components affecting the physical structure and biological richness of our forest rivers and streams. Their pure cold water is also essential for the survival of salmon, steelhead, resident trout and other species.

Large, fallen trees in various stages of decay contribute much-needed diversity to terrestrial and aquatic habitats in coniferous forests. If fallen timber and slightly decayed trees are removed, the entire system is gravely impoverished by more than a fifth of its fauna!

One researcher describes the decomposing wood of a fallen tree as "a savings account" of nutrients and organic material in the forest soil. In old growth Douglas-fir forests for example, about as much nitrogen accumulates in decaying, fallen trees as in the forest floor. Fallen trees contain myriad organisms, from nitrogen-fixing bacteria and fungi to a diverse variety of animals. Ancient ponderosa pine and other forest groves behave similarly. High overhead, nitrogen-fixing lichens produce from one to three pounds per acre per year of nitrogen that is contributed to the ecosystem through fixation and subsequent decomposition. This contribution directly benefits the host trees since nutrients are made available to saplings, seedlings and other understory vegetation as well.

Dead trees (snags) provide crucial nesting and feeding habitat for a wide variety of species. (Photo by Don DeFazio)

While the northern spotted owl is one the best known old growth-dependent species, many other animals (birds, mammals, reptiles, amphibians and invertebrates) find their optimum habitat in mature and old growth forest, including goshawk, Vaux's swift, Hammond's flycatcher, pine grosbeak, Townsend's warbler, pileated woodpecker and the ocean-going marbled murrelet. Old growth-dependent species that mostly inhabit eastern Oregon ponderosa pine and mixed-conifer forests include the flammulated owl, white-headed woodpecker and pygmy nuthatch. The bald eagle also depends on large old trees for nesting, perching and roosting. Marten and fisher are among the more notable ancient forest-dependent mammal species.

The pileated woodpecker, the largest in North America, provides an important role by excavating large cavities in snags that may later provide a home for bufflehead duck, great-horned owls, and even marten and raccoon. Except for a recent sighting in Cuba, the ivory-billed woodpecker (the East Coast and very similar relative of the pileated) was believed to have gone extinct after most of the native bald-cypress swamps and old growth forests in the southeastern United States were drained and destroyed.

These are important members of the forest community. For example, in western Oregon forests, 30 secondary hole nesters depend on 14 primary excavators, most of which find optimum habitat in old growth forests. But modern forest management does not value this habitat type very highly.

In theory, if not generally in practice, it may be possible to manage our forests to have some combination of either uneven age distributions, standing snags, down logs, broken top trees, nitrogen-fixing lichens, understory vegetation, or trunk rot cavities. When considered individually, none of these characteristics would need to be unique only to ancient forests. However, the old growth ecosystem is unique in possessing all these attributes simultaneously, and in addition, most likely contains a variety of others that scientists and forest ecologists have not yet discovered. ONRC encourages such "New Forestry" concepts be used as a restoration tool for cutover lands: "New Forestry for New Forests." The last old stands should be left intact for ecological purposes.

Despite their differences, geographically separated ancient forests may serve similar functions for the wildlife that inhabit them. On the east side of the Cascades, for instance, Rocky Mountain elk and mule deer seek shelter annually from harsh weather conditions (extreme heat and cold) in "stringers" of old growth. Thermal cover is also an important wildlife survival factor in the Cascades to reduce the stress of hot summers and cold winters. In the milder Coast Range, such thermal cover may be needed only once every ten winters—but it is just as vital to the survival of Roosevelt elk (and even black-tailed deer) when these conditions arise.

Additionally, a dense old growth forest provides important hiding and escape cover. Studies show that Rocky Mountain elk habitat is reduced by 69 percent where one mile of main road and one mile of secondary road per square mile of habitat is open to traffic. Many of the region's National Forests contain six to eight miles of road per square mile. In fact, the Pacific Northwest contains the highest road density in the entire National Forest System. Consequently, the few remaining roadless areas are a traditional high priority for conservationists, and they

7

often contain the largest and most functional blocks of ancient forest.

Lichens on fallen logs and branches also provide an important food source for elk and deer, especially during winter when otherwise abundant herbaceous food sources are not available. Foliose lichens such as *Lobaria oregana* (sometimes called Lungwort) are particularly important because of their nitrogen-fixing ability and high protein content. A single 400-year-old Douglas-fir tree may support 30 pounds of lichens. Once fallen to the ground, that translates into a lot of winter food for elk and deer.

Fallen trees also significantly shape the flow of energy and the cycling of nutrients, and greatly influence the physical structure of streams in the Douglas-fir, ponderosa pine and mixed-conifer forest regions. To the benefit of aquatic organisms, streams in natural old growth forest ecosystems contain vast quantities of large woody and organic debris.

The food base or energy supply of a stream in an old growth Douglas-fir forest is primarily litter from the adjacent forest, combined with algae produced in reaches of streams exposed to light. Pristine streams retain much of the forest litter. Fallen trees in a stream form "stairsteps" that allow over 70 percent of the litter to be retained long enough to be biologically processed by stream organisms, upon which trout and steelhead feed. Nitrogen fixation on fallen trees in streams accounts for five to ten percent of the annual nitrogen supply of the stream. Additional fallen trees and rootwads buffer the stream bank from swift currents. These trees form obstructions which dissipate some of the stream's energy and create pools used by salmon, steelhead and other fish.

The red tree vole is an example of a very specialized animal who may spend his or her entire life in the ancient forest canopy. (Photo by Chris Maser)

In addition to providing even flows of clear water for domestic water supplies, fisheries and recreation, ancient forests provide habitat for other freshwater organisms (including the tailed frog and Cope's giant salamander), which also benefit from the high water quality associated with old growth forests.

Have a Safe Trip

As you explore Oregon's forest legacy, don't forget that weather and other conditions can change rapidly. Although we have strived to include many relatively accessible, low-elevation sites to visit, these ancient forests grow in a rugged climate that can turn merciless without notice.

All travelers into Oregon's forests—no matter how brief or "easy" the trip may be—should carry a water-repellent parka and a rucksack with the following essentials (Sullivan, 1988):

1. Extra clothing
2. Extra food
3. Sunglasses
4. Knife
5. Firestarter (candle or butane lighter)
6. First aid kit
7. Matches in a waterproof container
8. Flashlight
9. Map (topographic maps are best)
10. Compass (and knowledge to use it)
11. Extra water

There are a few other obvious rules to observe. Be sure you notify someone of your plans, so if you get stuck or lost they will know you are missing. Lost hikers should stay put, and keep warm and dry. Lock your car, if yours locks. Be sure to leave gates as you find them.

Please remember that even though entries in the *Walking Guide* have been field-checked, mileages and descriptions are approximate. Conditions may change. Leave yourself a little breathing room time-wise, and don't take any unnecessary chances on bad roads, etc. Again, let us know of unexpected problems or conditions you encounter so that future editions of the *Walking Guide* are more accurate and useful.

Have fun, use common sense, and enjoy your adventures in the Great Oregon Forest.

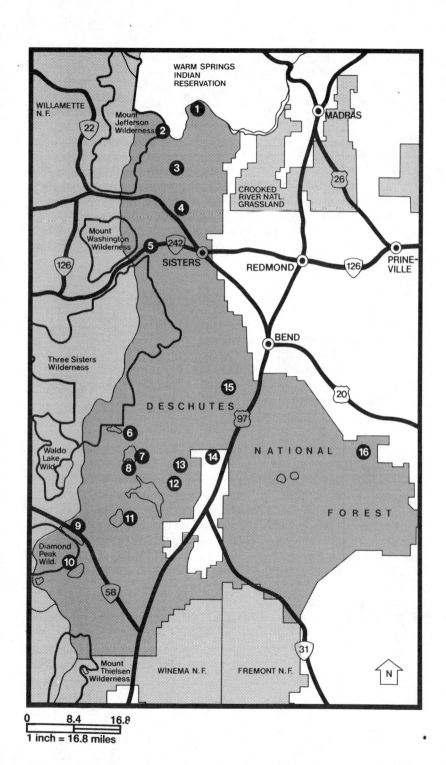

WARM SPRINGS
INDIAN
RESERVATION

WILLAMETTE
N. F.

Mount
Jefferson
Wilderness

MADRAS

CROOKED
RIVER NATL.
GRASSLAND

Mount
Washington
Wilderness

SISTERS

REDMOND

PRINE-
VILLE

Three Sisters
Wilderness

BEND

DESCHUTES

Waldo Lake
Wild.

NATIONAL

Diamond
Peak
Wild.

FOREST

Mount
Thielsen
Wilderness

WINEMA N. F.

FREMONT N. F.

N

0   8.4   16.8
1 inch = 16.8 miles

Deschutes National Forest

The Deschutes National Forest, headquartered in Bend, is named for the raging river which drains much of it. In many ways the Deschutes is the fastest changing National Forest in Oregon, as central Oregon's economy is quickly experiencing the classic transition from timber to a multi-faceted service-based economy, with emphasis largely on tourism and outdoor recreation, especially skiing, hunting and fishing. As the Bend-Redmond metropolis expands and Oregon's economy continues to diversify, growing public awareness of these last great pine forests may help protect them.

This 1.5-million acre National Forest includes the east side of the central Oregon Cascades and the edge of the high desert, including the newly designated Newberry National Volcanic Monument.

It is managed on the ground through four ranger districts.

The Deschutes Forest is home to some of Oregon's finest groves of ponderosa pine. As elsewhere throughout central and northeast Oregon, the big pine stands have been extensively high-graded, and true ancient ponderosa pine forests are extremely rare. But several areas on the Deschutes remain legendary, including the Metolius, which Oregon conservationists and local citizen and business groups propose be designated the Metolius National Conservation Area by Congress. Examples of old growth pine groves throughout the Deschutes National Forest are included in this *Walking Guide*.

Don't forget your Deschutes National Forest recreation map.

1. Metolius Breaks Wilderness (proposed)

Scattered ancient groves of ponderosa pine, Douglas-fir, incense-cedar, sugar pine and smaller western larch, along and above the beautiful Metolius River.

Sisters Ranger District
USGS 15' WHITEWATER RIVER (1961)

ABOUT THE AREA
The proposed Metolius Breaks Wilderness is a horseshoe-shaped roadless area bounded on the outside by a dirt road and trail along the Metolius River. The ex-

treme inside of the "U" high above the river canyon (the northernmost extension of Green Ridge) has already been roaded and logged. Ancient trees are scattered along the upper river benches and side canyons. The biggest trees, however, are on the steep, inaccessible slopes downstream from (north of) Candle Creek Campground and Bridge 99, on the west side of the roadless area, high above the Metolius.

In addition to the ancient forest walks noted below, rafting or kayaking the Metolius from Bridge 99 down to Monty Campground are popular ways to see the riverside old growth. Keep in mind this is a swift and strong river. (See the Upper Deschutes River Floats entry for discussion of more leisurely trips along central Oregon waterways.) While there are three Class III rapids along this stretch of the Metolius, the greatest dangers are partly submerged logs. (Large ponderosa pine may reach all the way across the river.) Also, the opposite bank of the river is on the Warm Springs Indian Reservation, and the public is not permitted to land boats or hike on that side of the river. Much to the credit of the Confederated Tribes of the Warm Springs Indian Nation, this area has been left in its natural condition and contains some of the nicest ancient pine groves along the river.

GETTING THERE

From US Highway 97 five miles south of Madras (or 15 miles north of Redmond), follow signs for Cove Palisades State Park to Billy Chinook Reservoir and the easternmost boat ramp. Stay on the paved road, which becomes Forest Service Road 64, for about 17.75 miles, crossing two bridges over the reservoir, all the way to the junction with FS Road 1170. From the intersection of FS Roads 64 and 1170, take FS Road 64 to the north and west—following signs for Forest Campgrounds—for 4.75 miles to Street Creek, or for 12 miles to the riverside trail (see below).

From the Willamette Valley, take US Highway 20/Oregon 126 six miles west of Sisters and turn north on Green Ridge Road (FS Road 11) for Indian Ford Campground. Follow FS Road 11 for about 17 miles (the first ten are paved) to the intersection of FS Roads 11, 1180 (on the left) and 1170 (on the right). Turn right on FS Road 1170, following signs for Lake (sic) Billy Chinook, and follow FS Road 1170 a total of about 20 miles to the junction with FS Road 64. From the intersection of FS Roads 64 and 1170, take FS Road 64 to the north and west— following signs for Forest Campgrounds—for 4.75 miles to Street Creek, or for 12 miles to the riverside trail (see below).

RECOMMENDED

From the east side of the proposed Metolius Breaks Wilderness, near Billy Chinook Reservoir, two trails are especially good—one along the Metolius River and another up Street Creek. The latter leads to cross-country routes into the roadless area's interior.

Metolius River Trail: Drive to the end of FS Road 64. The last four miles have some rough spots but can be carefully negotiated by vehicles with low clearance. At the very end of this road, an unmarked trail drops steeply down to the river and then follows the river bank for half a mile. In another half-mile, a trail to the right weaves onto a lovely river bench covered with big ponderosa pine and Douglas-fir. After this bench, the trail passes through a young forest and, in another half-mile, ends at the site of an old homestead on the river.

This end of the trail is also accessible by a rough ten-mile jeep road (FS Road 1499), which begins below (north of) Bridge 99 in the upper Metolius River Recreation Area several miles north of Camp Sherman. (This route is for high clearance vehicles only, preferably with four-wheel drive, or for hardy souls willing to climb to the biggest trees, high above the river.) This western side of the proposed Wilderness has outstanding views of the Metolius River Basin. Unfortunately, the Forest Service has selectively removed many of the really big trees along the road paralleling this portion of the river. To reach the riverside trail described above from this west side, go to the very end of the jeep road (beyond the homestead) and then bear right on an unmarked trail.

An old growth Pacific yew leans over the Metolius River. Trees from 12 to 20 inches in diameter range from 150 to 250 years of age.

Street Creek: This is probably the easiest way into the interior of the proposed Metolius Breaks Wilderness. The trailhead to Street Creek is west of FS Road 64, two miles beyond (north of) Perry South Campground, opposite gated FS Road 660 and beside a sign for "Monty Campground 3 miles." An unmarked but easily located trail follows the north side of the creek for a half-mile past a few large Douglas-fir and ponderosa pine in the canyon bottom. At the end of the trail, head up the hill on your right and continue upstream just above the older streamside forest; follow the same contour along the ill-defined deer trails. Vegetation on this south-facing slope is relatively sparse but includes lots of spring-blooming wildflowers. This eastern end of the proposed Wilderness Area is particularly interesting as a transition between Cascade montane forest communities and the more arid western juniper forests characteristic of eastern Oregon.

As you continue upstream, you'll pass dark basalt formations, cliffs of hardened white volcanic ash, and a cave sculpted by centuries of rain. About two miles up the canyon it is possible to hike straight to the top of the north (south-facing) rim along a smaller side canyon. Here is a mesa topped with ancient junipers and ponderosa pine, with an unobstructed view of the Street Creek drainage. Lovers of undisturbed landscapes will be pleased to note the absence of cattle in this open and pristine rangeland. You can follow this rim further into the proposed Wilderness, or walk back along the canyon from the direction you came.

Some of the biggest Douglas-fir trees on the east slope of the Cascades are found at this trailhead into the Mount Jefferson Wilderness.

2. Jefferson Lake Trail, Candle Creek

Record Rocky Mountain Douglas-fir at a trailhead for the popular Mount Jefferson Wilderness.

Sisters Ranger District
USGS 15' WHITEWATER RIVER (1961)

ABOUT THE AREA

This is a classic east Cascades wonderland, with the proposed Metolius Breaks Wilderness visible to the north. Impressive larch and ponderosa pine have struggled through lava flows here. At the beginning of this trail are several very large Rocky Mountain Douglas-fir *(Pseudotsuga menziesii* var. *glauca).* The largest, with a circumference of 24'7," is recorded in the American Forestry Association's register of champion trees.

Candle Creek was a major battleground in Congress's original Mount Jefferson Wilderness legislation. These trees would not be standing today if people hadn't insisted on reasonably low-elevation boundaries for the east side of the Mount Jefferson Wilderness in 1968.

GETTING THERE

Nine miles west of Sisters on US Highway 20/Oregon 126, turn north onto County and Forest Service Road 14. Proceed north on FS Road 14 for about 13 miles to just south of Lower Bridge Campground, and then cross Bridge 99 to FS Road 12. Stay on FS Road 12 for about one mile. Turn right on FS Road 1290, then left on FS Road 1292, following signs for the Jefferson Lake trailhead.

RECOMMENDED

Walk up Candle Creek at least a half-mile along a vine maple-lined trail, where most of the big trees occur.

14

3. Metolius River Trail

Largest stands of ponderosa pine along any trail on the Deschutes National Forest.

Sisters Ranger District
USGS 15' SISTERS (1959)
WHITEWATER RIVER (1961)

ABOUT THE AREA

The main trail in this area is along a nine-mile stretch on the west side of the scenic Metolius River, between Candle Creek and Lower Canyon Creek Campgrounds. On the way in, you'll probably want to visit Head of the Metolius Springs, just off FS Road 14. Also, to the east of FS Road 14 (on the other side of the river from Lower Canyon Creek Campground) is the Metolius Research Natural Area (RNA). Signs along the road will tell you when you enter and leave its domain. A short walk through this small RNA will help you distinguish a natural ponderosa pine forest from the sanitized versions that the Forest Service is creating almost everywhere else by repeated-entry logging.

GETTING THERE

Nine miles west of Sisters on US Highway 20/Oregon 126, turn north on County and Forest Service Road 14 for Camp Sherman. Proceed north on Route 14 (bearing right for the Head of the Metolius in 2.6 miles) for a total of 10.5 miles to Wizard Falls Fish Hatchery (paved all the way).

RECOMMENDED

The trail is most easily reached in the middle, from Route 14, at the Wizard Falls Hatchery. (Don't bother looking for Wizard Falls, as it no longer exists, having been diverted for the hatchery's use.) Locate the trailhead north and south immediately after crossing the bridge into the hatchery. While nice in either direction, the trail south is wildest, as it threads

through a rock-lined gorge with a gushing waterfall-like spring. It passes by a large rapid just before reaching Lower Canyon Creek Campground.

If you wish to begin on the southern end of the trail, Lower Canyon Creek Campground is a little over three miles north of Camp Sherman, off FS Road 1420. Turn right on FS Road 400 at a sign for "Canyon Creek Cpg. and W. Metolius Trailhead." Continue a half-mile to the trail heading downstream.

The northern trailhead, at Candle Creek Campground, is most easily reached by crossing Bridge 99 at the end of the

A nine-mile trail along the west side of the Metolius River provides a scenic and diverse old growth forest hiking experience.

paved road, 2.8 miles north of Wizard Falls. After crossing the bridge (from which you can also get to the trail), continue one mile on what becomes FS Road 12 and then turn right on FS Road 980, which dead-ends in 1.6 miles at the campground and trailhead. Head upstream from here.

4. Black Butte

A 360-degree scenic view, including the major snow-covered peaks of the Oregon Cascades.

Sisters Ranger District
USGS 15' SISTERS (1959)

ABOUT THE AREA
This popular two-mile hike passes through big ponderosa pine before reaching the open summit at 6436'. The wildflowers are best after the middle of June, but you might also consider a moonlight hike when the Cascades are dusted with snow if the trail up the butte isn't snowed in.

GETTING THERE
Nine miles northwest of Sisters on Highway 126, turn north on FS Road 11 at the turn-off for Indian Ford Campground. Continue on FS Road 11 for 3.9 miles and turn west (left) on FS Road 1110 at a sign for Black Butte Trailhead. Stay on FS Road 1110, which gains elevation and ends on the south side of the butte at a parking area in 5.3 miles.

RECOMMENDED
Black Butte Trail is not the only attraction. For a longer hike and to more fully enjoy the lower elevation ponderosa pine forest, consider arranging a ride and dropping down cross-country from near the top of the butte to Oregon Highway 126. A steep, unmarked trail starts down the hill 0.1 mile before the trailhead. Another trail begins on level terrain on the right in the elbow of the first sharp switchback, in the northeast corner of Section 33 (see the Deschutes National Forest recreation map). While many nice big pines still remain, both selective and clearcut logging continue at rampant levels in the immediate area.

5. McKenzie Pass Ski Tour

Outstanding cross-country ski tour up the gradual lower slopes on the east side of McKenzie Pass, through big ponderosa pine for the first two miles.

Sisters Ranger District
USGS 15' SISTERS (1959)
THREE FINGERED JACK (1959)

ABOUT THE AREA
Because of the mild grade, even novice skiers will have no problem, as long as conditions are not icy. If you have time, you may want to continue another three miles through lodgepole pine to Dee Wright Observatory at the summit, for outstanding views of the Three Sisters and most other prominent Cascade peaks. The author (*not* a great skier) made this

12-mile round trip in a comfortable five and a half hours.

GETTING THERE
From Sisters drive eight miles west on Oregon Highway 242 to the snow gate near the 84-mile post.

RECOMMENDED
From the snow gate, it is three miles to the first truly expansive look over the Mount Washington Wilderness lava fields to Belknap Crater, Mount Washington, Three Fingered Jack, Mount Jefferson, and visible in the distance, Mount Hood.

6. Cultus River, Benchmark Butte

Ancient ponderosa pine above Benchmark Butte at the headwaters of the Cultus River, one of Oregon's more spectacular streams.

Bend Ranger District
USGS 7.5' CRANE PRAIRIE
RESERVOIR (1981)

ABOUT THE AREA
Of Oregon's many "instant" rivers (including the Metolius, Fall, Spring, Wood and Ana Rivers and Jack Creek), the little-known Cultus River, with its broad headwaters, is perhaps the most striking. A river 200' wide forms in a stretch of about the same length. While the really big, ancient trees are on Benchmark Butte, the Cultus River winds by a nice grove of mature Engelmann spruce intermingled with lodgepole pine. Few people have discovered this area, but the Forest Service knows about it and has been selectively cutting old ponderosa pine and Douglas-fir on top of Benchmark Butte. Logging has not yet destroyed this beautiful place. (See also the following entry for Crane Prairie Osprey Management Area, about ten miles to the south.)

GETTING THERE
From Oregon Highway 58, turn east on Crescent Road at the sign for Davis Lake and Wickiup Reservoir, midway between the 72 and 73-mile posts. In 3.3 miles, turn north (left) on FS Road 46. Follow it for 25.5 miles to the area just north of Crane Prairie Reservoir (see the Deschutes National Forest recreation map). When you've gone 1.2 miles north of the paved turn-off to Cultus Lake Resort (FS Road 4635), turn west (left) on FS Road 4630, drive 0.2 mile across the Cultus River and park.

From Bend, travel west on the Cascade Lakes Highway, which becomes FS Road 46, and continue south to the area just north of Crane Prairie Reservoir, a total of 44.5 miles from Bend (see the Deschutes National Forest recreation map). Approximately one mile north of (before) the paved turn-off to Cultus Lake Resort (FS Road 4635), turn west (left) on FS Road 4630, drive 0.2 mile across the Cultus River and park.

From Highway 97 between Bend and Klamath Falls, turn west at signs for the Cascades Lakes Highway, 12 miles north of La Pine. After one mile, turn south on South Century Drive, which becomes FS Road 42. Follow it for 21 miles to the intersection with FS Road 46 and turn north (right). Follow FS Road 46 for 7.5 miles to the area just north of Crane Prairie

Big pine sentinels on Benchmark Butte overlook the gushing springs which form the Cultus River.

Reservoir. Approximately one mile north of the paved turn-off to Cultus Lake Resort (FS Road 4635), turn west (left) on FS Road 4630, drive 0.2 mile across the Cultus River and park.

RECOMMENDED

A poorly marked trail on the west side of the Cultus River follows the shore for a half-mile to the river's source at the base of Benchmark Butte. When you reach the springs, climb the hill and explore a south-facing bench where more big pines stand. A couple hundred feet up, Benchmark Butte also provides excellent views of the route you hiked along the river and of Cultus Mountain—an ecologically important area proposed for addition to the Three Sisters Wilderness—to the southwest.

7. Crane Prairie Osprey Management Area

Large ponderosa pine, ospreys calling overhead, and views of Cascade peaks along a semi-loop trail on the east shore of Crane Prairie Reservoir.

Bend Ranger District
USGS 7.5' CRANE PRAIRIE
RESERVOIR (1981)

ABOUT THE AREA

Like almost everywhere else east of the Cascade Crest, you will see evidence here of selective logging of ancient ponderosa pines. Still, because of the high value of snags (standing dead trees) and old trees for wildlife in this area, the concentration of big ponderosa pine is probably greater than anywhere else on the Bend Ranger District.

GETTING THERE

From Highway 58, turn east onto Crescent Road at the sign for Davis Lake and Wickiup Reservoir, midway between the 72 and 73-mile posts. In 3.3 miles, turn left on FS Road 46. Drive north for 18 miles, almost to Crane Prairie Reservoir (see the Deschutes National Forest recreation map) and turn east (right) on FS Road 42 at a sign for Twin Lakes and Crane Prairie.

Drive east on FS Road 42 for 3.8 miles, cross over the upper Deschutes River, and turn north (left) on FS Road 4270 at a sign for Crane Prairie Resort.

From Bend, travel west on the Cascade Lakes Highway, which becomes FS Road 46 and runs to the south well beyond Mount Bachelor. Follow FS Road 46 to its intersection with FS Road 42, about 52 miles from Bend. Turn east (left) on FS Road 42 for Twin Lakes and Crane Prairie. Drive east on FS Road 42 for 3.8 miles, cross over the upper Deschutes River, and turn north (left) on FS Road 4270 at a sign for Crane Prairie Resort.

From Highway 97 between Bend and Klamath Falls, turn west at signs for the Cascades Lakes Highway, 12 miles north of La Pine. After one mile, turn south on South Century Drive, which becomes FS Road 42. Follow it for just over 17 miles from Highway 97 to FS Road 4270, and turn north (right) at a sign for Crane Prairie Resort.

Just south of the 3-mile post on FS Road 4270, park at a gated road on the west side signed "Closed to vehicles to protect wildlife, Apr. 1 thru Sept. 30."

RECOMMENDED

Walk down this jeep road, which becomes FS Road 400, bearing left at the first two junctions. At the third junction, the road to the right leads immediately to the reservoir's shore and superb views of Cultus Mountain, Broken Top, South Sister and other nearby Cascade peaks. Continue back on FS Road 400, which winds around some big pine trees, several topped with osprey nests. About two miles from the beginning, go right on FS Road 430, which leads to the westernmost point along the eastern shoreline. Continue south again on FS Road 400 and bear left at FS Road 350. This will take you back to the highway (FS Road 4270) exactly 0.6 mile south of your car, for a total hike of about three miles. (None of these roads is marked on the Deschutes National Forest recreation map, but if you are in doubt as to where to turn after reaching the reservoir, almost any jeep road to the left will return you to FS Road 4270.)

A partial loop hike through the Crane Prairie Osprey Management Area includes views of the Cascades and some of the largest ponderosa pine on the Bend Ranger District. (Photo by Diane Kelsay)

8. Browns Mountain, Deschutes River

Medium and large ponderosa pine on several cross-country hikes.

Bend Ranger District
USGS 7.5' CRANE PRAIRIE
RESERVOIR (1981)
DAVIS MTN. (1981)

ABOUT THE AREA

Browns Mountain is close to Century Lakes Drive, the Crane Prairie Osprey Special Management Area, and several other popular water-related recreational sites. Nonetheless, much of this area's ancient ponderosa and mixed-conifer forest has been sold for timber by the Forest Service, diminishing the scenery for which this corridor is renowned. This area still contains some nice stands of ponderosa pine, both on the west side of Browns Mountain and along a short segment of the upper Deschutes River below Crane Prairie Reservoir.

A cross-country hike at Browns Mountain provides a sense of solitude among the big pines.

GETTING THERE

From Highway 58, turn east on Crescent Road at the sign for Davis Lake and Wickiup Reservoir, midway between the 72 and 73-mile posts. In 3.3 miles, turn left on FS Road 46. Drive north almost to Crane Prairie Reservoir (see the Deschutes National Forest recreation map) and turn east (right) on FS Road 42 at a sign for Twin Lakes and Crane Prairie.

From Bend, travel west on the Cascade Lakes Highway, which becomes FS Road 46, and follow it to the intersection with FS Road 42, a total of 52 miles from Bend. Turn east (left) on FS Road 42 for Twin Lakes and Crane Prairie, and continue 3.3 miles to the upper Deschutes River.

From Highway 97 between Bend and Klamath Falls, turn west at signs for the Cascades Lakes Highway, 12 miles north of La Pine. After one mile, turn south on South Century Drive, which becomes FS Road 42. Follow it for 17.7 miles to the upper Deschutes River.

RECOMMENDED

Browns Mountain lies to the north of FS Road 42. Recent logging has taken some of the biggest pine on the southern side of the mountain, and most of the remaining larger trees are on the northern side. The best way to see these trailless areas is to turn north on FS Road 4285 immediately west of the upper Deschutes River. FS Road 4285 circles Browns Mountain: once you're on the north side, take off cross-country to the top or explore other ancient forest groves.

An easier option is to take FS Road 42 another 0.1 mile east, to the east bank of the upper Deschutes River. Pull off on the jeep road which runs north along the east bank of the river. Follow this road through the big pine along this short stretch of rushing stream. (See also the earlier entry in this chapter for Crane Prairie Osprey Management Area, for a longer big tree hike only a few miles away.)

9. Rosary Lakes Trail, Maiden Peak Wilderness (proposed)

Large Douglas-fir along the first mile and a half of this three-mile section of the Pacific Crest Trail to Lower Rosary Lake; also a great cross-country ski trail.

Crescent Ranger District
USGS 7.5' WILLAMETTE PASS
(PROV. 1986)
ODELL LAKE (1981)

ABOUT THE AREA
This trail climbs gradually past a basalt outcrop to spectacular views of Eagle Peak above Rosary Lakes. The proposed Maiden Peak Wilderness to the north includes habitat wild and remote enough to harbor wolverine.

GETTING THERE
From the Willamette Pass Highway (Oregon 58) just east of the lodge at the summit of Willamette Pass, turn north for the Pacific Crest Trail (PCT). Bear right and drive east past a metal-roofed gravel storage barn to the trailhead. In the winter it is easier to park by Willamette Pass Lodge and ski to the trailhead.

RECOMMENDED
Follow the PCT as far as you like as it winds north into the biggest, wildest wilderness in the Oregon Cascades.

10. Crescent Lake, Diamond Peak Wilderness

The largest trees in the Diamond Peak Wilderness (along the first three miles of trail), with views of Crescent Lake and Cowhorn Mountain.

Crescent Ranger District
USGS 7.5' COWHORN MTN. (PROV. 1986)
CRESCENT LAKE (1981)

ABOUT THE AREA
Of Oregon's two million acres of "forested" Wilderness, only three hundred thousand scattered acres are classic, relatively low-elevation ancient forest. While Crescent Lake (at 4800') isn't really low-elevation, the forested slope above the north shore of Crescent Lake includes some very impressive trees. With the exception of this immediate area, the Diamond Peak Wilderness (like most forested Wilderness Areas east of the Cascade Crest) is dominated by stands of small diameter lodgepole pine.

GETTING THERE
From the Willamette Pass Highway (Oregon 58), turn west at Crescent Lake

Junction on FS Road 60 for Crescent Lake. In two miles turn right (continuing on FS Road 60) by a snow park area and a sign for Camp Makualla and Summit Lake. Continue another four miles along the north shore of Crescent Lake and turn right into Whitefish Campground at the extreme west end of the lake. Drive another half-mile to the far end of the campground. This is also the trailhead for Whitefish Creek Trail, which leads directly into the heart of the Diamond Peak Wilderness. Unfortunately, that trail is more typical of Oregon's Wilderness trails, with few big trees on it.

RECOMMENDED

The Metolius-Windigo Horse Trail starts at camp space #18. This section, which shows little use by horses, begins in a spindly lodgepole pine forest but soon (in only 0.1 mile) enters the big trees. As this trail follows FS Road 60 along the north shore of Crescent Lake, you can reach it anywhere along the road by walking uphill. The trail parallels the road too closely in places, but you have only to head uphill to be surrounded by

Douglas-fir (some over six feet in diameter), Shasta red fir and ponderosa pine. One mile from the southern trailhead there is evidence of an old spur road that crossed the trail, which provides a good route for a short cross-country trip deeper into this amazing Wilderness.

As you continue further east, large ponderosa pine begin to predominate before once again turning to solid stands of lodgepole pine above the eastern end of the lake. Unless you *really* like to explore lodgepole thickets, you should end (or begin) your hike 1.2 miles east of the snow park, where a barricaded road on the lake side dead-ends below the main road and where the big trees start along the road. If you enter the forest here, you may wish to first walk uphill across the trail to some benches with large ponderosa pine.

To cross-country ski here in winter, park at the snow park and head west following the orange diamonds, which will enter the big trees (away from the snowmobiles) in a little over a mile.

A wilderness trail paralleling the north side of Crescent Lake travels through some of the nicest old growth ponderosa pine forest on the Crescent Ranger District.

11. Davis Lake

Scattered groves of large ponderosa pine and Douglas-fir.

Crescent Ranger District
USGS 7.5' DAVIS MTN. (1981)
HAMNER BUTTE (1981)

ABOUT THE AREA

Near an impressive lava flow, one can walk through big ponderosa pine for three miles along the east shore of Davis Lake. Directly west across the lake is the proposed Maiden Peak Wilderness, with Maiden Peak itself at the crest of the Cascades. Besides terrific scenery, Davis Lake provides outstanding bird and wildlife viewing opportunities along its shores.

GETTING THERE

Turn east off the Willamette Pass Highway (Oregon 58) on Crescent Road at the sign for Davis Lake/Wickiup Reservoir, south of Crescent and midway between the 72 and 73-mile posts. In 3.3 miles turn left on FS Road 46, and drive 7.7 miles to a sign for Davis Lake Campgrounds.

RECOMMENDED

From Davis Lake Campgrounds, turn left and then immediately right, and drive north along the east shore of Davis Lake for three miles, following signs for Lava

Flow Campground to the northeast side of the lake. Along the south end of the lake, a trail through a riparian area connects East and West Davis Lake Campgrounds, though there are only a few big trees here.

For a short cross-country side trip, drive a total of 7.5 miles on FS Road 46 and park on the east side of the road, past a sign for Davis Lake Junction. (Just ahead, in 0.2 mile, is the turn-off for Davis Lake Campgrounds.) Opposite the next Do Not Pass sign, hike directly east (perpendicular to the road) into the woods. A just-visible trail leads past some nice ponderosa pine, large Douglas-fir and a few big western larch. The forest here is really just a narrow scenic corridor, and as you head east you'll enter a large shelterwood cut. Yet another option is an old skid road, which heads east (right) 0.8 mile north of the Davis Lake Campground turn-off, and leads through some more big pine.

12. Upper Deschutes River Floats

Some of the easiest and prettiest float trips in Oregon, past occasional large ponderosa pine, on a portion of the Deschutes designated a federal Wild and Scenic River in 1988.

Bend Ranger District
USGS 30' X 60' (1:100,000) LA PINE (1986)
USGS 7.5' WICKIUP DAM (1963)
LA PINE (1981)
PISTOL BUTTE (1981)
ANNS BUTTE (1981)

ABOUT THE AREA

The biggest trees on the Deschutes River are along this stretch, from just below Wickiup Reservoir to the La Pine State Recreation Area. Three of the best short

float trips are (heading downstream): from one mile above Bull Bend Campground to Wyeth Campground; from Pringle Falls Campground to just *before* Tetherow Campground; and from the Tetherow

Boat Launch to La Pine State Recreation Area. While it is possible to float downstream to the Big River Campground from the Tetherow Boat Launch without portaging, major falls at Tetherow, and especially at Pringle Falls, prohibit an uninterrupted float from Bull Bend to Big River. It is always a good idea to check with local agency personnel about conditions on and along the river before putting in, especially during high or low water.

The easiest river access is at Big River Campground, four miles downstream (north) of the La Pine State Recreation Area and about five miles west of US Highway 97 on County Route 42. If you are going from Tetherow Boat Launch to La Pine State Recreation Area, read the entry for Oregon's Biggest Ponderosa Pine in this chapter. (See also the following Upper Deschutes River, Pringle Falls Research Natural Area entry for other ancient forest hikes in the vicinity.)

GETTING THERE

Take US Highway 97 about 25 miles south of Bend. Turn west on County/FS Road 43 near the 165-mile post at Wickiup Junction, and drive about seven miles west to the intersection of FS Roads 43, 44 and 500, just before the Deschutes River.

To reach Wyeth and Bull Bend Campgrounds and the river above them, continue west on FS Road 43 for another 0.6 mile across the Deschutes to FS Road 4370. Turn south (left) on FS Road 4370 and drive 0.15 mile to Wyeth Campground. (This is the best place to pull out if you are canoeing above Pringle Falls. Another nice take-out is at Bull Bend

Campground, about 1.2 miles upstream on FS Road 4370.)

To reach Tetherow Boat Launch and Pringle Falls Campground below the falls—which are really a rapids—turn north (right) on FS Road 500. For Pringle Falls Campground, after 0.2 mile turn west (left) on the road marked Pringle Falls Campground and drive a half-mile through some large ponderosa pine. Otherwise, bear right (east), then follow the posted signs about three miles to Tetherow Boat Launch.

To reach Big River Campground from the Pringle Falls area, drive west on FS Road 43 for a half-mile and turn north on FS Road 4350. Drive two miles, then turn northeast (right) on FS Road 42. Continue eight miles to the campground.

RECOMMENDED

From Pringle Falls Campground to just *before* the Tetherow Boat Launch, be alert for two signs, posted on the left bank, warning of the rapids and logjam ahead. A 200-yard portage along the right bank is necessary but easy.

13. Upper Deschutes River, Pringle Falls Research Natural Area

Medium and large ponderosa pine along a beautiful river.

Bend Ranger District
USGS 7.5' LA PINE (1981)
PISTOL BUTTE (1981)

ABOUT THE AREA

A few small areas that escaped intrusion on the Deschutes National Forest are now protected as Research Natural Areas (RNAs). These lower elevation areas are about all that is left on the Deschutes Forest of the ponderosa forest that nature designed. The Pringle Falls RNA remained generally in a natural condition before protection was granted because it lacked really big trees. While heavy public use is discouraged (trails are not provided), it is not terribly difficult to get around this area, and it is fascinating.

For those who do not wish to walk cross-country through the RNA, there are some short hikes and drives with views of some larger ponderosa pine nearby along the upper Deschutes River. As well, several float trips in the vicinity are covered in the previous entry, Upper Deschutes River Floats.

GETTING THERE

From US Highway 97 turn west at Wickiup Junction a couple of miles north of La Pine. Take County/Forest Service Road 43 about 7.2 miles to the intersection with FS Road 43 (which continues west), FS Road 44 (to the south), and FS Road 500 (to the north). Each road offers something nice.

Canoe or hike by groves of ancient ponderosa pine along the upper Deschutes River, above or below Pringle Falls.

Pringle Falls Campground: Turn north (right) on FS Road 500. After 0.2 mile turn west (left) on the road marked Pringle Falls Campground, and drive a half-mile through some large ponderosa pine.

Upper Deschutes River scenic walk: Continue west (straight) on FS Road 43 for another 0.6 mile across the Deschutes River to FS Road 4370. Turn south (left) on FS Road 4370 and continue 0.15 mile to Wyeth Campground. Park here and walk another 0.7 mile upstream. Big ponderosa pine along the river's edge overlook a small marsh by a meandering hairpin loop in the river. Bird and wildlife watching can be excellent.

Pringle Falls Research Natural Area (RNA): Turn south (left) on FS Road 44 for 2.6 miles, and turn east on FS Road 4420 (not shown on the Deschutes National Forest recreation map). You may

park after the turn or continue 0.1 mile to the junction of three roads. FS Road 4420 continues on the left, the middle road is unmarked, and FS Road 010 is on the far right. Take the middle road. Park, if you haven't yet, at the bottom of the steep incline and continue on foot. The road/trail now bears right and continues to rise, heading south past small signs for the RNA. After a quarter-mile the road bears to the left, and you'll come upon some large sugar pine. At this point, veer to the left and you'll be heading into the RNA. You can make a broad, cross-country loop downhill and eventually return to your automobile.

About 0.3 mile upstream (south) of FS Road 44 on FS Road 4420, you'll find easy access to the east bank of the Deschutes River. This area has quite a few big pine trees, at least one of which supports an osprey nest.

14. Oregon's Biggest Ponderosa Pine

An 8'6"-diameter giant along a scenic stretch of the upper Deschutes River.

La Pine State Recreation Area
USGS 7.5' PISTOL BUTTE (1981)

ABOUT THE AREA
This tree was originally believed to be a national champion, but a slightly larger tree was later found growing near Plumas, California. (Also see previous descriptions in this chapter for the Upper Deschutes River Floats and Upper Deschutes River, Pringle Falls RNA entries.)

GETTING THERE
About 22 miles south of Bend on Highway 97 (or 7.5 miles north of La Pine), turn west and follow signs to the La Pine State Recreation Area. Continue 3.3 miles to the sign on the right for the Big Tree.

RECOMMENDED
A short trail leads to the river and the 500-year-old monarch. There are a few other large ponderosa pine scattered throughout the area.

Facing page: While big "bull pine" were once abundant south of Bend, the largest survivor stands alone by the Deschutes River at La Pine State Recreation Area.

A splendid grove of ancient ponderosa pine near Benham Falls was spared by early timber companies for their picnic site.

15. Benham Falls

A three-quarter mile walk to spectacular Benham Falls past lava flows, rock out-crops, a riverside meadow, still water and rapids, all surrounded by some of the largest ponderosa pine on the Fort Rock Ranger District.

Fork Rock Ranger District
USGS 7.5' BENHAM FALLS (1981)

ABOUT THE AREA
The Benham Falls area provides excellent opportunities for bird and wildlife viewing. Artifacts found in the area indicate this was a gathering site for native peoples for at least 7000 years. The big pines remain here only because this spot was used for company picnics by the Shevlin-Hixon Lumber Company, which began operations in the area in 1916 and rapidly logged out most of the ancient ponderosa pine elsewhere.

GETTING THERE
From US Highway 97 about eight miles south of Bend, turn west on FS Road 9702 for the Lava Lands Visitor Center.

Continue four miles to the end of this oversized Forest Service road to the picnic and parking area for Benham Falls.

RECOMMENDED
Take the wooden bridge over the Deschutes River and walk to Benham Falls. A half-mile beyond the falls, the trail passes through a few older trees and by an active osprey nest. Although there are not many more big trees, this trail continues along the river several miles downstream to Century Drive and Inn of the Seventh Mountain. Also you can follow a short historic trail from the pine-shaded picnic area upstream to an old wooden dock.

16. Pine Mountain

Gaze at the big trees by day and the stars by night.

Fork Rock Ranger District
USGS 7.5' PINE MTN. (1981)

ABOUT THE AREA

In summer, watch the stars and sky from Pine Mountain Observatory and camp among centuries-old ponderosa pine. In winter, cross-country ski along the 6600' ridgeline and among more big pines on the north slopes. The Pine Mountain Observatory is run by the University of Oregon Physics Department and is staffed year-round by a caretaker who plows the road in winter, providing cross-country ski access. (Four-wheel drive or traction tires are still needed to drive up Pine Mountain in winter.)

In the warmer months the caretaker gives nighttime star and planet lectures on Friday and Saturday evenings, beginning at sunset. A $2 donation is suggested for the star talk. (To check on snow conditions or for information on an astronomy tour, call the Pine Mountain Observatory at 382-8331.) Immediately opposite the observatory is a small Forest Service campground. There is no camping fee, but neither is there any water at the campground.

GETTING THERE

From Bend, travel 26 miles east on Highway 20 to FS Road 2017, immediately east of Millican. Turn south and drive eight miles to the observatory.

RECOMMENDED

The best snow is at the top of Pine Mountain, where FS Road 2017 narrows and continues along a ridge with scenic views of the Millican Valley to the north, Newberry Crater to the south, and the Cascades to the west. Bear left at the first junction and continue cross-country. In a half-mile look for a rocky butte that is visible to the left where the road swings sharply to the right and descends the south-facing slope. Stay on the north side of this butte, follow the contours of the slope northeast for a mile, and you will intersect FS Road 100 on the north-facing slope. Ski west (left) on this road back to the main road on which you drove in (and 500' lower than the observatory where you began). Obviously, it helps if someone in your party can pick you up below.

Other skiing opportunities: Beginning at the observatory, drive back down FS Road 2017 for 0.75 mile. Here an unobtrusive road (FS Road 100) winds west along the north slope through ancient ponderosa pine. Another 0.6 mile further, FS Road 100 takes off to the east (see above). For an easy downhill run, cut off from this road. The canyon contour will channel you back down to the main road in another 1.5 miles, at the junction with FS Road 250.

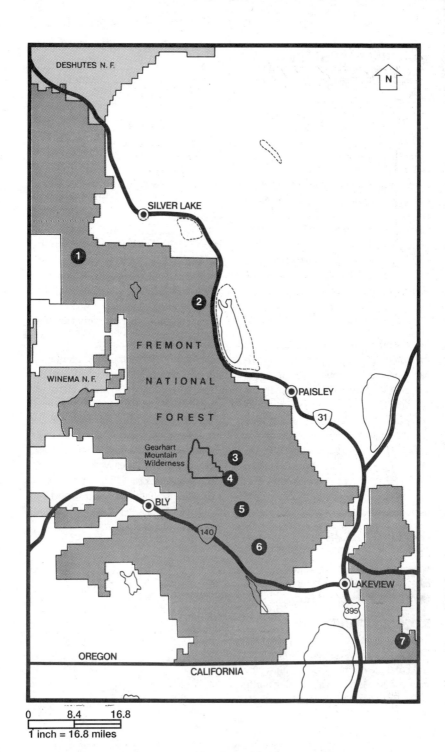

DESHUTES N. F.

N

SILVER LAKE

1

2

FREMONT

NATIONAL

WINEMA N.F.

FOREST

PAISLEY

31

Gearhart
Mountain
Wilderness

3

4

BLY

5

140

6

LAKEVIEW

395

7

OREGON

CALIFORNIA

0   8.4   16.8
1 inch = 16.8 miles

Fremont National Forest

The Fremont Forest is one of only two Oregon National Forests named for early Caucasian explorers, in this case John C. Fremont. Along with the Winema, the Fremont National Forest is viewed by many as a "stepchild" forest of Region Six, more isolated than most and unique in its south-central Oregon setting. Based in Lakeview, its four ranger districts encompass 1.2 million acres. It includes the northernmost extension of the Warner Mountains, reaching up from California.

Like the Deschutes and other east-side forests, the most renowned and prized ancient forests on the Fremont are the park-like stands of big ponderosa pine. Although much of the Fremont has been intensively logged, stunning groves of these "yellow-bellies" can still be found; the most magnificent pine forests thrive in the Fremont Forest roadless areas, which are the last remaining undisturbed drainages in south-central Oregon. For example, Coleman and Deadhorse Rims contain some of the finest ponderosa pine stands in the world.

Don't forget your Fremont National Forest recreation map.

1. Buck Creek, Yamsay Mountain Wilderness (proposed)

Some of the most easily reached ancient ponderosa pine on the forest, along a beautiful perennial stream full of small but hungry trout.

Silver Lake Ranger District
USGS 7.5' RODMAN ROCK (1968)
USGS 15' YAMSAY MTN. (1960)

ABOUT THE AREA

The proposed Yamsay Mountain Wilderness is a 20,000-acre roadless area on the Fremont and Winema National Forests. It's a classic south-central Oregon forest of ponderosa pine, mixed-conifers, and some memorable lodgepole thickets. (Also see the Jackson Creek, Yamsay Mountain description in the Winema National Forest chapter.)

GETTING THERE

Turn west off Oregon Highway 31 one mile north of the town of Silver Lake (or 48 miles south of La Pine) on Bear Flat Road/County Route 4-10. (This road becomes County Route 676, which in turn is known as the Silver Lake Road on its western end, near US Highway 97.) Drive 10.6 miles west on County Route 676 and turn south (left) on FS Road 2804,

Lots of big trees can be found along Buck Creek in the proposed Yamsay Mountain Wilderness.

initially following signs for Thompson Reservoir. Turn right on FS Road 015 about 0.8 mile after the five-mile post on FS Road 2804. Turn right again in 2.8 miles on FS Road 7645 and proceed 1.25 miles to Buck Creek.

RECOMMENDED

Some of the nicest ponderosa pine forest is downstream—but this is a moderately difficult cross-country hike. To head into the proposed Wilderness Area instead, hike cross-country along deer trails upstream along the east side of Buck Creek. In 100 yards, walk uphill and you'll come to the end of a logging spur road which permitted the selective logging of portions of this forest (like most of the ponderosa pine under federal management). Continue uphill along this road, and when you arrive at a "Y" bear right to descend back to the creek. You are now about a mile upstream and on your own to scramble up the creek and further into the roadless area. If you persevere through some legendary lodgepole thickets and across loose pumice slopes, you'll reach large scenic meadows surrounded by lodgepole pine along the upper reaches of Buck Creek.

2. Fremont Point

Ancient ponderosa pine along Winter Ridge, overlooking Summer Lake 3000' below.

Silver Lake Ranger District
USGS 7.5' FREMONT POINT (1980)

ABOUT THE AREA

Winter Ridge and the summit of Fremont Point (7134') are among the most spectacular viewpoints on the Fremont National Forest. On the road in, you can see the Three Sisters to the northwest; due east from the rim is the famous notch in Steens Mountain, Kiger Gorge.

GETTING THERE

From Oregon Highway 31, turn west on FS Road 2901. This turn is near Picture Rock Pass, just north of the north end of Summer Lake, about 17 miles south of Silver Lake and 34 miles north of Paisley. Continue on FS Road 2901 for 12.7 (mostly paved) miles. Bear left on FS Road 2901 one-third mile after the junction with FS Road 3012 (to the right), then take the next left onto an unmarked red cinder road, FS Road 3004C. In 1.2 miles FS Road 3004C joins FS Road 3004, which follows the rim. Turn right and drive another 1.5 miles to a barbed wire fence and gate across the road. (Neither FS Road 3004 nor FS Road 3004C are shown on the Fremont National Forest recreation map.)

RECOMMENDED

You can drive all the way to the summit at Fremont Point, but the road gets a lot worse after the fence. To enjoy the ponderosa pine forest and scenic views along the rim, park at the fence and walk another two miles south along the road (or cross-country along the top of the ridge) to Fremont Point. You'll find a fire lookout tower and a small cabin.

For a longer hike, descend from the top of the rim to Summer Lake and Highway 31. The poorly defined Harris Trail winds down from Winter Ridge to the northeast through a little-disturbed ponderosa pine forest, beginning about 150 yards north of (before coming to) the fence. A post on the left, but not a sign, also marks the rough beginning of this trail from FS Road 3004. Harris Trail meets Highway 31 at an unmarked trailhead three-quarters of a mile south of the 73-mile post, opposite an abandoned schoolhouse. As this is a major descent, a car shuttle is recommended.

Old growth ponderosa pine grow to the top of Winter Ridge, over- looking Summer Lake.

33

3. Dead Horse Rim Wilderness (proposed)

*One of the last two large, unroaded stands
of ancient ponderosa pine in Lake County.*

Paisley Ranger District
USGS 7.5' LEE THOMAS CROSSING (1980)
COFFEEPOT CREEK (1980)

ABOUT THE AREA

This 12,500-acre roadless area is just east of Gearhart Mountain Wilderness and north of the equally spectacular and threatened Coleman Rim. One of the reasons the roadless areas around Dead Horse and Coleman Rims have not received the protection they deserve is that—unlike the Gearhart Mountain area—they contain quite a few big and valuable old trees. In fact, the ponderosa pine forest below Dead Horse Rim has probably the greatest concentration of ancient ponderosa—some as large as four feet thick—in Oregon. (Also see the following Coleman Rim entry in this chapter.)

Described below are three routes into the western, southern and eastern sides of the proposed Dead Horse Rim Wilderness, each of which has its own charm and character. Together, Dead Horse Trail #139, which runs along the rim itself, and Cache Creek Trail #140A, which follows Augur Creek up into the heart of the roadless area, make an 11-mile loop hike around the area (see map, opposite page).

The loop could begin either at Wagon Wheel Flat on the west or Augur Creek on the south—or from the developed campgrounds at Campbell and Dead Horse Lakes, on the northern edge of the proposed Dead Horse Wilderness. The directions given for each area correspond to the three primary routes and population centers near this eastern portion of the Fremont National Forest: Oregon Highway 31 at Paisley to the northeast, Oregon Highway 140 at Bly to the southwest, and Oregon Highway 140 and US Highway 395 at Lakeview to the southeast.

West Side of Dead Horse Rim, Wagon Wheel Flat

ABOUT THE AREA

Wagon Wheel Flat is a half-mile-long aspen meadow on both sides of FS Road 3372—the road which separates the Dead Horse Rim roadless area from the Gearhart Mountain Wilderness. On the uphill (Dead Horse Rim) side, the "flat" is bounded by large ponderosa pine and white fir. It is an excellent place for a short hike to the top of the Dead Horse Rim escarpment (from the easy side) through big trees and striking meadows. You'll find great views of the Gearhart Mountain Wilderness on the way up, and a spectacular perspective on the proposed Dead Horse Rim Wilderness area from the top.

GETTING THERE

From Oregon Highway 140 at Paisley, turn west on Mill Street, which becomes FS Road 33. (There are several good campsites off FS Road 33 along the Chewaucan River.) After 20 miles, turn northwest (right) on FS Road 28 for Dead Horse and Campbell Lakes. In 2.5 miles, turn southwest (left) on FS Road 34 and drive 6 miles to the intersection with FS Roads 3372 and 3428. Turn northwest (right) on FS Road 3372.

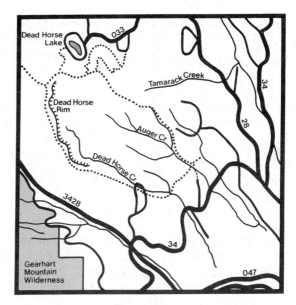

DEAD HORSE RIM. Ancient forest hikes along FS Trails #139 and #140A are best reached by cross-country routes (see text, facing page).

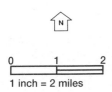

0   1   2

1 inch = 2 miles

From Lakeview, take Thomas Creek Road—which becomes FS Road 28—to the north and west. Stay on FS Road 28 for about 35 miles, following signs for Dairy Point Campground. From Dairy Point, drive to the intersection of FS Roads 34, 3372 and 3428—a bit more than seven miles—on either FS Road 047 (off FS Road 28 after the Dairy Creek bridge) or FS Road 3428. At that intersection, turn right (northwest) on FS Road 3372. (See the Fremont National Forest recreation map for details.)

To get to Dead Horse Rim from the southwest, take Highway 140 to the Quartz Mountain Summit, 13 miles east of Bly. Turn north (left) on FS Road 3360 and drive 13.5 miles to FS Road 34 (the first two-thirds are paved). Make a sharp right on FS Road 34 and follow signs for Dairy Creek. In 4.5 miles FS Road 34 meets FS Roads 3428 and 3372. Turn left (northwest) on FS Road 3372.

RECOMMENDED

Drive north on FS Road 3372 for 4.75 miles to Wagon Wheel Flat and park. Be careful not to confuse it with a steeper aspen meadow which is only four miles from the junction.

Dead Horse Trail #139—and a fabulous view over the rim—are a bit more than a mile directly uphill from the north end of Wagon Wheel Flat. Looking back, nice views of the east side of Gearhart Mountain reward you as you negotiate the meadow. Once you reach the rim and Dead Horse Trail #139, take careful note of where you hit the trail if you wish to return as you came. From the trail, you can see that the point on the rim above Wagon Wheel Flat is also where the forest changes from fir and lodgepole pine to exclusively pine. (The meadow, however, is not visible from the rim trail.) Although there are some large lodgepole pine (two feet in diameter) along the rim, in general the trees get smaller as you approach the top.

If you walk south down Dead Horse Trail #139 (the rim trail), you will re-enter the big old trees, and eventually a Weyerhaeuser clearcut, before you reach Dead Horse Creek in the canyon below the rim.

If you hike north on Dead Horse Trail #139, look for a place where the trail approaches the edge of the rim in about a half-mile. Here you can see a small un-named lake and make a steep descent into the canyon down the face of the rim. A few miles further north on Dead Horse Trail #139, you pass through old growth whitebark pine, and enjoy good views of Dead Horse and Campbell Lakes. You can join Cache Cabin Trail #140A from Dead Horse Trail #139 just over the next ridge and walk down Augur Creek.

South Side of Dead Horse Rim, Augur Creek

ABOUT THE AREA

Of the entire forest in the roadless area below Dead Horse Rim, the big trees along Augur Creek are the most threatened by logging and roadbuilding. The dreaded Augur Creek Timber Sale, scheduled by the Paisley Ranger District for 1990, was withdrawn on conservationists' appeal, but the forest remains imperiled until permanent protection is secured.

GETTING THERE

Recommended access to Augur Creek is in Section 28 (T35S R17E), where FS Road 34 crosses the stream in a large, flat meadow surrounded mostly by Weyerhaeuser clearcuts which border the roadless area.

From Oregon Highway 140 at Paisley, turn west on Mill Street, which becomes FS Road 33. (There are several good campsites off FS Road 33 along the Chewaucan River.) After 20 miles on FS Road 33, turn right (northwest) on FS Road 28 for Dead Horse and Campbell Lakes. In 2.5 miles, turn left (southwest) on FS Road 34 and drive two miles west to Augur Creek.

From Lakeview, take Thomas Creek Road—which becomes FS Road 28—to the north and west. Stay on FS Road 28 for about 35 miles, following first the signs for Dairy Point Campground, then signs for Dead Horse and Campbell Lakes. As above, turn southwest (left) on FS Road 34 and drive two miles west to Augur Creek.

To get to Augur Creek from the southwest, take Highway 140 to the Quartz Mountain Summit, 13 miles east of Bly. Turn north (left) on FS Road 3360 and drive 13.5 miles to FS Road 34 (the first two-thirds are paved). Make a sharp right on FS Road 34 and follow signs for Dairy Creek. In 4.5 miles FS Road 34 meets FS Roads 3428 and 3372. Continue straight through (uphill) on FS Road 34 and drive another four miles to Augur Creek.

RECOMMENDED

A logging road turns north 0.1 mile west of Augur Creek. Drive or walk a quarter-mile up this road along the west side of the creek. At the National Forest boundary, cross the creek and look for an unmarked trail that follows the east bank. This trail is poorly defined, but it stays within 50 yards of the creek. In another quarter-mile the trail you're on intersects a vehicle track (not really a road). This track is Dead Horse Trail #139, which you may follow in either direction. The track to the east (right) leads in another quarter-mile to a large, spectacular meadow surrounded by ancient ponderosa pine and groves of quaking aspen. The track to the west (left) connects to the main trails through the proposed Dead Horse Wilderness.

To continue up Augur Creek, follow the vehicle track to the west but immediately look for prominent blazes on trees to the right (north). This is Cache Cabin Trail #140A, which follows Augur Creek through more big ponderosa pine to Dead Horse and Campbell Lakes and the northern end of the proposed Wilderness. You can make an 11-mile loop along the edge of Dead Horse Rim back to Augur Creek by following Cache Cabin Trail #140A to Dead Horse Trail #139 on the north end of Dead Horse Rim (see map, page 35). Only the northern part of Cache Cabin Trail #140A is marked on the Fremont National Forest recreation map, but Dead Horse Trail #139 is shown. The northern part of the roadless area contains principally lodgepole pine, with some whitebark pine.

To see the southern end of Dead Horse Rim, follow the vehicle track (Dead Horse

The largest ponderosa pine groves in eastern Oregon occur along Augur Creek in the proposed Deadhorse Rim Wilderness.

Trail #139) to the left, past the blazes which mark Cache Cabin Trail, to its end at Augur Creek. Cross the stream and follow the foot trail west through a small meadow into a lodgepole pine forest, and to Dead Horse Creek. After Dead Horse Creek, the now-obscure trail heads up the rim and through a large Weyerhaeuser clearcut in Section 30 on the southwest edge of the Dead Horse roadless area. (You might want to follow Dead Horse Creek upstream just past the clearcut and then climb uphill to pick up Dead Horse Trail #139 on the ridgetop.)

East Side of Dead Horse Rim, Tamarack Creek

ABOUT THE AREA
This is a cross-country route into the east side of the proposed Dead Horse Rim Wilderness, through mammoth ponderosa pine and large white fir to a ridge east of Augur Creek. The number and size of big old trees in the Tamarack Creek area is incredible—probably the greatest volume of biomass per acre in eastern Oregon.

GETTING THERE

Both Tamarack Creek and Cold Creek (which is actually the best route into Tamarack Creek) are in Section 9 of T35S R17E.

From Paisley, take FS Road 33 south for 20 miles, as described above, and turn right at the intersection with FS Road 28. Drive a little more than six miles north, following the signs for Campbell and Deadhorse Lakes. Look for a sign saying "Campbell Lake 9 miles" and check your odometer—it's exactly 3.7 miles further to Cold Creek.

Of course, if you're coming from Lakeview, you're already on FS Road 28. Stay on FS Road 28 past both the Dairy Point Campground, where it makes a sharp right across Dairy Creek, and the intersection for Paisley, where FS Road 28 bears to the left, following signs for Coleman and Dead Horse Lakes. As above, watch for the sign for "Campbell Lake 9 miles."

From Bly and points southwest on Oregon Highway 140, drive to the Quartz Mountain Summit, 13 miles east of Bly. Turn north (left) on FS Road 3360 and drive 13.5 miles to FS Road 34 (the first two-thirds are paved). Make a sharp right on FS Road 34 and follow signs for Dairy Creek. In 4.5 miles FS Road 34 meets FS Roads 3428 and 3372. Continue straight through (uphill) on FS Road 34 and drive six miles (passing Augur Creek at about four miles) to FS Road 28. Turn north (left) and proceed as above, keeping an eye out for the "Campbell Lake 9 miles" sign.

You can identify the place to stop for Cold Creek in two ways: first, a spring is channelled through a narrow wooden trough next to the road; and second, you'll have been driving through Weyerhaeuser clearcuts, and Cold Creek is as close as FS Road 28 gets to real forest in the unlogged roadless area. (See Section 9 of T35S R17E on the Fremont National Forest recreation map for clarification.)

RECOMMENDED

Park at the spring and follow the south bank of Cold Creek upstream (west) through the clearcut into the dense forest. About 100 yards into the forest, bear left and walk up the small rise which separates Cold Creek from Tamarack Creek. Follow this ridge and a series of benches up to the west and a bit south. For over a mile and a half you will walk through almost continuous groves of extremely large ponderosa pine. The big ponderosa pine eventually give way to big lodgepole pine, and you come to a ridge which runs basically north to south. The upper reaches of Augur Creek are below and west of this unnamed ridge.

Follow the ridge to the north and west and you will meet Cache Creek Trail #140A, which you can then follow down Augur Creek or upstream to Upper Lakes Trail #140 on the rim above Campbell and Dead Horse Lakes. To the east, Upper Lakes Trail #140 descends through lodgepole and whitebark pine forests to the developed Campbell Lake and Dead Horse Lake Campgrounds, which define the northern border of the proposed Wilderness. To the west, Upper Lakes Trail #140 meets Dead Horse Trail #139, which hugs the rim on the west side of the roadless area near the proposed Wilderness Area boundary.

4. Gearhart Mountain Wilderness

Large old growth ponderosa pine and some true fir on the scenic south side of Gearhart Mountain Wilderness.

Bly Ranger District
USGS 7.5' GEARHART MOUNTAIN (1988)

ABOUT THE AREA

The 18,709-acre Gearhart Mountain Wilderness Area, designated in 1964 with passage of the original Wilderness Act, is forested primarily with lodgepole pine. However, the first three miles of trail in the southeast corner of the Wilderness pass through a grove of stupendous old growth ponderosa pine.

The latest Fremont National Forest recreation map (1987) includes an inset topographic map of the Gearhart Mountain Wilderness. For more information about the area, you may wish to obtain the Forest Service's Gearhart Mountain Wilderness map (which includes color pictures, topographic lines and written descriptions of the area), as well as William Sullivan's *Exploring Oregon's Wild Areas.*

GETTING THERE

One mile east of Bly on Oregon Highway 140, turn north at a sign for "Gearhart Mountain Wilderness 17 miles." In another half-mile, turn right on gravel FS Road 34 and drive 14.5 miles, still following signs for the Gearhart Mountain Wil-

derness. Turn left on FS Road 012 at a sign for Corral Creek Campground, next to a meadow along the headwaters of the Sprague River. This nice campground is not shown on the Fremont National Forest recreation map.

RECOMMENDED

Gearhart Mountain Trail #100 begins just less than two miles up FS Road 012, a mile and a half past the campground. Follow the trail into the big pines. You'll come to Palisade Rocks in a mile and The Dome, at 7380', in another two miles. By this point the old growth ponderosa and fir are behind you, but Gearhart Mountain Trail #100 continues through spectacular cliffs and meadows, up and over 8354' Gearhart Mountain and out the northeast side of the Wilderness, a total of 12 miles.

If you don't choose to hike into the Wilderness but want an exciting view of the forest close to the parking area, walk down a short (gated) road and trail from just east of the Gearhart Mountain Trail #100 trailhead to the fire lookout on Lookout Rock.

5. Coleman Rim Wilderness (proposed)

The second of the last two extensive uncut and unroaded stands of ponderosa pine in Lake County.

Bly Ranger District
USGS 7.5' COLEMAN POINT (1980)

ABOUT THE AREA

More than half of this roadless area is covered by ancient ponderosa pine and white fir forest, including some of the

largest ponderosa pine found anywhere in Oregon—many three to four feet in diameter. Coleman Rim is separated from Dead Horse Rim (see the preceding description in this chapter) to the north by only two roads; together the Rims' roadless areas contain the last large untouched stands of ancient forest on the west side of the Fremont National Forest. In addition to their recreational, biological and spiritual values, the Rims are geologically fascinating: Dead Horse Rim is what remains of a long-dead volcano's caldera, while Coleman Rim is an excellent example of fault block formation. The proposed 8400-acre Coleman Rim Wilderness was included in the House version of the 1984 Oregon Forest Wilderness Act, but was deleted (along with Dead Horse Rim Wilderness) from the final version of the bill by Senator Hatfield.

Described below are two different ways to explore the roadless area around Coleman Rim. The first route leads to two great options for hikes along and through the top of the rim. It comes in from the west, on FS Road 3660 off Oregon Highway 140 between Bly and Lakeview. The second approach winds into the canyons below Coleman Rim, off FS Road 28 on the east side of the roadless area, and is accessible from Paisley to the north, Lakeview to the southeast, and Bly to the west.

West Side, Top of the Rim

ABOUT THE AREA

The roadless area above Coleman Rim is approximately a mile wide and seven miles long. It includes several big meadows surrounded by huge pine and fir. The view from the rim over the southern headwaters of the Chewaucan River is grand!

GETTING THERE

Take Oregon Highway 140 to the Quartz Mountain Summit, 13 miles east of Bly, and turn north on paved FS Road 3660. Drive 9.25 miles on FS Road 3660, then turn east (right) on FS Road 3611 opposite a sign for Bare Flat. Proceed one mile to the intersection with FS Road 3674 and the campground and meadow at Lantern Flat. (Neither FS Road 3611 nor FS Road 3674 are shown on the Fremont National Forest recreation map, but both Bare Flat and Lantern Flat are marked.)

RECOMMENDED

A grove of large ponderosa pine can be found directly east of Lantern Flat, which extends into the roadless area, but each of the two hikes below provides a broader experience. Both include some cross-country travel, but the walking is relatively easy, up a gradual slope through open forest to the east-facing rim.

1.5-mile hike to the top of the rim: Turn south (right) on FS Road 3674 at Lantern Flat, drive three-quarters of a mile, and park opposite a big, aspen-filled meadow (shown on the Fremont National Forest recreation map as Shepard Camp). Walk southeast, directly up into the meadow. When you think you've reached the top, bear right along a creek bed and you'll come to another meadow. At the top of this meadow, walk directly uphill. From here to the rim overlooking the Chewaucan River Valley, the ponderosa pine give way to large white fir. For an even better view over the rimrock, walk an-

Facing page: Beautiful quaking aspen and adjacent meadows provide additional habitat diversity to the proposed Coleman Rim Wilderness.

other half-mile south. Be careful to note where you emerged from the forest onto the rim (in Section 10 of T37S R17E) so you may return as you came. If you head back from too far south on the rim you will enter Section 9, which is not part of the proposed Wilderness and has seen both selective and clearcut logging.

Gentle descent through a break in the rim to the Chewaucan River headwaters: This hike will take you into the northern portion of the roadless area. At Lantern Flat bear left (north) and drive three-quarters of a mile on FS Road 3611 to the junction with FS Road 17 on the

left. Park here (or just ahead) and walk along FS Road 3611, which enters the old forest and becomes a poorly defined jeep road. Follow this track for about three-quarters of a mile among big pine and fir. After the trail bears to the left (north) and begins to descend, watch for a fork to the right crossed by a barbed wire gate. Follow this track to the right into a long, continuous, aspen-filled meadow. This is the uppermost headwaters of the South Fork of the Chewaucan River. For a true wilderness experience, follow the canyon down past small springs and more outstanding ancient forest.

East Side, Below the Rim

ABOUT THE AREA

The forest below Coleman Rim is punctuated by spacious meadows graced with surrounding quaking aspen, mammoth ponderosa pines and white fir. There are also big old western white pine and a few old growth western junipers on the edge of some of the drier meadows. The suggested route begins with some very steep grades above South Creek, but after a quarter-mile you reach the top of the ridge and the terrain levels out. From the ridgetop there are countless opportunities to follow relatively gentle contour routes to the north or south below the Coleman Rim escarpment.

GETTING THERE

From Paisley, turn west off Highway 31 on Mill Street, which becomes FS Road 33. Drive south for 20 miles. (There are some good camping spots in the stretch along the Chewaucan River.) Bear left at the junction with FS Road 28, drive two

miles to Dairy Creek, and follow FS Road 28 another seven miles to FS Road 016. Turn right.

From Bly, drive south and east on Oregon 140 for 20 miles. Turn north (left) for Cottonwood Meadows Lake a quarter-mile before the 74-mile post, on paved FS Road 3870. Drive five miles, turn north (left) on FS Road 3724, drive 9.3 miles and turn left again on paved FS Road 28. Drive five miles north on FS Road 28 to the second turn for FS Road 016 on the left. (Do not take the first left for FS Road 016 in 3.5 miles, at the north end of Cox Flat. It is not a shortcut.)

From Lakeview, take Thomas Creek Road—which becomes FS Road 28—to the north and west for a total of 22.5 miles, again to the second turn for FS Road 016 on the left. (This route has the advantage of being paved all the way to FS Road 016.)

RECOMMENDED
From the intersection of FS Roads 28 and 016, drive 2.1 miles west on (gravel) FS Road 016. Then bear right on FS Road 046, which dead-ends in a little over three miles near the southeast edge of the roadless area.

Park at the end of FS Road 046 and follow a jeep track off the left side of the road for a tenth of a mile. When the jeep road ends, keep walking north (the direction FS Road 046 was heading when it dead-ended) over a small rise and then down to South Creek in its steep V-shaped canyon. Cross the creek and walk directly uphill (north to northwest) for a quarter-mile to a gradually sloping dry meadow on the ridgetop above.

From the ridge, there are almost endless opportunities for cross-country exploration. If you follow the canyon edge to the left—don't lose track of the steep canyon below—you will come to a one-acre pond shaded by big white fir and ponderosa pine. At the top of the canyon, the steep V shape ends suddenly in an open meadow surrounded by more huge pines and scattered quaking aspens.

6. Cottonwood Meadows Lake

On the way to Coleman Rim from Bly, camp among the big ponderosa pine on the north shore of this medium-sized lake.

Bly Ranger District
USGS 7.5' COUGAR PEAK (1980)

ABOUT THE AREA
Cottonwood Meadows is on the southern end of a the relatively intact area below Cougar Peak. Trails and jeep roads or cross-country walking brings you to big pines, aspen-lined meadows, and pretty streams. Unfortunately, only Cougar Peak's name remains—like Grizzly Peak to the south and countless Wolf Creeks throughout Oregon—to remind us of the species which flourished here until little more than a century ago. (Unlike grizzly

Big trees on the Fremont are going fast.

bears and wolves, cougars are found in other portions of Oregon, thankfully.)

GETTING THERE
From Bly, drive south and east on Oregon Highway 140 for 20 miles. Turn north (left) for Cottonwood Meadows Lake a quarter-mile before the 74-mile post, on paved FS Road 3870. Drive about six miles, and when the pavement ends, bear left on FS Road 024.

RECOMMENDED
In 0.7 mile turn left on FS Road 388 at a sign for "Cougar Peak Trail 2 miles." This road, which goes to the campground, is barricaded in one-third mile. A newly constructed (and as yet unsigned) trail to Cougar Peak leaves the right side of the road 25 yards past the rail fence.

Another option is to drive to the end of FS Road 024 around the north side of the lake. A beautiful grove of large (15 to 20 inches in diameter) aspen can be found at the north end of a wet meadow, across from the boat launch. You can begin hiking north here on a jeep road (FS Road 011). The trail to Cougar Peak (again unsigned) takes off to the left at the top of the meadow, where the jeep road veers to the right.

Deep Creek Campground is an ideal place to see big trees at the edge of Crane Mountain.

7. Crane Mountain Wilderness (proposed)

The most southeastern expanse of old growth ponderosa pine forests in south-central Oregon.

Lakeview Ranger District
USGS 7.5' CRANE MT. (1980)

ABOUT THE AREA

The Crane Mountain roadless area is one of the wildest places on the Fremont National Forest—sadly, the only one where cougars still survive. The Crane Mountain National Recreation Trail runs north and south along the ridge of Crane Mountain, often above timberline. In truth, there is very little old growth ponderosa pine and white fir in what is left of the roadless area. For the best scenery and biggest trees, enter the roadless area from the east at Deep Creek Campground (photo, facing page).

GETTING THERE

From Lakeview drive 4.5 miles north on US Highway 395 to the junction with Oregon Highway 140. Turn east (right) and drive about seven miles on Highway 140, then turn south (right) on South Warner Road (FS Road 3915) for Deep Creek Campground. Drive 15.3 miles on this mostly surfaced road and turn right on FS Road 4015 at a sign for Deep Creek Campground. In one mile, when the road divides for the campground, bear right on FS Road 018. Continue 0.3 mile, drive past the campground and cross a bridge over Deep Creek.

RECOMMENDED

Unless you have a high clearance vehicle, park after the Deep Creek bridge and walk two miles up the narrow jeep road (FS Road 018) along the northern bank of the stream—actually the North Fork of the Middle Fork of Deep Creek. This route passes ancient ponderosa pine, cottonwoods, and extensive wet and dry meadows. If you walk roughly another five miles uphill, you will reach the ridgetop and the Crane Mountain National Recreational Trail. This is probably the best way to reach the ridge trail from Deep Creek, as the trail from a more northern trailhead—about five miles back on FS Road 3915—begins in a dense forest of small lodgepole pine, after two miles of travel on an extremely rough and rocky road.

For a shorter loop hike, follow FS Road 018 along Deep Creek to the road's end (as described above) beside a big meadow, then follow the track up the hill to more big trees. If you head south from this area, you can follow one of the more southern tributaries of the Middle Fork of Deep Creek downstream to the main stem and back to Deep Creek Campground.

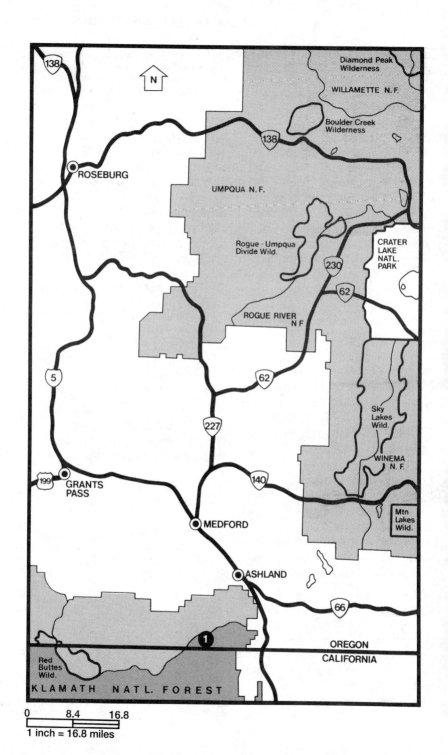

Klamath National Forest

The 1.7-million acre Klamath Forest is the only National Forest in Oregon which is not headquartered in the state. Technically, the Klamath is part of the Forest Service's Region Five (California), rather than Region Six (Oregon and Washington). At the north end of the Klamath National Forest, which is based in Yreka, California, the Oak Knoll Ranger District includes 30,720 acres in extreme southern Oregon. Since this *Walking Guide* is intended to be comprehensive, it seems appropriate to include at least one sample of the Klamath's native ancient forests.

Northwest old growth forests don't stop at the Oregon border. The ancient forests of concern span the region from southeast Alaska to California, including British Columbia, Washington, Idaho, western Montana and Wyoming, and beyond.

Don't forget your Klamath National Forest recreation map.

1. Cow Creek Trail

Only ancient forest streamside trail on Oregon's portion of the Klamath National Forest.

Oak Knoll Ranger District
USGS 7.5' SISKIYOU PEAK (1983)

ABOUT THE AREA

Approximately 48 square miles of the Klamath National Forest extend from California into Oregon south and west of Ashland. (This is the only National Forest land in Oregon supervised from outside the state.) The abandoned Cow Creek Trail follows a rushing stream lined with ancient mixed-conifer forest. Although it is crossed by roads in the upper watershed, the trail extends to Observation Gap, about five miles upstream.

GETTING THERE

You can reach the Cow Creek Trail either by leaving I-5 for Mount Ashland or by continuing down I-5 over the Siskiyou Pass into California for one mile. Both routes are described below, and a loop auto tour is recommended to fully appreciate Oregon's portion of the Klamath National Forest.

Higher elevation approach: From I-5, take Exit 5 for Mount Ashland and follow signs to the ski area for almost eight miles. The Rogue River National Forest is north of this road, while the Klamath National Forest is south and west. About 0.1 mile after the pavement ends, take the first turn to the south (left) on FS Road 40S15, opposite a sign for Dutchman Peak. This gravel road drops down the south side of Mount Ashland for 6.5 miles through old growth Shasta red fir and wildflower meadows. Pass by the first turn to the right for FS Road 40S16, but take the second turn to the right just ahead on FS Road 40S16, opposite the junction with FS Road 40S06. Drive 2.5 miles on FS Road 40S16 and turn west (right) on FS Road 41S15.1 at a sign for "Sterling Mt. 5 miles." In 0.3 mile, before a bridge over Cow Creek, continue ahead to the camp area and the unmarked trailhead.

Lower elevation approach: One mile south of the Oregon/California border, turn off I-5 at Hilt. Cross the railroad tracks in downtown Hilt and drive 13 miles west on a mostly surfaced road which becomes FS Road 11. Turn right at a sign for Mount Ashland on FS Road 40S16, and continue approximately four miles to the junction with FS Road 41S15.1 (see above).

RECOMMENDED

The lower, unmarked trailhead is at the end of a spur off FS Road 41S15.1. A perfect camping spot is located on a broad old growth-covered bench beside the stream 0.1 mile before the spur road turns into a trail.

The trail follows the north side of Cow Creek. Dominant tree species on the lower elevation trail are (in order of abundance) Douglas-fir, white fir, sugar pine, Port-Orford-cedar and ponderosa pine. Bigleaf maple and Pacific yew are also plentiful along the stream.

Facing page: Big Port-Orford-cedar are among the many conifers along Cow Creek.

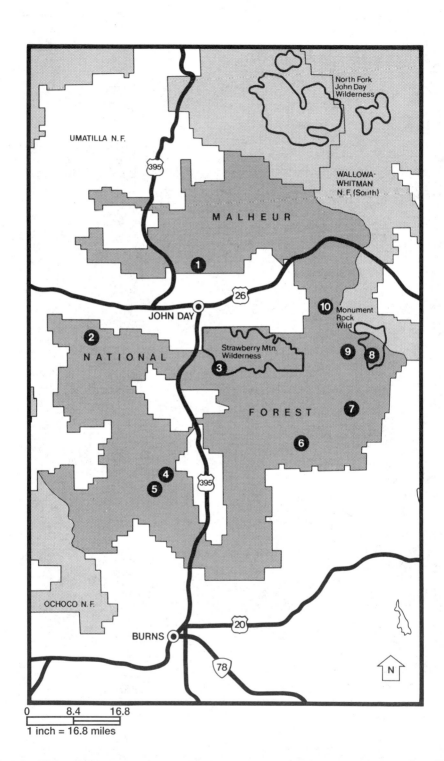

North Fork
John Day
Wilderness

UMATILLA N.F.

395

WALLOWA-
WHITMAN
N.F. (South)

MALHEUR

1

26

10 Monument
Rock
Wild

JOHN DAY

2

9   8

NATIONAL

Strawberry Mtn.
Wilderness

3

FOREST

7

6

4

5

395

OCHOCO N.F.

20

BURNS

78

N

0   8.4   16.8
1 inch = 16.8 miles

Malheur National Forest

Names of National Forests can be intriguing. This beautiful forest is very popular, regardless of the fact that its name has a French origin meaning roughly "bad feeling." Times weren't always easy on the frontier! But the Malheur National Forest, with more old growth ponderosa pine than any other, contains some of the most hallowed ancient forests in Oregon. It also enjoys a history of citizen involvement that has resulted in many conservation victories over the decades.

Serving as the headwaters for a large and significant river system of the same name, the John Day-based Malheur Forest is managed through four ranger districts which comprise 1.5 million acres. It contains a series of small but important roadless areas across the forest, and is best known for its east-west Strawberry Range, which is largely protected in the Strawberry Mountain Wilderness.

Don't forget your Malheur National Forest recreation map.

1. Magone Lake, Nipple Butte Wilderness (proposed)

Scattered park-like groves of big ponderosa pine, Douglas-fir, white fir and larch surround this picturesque, 45-acre lake near the proposed Nipple Butte Wilderness Area.

Long Creek Ranger District
USGS 15' SUSANVILLE (1949)

ABOUT THE AREA
Over 70% of this 11,525-acre roadless area is forested. About one-quarter of the forest—roughly 2000 acres—is old growth, largely in the canyon bottoms. Ponderosa pine is the dominant species, intermingled with juniper and mountain-mahogany on some upland flats and side slopes. White fir and Douglas-fir proliferate in the moister areas.

A half-mile nature trail at Magone Lake provides an easy way to begin a cross-country hike from a ridgetop to the bottom of McClellan Creek through the proposed Wilderness. Also, the one-mile long FS Trail #352 circles the lake, providing fishing and birding opportunities. Beaver activity in the lake is apparent, and a lodge is visible near the north end of the day use area.

GETTING THERE
From Mount Vernon take US Highway

At Magone Lake you can camp and fish under big pines, and hike the proposed Nipple Butte Wilderness.

395 north for ten miles and turn right on FS Road 36, which parallels the East Fork of Beech Creek. Continue eight miles on FS Road 36 and bear north (left) on FS Road 3620. Drive 1.5 miles on FS Road 3620, and another 1.5 miles on FS Road 3618 to the day use area after the campground. FS Road 3618 makes a one-way, two-mile loop from Magone Lake down a scenic canyon to FS Road 36 and Beech Creek.

RECOMMENDED

FS Trail #353 leads northwest from the uphill side of FS Road 3618 just before the turn into the day use parking area. On the left fork of the trail you can easily see where a landslide occurred in the early 1800's, creating Magone Lake and causing many tall trees to lean. Where the trail forks to the right and ends, you may wish to continue uphill to the ridgetop for a good view of the McClellan Creek drainage or to hike cross-country down through the proposed Nipple Butte Wilderness. If

you contour around the steep areas down the ridge to McClellan Creek, you can follow the stream back to FS Road 36 and East Fork Beech Creek.

To get to McClellan Creek from the bottom, take FS Road 36 about 3.5 miles east of the junction with Highway 395 (and a half-mile beyond a sign for Thompson Creek, which also flows through the proposed Wilderness). McClellan Creek crosses under FS Road 36 and enters East Fork Beech Creek just past a cattle stockade on the north (left) side of the road. Park here and walk around the fenced private inholding and up McClellan Creek into the roadless area. This stream has been noticeably damaged by grazing, but will recover nicely when the cows are gone.

2. Murderers Creek Wilderness (proposed)

Spectacular vistas along the drive to the dramatic Aldrich Mountain Lookout at 6991'.

Bear Valley Ranger District
USGS 7.5' BIG WEASEL SPRINGS (1938)
ALDRICH MTN. SOUTH (1983)

ABOUT THE AREA

The rugged Aldrich Mountain–Murderers Creek area is renowned wildlife habitat. It supports healthy herds of bighorn sheep, Rocky Mountain elk and mule deer, and robust populations of many other animals. White fir and larch grow on the mountain's north-facing slopes, while old growth ponderosa pine thrive on ridges and in canyons with southern exposure. Most of the area is scheduled for clearcutting in the Malheur National Forest Plan.

The proposed Murderers Creek Wilderness includes the Forest Service's Dry Cabin and Aldrich Mountain roadless areas, and the BLM's Aldrich Mountain Wilderness Study Area to the west. Altogether, 30,000 roadless acres are currently proposed for congressional protection as Wilderness. Just south of the proposed Wilderness is the Oregon Department of Fish and Wildlife's Murderers Creek Wildlife Management Area, which encompasses another 17,000 acres and is managed as part of the larger natural habitat area.

GETTING THERE

Take US Highway 26 to the 144-mile post 13 miles east of Dayville (or 18 miles west of John Day), and turn south on Fields Creek Road, also called FS Road 21. Follow this scenic paved road ten miles to the ridge of the Aldrich Mountains, and turn west (right) on FS Road 2150 at a sign for "Aldrich Moun-

tain Lookout–15 miles" and "Cedar Grove Trail #203A."

RECOMMENDED

In six miles watch for a trailhead to the Cedar Grove Botanical Area. It's on the right, 0.6 mile after the junction with FS Road 070. This moderately steep one-mile trail leads through old growth ponderosa pine and white fir to a small, botanically unique remnant grove of Alaska yellow-cedar, growing here at the eastern limit of its range. While these trees are not dramatically large, they could be quite old: yellow-cedars only 15" to 20" in diameter typically range from 200 to 300 years old. In fact, the incredibly hardy Alaska yellow-cedar may well be the longest-lived plant species in the Pacific Northwest.

In another two miles, FS Road 2150 enters a grove of large white fir in Section 16 (T14S R28E), near Frankie and Johnny Spring. Continuing to the lookout, two abandoned Forest Service trails lead down from the road on the big pine-lined ridges to just above Murderers Creek Wildlife Management Area, in Section 3 (T15S R27E). The first (unmarked) trail begins on the south (downhill) side of FS Road 2150, in approximately the middle of Section 18 (T14S R28E) on the ridge between Dry Cabin Creek and Cabin Creek. The next trail descends in Section 11 (T14S R27E) on the west side of Cabin Creek before FS Road 540 (which is not shown on the Malheur National

Forest recreation map and is closed to vehicles). Proceed to the lookout on Aldrich Mountain for spectacular views

of Bottle Rock and the wild Smoky Gulch Canyon, key summer range for bighorn sheep.

3. Strawberry Mountain Wilderness

A beautiful trail in a magnificent Wilderness Area only 17 miles from downtown John Day.

Prairie City Ranger District
USGS 7.5' PINE CREEK MTN. (1983)
CANYON MTN. (1983)

ABOUT THE AREA
This easy, lower elevation trail along the East Fork of Canyon Creek (in the southwest corner of the Strawberry Mountain Wilderness) follows one of the prettiest riparian zones on the Malheur National Forest through ponderosa pine, western larch, white fir, black cottonwood, and smaller lodgepole pine and quaking aspen. The Canyon Creek drainage has been of particular concern in the long fight to protect the Strawberries through several expansions of the Wilderness boundaries by Congress. Because of

conservationists' victories here, this unique east-west mountain range has come to represent successful citizen activism in eastern Oregon.

GETTING THERE
From John Day, travel ten miles south on US Highway 395 and turn south (left) on Grant County Route 65 (which becomes FS Road 15) at a sign for Wickiup and Canyon Meadows Campgrounds. Drive 2.8 miles, turn left on FS Road 6510, and follow signs for "East Fork Canyon Creek Trail No. 211." In 1.6 miles turn right on FS Road 812 and follow it 2.7 miles to the trailhead at the road's end.

RECOMMENDED
The trail crosses rock outcrops and reaches the creek in less than a half-mile; it then climbs along the lush, streamside old growth ponderosa pine in the Canyon Creek Research Natural Area (RNA). FS Trail #211 leads to some popular high-elevation routes which penetrate deeper into this legendary 68,000-acre Wilderness.

Western larch is the tallest and most massive of the American larches. Trees 16"– 20" in diameter are usually between 250 and 300 years old.

4. Myrtle Park Meadows

A great place to visit or camp near majestic park-like stands of 300-year-old ponderosa pine, on the way to the proposed Myrtle-Silvies Wilderness.

Bear Valley Ranger District
USGS 15' LOGDELL (1961)
WEST MYRTLE BUTTE (1959)

ABOUT THE AREA

Extensive grazing over the years has converted most of what used to be a meadow community of plant species to a drier sagebrush type. But the open expanse, surrounded by big ponderosa pines, is still truly impressive. The author camped here while investigating the area. At dusk a short-eared owl flew over our heads at our camp on the prairie's edge, and coyotes yipped and serenaded us through the night. (Also see the following description of the proposed Myrtle-Silvies Wilderness entry.)

GETTING THERE

South of Seneca on US Highway 395, turn west on FS Road 37. About one-tenth of a mile before the junction of FS Roads 37 and 31, turn east on FS Road 861 and drive one and a half miles to the sage flats.

RECOMMENDED

Park and walk uphill (east) to a 300-acre grove of big trees above the sage flats. If you'd like to walk across the meadow for more big trees, stay on FS Road 861 a total of 3.25 miles and park at a gate at the private quarter-section in the northwest corner of Section 26 (T18S R30E). Walk south along the fenceline to Mill Creek in the lower meadow and the big trees beyond.

5. Myrtle-Silvies Wilderness (proposed)

The biggest trees in Harney County.

Burns Ranger District
USGS 15' WEST MYRTLE BUTTE (1959)

ABOUT THE AREA

The proposed 11,747-acre Myrtle-Silvies Wilderness includes the canyons of the Silvies River and Myrtle Creek drainages. These canyons are fairly wide (averaging a mile across) and steep with prominent rock outcroppings. The narrow creek valleys (50'-200' across) sometimes drop more than 600' below the top of the deeply incised plateau. An 8.6-mile canyon trail follows Myrtle Creek downstream through benches of old growth ponderosa pine, some up to 40" in diameter. The deeper pools contain small, catchable trout.

Myrtle-Silvies is one of several roadless areas with a long controversial history. The area has been allocated in the Malheur National Forest Plan for "semi-primitive non-motorized recreation use." A major conflict concerns grazing along portions of the stream, and its impact on water quality and flows. While the Forest Service may argue that none of the cows have motors, it is hard to see these hoofed locusts as either semi-primitive or recreational. (Also see the above description for the Myrtle Park Meadows entry.)

GETTING THERE

Take Highway 395 south from John Day for 31 miles (four miles south of Seneca) and turn west (right) on FS Road 37. Travel 12.6 miles (the first seven are paved) to Cheatem Holler and Myrtle Creek at the junction with FS Road 31. Make a hard left, drive *south* on FS Road 31 for 6.1 miles, and cross Myrtle Creek again at the south end of Myrtle Park Meadows. Turn right for the trailhead at a prominent sign for "Myrtle Creek Trail No. 308."

From Burns, travel north on Highway 395 about one mile past Idlewild Camp-ground and turn west (left) on FS Road 31. Drive 13 miles to the trailhead.

RECOMMENDED

Myrtle Creek Trail #308 ranges in pitch from level to moderately steep. It begins at 5400' and meanders alternately above and along the stream. You must cross Myrtle Creek or its tributaries at low banks several times along the route, which poses no significant problem except when it's running high in early spring. As Myrtle Creek Trail #308 ends where Myrtle Creek enters the Silvies River on private land, the trail can be reached only from the north.

6. Malheur River Canyon Wilderness (proposed)

Virgin groves of big ponderosa pine, Douglas-fir and western larch along the steep slopes and flat river benches of this stunning rimrock canyon.

Prairie City and Bear Valley Ranger Districts
USGS 15' LOGAN VALLEY (1961)

ABOUT THE AREA

This 7000-acre Wilderness proposal includes Malheur River Trail #303, an eight-mile National Recreation Trail along the west bank of one of the area's largest and best fishing streams.

The Malheur River gained national Wild and Scenic River status in 1988, with seven miles classified as "wild" below Malheur Ford, and 5.3 miles designated as "scenic" above the Ford.

The directions below, to the east and west sides of the lower Logan Valley, take you to the corresponding sides of the Malheur River. From Logan Valley's east side, you must cross the river at Malheur Ford to reach the trail along the west bank. As the Malheur River is really a river (not a large creek, like many eastern Oregon "rivers"), crossing is possible only dur-ing lower, late season flows. In other words, stick to the west side in the spring.

While the trail below Malheur Ford leads through some beautiful unmolested ponderosa pine forests, in 1988 the Forest Service clearcut many of the big old pines just where the road enters the river canyon on the east side. Unfortunately, the area farther west has suffered too. FS Road 1643 from upper to lower Logan Valley passes mile after mile of monotonous, even-aged plantations of young pine—a grim reminder of what the government and timber industry have in mind for most of eastern Oregon's remaining ancient ponderosa groves.

GETTING THERE

From Prairie City and Highway 26, drive south on Grant County Route 62/FS Road 14 for 23 miles to Summit Prairie, and turn west (right) on FS Road 16. To reach the east side of Logan Valley, drive 5.2 miles west on FS Road 16 and turn south on FS Road 1647. Bear right at all major intersections, turn right on FS Road 1651 in four miles, and continue to Malheur Ford, a total of 7.3 miles from FS Road 16. For the west side of Logan Valley, drive 8.5 miles west on FS Road 16 and turn south (left) onto FS Road 1643. Drive south on FS Road 1643 for 8.5 miles to the junction with FS Road 1651.

From Seneca and Highway 395, travel 14 miles east on FS Road 16. For the east side, continue west on FS Road 16 and turn south at FS Road 1647. For the west side, turn south (right) on FS Road 1643 just before Logan Valley. In either case, follow the directions above for FS Roads 1643 and 1647 to the Malheur River.

RECOMMENDED

East side: As noted above, you must cross the river at Malheur Ford to reach the northern trailhead on the west bank, which is possible only during low water.

West side (northern trailhead): Turn left on FS Road 1651 at a sign for Dollar Basin. Continue 1.2 miles to the Malheur River Trail's northern trailhead. FS Trail #303 tumbles downstream from below a parking and dispersed camping area off of FS Road 1651.

West side (southern trailhead): From the southern trailhead Malheur River Trail #303 drops from the canyon rim to the river's edge. From the junction with FS Road 1651, continue south on FS Road 1643 for another six miles to Hog Flat, an open scabland plateau, and turn east (left) on FS Road 142 at a sign for Malheur River Trail #303. It is 1.2 miles to the trailhead, with scenic vistas up and down the canyon.

Most of the state's remaining large western larch and ponderosa pine are in the roadless canyons of eastern Oregon's national forests and BLM districts.

7. North Fork Malheur River Wilderness (proposed)

A trail through ancient ponderosa pine along a Wild and Scenic River.

Prairie City Ranger District
USGS 15' FLAG PRAIRIE (1970)

ABOUT THE AREA

A 12.2-mile north-south trail follows Crane Creek, a tributary of the North Fork Malheur River, through park-like stands of old growth ponderosa pine and big old western larch. The North Fork Malheur was designated a National Wild and Scenic River by Congress in 1988, and is included in 18,300 acres of wild lands which have been proposed for protection as the North Fork Malheur River Wilderness.

GETTING THERE

From Highway 26 in Prairie City, turn south on Main Street at a sign for "Bl. Mt. Springs," drive 0.4 mile to an intersection, and bear left on Grant County Route 62

An ancient ponderosa pine with four tops marks the northernmost trailhead for the proposed North Fork Malheur Wilderness.

(FS Road 14). Drive eight miles east and turn left on FS Road 13 (Deardorff Creek Road), which is paved after the first 7.75 miles. Follow FS Road 13 about 16 miles to its end at the Forest Service's Short Creek Guard Station. Bear right on FS Road 16 for "N. Fk. Campground." Drive 2.2 miles and turn left on FS Road 1675 at a sign for "N. Fk. Malheur River Trail— 4 miles." Continue to the trailhead (it's actually only 3.25 miles).

RECOMMENDED

The trail begins at a log bridge over the river near a remarkable old ponderosa pine with four separate tops. Follow the trail south its entire ten-mile length down the ever-deepening rimrock canyon; or, in 2.5 miles head west up Crane Creek to a nice grove of big ancient western larch (which turn a brilliant golden by mid-October). Just before Crane Creek take an old wagon road to the right along Crane Creek. This is the Dalles to Boise Military Road, which ends at Crane Prairie, in the western part of the proposed Wilderness.

To reach the west end of the old wagon road at Crane Prairie, drive another 10.8 miles on FS Road 16 from the junction with FS Road 1675. Turn left just before the 29-mile post on gravel FS Road 1663, which runs along the east side of Crane Prairie, and continue one mile to FS Road 809 on the left, just before a cattle guard. Cross the fence and walk past tall pines down the historic wagon road (FS Road 809). The best old growth trees start in about one and a quarter miles, after the confluence of Buttermilk and Crane

Creeks. From this unmarked Crane Prairie trailhead, the most direct route back to Highway 26 and Prairie City is to continue on FS Road 16 another 4.2 miles to Summit Prairie, and take FS Road 14 north 23 miles to Prairie City.

8. Monument Rock Wilderness

A 7.2-mile trail along the Little Malheur River, lined with old growth ponderosa pine and western larch.

Prairie City Ranger District
USGS 7.5' BULLRUN ROCK (1983)

ABOUT THE AREA

Two entries into this Wilderness Area are described below. The south trailhead offers more gratification for those seeking the big, old forest. From the turn-off at FS Road 16, there are many large ancient ponderosa pine, western larch and black cottonwoods along the road, river and Wilderness boundary. This side also offers many dispersed camping opportunities in the last 3.6 miles of road, and fishing is best in this southern portion of the Little Malheur River. However, cattle grazing is still permitted in the Wilderness Area and continues to significantly degrade both the aesthetic and riparian values of this otherwise pristine land.

On the other hand, the north trailhead, which does not immediately lead to a lot of old growth forest, is conveniently close to the scenic Table Rock Lookout. The 360-degree panoramic view from the lookout at Table Rock includes much of the Monument Rock Wilderness, the eastern Malheur National Forest, and the southern portion of the "south half" of the Wallowa-Whitman National Forest.

GETTING THERE

From US Highway 26 in Prairie City, turn south on Main Street at a sign for "Bl. Mt. Springs," drive 0.4 mile to an intersection, and bear left on Grant County Route 62 (FS Road 14). Drive eight miles east and turn left on FS Road 13 (Deardorff Creek Road), which is paved after the first 7.75 miles.

RECOMMENDED

North trailhead: Drive 11.8 miles on FS Road 13 and turn left on FS Road 1370, following signs for "Little Malheur Trail No. 366." Except on the ridge west of the Little Malheur River, there are no old growth trees along the first two miles of this Wilderness trail. From the north trailhead, it is only 5.3 miles on FS Road 1370 to Table Rock Lookout. About a mile of this road (the section after Elk Creek Campground) is very rough, and walking is recommended.

South trailhead: Drive 16.1 miles on FS Road 13 and bear left on FS Road 16, towards Unity. Stay on FS Road 16 for 11 miles, cross the Little Malheur River, and turn left on FS Road 1672 at a sign for Little Malheur Trail #366. In one mile continue straight ahead on FS Road 457, which ends at the trailhead.

Other good routes in the area include: cross-country hikes up Larch Creek; off FS Road 457 before the south trailhead; up Rock Creek (Section 32); and up Lunch Creek (Sections 8 and 9). To reach Rock and Lunch Creeks, take the Little Malheur River Trail to the appropriate stream. For Lunch Creek (which is two miles from the south trailhead), follow a small draw which begins just north of Lunch Creek to the east; hike above

Lunch Creek and perpendicular to the Little Malheur River. You'll drop down into a scenic rock grotto with a waterfall.

9. Spring Creek and Glacier Mountain Wilderness (proposed)

One of the nicest ponderosa pine groves on the Malheur National Forest, near the proposed Glacier Mountain Wilderness.

Prairie City Ranger District
USGS 7.5' LITTLE BALDY MTN. (1983)

ABOUT THE AREA

The proposed 19,500-acre Glacier Mountain Wilderness was included in the 1984 Oregon Forest Wilderness Act passed by the House of Representatives, but was removed by Senator Hatfield in the final bill. Old growth trees are concentrated in small scattered groves throughout the area, although there are numerous down trees and snags along Spring Creek and the North Fork Malheur River.

The proposed Glacier Mountain Wilderness contains some old growth forest, but it is difficult to reach. The Spring Creek ponderosa stand is directly across

the North Fork Malheur River, east of the proposed Glacier Mountain Wilderness. A good dispersed camping spot is located only an eighth of a mile from the main entryway to the Spring Creek grove.

GETTING THERE

From Highway 26 in Prairie City, turn south on Main Street at the sign for "Bl. Mt. Spring." Drive 0.4 mile and bear left at an intersection on Grant County Route 62 (FS Road 14). Continue eight miles to FS Road 13, Deardorff Creek Road, and turn east (left). Stay on FS Road 13 for a total of 14 miles; it's paved after the first 7.75 miles. Directly opposite the 14-mile post, turn left onto a visible tire track (FS

Park-like stands of ancient ponderosa pine, like these at Spring Creek, provide important thermal cover for deer, elk and other wildlife.

Road 342). Continue a quarter-mile and park or camp beside the big ponderosa pine on the west side of the stream.

RECOMMENDED
Cross the river on down logs just upstream from the big pine and head directly uphill. After you cross a barbed wire fence, the grade becomes more gradual. Continue walking uphill, following deer trails through this cathedral-like ponderosa pine forest. To reach Sheep Creek Trail #371 to Lookout Mountain, which is inside the proposed Glacier Mountain Wilderness, continue another mile on FS Road 13 before parking. The trailhead is on the right just before the 15-mile post.

10. Reynolds Creek, Wildcat Backcountry (proposed)

Mixed coniferous forest of ponderosa pine, western larch, white fir, Douglas-fir, lodgepole pine and western juniper.

Prairie City Ranger District
USGS 7.5' DEARDORFF MTN. (1983)

ABOUT THE AREA
With the notable exception of a few really big pine and fir on the upper slopes, few large trees live along the beautiful canyon of Reynolds Creek. However, at 24" to 32" in diameter, they are typical of what the Forest Service identifies as "old growth" in eastern Oregon. This hike is included because it's easy to reach (only 12 miles from US Highway 26 in Prairie City), and because it's very scenic. The trail follows a rushing mountain stream (one of the few left ungrazed on the Malheur National Forest) to a geologically interesting arch rock a short distance from its end.

The proposed Wildcat Backcountry is a modest 6700-acre roadless area. Backcountry Areas are designated by agency administrators, not by Congress; although the administrative protection granted is not as strong or permanent as legislation, it is otherwise similar to a Wilderness classification.

GETTING THERE
From Highway 26 in Prairie City turn south on Main Street at the sign for "Bl. Mt. Spring." After 0.4 mile bear left on Grant County Route 62, which is FS Road 14. Continue 7.5 miles, then turn left on FS Road 2635. Drive exactly four miles to Reynolds Creek Trail #264.

RECOMMENDED
Only a wooden post marks the trailhead to the right, immediately after FS Road 2635 crosses Reynolds Creek and before a side road intersects from the left. To reach the arch (one of three on the Malheur National Forest), hike two miles to where the trail suddenly ends after crossing a small draw to the left. Continue up the main canyon on elk and deer trails another quarter-mile to a massive rock on your left (north), which comes all the way to the creek and is largely moss-covered. The arch is 200 yards straight up from here. The view down the pristine canyon from above the arch is impressive. Another quarter-mile upstream you will come to a lovely Engelmann spruce grove and two elk wallows along the creek.

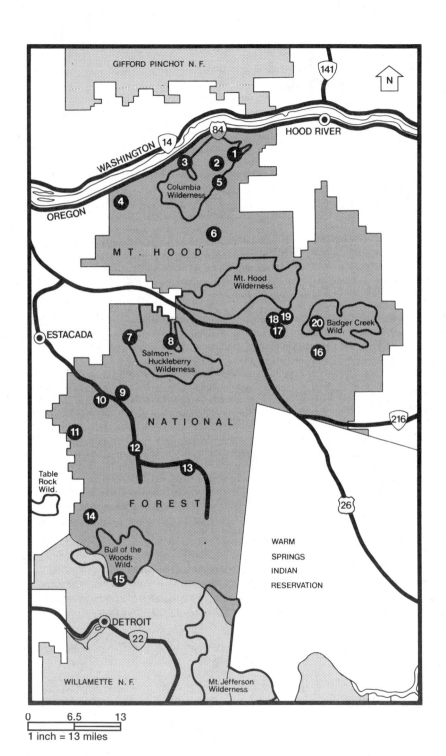

GIFFORD PINCHOT N. F.

141

N

WASHINGTON

14

84

HOOD RIVER

OREGON

3
2
1

5

Columbia
Wilderness

4

6

M T.   H O O D

Mt. Hood
Wilderness

18 19
17

20 Badger Creek
Wild.

ESTACADA

7

8

16

Salmon-
Huckleberry
Wilderness

10 9

N A T I O N A L

216

11

12

13

Table
Rock
Wild.

F O R E S T

14

WARM

SPRINGS

INDIAN

RESERVATION

26

Bull of the
Woods Wild.

15

DETROIT

22

WILLAMETTE N. F.

Mt. Jefferson
Wilderness

0   6.5   13

1 inch = 13 miles

Mount Hood National Forest

The Mount Hood is Oregon's most urban national forest. Featuring and named for Oregon's highest peak, one of the most frequently climbed mountains in the West, Mount Hood is one of the workhorse forests. Despite its proximity to Portland and the surrounding metropolis, this heavily logged landscape is the most over-cut National Forest in the Oregon Cascades. Its old growth strongholds include the east-side Badger Creek drainage, the Salmon and Roaring Rivers, and the famous Bull Run Watershed, source of Portland's renowned drinking water.

The Mount Hood National Forest's seven ranger districts encompass over a million acres. It is the only National Forest in Oregon to span the Cascades, and includes forest types typical of both the western and eastern Cascades. From the awesome Columbia Gorge south to Bagby Hot Springs and Bull-of-the-Woods, the Mount Hood Forest contains a wealth of ancient forest groves, although they're getting harder and harder to find.

Don't forget your Mount Hood National Forest recreation map.

1. North Lake

A one-mile hike to an impressive grove of fir and western red-cedar, passing a scenic, cliff-surrounded lake at 3900' in the Columbia Wilderness.

Columbia Gorge Ranger District
USGS 7.5' MOUNT DEFIANCE (1979)

ABOUT THE AREA
Although the forest is nice all along the trail, you don't enter the grove of really big trees until you're just north and east of North Lake. The lake and the old cedars make a fine, easily reached destination along this Wilderness trail.

GETTING THERE
From Portland take I-84 to Hood River (about one hour). Turn off at Exit 62 on Highway 30 East (West Cliff Drive), which becomes Cascade, then Oak Street.

In approximately one mile turn right at a flashing traffic light, proceed uphill on 13th Street, and follow signs for Odell through Hood River. In five miles, just after crossing the Hood River, bear right on Dee Highway past Tucker Park. Drive along the river for six miles and bear right at a sign for Dee.

Cross the bridge over the Hood River and bear right on Punch Bowl Road (which becomes FS Road 2820), following signs for Rainy Lake. Continue on gravel FS

Road 2820 for nine miles to the trailhead for Wyeth Trail #411 and Mount Defiance on the right one mile before Rainy Lake.

RECOMMENDED
Take the Wyeth Trail (not the Mount Defiance Trail, which forks to the right) a half-mile to North Lake (the sign says one mile). Walk another half-mile along the Wyeth Trail as it drops downhill and

enters a forest of old noble fir and then Douglas-fir. After a large rockslide on the left, the trail heads uphill into a forest of smaller trees. Here, leave the trail and walk cross-country downhill to the right (heading east and a little north) to a small stream surrounded by some prime western red-cedar. If you choose to walk all the way down the trail to the Columbia Gorge, it is 6.2 miles to the Wyeth Trail's northern trailhead, off I-84 at Exit 51.

2. Herman Creek Ancient Cedar Grove

A large stand of western red-cedar estimated to be a thousand years old, in the Columbia Wilderness.

Columbia Gorge Ranger District
USGS 7.5' CARSON (WA) (1979)
WAHTUM LAKE (1979)

ABOUT THE AREA
The great Columbia Fire of 1902 and subsequent smaller fires burned most of the ancient forest in the Columbia River Gorge, leaving only remnant stands of old trees here and there. One outstanding example of such a grove lies along Herman Creek Trail #406 in Sections 26 and 35 (T2N R8E), mostly north but also south of the junction with Herman Creek Cutoff Trail #410. While FS Trail #406 can be reached from the Gorge, the shorter hike is from FS Road 2820 south of Rainy Lake (at 4000'). This is a moderately strenuous walk; in addition to the cedar grove, there are many wildflowers in the spring, waterfalls, and young Douglas-fir and western hemlock stands. It leaves one with the sense of having truly experienced the inner Gorge.

GETTING THERE
To get to this area from below, take Exit 44 from Highway I-84 for US 30 East–Cascade Locks. Approximately 1.75

Thousand-year-old cedars on the Herman Creek Trail make a fine destination for a Columbia River Gorge hike.

64

miles from the turn-off, after driving east through Cascade Locks, you pass underneath I-84. Make the next possible right turn or you will find yourself back on the freeway. Drive 1.6 miles paralleling I-84 (on your left) to just past the Columbia Gorge Work Center, and turn right by the sign for Herman Creek Campground and Trailhead. It is 0.3 mile to the parking area and trailhead.

RECOMMENDED

Take Herman Creek Trail #406 past the junction on the left with Nick Eaton Trail #447. At Casey Camp, in four miles, you will find fire-scarred old growth Dou-

glas-fir trees and snags. From Whiskey Creek to Cedar Swamp Shelter (6.0 and 7.3 miles from the trailhead, respectively), you'll encounter very old cedar groves. At the shelter, FS Trail #410 cuts off to the left (east) and climbs steeply up Greenpoint Mountain to Rainy Lake, an upper access point for the region and home to more ancient trees.

A nice pocket of old growth Douglas-fir can be found east of (above) Herman Creek, near Deadwood Camp in Section 11 (T2N R8E). It can be reached on either Gordon Creek Trail #408 or Nick Eaton Trail #447.

3. Wauna Viewpoint Trail

The most accessible ancient forest in the Columbia River Gorge.

Columbia Gorge Ranger District
USGS 7.5' BONNEVILLE DAM (WA) (1979)

ABOUT THE AREA

This two-mile trail leads past old growth trees and outcrops of basaltic rock to a beautiful viewpoint 880' above the Gorge. (It should not be confused with Wauna *Point* Trail #401.)

GETTING THERE

From I-84 take Exit 41, turn right for Eagle Creek Park, and pull into the picnic area.

RECOMMENDED

A suspension bridge spans Eagle Creek at the trailhead for both the short and easy Shady Glen Interpretive Trail and the Wauna Viewpoint Trail. Each wanders through a forest of mature and old growth (up to 450-year-old) Douglas-fir interspersed with alders and maples.

For more stunning scenery, continue by vehicle another 0.3 mile upstream, past

the suspension bridge, to the very popular Eagle Creek Trail #440. It is noted for spectacular waterfalls along the narrow canyon from Eagle Creek's headwaters at Wahtum Lake. (See also the following description for the Wahtum Lake, Columbia Wilderness entry.) Enjoy the Eagle Creek Campground and picnic area, which contain many large old Douglas-fir trees.

4. Larch Mountain Unit, Multnomah Basin Additions to Columbia Wilderness (proposed)

One of the largest and most accessible groves of big western hemlock and Douglas-fir in the Columbia Gorge National Scenic Area.

Columbia Gorge Ranger District
USGS 7.5' MULTNOMAH FALLS (1986)

ABOUT THE AREA

Larch Mountain contains impressive groves of western hemlock, Douglas-fir and (occasionally) noble fir, but not larch. Many trees are 400 years old or more. Only 37 miles from downtown Portland, it's worth the trip any day. The suggested seven-mile loop trail includes segments of four different trails. Because this loop has seven trail junctions, a detailed map is indispensable. The Forest Service's large-scale, topographic map, "Forest Trails of the Columbia Gorge," which

can be obtained for $2 from local agency offices, is especially good.

Although elevations range only from 2700' to 3400' in the Multnomah Basin, there is often a heavy winter snowpack. Mid-May or even June is usually the earliest you can make this hike without crossing a lot of snowbanks. When snow blocks higher elevation routes, the Multnomah Basin can be reached from Multnomah Falls on I-84 (Exit 31) via Larch Mountain Trail #441. The end of

Multnomah Basin, on the north slope of Larch Mountain, is the largest contiguous ancient forest grove in the Columbia Gorge, and a classic example of a climax ancient hemlock forest.

this trail is the rock stairs on the east side of the lodge.

GETTING THERE
East of Portland on I-84, take Exit 22 for Corbett. Proceed uphill 1.6 miles on NE Corbett Hill Road. At the top of the hill turn east (left) on the Columbia Gorge Scenic Highway, and follow signs for Crown Point and Multnomah Falls. In two miles bear right on Larch Mountain Road. Continue 14 miles through a corridor of second growth forest to the trailhead parking area at the end of the road. Signs along this corridor indicate that no timber cutting is allowed within 200' of the road. (You don't want to know what it's like beyond the 200' limit.)

RECOMMENDED
The seven-mile loop begins (reading clockwise on the map) on Larch Mountain Trail #441, turns onto Multnomah Spur Trail #446, then Oneonta Trail #424, and finally Multnomah Way Trail #444, which will take you back to your car at the end of Larch Mountain Road (or to the Larch Mountain Picnic Area). If you have the energy for a side trip, the Bell Creek Trail (which takes off from One-onta Trail #424 in Section 27) reaches some of the largest old trees in the basin along another mile and a half of trail (marred by a quarter-mile blowdown salvage). The trees east of Bell Creek in Section 23 are especially big ones! (Check a Mount Hood National Forest recreation map for section numbers.)

You can take a shorter, five-mile loop hike (with many switchbacks) by taking FS Trail #441 to FS Trail #446 and immediately returning on FS Trail #444. When you cross the first log footbridge over Multnomah Creek, turn right on FS Trail #444 and you will soon pass a marshy meadow with a view of the top of Larch Mountain. A half-mile from the bridge FS Trail #444 enters a beautiful ancient forest grove in Section 28. You can reach this grove in 1.5 miles on Larch Mountain Trail. From the Larch Mountain Road a half-mile east of the 11-mile post, turn east on FS Road 315. Unless you have a high clearance vehicle, park in the gravel quarry just ahead and walk up the road another quarter-mile, watching for the trail which starts downhill to the left just before the gravel road ends.

5. Wahtum Lake, Columbia Wilderness

Ancient noble fir and western hemlock at the headwaters of Eagle Creek.

Columbia Gorge Ranger District
USGS 7.5' WAHTUM LAKE (1979)

ABOUT THE AREA
Most of this area, including the popular Eagle Creek Trail, is now protected in the Columbia Wilderness Area. Big trees surround this lake basin and extend beyond along the area's trails. While the trail to Wahtum Lake itself is steep, it's close enough to the road to carry in a raft or canoe, yet still find seclusion and solitude.

GETTING THERE
From Portland take I-84 to Hood River (about one hour). Turn off at Exit 62 on

Highway 30 East (West Cliff Drive), which becomes Cascade, then Oak Street. In approximately one mile turn right at a flashing traffic light, proceed uphill on 13th Street, and follow signs for Odell through Hood River. In five miles, just after crossing the Hood River, bear right on Dee Highway past Tucker Park. Drive along the river for six miles and bear right at a sign for Dee.

Cross the bridge over Hood River and bear left on Lost Lake Road. In another five miles bear right on FS Road 13 for Wahtum Lake. Take FS Road 13 for four miles and bear right on Scout Lake Road (FS Road 1310). Continue on FS Road 1310 for six miles to a pull-out on the right. If the paved road turns to gravel, you've gone too far. Wahtum Lake is in the basin directly below the pull-out.

RECOMMENDED

A fairly steep trail leads a quarter-mile downhill and joins the Pacific Crest Trail (PCT) on the southwest end of the lake. To the right, the PCT reaches up high around the lake past many large noble firs.

For a leisurely hike through wildflowers beneath large noble fir, Pacific silver fir and western hemlock, walk to the left on the PCT along the southern lakeshore. The PCT soon forks; bear right and follow Eagle Creek along the Eagle Creek Trail for another mile among big old trees.

For an all-day 13-mile hike, arrange a car shuttle and follow Eagle Creek Trail #440 to the bottom of the Gorge through one of the Columbia River's classic waterfall-lined, emerald-green side canyons. The trail drops 3600' from Wahtum Lake to the mouth of Eagle Creek on the Columbia River, so you may want to hike downhill rather than up.

From ancient Douglas-fir and western hemlock at Wahtum Lake, the middle and lower segments of Eagle Creek Trail pass through an emerald-colored world of waterfalls and gorges. (Photo by Diane Kelsay)

6. Lost Lake

Nicest ancient forest left on the Hood River Ranger District.

Hood River Ranger District
USGS 7.5' BULL RUN LAKE (1985)

ABOUT THE AREA

This old grove, about 27 miles from the town of Hood River, is worth a special trip at any time. It is unquestionably the most impressive remnant of ancient forest left on the heavily logged Hood River Ranger District. If ancient forests were rated like restaurants, this one would receive five stars!

GETTING THERE

From Portland take I-84 to Hood River (about one hour). Turn off at Exit 62 on Highway 30 East (West Cliff Drive), which becomes Cascade, then Oak Street. In approximately one mile turn right at a flashing traffic light, proceed uphill on 13th Street, and follow signs for Odell through Hood River. In five miles, just after crossing the Hood River, bear right on Dee Highway past Tucker Park. Drive along the river for six miles and bear right at a sign for Dee.

Cross the river, bear left on Lost Lake Road, and in another five miles bear left on FS Road 13 for Lost Lake. Continue on FS Road 13 approximately 5.5 miles past the junction with FS Road 18 to FS Road 1341, which leads directly to Lost Lake. Bear right at the lake, past the campground, boat rental, cabins and general store. Cross the small bridge at Lake Branch Creek and park at the road's end at the trailhead for Lost Lake Nature Trail.

RECOMMENDED

The Lost Lake Nature Trail makes an easy three-mile loop around the lake, with the last mile along the road and campground. The first mile of trail passes through a stunning forest of western redcedar and giant old growth fir with postcard-perfect views of snow-capped Mount Hood above the lake. In three-quarters of a mile you'll cross a boardwalk through a skunk cabbage marsh surrounded by more big cedars.

Another engaging hike, even shorter than Lost Lake Nature Trail, starts from the bridge at Lake Branch Creek described above. The trail leads immediately into the forest along the stream among more big fir and majestic cedars.

Huckleberry Mountain Trail #617 takes off from the south side of the loop around Lost Lake. It climbs 900' in two miles to join the Pacific Crest Trail (PCT), which follows a ridge at 4100' above the Bull Run Watershed. You can also pick up Huckleberry Mountain Trail #617 at a trailhead on FS Road 620, a spur off of FS Road 1340 south of Lost Lake. In the last half-mile before the PCT, the trail passes through a beautiful old growth Pacific silver fir forest. Mount Hood looms spectacular over Bull Run Reservoir from the ridge above the trail, but the area is closed to the public to protect Portland's water supply. Incredibly, while you can't enter the watershed, loggers can.

7. Eagle Creek, Salmon-Huckleberry Wilderness

Large old growth Douglas-fir trees along a beautiful six-mile, low-elevation trail following Eagle Creek in the Salmon-Huckleberry Wilderness.

Zigzag Ranger District
USGS 15' CHERRYVILLE (1955)

ABOUT THE AREA

This is the "other" Eagle Creek on the Mount Hood National Forest, the one that's *not* in the Columbia Gorge. (To visit the Eagle Creek that *is* in the Gorge, see the preceding entries in this chapter for Wauna Viewpoint Trail and Wahtum Lake, Columbia Wilderness.) Although you begin seeing ancient trees a half-mile before the Wilderness boundary, the lower portion of the trail has been (and still is) threatened by logging.

GETTING THERE

From Oregon Highway 211/224 about four miles north of Estacada, turn east on SE Wildcat Mountain Drive. Look for a sign to "Eagle Fern Park—Dover District;" from this point it is 11 miles to the trailhead. In a mile and a half bear right at a "Y" on SE Eagle Fern Road. You will pass Eagle Fern Park in 2.5 miles. In another half-mile Eagle Fern Road becomes SE George Road. Near the end of this road, where SE George becomes SE Clausen Road, turn right on SE Harvey Road and look for a sign for "Eagle Cr. Tr. No. 501 2 miles" (really 2.5 miles). Stay on the main road, holding left at the first three "Y's." Take the fourth "Y" to the right on FS Road 335, then park on the right at the next "Y," before you come to a dead-end uphill in a clearcut. Do not drive down this last right-hand spur— the road immediately worsens, then narrows to become the trail in another mile.

RECOMMENDED

From where you park, it is a two-mile walk down the spur road and on FS Trail #501 to some large old trees. The ancient forest continues for another two miles in its greatest concentration along this Wilderness stream. Wear appropriate footwear in winter, as the trail is muddy. Otherwise, the going is easy.

On your way in or out, you may want to stop briefly at Eagle Fern Park to see some large old western red-cedar and Douglas-fir. If you ford the river or hike above the road it is possible to get a glimpse of how the entire valley looked before it was logged. A nice (but very small) bench of old growth cedar and fir is easily located above and below the intersection of SE Kitzmiller and SE Eagle Fern Roads.

8. Salmon River Trail

Low-elevation old growth Douglas-fir, hemlock and cedar forest on the easy 2.6-mile Old Salmon River Trail.

Zigzag Ranger District
USGS 7.5' RHODODENDRON (1980)

ABOUT THE AREA

Although FS Trail #742 follows FS Road 2618 and is within view of it several times, this is somehow still a wild and enchanting walk. The proximity and constant sounds of the nearby river, as well as the lushness of the forest and outstanding displays of wildflowers in spring and early summer, make this one of the most enjoyable hikes on the Zigzag Ranger District.

When snow accumulates in the lower elevations, the road just beyond the National Forest boundary provides good novice-level cross-country skiing. On one January outing, we walked the Old Salmon River Trail first, then skied south on FS Road 2618 to a second bridge across the South Fork of Salmon Creek, where we happened to spot an otter fishing in this old growth forest-lined stream.

GETTING THERE

Follow US Highway 26 about 18 miles east of Sandy. Turn south (right) on Salmon River Road (FS Road 2618) just west of the Zigzag Ranger Station. Follow FS Road 2618 for 2.7 miles to the northern trailhead (at the first pull-out on the right after the National Forest boundary) or for 4.7 miles to Green Canyon Campground and trailhead.

RECOMMENDED

The "Old" Salmon River Trail runs downstream from Green River Campground near the road. Salmon River Trail #742 continues into the Salmon-Huckleberry

Wilderness up the North Fork Salmon River. As usual, the old trees do not extend very far into the Wilderness Area itself, as certain politicians drew the Wilderness boundaries to exclude them.

Green Canyon Way Trail #793A, which climbs the ridge of Hunchback Mountain to Devil's Peak above the North Fork Salmon River Canyon, begins just beyond Green Canyon Campground, on the left side of FS Road 2618.

The Salmon River Trail is the finest streamside ancient forest trail on the Zigzag Ranger District. The nearby road provides an easy cross-country ski route among big trees in winter. (Photo by Diane Kelsay)

9. Roaring River Wilderness (proposed)

A small but significant ancient forest grove
a half-mile into this scenic roadless area,
which conservationists are asking Congress
to designate as Wilderness.

Estacada Ranger District
USGS 7.5' THREE LYNX (1985)

ABOUT THE AREA
The first part of this trail harbors many large old growth and mature Douglas-fir trees, standing snags and down logs. To a forester, this area is "decadent." To a salamander, it's just right. The Roaring River Campground shelters an impressive grove of western red-cedar.

GETTING THERE
Drive 18.2 miles southeast of Estacada on Oregon Highway 224 along the Clackamas River, and turn left into the Roaring River Campground.

RECOMMENDED
Follow Dry Ridge Trail #518, which begins at camp space #7. The trail is near the river at first, but almost immediately turns to the right and enters the forest. A primitive fishermen's trail continues a half-mile upstream and dead-ends after it passes a massive moss and wildflower-covered rock. Beyond the ancient grove the trail switchbacks sharply up to Grouse Point Trail #517, approximately six miles from the campground. About two miles southeast on FS Trail #517 is a junction with FS Trail #512 to Serene Lake and the Rock Lakes. While it lacks old trees, the popular high-elevation Rock Lake Basin (generally approached from Frazier Turnaround) is also deserving of protection, and is included in the proposed Roaring River Wilderness Area.

A young northern spotted owl perches on a Pacific yew in the shelter of the ancient forest canopy. (Photo by Gary Braasch)

"The first rule of intelligent tinkering is to save all the pieces."
—Aldo Leopold
(Photo by Phillip Renault)

10. Clackamas River Trail

Big trees, big rocks and a big waterfall, along a riverside trail.

Estacada Ranger District
USGS 7.5' BEDFORD POINT (1986)
THREE LYNX (1985)
FISH CREEK (1985)

ABOUT THE AREA
A 7.8-mile trail follows the southwest side of the river past riparian old growth, rock outcrops and the 100'-high Pup Creek Falls. There are two trailheads, one at Fish Creek and the other upstream across from Indian Henry Campground.

GETTING THERE
Take Oregon Highway 224 roughly 15 miles south of Estacada and bear right at Fish Creek Road, FS Road 54. Cross the Clackamas River bridge and park on the right.

RECOMMENDED
Clackamas River Trail #715 begins on the left side of the road. You will find exceptionally nice old growth forest flats close to the river 2.3 and four miles down the trail. It's three and a half miles upstream to the Pup Creek Falls viewpoint.

An alternative is to walk on the less-traveled southern end of the trail, which is perched 600'-800' above the Clackamas River. Drive another seven miles on Oregon Highway 224 and turn right on Sandstone Road (FS Road 4620). Proceed one-third mile to the trailhead and parking area on the right, across from Indian Henry Campground. This portion of FS Trail #715 (heading downstream to the Fish Creek bridge) passes through a "half-cave" behind a small waterfall one and a half miles from Indian Henry Campground.

11. Memaloose Lake

A small Cascades lake surrounded by old growth Douglas-fir and western red-cedar, skunk cabbage, huckleberries and abundant wildflowers.

Estacada Ranger District
USGS 7.5' WANDERS PEAK (1985)
SOOSAP PEAK (1986)

ABOUT THE AREA
The one-mile trail to Memaloose Lake is moderately steep. The area is best visited from June through November. From the nearby South Fork Mountain Lookout there are good views of Mount Jefferson, Mount Hood and Mount Adams, as well as the sea of clearcuts which surrounds them.

GETTING THERE
Take Oregon Highway 224 about 9.5 miles southeast of Estacada, and make the first possible right turn across the Clackamas River on Memaloose Road (FS Road 45). Proceed for eleven curvaceous miles, and turn right on a gravel road at a sign for Memaloose Lake Trail. The trail begins to the left in one mile, where a post marks the trailhead.

RECOMMENDED
Memaloose Lake Trail #515 continues half a mile beyond the lake through more old growth forest. It ends at South Fork Mountain Lookout, which can also be reached from FS Road 140 off FS Road 4540.

Beargrass, Xerophyllum tenax, was an important article of trade by the Indians, who constructed baskets, hats, pouches and watertight cooking pots from its fibrous leaves. (Photo by Diane Kelsay)

12. Riverside Trail

A lush rainforest with an easy hiking trail along the Clackamas River.

Clackamas (Ripplebrook) Ranger District
USGS 7.5' FISH CREEK MTN. (1985)

ABOUT THE AREA
This forest has a majestic cathedral quality, and there are several great views along the trail from cliffs overlooking the river. The Riverside National Recreation Trail was designated by the Secretary of Agriculture under the National Trail Systems Act because of its outstanding scenic qualities and accessibility to urban areas. Unfortunately, despite the hype, logging is permitted along most of the Forest Service's "protected" National Recreation Trails, including all of them in Oregon.

GETTING THERE
Travel twenty-six miles south of Estacada on Oregon Highway 224 to Rainbow Campground, which is on the right after the highway incorporates FS Road 46 a half-mile past the Ripplebrook Ranger Station.

RECOMMENDED
FS Trail #723 begins at the south end of Rainbow Campground. Four miles long, it follows the east bank of the Clackamas River, crosses several log bridges, and ends at Riverside Campground. The nicest old growth trees (four to five feet in diameter) are a little over one mile from the trailhead at Rainbow Campground. Another option is to drive a few miles further south on Oregon 224 (FS Road 46) to Riverside Campground and walk the other direction.

13. Big Bottom

The nicest old growth forest grove on the Clackamas Ranger District.

Clackamas Ranger District
USGS 7.5' MT. MITCHELL (1985)
MT. LOWE (1986)

ABOUT THE AREA
Drive down an unobtrusive single-lane dirt road and hike cross-country into a magnificent ancient forest along the upper reaches of the Clackamas River. Segments of the Clackamas were designated "scenic" and "recreational" by Congress in the 1988 Oregon Wild and Scenic Rivers Act, but that may not protect the old growth groves at Big Bottom from chainsaws in the near future.

GETTING THERE
Take Oregon Highway 224 up the Clackamas River about five miles past Austin Hot Springs. Turn right on FS Road 4650 (paved) and then left on FS Road 4651 (gravel). Proceed 3.5 miles to FS Road 120 and make a hard left. This is poorly marked but is the first possible turn to the left. (The gate on FS Road 120 is closed from December to April.) Drive one mile to the road's end. A turn either way onto FS Road 140 takes you through the cathedral forest. Drive to the north (left) end of FS Road 140 and park.

RECOMMENDED
Wander northward. Besides seeing some fine stands of old growth, you'll also

enjoy the Clackamas River, some extensive wetlands, and lots of wildlife. Should the gate be closed, or if you'd like to avoid a clearcut between Big Bottom and FS Road 4651, drive a half-mile back on FS Road 4651 to an old growth grove at the top of the hill. Walk cross-country three-quarters of a mile to the east and you will come to the really big trees along the river.

Big Bottom on the Clackamas River is the finest example of cathedral forest on the Clackamas Ranger District.

14. Bagby Hot Springs, Bull-of-the-Woods Wilderness

Take a towel and soak in Bagby Hot Springs, among giant old growth Douglas-fir.

Estacada Ranger District
USGS 7.5' BAGBY HOT SPRING (1985)

ABOUT THE AREA

The Hot Springs Fork of the Collawash River contains outstanding groves of ancient Douglas-fir forest. It's an easy mile and a half hike to the hot springs, but don't expect to find solitude at this popular location. (Consider visiting on a weekday to avoid crowds.) Regardless, the big trees and hot water beckon.

GETTING THERE

From Estacada, travel south up the Clackamas River Gorge on Oregon Highway 224 to FS Road 63, about five miles past Ripplebrook Ranger Station. Bear right on FS Road 63, following signs for Bagby Hot Springs for three and a half miles; turn right on FS Road 70, and drive six miles to the Bagby parking area.

RECOMMENDED

Take FS Trail #544 from the parking area. The trail continues south for many miles beyond the hot springs, into the wondrous old growth forest of Bull-of-the-Woods Wilderness and its adjacent roadless but unprotected lands.

15. Elk Lake, Bull-of-the-Woods Wilderness

Large old Douglas-fir and Alaska yellow-cedar along Elk Lake and a scenic Wilderness trail.

Estacada Ranger District
USGS 7.5' MOTHER LODE MTN. (1985)

ABOUT THE AREA

Although this area is in the Mount Hood National Forest, it is administered by (and accessible principally from) the Detroit Ranger District of the Willamette National Forest. A splendid old growth forest begins in the last half-mile of road before the lake.

GETTING THERE

Take North Santiam Highway 22 to Detroit and turn north (left) on FS Road 46, also known as Oregon Highway 224. Follow it along the Breitenbush River for a little over four miles to the Elk Lake turn-off, FS Road 4696. In less than a mile turn left on FS Road 2209 and follow signs to Elk Lake. While it is less than six miles, the last two miles are exceedingly rough (like driving up a dry streambed) and should not be attempted with low clearance vehicles.

RECOMMENDED

Superlative old growth Alaska yellow-cedar trees can be found to the east of FS Road 2209 and along the south shore of Elk Lake. Another nice old grove is located on the west side of Elk Lake. From here, follow the stream cross-country about three-quarters of a mile to a meadow and two ponds with lots of beaver, bear and elk sign.

Approximately 0.2 mile after the road crosses Elk Lake Creek (on the east end of the lake), Elk Lake Trail #559 begins at the Bull-of-the-Woods Wilderness boundary and passes through large trees

for the first mile. The Battle Creek Shelter and another outstanding ancient forest grove are four miles from Elk Lake. FS Trail #559 is also accessible from the upper Collawash River, 47 miles south of Estacada. Battle Creek Shelter is five miles in from the trailhead, in a clearcut at the southern end of FS Road 6380.

Beaver, black bear, Roosevelt elk, ancient Alaska yellow-cedar, and the nearby Bull-of-the-Woods Wilderness make Elk Lake a special place. (Photo by Diane Kelsay)

16. Boulder Creek to Boulder Lake

Mile after mile of cathedral-like Douglas-fir and Engelmann spruce forest, with a detour to a special Cascades lake.

Barlow Ranger District
USGS 7.5' BADGER LAKE (1979)
POST POINT (1985)

ABOUT THE AREA

This relatively pristine area off Mount Hood's southeast flank lies just south of the Badger Creek Wilderness. It includes three pretty alpine lakes, numerous trails, and many magnificent old trees. At Boulder Lake you can sit quietly and hear woodpeckers softly tapping on old growth trees, while pikas (mammals related to rabbits) give their high-pitched, one-note calls from talus slopes above the lake.

GETTING THERE

From US Highway 26 about 14 miles south of Government Camp (0.2 mile south of the 68-mile post), turn north on FS Road 43, Cedar Burn Road, and follow signs for White River. About six miles after FS Road 43 crosses the White River, turn right on FS Road 48, the White River Road. (You can also reach this point by following FS Road 48 south for nine miles from near the 62-mile post on Oregon Highway 35.) Drive 6.75 miles south on FS Road 48 from the junction with FS Road 43, and turn left on FS Road 4870 just before Lost Creek. Take this gravel road exactly three miles, bearing left at an unmarked fork in 1.5 miles.

To shorten the walk to Boulder Lake (you'll miss the best trees), turn left on FS Road 4880 off FS Road 48, about one and a half miles before FS Road 4870, the recommended route.

RECOMMENDED

The trailhead is on a narrow spur road that veers downhill to the left from the unmarked road off FS Road 4870. An old, barely legible sign reads "Crane Creek Trail #478," and "47" is painted on

Boulder Lake is a fine destination for the cathedral forest trail along Crane Creek.

another small sign. Follow the spur road as it becomes a trail, which begins on private land in Section 16 (see your Mount Hood National Forest recreation map). The first half-mile is still mostly shaded by standing trees, but previous logging activity is quite evident. Just before the stream you'll enter the old forest, and you'll agree it's well worth the hike. The first mile of trail follows Boulder Creek through park-like meadows lined with old growth Engelmann spruce. In two miles an impressive grove of ancient Douglas-fir awaits you.

About a quarter-mile after the three-mile trail marker you can either continue on FS Trail #478 another 1.5 miles to Crane Prairie (a large meadow at the headwaters of the canyon), or turn left on FS Trail #463 for Boulder Lake. FS Trail #478

winds by relatively small old growth mountain hemlock and some proud noble fir on its way to Badger Lake. While there is an upper trailhead for Crane Creek Trail #478 off FS Road 3530 and Bennett Pass, these roads are so rough that they should, for all practical purposes, be regarded as inaccessible by vehicle. (See the description for the Badger Creek Wilderness entry later in this chapter.)

FS Trail #463 crosses a footbridge over Boulder Creek and heads uphill. It crosses FS Road 4880 in half a mile and reaches Boulder Lake in another half-mile. While the big trees tend to hug the stream, old Douglas-fir and noble fir extend all the way to Boulder Lake and beyond on a 1.75-mile trail north to Bonnie Meadows. Another 1.75-mile trail will lead you to Little Boulder Lake.

17. White River

An easy, two-mile trail along a Wild and Scenic River through the largest trees left on the Bear Springs Ranger District.

Bear Springs Ranger District
USGS 7.5' MOUNT HOOD SOUTH (1980)
BADGER LAKE (1979)

ABOUT THE AREA

The Barlow Wagon Road, built in 1845-46 and named for its builder, Samuel K. Barlow, was the first road ever constructed over the Cascade Range. Visitors to this area often comment on the irony of the Forest Service's "No Wood Cutting" signs along the historic Barlow Road, as the agency logs the centuries-old trees within sight of the road. This lower portion of the Old Barlow Road (which is better walked than driven) contrasts dramatically with today's typical Forest Service haul roads, and demonstrates how different forest roads could be if built for

recreation and public use rather than just log trucks. Several big trees can be found along this lower portion of the Old Barlow Road, and along Barlow Creek beyond Klinger's Camp.

Between the second and third clearcut on FS Road 240 you'll pass "Arnie's Island," named by Forest Service timber managers for a former ranger on the Bear Springs Ranger District. This remnant ten-acre grove, cut on three sides and abutting the White River on its fourth, contains some of the greatest trees remaining on the district. (Poor Arnie must

79

have taken a lot of ribbing for having left a few big ones standing.) Fortunately, still more large trees reside in the uncut canyon along the trail ahead.

GETTING THERE

From US Highway 26 about 14 miles south of Government Camp, turn north on FS Road 43. After 5.25 miles, turn left (north again) on the Old Barlow Road (FS Road 3530). Or take the White River Road, FS Road 48, from Highway 35 and turn right at the junction of FS Roads 43 and 48, and then right again on FS Road 3530 after crossing the White River.

Drive 2.25 miles up the Old Barlow Road past Barlow Crossing and Barlow Creek Campgrounds. A tenth of a mile

The biggest trees on the Bear Springs Ranger District are on a Boy Scout trail along the congressionally designated Wild and Scenic White River.

before Klinger's Camp (a historic landmark, from which point the Old Barlow Road significantly worsens), turn right on FS Road 240 and drive 1.3 miles to the end of the road where the trail begins. The Forest Service went to great lengths to protect the Old Barlow Road itself by constructing a major log haul road on the other side of Barlow Creek (parallel to the Old Barlow Road). FS Road 240 is an extension of that logging road, and three large clearcuts greet you before the trail does.

RECOMMENDED

The trailhead at the end of FS Road 240 is unmarked, but the trail continues directly in line with the road after a small creek. Boy Scouts built this trail, which is not shown on any maps. It continues about four miles to the Boy Scout camp at the base of Mount Hood, near the junction of FS Road 48 and Oregon Highway 35.

Now the cathedral forest begins. Large diameter Douglas-fir, western red-cedar and various true fir occur along the next two undisturbed miles of trail. You may wish to leave the trail and walk cross-country down to the river. About where the biggest trees stop, the trail leads to the river, where large rocks provide a good stream crossing. From here the trail runs along a stabilized sandbar of volcanic ash among lodgepole pine, fir and some big cottonwoods. It continues up the old road for a couple of miles toward Mount Hood, through a riparian zone along a glacial moraine between the White River and Iron Creek.

18. Barlow Pass

A half-mile walk to a small but lovely old growth grove beside Barlow Creek.

Bear Springs Ranger District
USGS 7.5' MOUNT HOOD SOUTH (1980)

ABOUT THE AREA

This is a fine place for a short hike in summer, mushroom collecting in fall, or intermediate-level cross-country skiing in winter.

GETTING THERE

Take Highway 26 to Mount Hood and the Hood River Highway 35 North turn-off. Proceed 2.5 miles on Highway 35 to the 60-mile post and Barlow Pass, and turn right on FS Road 3531. A parking area for the Pacific Crest Trail (PCT) and Barlow Ridge Trail #670 is just ahead on the right, after the Highway 35 turn-off.

RECOMMENDED

While FS Road 3530 (which takes off to the left) is identified as the historic Barlow Wagon Road, portions of the actual roadbed also followed (and are visible along) Barlow Ridge Trail #670. Follow this trail across the "developed" Barlow Wagon Road and downhill; this stretch is also called Mineral Jane Ski Trail. Continue ahead on FS Trail #670 past a junction on the left for Barlow Butte and FS Trail #485, through a meadow and into a grove of large 400 to 500-year-old noble fir, Douglas-fir, western hemlock and western red-cedar.

19. Bennett Ridge Connector Cross-Country Ski Tour

Easy cross-country ski route through the biggest high-elevation trees on Mount Hood, en route to the Bennett Ridge Connector.

Bear Springs Ranger District
USGS 7.5' MOUNT HOOD SOUTH (1980)

ABOUT THE AREA

The Bennett Ridge route should not be confused with the Giant Trees Loop described in Klindt Vielbig's *Cross-Country Ski Routes of Oregon's Cascades,* which the Forest Service has clearcut. However, this area's ancient trees were also scheduled for clearcutting. Fortunately, the Forest Service withdrew the threatening Fishhook Timber Sale following a 1988 lawsuit filed by the Sierra Club Legal Defense Fund on behalf of the Oregon Nordic Club and Oregon Natural Resources Council. This pro-

posed timber sale near the popular White River Snow Park would have eliminated a host of ancient forest and recreational values, including completion of the final portion of the 20-mile Wy'East Skiing Loop, which follows a historic wagon road through areas of outstanding old forest.

The cross-country ski route described below provides novice skiers with easy opportunities to experience some impressive old growth Douglas-fir and noble fir. The route becomes increasingly difficult (or challenging, depending on your perspective) as it continues on to Bennett Ridge on the steep, winding Bennett Ridge Connector. When you see these big trees, please remember how close they came to falling to the saw. Watch for the small (souvenir!) paper signs on the big trees which declare Boundary Fishhook Timber Sale, and rejoice that this part of the forest is, at least for now, no longer slated for logging.

GETTING THERE

From Portland take Highway 26 to Mount Hood and the Hood River Highway 35 North turn-off. Proceed 4.5 miles on Highway 35 to White River East Snow-park on the east side of the road.

RECOMMENDED

Ski down FS Road 48, which parallels Iron Creek and the White River deep in its canyon below. In 0.7 mile the road crosses Iron Creek. Another quarter-mile down FS Road 48, Mount Hood's massive slopes loom above you. After Iron Creek, head up FS Road 530 to the left, to a nice grove of noble fir, Engelmann spruce and mountain hemlock. Or bear right and continue on FS Road 530 another 0.8 mile to another spur road (to the left) and the Bennett Ridge Connector Trail, through large noble and Douglas-fir.

One of the finest ancient forest cross-country ski routes on Mount Hood was saved from clearcutting by an ONRC lawsuit.

20. Badger Creek Wilderness

Classic eastern Cascades old growth mixed-conifer forest, including a nice stand of western red-cedar.

Barlow Ranger District
USGS 7.5' BADGER LAKE (1979)

ABOUT THE AREA

Ancient forest groves are concentrated near stream bottoms where cooler and moister environments have conferred greater resistance to fire. The biggest trees are in a two-mile corridor along Badger Creek from a half-mile below Badger Lake to just below the mouth of Gumjuwac Creek. (This stream is named for Gum Shoe Jack, a French Canadian sheepherder.) Fifteen species of conifers can be found along these trails! In years with heavy snowpacks, it may not be possible to reach the area before the end of June.

GETTING THERE

From the junction of US Highway 26 and Oregon Highway 35 on Mount Hood, continue on Highway 35 for two and a half miles past Robin Hood Campground to FS Road 44. Turn right on FS Road 44 for 3.8 miles, then right again on FS Road 4410 at a sign for "High Prairie 6 miles." Drive 4.8 miles on FS Road 4410, and turn right on the Bennett Pass Road (FS Road 3550). There will be two trailheads in 1.9 miles on your left, on both sides of a big sign explaining about Gum Shoe Jack.

It is also possible to drive to Badger Lake beginning on FS Road 3530 from Bennett Pass, near the 64-mile post on Highway 35. While it looks tempting on the map, this route is not recommended. The author drove in—once. The first two miles are okay, but the last ten are strictly for high clearance four-wheel drive vehicles (if you want to get back out). Even with such a vehicle, it takes about an hour and a half to drive in on this road. This is the kind of road that keeps wheel alignment shops in business. Take it on faith—walking is faster and far less grueling. Besides, this is a "walking" guide!

RECOMMENDED

From Gumjuwac Saddle, a 6.75-mile loop hike is the easiest way to see both Badger Lake and the ancient forest along Badger Creek. Take FS Trail #480 (just before the sign) which drops two miles down to the junction of Gumjawac Creek and Badger Creek. You'll pass through meadows and a few big Engelmann spruce and Douglas-fir along the way. When you reach Badger Creek the more impressive old groves begin. Turn right and head upstream along Badger Creek on FS Trail #480 for 2.25 miles to Badger Lake. To complete the loop take FS Trail #458 from the north end of Badger Lake two and a half miles back to Gumjawac Saddle. This last trail passes only a few big trees, but provides great views of the lake and the Wilderness canyon.

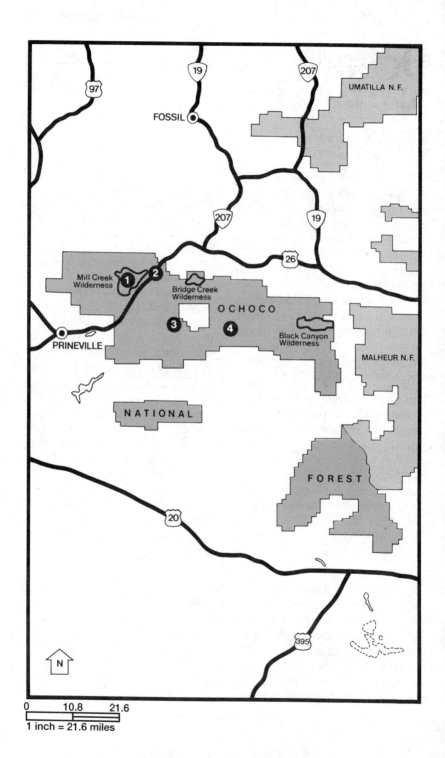

19 207 UMATILLA N. F.

97

FOSSIL ●

207

19

26

Mill Creek Wilderness ① ②

Bridge Creek Wilderness

OCHOCO

③ ④

Black Canyon Wilderness

MALHEUR N. F.

PRINEVILLE ◉

NATIONAL

FOREST

20

395

⬆ N

0   10.8   21.6
1 inch = 21.6 miles

Ochoco National Forest

The Paiute word "ochoco" means "willow." To most people, however, the forests of the Ochoco Mountains in central Oregon are better known for their stupendous stands of old growth ponderosa pine, which once blanketed the region. The 950,000-acre Ochoco National Forest encompasses the Ochoco Mountains and its satellite range, the Maury Mountains. Together these mountains comprise the western end of the Blue Mountains physiographic province, which covers most of northeast Oregon.

The Ochoco National Forest, with its supervisor's office in Prineville, has five ranger districts, one of which is Oregon's only National Grassland, Crooked River. In 1984, three Wilderness Areas on the Ochoco were established by Congress. One of them, Mill Creek, contains the grandest and most extensive ponderosa pine forests currently protected in the National Wilderness System, bar none. Many people believe the finest groves of big pine in Oregon are those found in Lookout Mountain, an unprotected roadless area on the Ochoco Forest long proposed for congressional Wilderness classification by local and statewide conservation and sportsmen organizations.

Don't forget your Ochoco National Forest recreation map.

1. Mill Creek Wilderness and Green Mountain

Groves of big ponderosa pine on the way to Twin Pillars (200' rock monoliths) in this 17,400-acre Wilderness.

Prineville Ranger District
USGS 7.5' WILDCAT MTN. (1985)

ABOUT THE AREA
This is the Ochoco National Forest's only designated Wilderness Area with really big pine trees. It contains almost continuous stands of classic "yellow belly" ponderosa pine, several stream systems, striking rock formations, and a unique wilderness resource. Mill Creek, also known as Big Pine, was one of conservationists' "most wanted" areas for decades; it was finally classified as Wilderness by Congress in the 1984 Oregon Forest Wilderness Act.

GETTING THERE
Drive east of Prineville on US Highway 26 for eight miles, just past the 28-mile post. Turn north (left) on Mill Creek Road (FS Road 33) at a sign for Wildcat Camp, and continue north for ten miles to Wildcat Campground. All but the last few miles are paved.

RECOMMENDED

Mill Creek–Twin Pillars: The trailhead to the Wilderness Area begins at Wildcat Campground, rich with ancient pines. The trail follows Mill Creek the first three and a half miles, with frequent stream crossings over small wooden footbridges and hewn logs. In the next two miles the trail moves into the nicest pine stands (which are above the canyon bottom) as it climbs to Twin Pillars. Follow the trail a half-mile beyond the pillars for another outstanding view of the "rock" and to see some of the area's biggest pines, white firs and larch, next to and just above the trail.

Green Mountain: The Green Mountain roadless area, immediately west of Mill Creek Wilderness, contains ample opportunities for hiking and sightseeing. Both the northern and southern trailheads to an eight-mile trail into the Green Mountain area are near the Mill Creek Wilderness, just off Mill Creek Road (FS Road 33). The biggest old growth white fir and pine are closer to the north end of the trail. The northern trailhead is 4.3 miles past Wildcat Campground, on the left after the junction with FS Road 3320.

From its south end, the trail leads through the lower elevation portion of the roadless area along a dry, open ridge with scattered old growth ponderosa pine and western juniper. To reach that southern trailhead, take Mill Creek Road/FS Road 33 north from Highway 26 for five miles to the end of the pavement, and turn left on FS Road 3370. Drive a quarter-mile, turn left again on FS Road 3380, and continue 3.3 miles to the signed trailhead on the right.

2. Ochoco Summit and Bandit Springs Rest Area

Hiking and cross-country skiing through open meadows and tall ponderosa pine.

Big Summit Ranger District
USGS 15' LOOKOUT MTN. (1951)
USGS 7.5' STEPHENSON MTN. (1985)

ABOUT THE AREA

Beginning 17 miles east of Prineville, US Highway 26 toward Mitchell winds through park-like stands of ponderosa pine for about 12 miles. The area's extensive meadows and ancient pines provide a variety of fine places to hike and camp. Unfortunately, the Forest Service continues logging the biggest yellow belly pines, even in the scenic corridor along the highway. You'll notice some of their recent mischief west of the summit south of the highway.

GETTING THERE

The Bandit Springs rest area, near the 49-mile post on Highway 26, is a good place to start exploring. Another easy first stop is Ochoco Divide Campground, where many ancient trees still stand. It is just south of the main highway at the summit, one mile north and east of the rest area.

RECOMMENDED

From the rest area, several cross-country ski trails follow the meadows, ridges and logging roads north of Highway 26. They are marked with blue diamond signs.

For a nice hike into some "unmanaged" old growth ponderosa pine, follow FS Road 400 from the Bandit Springs rest area. (The Ochoco National Forest recreation map does not show this road.) As soon as you come to the cattle gate turn north (left), cross the meadow, and follow the fenceline into the woods.

For a longer ski or auto excursion, turn north on FS Road 27, a half-mile north and east of Bandit Springs rest area. In

0.6 mile on the right is a pretty meadow surrounded by old growth pine. On the left, a narrow gravel road, FS Road 650 (not marked on the Ochoco National Forest recreation map), heads east above and through the ancient forest. If you follow FS Road 27 for about five miles, you'll come to a viewpoint (elevation about 6000') overlooking the Mill Creek Wilderness and Round and Lookout Mountains to the south and west, and the John Day and Mitchell Valleys to the east.

3. Lookout Mountain Wilderness (proposed)

This exhilarating and accessible proposed Wilderness Area includes the nicest groves of ancient ponderosa pine on the Ochoco National Forest.

Big Summit Ranger District
USGS 15' LOOKOUT MTN. (1951)

ABOUT THE AREA
Conservationists have proposed a 16,577-acre Lookout Mountain Wilderness to protect this critical area from logging, grazing and other depredations. The proposed Lookout Mountain Wilderness contains, in the author's opinion, the finest old growth ponderosa pine stands on the Ochoco National Forest, along Polie Creek.

GETTING THERE
From the Prineville Ranger District office at the east end of Prineville, drive 15 miles east on US Highway 26. Turn right on FS Road 22 at a sign for Ochoco Creek and Ranger Station, and drive east for eight miles.

RECOMMENDED
Next to the Ochoco Ranger Station is a delightful, non-fee campground. About

0.1 mile beyond the ranger station is the trailhead for Lookout Mountain Trail #804, which follows a ridge to the summit. It bisects the roadless area from north to south for its 7.5-mile length. The first three to four miles of this trail pass through some medium to large ponderosa pine, with old western juniper surrounding flat rocky openings. Some great views emerge as the trail climbs 3000' to Lookout Mountain's nearly 7000' summit, from where the Oregon Cascades are visible to the west.

To reach the east side of the proposed Wilderness and some classic flat, open stands of ancient ponderosa pine with broken tops (excellent wildlife habitat), continue 0.3 mile past the ranger station and turn south (right) on FS Road 42. Just after the 12-mile post turn right on FS

Road 250 (not marked on the Ochoco National Forest recreation map) along Brush Creek. A quiet, undisturbed campsite awaits you at the end of this gravel road. The north-facing slope (on your left, to the south) is largely white fir forest. To the north (your right) are some stunning ponderosa pine groves, especially in Sections 23 and 24. Explore the magical pine forest to the north, through mountain meadows and over the ridge to aspen-lined Polie Creek. Carpets of yellow Arnicas (sunflowers) bloom in July.

To reach the summit of Lookout Mountain and the Lookout Mountain Trail from the east (and do most of the climbing in your car), continue another quarter-mile beyond FS Road 250 and turn right on FS Road 300. Follow this gravel road five miles to its end. (You will have to open and close a cattle gate in three miles.) A poorly defined trail, nearly obliterated by a recent Forest Service clearcut, begins at the end of FS Road 300 and follows the ridge west between Brush and Lookout Creeks. Follow the main skid road through the clearcut to the northwest, and pick up the trail in about 150 yards. It is nearly flat for its first two miles, then rises to the summit in a little over one more mile.

FS Road 42 is a pleasant drive on a paved road through ponderosa pine and mixed-conifer forests along the east side of Lookout Mountain. In winter you might drive up FS Road 42 to snowline and cross-country ski to Independent Mine, about a mile from FS Road 42 on FS Road 4205. Bear right at the first fork, at the Round Mountain Trail sign. The latter road leads to the right just after the summit of FS Road 42, as it begins downhill. From the mine a steep trail climbs to the top of Lookout Mountain.

With chainsaws in abundance, Wendell has to work hard to keep the trees standing. (Polie Creek, with its impressive groups of ponderosa pine and quaking aspen intermingled with wet meadows, is included in the proposed Lookout Mountain Wilderness.)

4. North Fork Crooked River

Big ponderosa pine (with some Douglas-fir and western larch) in a scenic rimrock canyon.

Big Summit Ranger District
USGS 7.5' KEYS CREEK (1985)

ABOUT THE AREA

The route described below is an easy, enjoyable cross-country hike along the ponderosa pine-lined North Fork Crooked River—a national Wild and Scenic River—from a campground among the big trees. The North Fork Crooked River is a medium-sized river (crossing it in late winter might be tricky) which flows through a rimrock canyon. From forest in the river bottoms to sagebrush on the canyon rims, the area provides a rich diversity of habitats for wildlife, including Rocky Mountain elk, mule deer, antelope, ruffed and blue grouse, California and mountain quail, and many small fur-bearing animals.

GETTING THERE

Follow the directions for Lookout Mountain (see previous description), but continue on FS Road 42 for a total of 23 paved miles to Deep Creek Campground, where you can park.

RECOMMENDED

South of the campground, follow a jeep trail which parallels Porter Creek and then fords the Crooked River. Shortly after this stream crossing, the jeep road becomes less obtrusive, and ends in a half-mile. A cattle trail continues downstream, and hiking is not difficult except during high water. Some of the largest yellow bellies are two miles down the canyon, near the confluence with Donnelly Creek. This part of the canyon can also be reached by turning east on FS Road 4240 near Donnelly Creek (Section 5 of T15S R22E), four miles before Deep Creek Campground on FS Road 42. Stay on FS Road 42 for 7.5 miles. Park and hike down below the rim to the river.

Except for a couple of mesas over the river, the best places to camp are the grassy forested draws (stringers) with small tributary streams. Expect to see and hear a lot of wildlife if you spend the night.

The ancient ponderosa-lined canyon bottoms provide important thermal cover for eastern Oregon's mule deer. (Photo by Diane Kelsay)

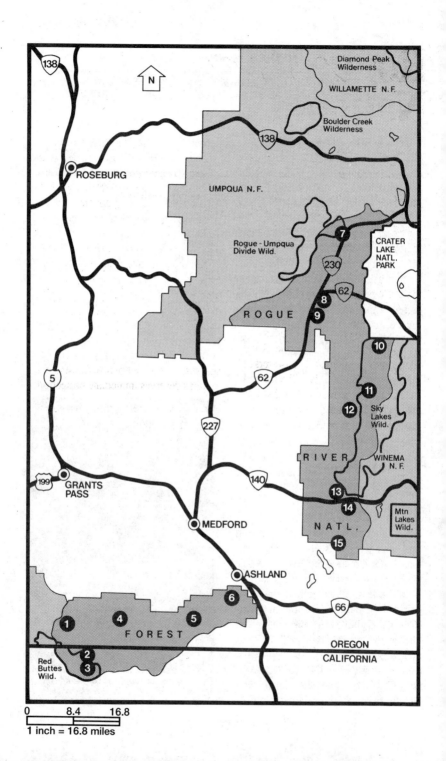

138

N

ROSEBURG

138

Diamond Peak
Wilderness

WILLAMETTE N. F.

Boulder Creek
Wilderness

UMPQUA N. F.

Rogue - Umpqua
Divide Wild.

7

230

CRATER
LAKE
NATL.
PARK

8
9

62

10

5

62

11

12

Sky
Lakes
Wild.

227

R I V E R

WINEMA
N. F.

199

GRANTS
PASS

140

13

14

Mtn
Lakes
Wild.

MEDFORD

N A T L.

15

ASHLAND

6

66

4

1

5

F O R E S T

OREGON

2

CALIFORNIA

3

Red
Buttes
Wild.

0   8.4   16.8

1 inch = 16.8 miles

Rogue River National Forest

The 628,000-acre Rogue River National Forest spans the western slopes of the southern Oregon Cascades, from the edge of Crater Lake National Park to the California border. A disjunct portion lies to the southwest in the Siskiyou-Klamath Mountains and slips partly into California. The supervisor's office is in Medford.

The Rogue River Forest includes not only most of the upper Rogue River drainage itself, but also the headwaters of the Applegate River. It is a diverse and beautiful forest; its four ranger districts encompass portions of two different physiographic provinces and serve as a corridor between them.

For all its scenic grandeur and recreational reputation, this relatively small national forest has been heavily logged. Along with the Winema, Fremont and Siuslaw, the Rogue River National Forest contains only modest ancient forest reserves. Even highly sensitive areas like the Rogue River corridor and boundaries with Crater Lake National Park are managed for serious timber production. The sparse amount of old growth forest which remains deserves immediate protection.

Don't forget your Rogue River National Forest recreation map.

1. Miller Lake

High-elevation old growth mixed-conifer forest, featuring a grove of Siskiyou cypress, one of Oregon's rarest trees.

Applegate (Star) Ranger District
USGS 15' OREGON CAVES (1954)

ABOUT THE AREA
Miller Lake, a popular fishing hole, sits in a pretty basin surrounded by ridges of big true firs and pines. Although the lake has been partially converted to a collection basin for irrigators down Thompson Creek, it remains a wonderfully diverse place. Above Miller Lake is a smaller lake full of yellow water lilies. Trails from the eastern and western sides of the basin climb to the small lake, the wild-flower meadows and big trees above. From the tops of the rocky ridges are outstanding views of Greyback Mountain to the north.

The Siskiyou cypress grove is about a quarter-mile directly east of the northern end of Miller Lake. Simply follow the contours and do not go steeply uphill. Siskiyou cypress (*Cupressus bakori matthewsii*) is rare, known only in a few sites in southern Oregon and northern California. Black lichen grow on the reddish bark of these impressive trees, a few of which are more than 30" in diameter. In addition to the cypress grove, a small stand of the uncommon Brewer spruce can be found on the western ridge above

This old growth Siskiyou cypress near Miller Lake is one of Oregon's rarest conifers.

Miller Lake. (For the best Brewer spruce grove in this guide, see the Babyfoot Lake, Kalmiopsis Wilderness entry in the Siskiyou National Forest chapter.)

GETTING THERE
From I-5 at Grants Pass, take Oregon Highway 238 south for 18 miles to the town of Applegate. Turn south on Thompson Creek Road, which becomes FS Road 10. Drive 11.75 miles and, at a sign for "FS Road 1020 2 miles," make the first possible right turn after the pavement ends, onto FS Road 1010. In 1.5 miles turn right on FS Road 1020. Stay left for three miles and, following signs for Miller Lake, continue straight ahead on FS Road 400 for 3.5 miles to the Miller Lake trailhead at the road's end.

RECOMMENDED
It is only a half-mile from the trailhead to the lake. Because there are no other trails in the valley, exploring this area requires some steep cross-country hiking. Additional trails along the ridges and across the upper lake basin are planned.

2. Middle Fork Applegate River Trail

A lovely streamside trail which passes old miners' cabins and crosses a log foot-bridge among old growth Douglas-fir, ponderosa pine, canyon live oak, madrone, dogwood, and bigleaf and vine maple.

Applegate Ranger District
USGS 15' SEIAD VALLEY (1955)
HAPPY CAMP (1956)

ABOUT THE AREA
Beginning at about 2500', the three-mile Middle Fork Trail #950 is usually accessible year-round. It borders the Red Buttes Wilderness (which straddles the Oregon-California state line), connecting at

several points with trails which climb into the Wilderness Area. Although Middle Fork Trail #950 is actually in California, you'd never know it; this is an easy, cool hike, even on the hottest summer days.

GETTING THERE

From I-5, take Oregon Highway 238 south and east for 27 miles from Grants Pass (or south and west for eight miles from Jacksonville) to the small town of Ruch. Turn south on Applegate Road and drive 19 miles to the upper end of Applegate Reservoir. At the "T" junction of Applegate and Carberry Roads, turn left on Applegate Road and continue 1.3 miles on what becomes FS Road 1040. When the pavement ends (just before the big ponderosa pine at the state line), make the next possible (hard) right turn to stay on FS Road 1040. Drive 5.25 miles along the Middle Fork Applegate River, continuing ahead at the forks, both where FS Road 1040 veers left over a bridge and FS Road 1035 leads right to Whiskey Peak. (The road you end up on is marked, but not numbered, on the Rogue River National Forest recreation map.)

RECOMMENDED

The trailhead for Middle Fork Trail #950 is on the left, 0.2 mile up the road along

the river. For the first quarter-mile the trail follows an old jeep road; when it descends toward the river, continue straight ahead on the footpath.

Northwest old growth forests, including those along the Applegate River, contain more organic material per acre than tropical rainforests.

3. Red Buttes Wilderness

Follow the scenic Butte Fork of the Applegate River to its headwaters at Azalea Lake.

Applegate Ranger District
USGS 15' SEIAD VALLEY (1955)
HAPPY CAMP (1956)

ABOUT THE AREA

Most of the existing 20,323-acre Red Buttes Wilderness is located in California. For the Oregon side of the state line, the House of Representatives passed a modest 25,895-acre bill in 1983, only to have it reduced to 3821 acres by Senator Hatfield in the final version. Conservationists' original proposal would have extended the Wilderness boundary

through the Craggy Mountain Scenic Area to Miller Lake, Bigelow Lake and Oregon Caves National Monument, for a two-state total of about 42,000 acres. The still-wild lands that were excluded from the designated Wilderness Area are now threatened with increased high-elevation clearcutting in both Oregon and California. The Red Buttes Wilderness desperately needs expansion.

Butte Fork Trail #957, in California, reaches some of the nicest stands of old growth within the protected Wilderness, and provides a marvelous introduction to these untrammeled and botanically diverse forestlands. You will see big sugar pine, Port-Orford-cedar, Douglas-fir, and sizeable golden chinquapin on this walk.

GETTING THERE

From I-5, take Oregon Highway 238 south and east for 27 miles from Grants Pass (or south and west for eight miles from Jacksonville) to the small town of Ruch. Turn south on Applegate Road and drive 19 miles to the upper end of Applegate Reservoir. At the "T" junction of Applegate and Carberry Roads, turn left on Applegate Road and continue 1.3 miles on what becomes FS Road 1040. When the pavement ends (just before the big ponderosa pine at the state line), make the next possible (hard) right turn to stay on FS Road 1040. Continue on FS Road 1040 about five miles along the Middle Fork Applegate River, turn left at a bridge over the river (staying on FS Road 1040), and climb the north-facing slope above. Drive 2.5 miles up the logging road from the bridge.

RECOMMENDED

The head of Butte Fork Trail #957 is on the left. In the first half-mile the trail switchbacks through enormous sugar pine and mature "zebra-striped" chinquapin. It then levels out and follows the river deep into the Red Buttes Wilderness. Large Douglas-fir in the lower reaches and a gorgeous Port-Orford-cedar grove at Cedar Basin are among the many highlights of this Wilderness trail.

Massive, ancient sugar pine are not uncommon along the lower elevation trails in Red Buttes Wilderness.

4. Applegate Wilderness (proposed)

*A pristine example of mixed-conifer/
oak woodlands.*

Applegate Ranger District
USGS 7.5' CARBERRY CREEK (1983)

ABOUT THE AREA
While the proposed Applegate Wilderness contains little classic old growth forest, it does include pristine examples of mixed-conifer/oak woodlands (punctuated by grassy areas and outcrops of bedrock) that blanket southern Oregon. In a pattern typical of drier regions, the large trees that do occur are widely dispersed, except in the canyon bottoms. This area is included here because it is easy to reach year-round, and because of its many varied trails.

The two units of the proposed Wilderness, which straddle the Applegate River around Applegate Dam, embrace a range of geologically and botanically diverse sites. The Kinney Mountain Unit, west of the Applegate River, contains the Collings Mountain and Grouse Loop Trails described below. The Little Greyback Unit is east of the Applegate River, and includes trails up Little Greyback, Mule Mountain and Baldy Peak.

In addition to the Rogue River National Forest recreation map, you may want to consult the Applegate Ranger District fireman's map for detailed information.

GETTING THERE
From I-5 at Grants Pass, take Highway 238 south and east for 27 miles (or south and west for eight miles from Jacksonville) to the small town of Ruch. Turn south on Applegate Road and drive 16.5 miles to Hart-Tish Park on Applegate Reservoir.

RECOMMENDED
Grouse Loop Trail #941, which is marked by a small sign, begins at the picnic area and crosses the road 0.1 mile south of the turn-off. Walk down the road a bit further south to Grouse Creek and Collings Mountain Trail #943, which follows the stream above the canyon's headwalls. In its first mile, Collings Mountain Trail #943 crosses two footbridges over Grouse Creek and passes a grove of old growth Douglas-fir, a miner's cabin and mine shaft. The trail winds through the forest for another four miles before descending at the southern end of the reservoir.

5. Seven Mile Ridge, Red Mountain Special Interest Area

*The largest remnant of roadless ancient
forest in this watershed.*

Applegate Ranger District
USGS 7.5' SISKIYOU PEAK (1983)

ABOUT THE AREA
This portion of the mountainous headwaters of the Little Applegate Valley ranges from low-elevation riparian ancient forest to the high Siskiyous Crest. It is endowed with diverse plant communities, abundant wildlife, reaches of three free-flowing creeks, sweeping meadows, giant trees, high mountain lakes, a 300'

waterfall, and an interesting but unmaintained trail system.

This premier Siskiyou Mountains old growth forest had been threatened by two large timber sales and a proposed road on Hells Peak. These projects have been postponed for now, thanks to the involvement of local conservationists. A Red Mountain Special Interest Area was proposed by the Little Applegate Watershed Council and the Rogue Group Sierra Club, in order to protect and enhance the priceless and irreplaceable watershed and wildlife values of this spectacular forest. Only part of the area was so designated.

GETTING THERE
From I-5 south of Medford, take the Talent exit. One block after the main stoplight in Talent, turn left on old Highway 99. Turn right on Wagner Creek

Big "bull" pine along the trail midway up Seven Mile Ridge.

Road and drive five miles to the end of the pavement. Follow the main dirt road up Wagner Creek for five miles to Wagner Gap.

RECOMMENDED
From Wagner Gap there are two attractive options. Note that you can reach the Seven Mile Ridge Trail from either trailhead, although it's a cross-country hike from the Pacific Crest Trail (PCT). The Seven Mile Ridge Trail route is the shortest way to the big trees, and the best option if you are not familiar with the terrain.

Seven Mile Ridge Trail (Glade Creek Trailhead): From Wagner Gap turn right on FS Road 2250. Drive seven miles to FS Road 2030 and turn left. Cross the bridge over Glade Creek, bear left at the fork in the road, and drive three miles up Glade Creek to the Seven Mile Ridge Trail sign. On the trail, you'll pass through riparian old growth Douglas-fir which has been partially logged. Cross Glade Creek on a log and enter the roadless area, passing through superb groves of giant incense-cedar and Douglas-fir. The trail follows a pleasant spring gulch, then begins switchbacks up through ancient ponderosa and sugar pine.

You'll probably notice the proposed clearcut survey ribbons, which for now help define the trail. Nice bluffs and open slopes along the way afford sobering views of the advancing clearcuts. About 2.5 miles up the trail is Hells Peak Saddle, a great spot for a lunch break in a magnificent grove of giant ponderosa pine. The trail continues through dense forest up Seven Mile Ridge to Jack Flat and Red Mountain.

Pacific Crest Trailhead: Turn left at Wagner Gap on FS Road 22, and drive eight miles to the junction with FS Road 20. Turn right on FS Road 20, and continue seven miles to Wrangle Gap and the trailhead for the Pacific Crest Trail. It's an easy hike on the PCT into the exquisite Red Mountain-Monogram Lakes Basin.

Before reaching the lakes, you can drop down along the spine of Seven Mile Ridge cross-country for .5 mile and pick up the Seven Mile Ridge Trail. This is a moderately difficult hike through steep high-elevation meadows, ridgecrests, and old growth Shasta red fir and western hemlock. At Jack Flat Meadow, an old miner's cabin commands spectacular views of the Applegate Valley. The trail continues down Seven Mile Ridge, deep into the roadless old growth forest.

6. City of Ashland Watershed

Old growth mixed-evergreen forest, including large ponderosa and sugar pine along a little-used trail.

Ashland Ranger District
USGS 7.5' MOUNT ASHLAND (1983)
ASHLAND (1983)

ABOUT THE AREA

Ashland's water is supplied to its Reeder Reservoir by the forested hills between the city and Mount Ashland, which are designated the Ashland Watershed. On the east side of the watershed, a long section of canyon along the East Fork of Ashland Creek has been classified the Ashland Creek Research Natural Area (RNA) to protect it from logging. Two of the three trails described below lead through undisturbed Douglas-fir and ponderosa pine (and wildflowers in the spring) in the RNA. The third option, which takes you to the most ancient trees, is along the West Fork of Ashland Creek, above the reservoir. In the spring of 1990, ONRC appealed a Forest Service plan to helicopter-log some of the largest trees and standing snags in the watershed.

Please note: National Forest boundaries here are gated. Check with the Ashland Ranger District (482-3333) before your trip to ensure passage to the trailhead. If you wish to enter the Ashland Watershed from the bottom rather than the top, as in the following description, you must obtain access authorization by calling 482-3211, ext. 25 in Ashland. The lower watershed and area around the reservoir is patrolled by the Ashland City Police, who issue citations for unauthorized entry. It's less hassle to explore the upper watershed, which contains the most impressive trees anyway.

GETTING THERE

From downtown Ashland turn west off East Main on Winburn Way for Lithia Park. Drive 1.5 miles on Winburn Way through the park (past the first turn for Granite in 0.7 mile) to the intersection of Winburn Way, Granite and Grandview.

If you're heading for the recommended trail on and above the West Fork of Ashland Creek, turn right on Granite. Stay on this road, which narrows and becomes FS Road 2060, for 3.6 miles to FS Road 200 on the left. Turn left and drive 4.6 miles to the end of FS Road 200 and the trailhead. A spur road on the left, FS Road 270, is not the trail.

For the East Fork of Ashland Creek and the Research Natural Area, turn left on Grandview instead. Drive 0.4 mile and make a sharp right on Ashland Loop Road. In another 0.4 mile, at the junction of Terrace Street and Ashland Loop Road, bear right and continue 2.7 miles on Ashland Loop Road to a pull-out on the right and a sign for the Ashland Nature Trail. The first mile and a half of Ashland Loop Road (before it enters the National Forest) are deeply rutted, but passable in a regular passenger car.

RECOMMENDED
The trail to the West Fork of Ashland Creek spills gradually downhill for 1.5 miles, to just below the upper forks of the

stream. From here a jeep road runs downstream along the west bank to Reeder Reservoir. It comes out on FS Road 2060 near the bottom of the canyon.

The easy, mile-long Ashland Nature Trail leads to good views of Mount Ashland and the canyon above the East Fork of Ashland Creek. Markers along the trail identify the area's common trees and shrubs; in spring, wildflowers abound. A special bonus: large trees and snags have fallen across the trail, attesting to the natural character of this unique and special area.

Directly behind the Ashland Nature Trail sign, a steep and primitive half-mile trail heads downhill to the new mouth of the East Fork of Ashland Creek, where it enters the reservoir. This area is signed "No overnight camping."

7. Muir Creek

Scattered groves of large old Douglas-fir along a lovely stream and wide beaver marsh.

Prospect Ranger District
USGS 7.5' HAMAKER BUTTE (1985)

ABOUT THE AREA
This is an impressive higher elevation ancient forest walk, with big trees and sizeable bogs and meadows. Beaver dams and lodges can be seen from vistas overlooking the marsh. Signs of elk and other wildlife abound. There are no facilities, but pleasant campsites can be found on either side of Muir Creek.

GETTING THERE
Follow the directions under the Upper Rogue River Trail and Scenic Drive entry (following in this chapter) to the junction of Oregon Highway 62 and Oregon Highway 230. Take Highway 230 north toward

Diamond Lake and the north entrance of Crater Lake National Park. The Muir Creek trailhead is on the west side of the road, one-third mile north of the ten-mile post and south of the bridge over the creek.

RECOMMENDED
Muir Creek Trail #1042 climbs over a hill to reveal a fantastic marsh fed by a meandering stream. The trail, steep in places, leads around the marsh and up the West Fork of Muir Creek to Buck Canyon Trail #1046, a total of 3.5 miles. You can also reach this upper portion of the trail, which leads into the Rogue-Umpqua Divide Wilderness, from High-

way 230. Turn west (left) on FS Road 6560 about a quarter-mile north of the 12-mile post, and then turn left again, in a little over a mile, on FS Road 190. The trailhead is at the end of FS Road 190, one mile past Ice Creek, which flows into

Muir Creek. For Muir Creek, take the first fork to the left, a quarter-mile down the trail. The straight-ahead fork leads up Buck Canyon into the Rogue-Umpqua Divide Wilderness. See the Rogue River National Forest recreation map for details.

8. Union Creek

Acre for acre, the nicest old growth forest trail on the Rogue River National Forest.

Prospect Ranger District
USGS 15' PROSPECT (1956)

ABOUT THE AREA
Easy access, a splendid streamside trail, waterfalls, and super old growth Douglas-fir make this a "five star" ancient forest walk. You'll wish the 4.4-mile trail would never end.

Across the road a novice level, 1.3-mile cross-country skiing trail glides through big old trees and across two wooden footbridges in the Union Creek Campground, at the confluence of Union Creek and the Rogue River. This short ski tour is possible only when snow reaches the lower elevations. (Union Creek Campground is at 3300'.) For snow information, call the Union Creek Resort at 560-3565.

GETTING THERE
Follow the directions under the Upper Rogue River Trail and Scenic Drive entry (next) to Oregon Highway 62. Drive north past Prospect to Union Creek, at the 56-mile post.

RECOMMENDED
The trailhead for Union Creek Trail #1035 is on the east side of Highway 62, just south of Union Creek Resort and a bridge over Union Creek.

The upper trailhead (at the eastern

terminus of Union Creek Trail #1035) can also be reached from Highway 62. Follow it towards Crater Lake National Park; at 0.3 mile east of the 59-mile post, turn south (right) on FS Road 600, then left on FS Road 610, following signs for Union Creek Trail. The trailhead is a half-mile from Highway 62.

The author's wife, Kathy, examines the thick bark that has helped this ancient giant survive over time.

9. Upper Rogue River Trail and Scenic Drive

Some of the most impressive old growth Douglas-fir and mixed-conifer forests left on the Prospect Ranger District, along a 47-mile trail.

Prospect Ranger District
USGS 15' PROSPECT (1956)
ABBOTT BUTTE (1944)

ABOUT THE AREA

While old growth forests are best appreciated on foot, unobstructed by your car's roof and unblurred by its speed, the big trees along the heavily travelled Oregon Highway 62 corridor make it one of the nicest drives in the state. In addition to ancient forests, a kaleidoscope of scenery includes the wild Rogue River and striking geologic formations like Takelma Gorge, Natural Bridge, Rogue Gorge and the pumice canyons.

In the 3.5 miles between the Rogue Gorge and Natural Bridge, the Rogue River provides a spectacular setting for two of the finest riverside trails in Oregon. Upper Rogue River Trail #1034, which follows the river's west bank for 47 miles, is complemented in this brief section by Rogue Gorge Trail #1034A, which follows the east bank, between the river and Highway 62. Some lovely ancient forest groves can be found along the river for another 7.5 miles downstream, as far as River Bridge Campground.

The Forest Service has maintained a quarter-mile buffer strip along Oregon Highway 62 and the Rogue River, but does not protect the forest between them. While many large old growth trees remain, the agency's management goal is not ancient forest protection but "scenic retention," which allows the removal of individual old growth trees as younger trees grow up to hide logging otherwise visible from the highway and trail.

What scenic retention really means is that the Forest Service can continue to cut down big trees in what should be completely protected zones. Camper safety, root rot and bark beetles provide the most frequent excuses for removal of the old giants. The greatly compromised Mammoth Pines Loop Trail is a case in point. You will encounter many stumps and some skid roads along the trail. When the trail descends through low ravines, if the forest above is not visible from the trail, most likely it is no longer there. If the biological diversity and scenic grandeur are to remain, all the remaining big trees should be truly protected, not salvaged.

GETTING THERE

If you are coming from the north on I-5, take the Canyonville exit to Oregon Highway 227. Enjoy this rural and mountainous drive, which crosses the southern end of the Rogue-Umpqua Divide and brings you to the town of Trail. Turn left on Oregon Highway 62, following signs for Prospect. From the south on I-5, take the Highway 62 exit at Medford for Prospect. Drive north on Highway 62 past Prospect.

From the Bend area, take US Highway 97 south to Oregon Highway 138, drive west to Oregon Highway 230, and continue west and south on Oregon 230 to Oregon Highway 62 at the Rogue Gorge. If you're down by Klamath Falls, just follow Highway 62 through Crater Lake National Park to the Rogue River Gorge.

The ancient forest along the upper Rogue River Trail provides the ecosystem structure necessary for diverse wildlife and fisheries habitat.

RECOMMENDED

The largest trees are along ten miles of a dramatic stretch of the Rogue River. This section of river and the trail along its banks are described below in three sections, from River Bridge Campground upstream to the Woodruff Bridge picnic area, Natural Bridge Campground and the Rogue River Gorge. (You may, of course, walk the sections in either direction.)

For a short but nice drive along this part of the river, turn west into the Natural Bridge and Union Creek Campgrounds near mile posts 55 and 56, and drive through the big trees on flat river terraces. Even though many "hazard trees" have been salvaged, these are some of the nicest old groves found anywhere on the Rogue River National Forest. If you think this kind of forest is still common, just take any side road.

River Bridge Campground to Woodruff Bridge picnic area (4.6 miles): From Prospect take Highway 62 north for 3.6 miles past the Prospect Ranger

District Office, and turn left for River Bridge Campground a quarter-mile north of the 49-mile post. The trailheads (upstream and downstream) are on the east side of the river before the bridge. The trailhead to the left leads back towards Prospect to a section of river which has been heavily logged a short way downstream, and is not recommended for an ancient forest walk.

Instead, turn right into River Bridge Campground. The trailhead (and parking) for the trail upstream along the east shore is on the left. A key attraction on this portion of the Upper Rogue River Trail is the wild, raging Rogue itself, as it passes through Takelma Gorge. This gorge begins a mile and a half downstream from Woodruff Bridge picnic area, the easiest access point for the gorge.

Woodruff Bridge picnic area to Natural Bridge and Natural Bridge Campground (3.5 miles): Two miles north of the River Bridge turn-off on Highway 62, turn west on FS Road 68 at a sign for "Abbott Camp 3 miles." Drive 1.8 miles on FS Road 68 to the up- and down-stream trailheads, which are just before an auto bridge across the Rogue River and just past the turn-off into the Woodruff Bridge picnic area. Walk downstream for Takelma Gorge. If you walk upstream you will come to Natural Bridge Geologic Area, where the entire Rogue River passes through a series of lava tubes. A man-made bridge provides good views of the area, and access to both an interpretive trail and the continuation of Upper Rogue River Trail #1034 on the west bank of the river.

Natural Bridge Campground to Rogue River Gorge (3 to 6 miles): Approximately 3.4 miles north of the Woodruff Bridge picnic area on Highway 62 (just south of the 55-mile post), turn west on FS Road 300 for Natural Bridge and the Natural Bridge Campground. A large parking area for Natural Bridge is ahead on the left. You can get to the eastside Rogue Gorge Trail #1034A from anywhere on the far eastern end of the campground along the river shore.

A mile upstream from Natural Bridge, a footbridge crosses the Rogue River. The Upper Rogue River Trail follows the Rogue's west bank another five miles to the Big Bend trailhead, which is accessible from FS Road 6510 off Highway 230. For a view of the spectacular Rogue Gorge and more big trees up Union Creek (see previous description in this chapter), do not cross the footbridge. Instead, continue another two miles upstream along the east side of the river on Rogue Gorge Trail #1034A, to where the trail joins Highway 62 at the Rogue River Gorge Visitor Area, just beyond the Union Creek Resort.

10. Red Blanket Creek, Sky Lakes Wilderness

A closed canopy of mature grand fir and old growth Douglas-fir.

Prospect Ranger District
USGS 7.5' UNION PEAK (1985)
RED BLANKET MTN (1985)

ABOUT THE AREA
The Red Blanket Trail, which follows the stream of the same name high into the northern reaches of Sky Lakes, begins at the northwest corner of the Sky Lakes Wilderness Area, only several hundred yards from the southwest corner of Crater Lake National Park. At the trailhead is a lovely little pond on the left and a bubbling spring on the hillside high above. The large trees in this area grow on relatively dry lands, and are a critical component of this important big game habitat. The area serves as a key migration corridor and provides thermal cover for elk and deer.

GETTING THERE
Follow directions in the preceding Upper Rogue River Trail and Scenic Drive entry for Oregon Highway 62 to Prospect. In downtown Prospect turn east on the Butte Falls-Prospect Road (unmarked) at the turn for Red Blanket Road and the airport. In one mile turn left on Red Blanket Road, then bear left in 0.3 mile on FS Road 6205. Stay on this gravel road for 12 miles to the Red Blanket trailhead at its end. (Note: FS Road 6205 is closed from December 1 to April 15 for purposes of protecting elk wintering and calving activities during this crucial time.)

RECOMMENDED

After a quarter-mile the trail switchbacks twice, then climbs steeply for two miles to take wilderness travelers above cascading waterfalls and a deep ravine. It then joins the stream, which you can't see from the trail before this point.

If you are not planning an extended trip into the Sky Lakes Wilderness Area, open stands of ancient forest close to the trailhead create attractive cross-country walks that are in many ways easier than the trail. Before the first hairpin switchback, cut downhill to benches along Red Blanket Creek where the largest trees still stand. Watch for elk sign, which is often in abundance here.

The Red Blanket Creek old growth corridor on the southwest corner of Crater Lake National Park is an important elk migration route between the Park and National Forest lands.

11. King Spruce Trail, Sky Lakes Wilderness

A Wilderness trail into the dramatic Seven Lakes Basin, through some large Engelmann spruce.

Butte Falls Ranger District
USGS 7.5' IMNAHA CREEK (1985)

ABOUT THE AREA

King Spruce Trail #980 is more of a wilderness hike than an ancient forest walk, but big old Engelmann spruce along and above a pretty meadow make the trip worthwhile even for big tree fanatics.

Although they do not form the closed canopy seen in lower elevation old growth forests, these spruce are quite large for this relatively high elevation. It is easy to identify Engelmann spruce by their grey flaky bark and sharp needles.

Although the author has hiked this area (through snow) as early as May 10, it is often early June before King Spruce Trail #981 is really accessible. Check trail conditions with the Butte Falls Ranger District (865-3581).

GETTING THERE

Follow the directions in the preceding Upper Rogue River Trail and Scenic Drive entry for Highway 62 to Prospect. Turn east on the Butte Falls-Prospect Road (which is not marked) at the turn for Red Blanket Road and the airport. Drive about two miles east and turn left on Bessie Creek Road (FS Road 37). Stay on FS Road 37 for 12 miles, then turn left on gravel FS Road 3780 at the sign for "Seven Lakes Trail 4 miles." There is a large pull-out at the trailhead.

RECOMMENDED

The first, steep half-mile of trail (which may be marked as FS #980 or #981) travels through a younger forest of true fir and mountain hemlock. At the trail junction, bear left on King Spruce Trail #980 (for Lake Alta). After a mile on this more level trail, which traverses a north-facing slope high above the forks of Sumpter Creek, you'll find a spectacular mountain meadow and the first large Engelmann spruce. Above the meadow giant true fir trees tower over wildflowers fed by many springs. The trail leads to the upper end of the meadow and a few more big spruce, then switches back on the opposite slope. It is on this south-facing slope, about 2.5 miles from the trailhead, that the largest grove of spruce lives. Some are three feet in diameter.

12. South Fork Rogue River Trail

Excellent views of the river and a stand of large conifers.

Butte Falls Ranger District
USGS 7.5' IMNAHA CREEK (1985)
RUSTLER PEAK (1985)

ABOUT THE AREA

This pleasant and easy 5.3-mile trail is one of the nicest on the Butte Falls Ranger District. It is actually a recently constructed downstream section of South Fork Trail #988, which follows the South Fork Rogue River further upstream into the Sky Lakes Wilderness. Lower South Fork Trail #988 leads to five footbridges, beautiful views of the river, and a really nice stand of large mixed-conifers. Brook trout beckon you to bring a fishing pole.

GETTING THERE

From Prospect: Follow directions for King Spruce Trail #980 (see above). Instead of turning left on FS Road 3780,

hold to the right and drive exactly one half-mile further on FS Road 37 to FS Road 34. The downstream trailhead is 0.1 mile further west.

From Butte Falls: Take the main road from town about one mile east to the Prospect-Butte Falls Road. Turn north and drive about nine miles to FS Road 34 (Lodgepole Road). Turn east on FS Road 34 and continue over the South Fork Rogue River to just before the junction with FS Road 37. This is a total of about 18 miles, paved all the way.

RECOMMENDED

A quarter-mile east of the FS Road 34 bridge over the South Fork Rogue River (and about one-tenth of a mile west of the junction of FS Roads 34 and 37) is a large, signed parking area for South Fork Trail #988. The trail leads to the South Fork Rogue River through park-like stands of mixed-conifers, including some large old growth ponderosa pine. It then follows the east bank of the river upstream.

For the upstream trailhead, drive south on FS Road 37 from the junction with FS Road 34. Continue about five and a half miles (0.1 mile past FS Road 720) to the trailhead and a parking area on the right, just before the bridge over the South Fork Rogue River. To reach a small rustic

camping area on the river's west bank, turn right on FS Road 3450 after the South Fork bridge, then take the next right on FS Road 800 in a half-mile.

If you want to hike the upper portion of South Fork Rogue River Trail #988 into the Sky Lakes Wilderness Area, turn south off FS Road 37 on FS Road 720 (just east of the upper South Fork bridge) and drive one mile to the trailhead at the end of the road. Regrettably, as is so often the case, the big trees stop just beyond the Wilderness boundary. A large shelterwood cut east of FS Road 37 similarly defines the congressionally designated boundary there.

13. Rye Spring

A cross-country hike through a cathedral forest of Douglas-fir, Shasta red fir and western white pine.

Butte Falls Ranger District
USGS 15' MOUNT MCLOUGHLIN (1955)

ABOUT THE AREA
One of the most magnificent ancient forest groves left on the Prospect Ranger District, Rye Spring is adjacent to (but unprotected by) the Sky Lakes Wilderness. It is a pleasant walk, with nearby cross-country skiing opportunities in the winter. Just north of Fish Lake, this area is near many popular recreation sites. As you drive up FS Road 3740, you'll notice the native trees along Oregon Highway 140 constitute only a scenic corridor, although one gorgeous old grove survives on the east side of FS Road 3740 on your way in.

GETTING THERE
From Oregon Highway 140, turn north a quarter-mile east of the 29-mile post on

FS Road 3740, at a sign for "Rye Spring 2 miles" (it's actually 2.3). Immediately after the turn, a cross-country ski trail (paralleling the main highway, but through big trees) heads off to the east (right). Also, the first road to the right(FS Road 900) is a good two-mile cross-country ski trail through big trees.

At the next sign for Rye Spring, turn right on FS Road 600, which dead-ends at a barbed wire fence around Rye Spring in 0.1 mile. The spring was dug to create a pool for fire pump trucks (an ignominious fate). Together with the large clearcut on the right, they create the impression that something more was here when the Forest Service first began advertising it for public use.

RECOMMENDED

Follow the edge of the clearcut above the spring and up the hill. A short spur road leads from the northwest corner of the clearcut into the cathedral forest. Although you will cross the Sky Lakes Wilderness boundary if you continue ahead (north), most of the grove is not protected by classified Wilderness. This is a common problem in Pacific Northwest Wilderness Areas, and an especially serious one throughout Oregon.

14. Fish Lake

Ancient Douglas-fir and Shasta red fir between Fish Lake and Oregon Highway 140.

Ashland Ranger District
USGS 15' MOUNT MCLOUGHLIN (1955)

ABOUT THE AREA

Some of the largest old trees left on the Butte Falls Ranger District stand along the Highway 140 scenic corridor from three miles west of Fish Lake to just east of Lake of the Woods. (Also see the Lake of the Woods entry in the Winema National Forest chapter.) Unfortunately, the Forest Service is now planning to sell the big trees in these visual corridors.

GETTING THERE

After visiting Rye Springs (see the previous description in this chapter), turn south off Oregon Highway 140 about 0.1 mile east of the 29-mile post (and 0.15 miles west of the Rye Springs turn-off) on FS Road 190 and park.

RECOMMENDED

Walk along the narrow dirt roads through this old growth fir forest. Please respect the privacy of homeowners along the north shore of Fish Lake and do not drive all the way in. To reach the lake but not the summer homes, bear to the left (southeast) through some really big Douglas-fir. Keep in mind this can be a busy spot on weekends.

Another impressive but lesser-known trail, with fewer big trees, skirts a nifty little marsh along Little Butte Creek. This trail begins across from the North Fork Campground on FS Road 37, just west of Fish Lake. (See the Rogue River National Forest recreation map.)

15. Big Draw

A short cross-country hike through old growth grand fir and Douglas-fir on the way to Lake of the Woods.

Ashland Ranger District
USGS 15' MOUNT MCLOUGHLIN (1955)

ABOUT THE AREA

While there are neither roads nor trails in this area, the route recommended below is an easy cross-country hike through a great ancient forest to a pristine meadow.

GETTING THERE

From I-5 at Ashland, take Exit 14 to Oregon Highway 66 and drive east toward Klamath Falls. In 0.6 mile turn left on Dead Indian Road. Turn right on FS Road 2520 about 0.7 mile east of the 27-mile post, at a sign for Old Baldy and Keno Access Road. Drive one mile on FS Road 2520.

RECOMMENDED

Fifty feet past the one-mile post, walk down an old spur road on the right across a creek. Continue heading (mostly) perpendicular to FS Road 2520, but slightly downhill. In a quarter-mile you'll come to a stunning meadow surrounded by old growth forest.

The berries of mountain Oregon grape (Berberis nervosa) *provide an important food source for blue grouse and other ancient forest denizens.*

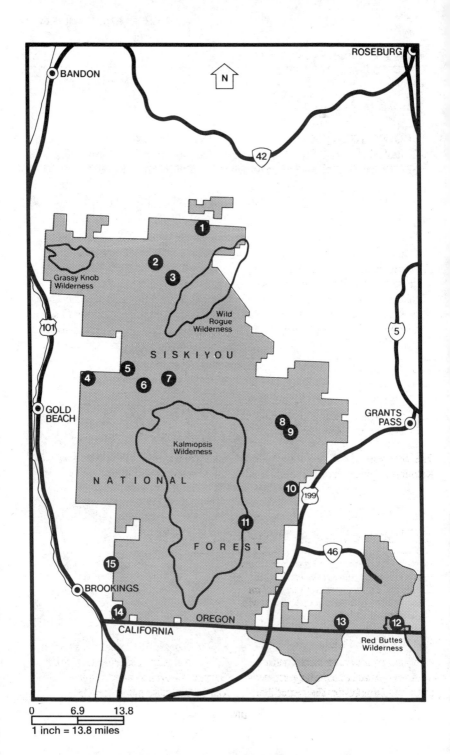

Siskiyou National Forest

The Siskiyou National Forest in southwest Oregon (and just a bit in California) is perhaps the state's most renowned federal forest. It contains one of the oldest and most diverse botanical landscapes in North America; scientists refer to the Siskiyous as the "Smoky Mountains of the West."

The million-acre Siskiyou National Forest is administered through five ranger districts, and headquartered in Grants Pass. It contains five federal Wild and Scenic Rivers (the Rogue, Illinois, Chetco, Elk and North Fork Smith) and three Wilderness Areas. Oregon's only ancient redwoods can be found here as well.

The Siskiyou Forest is home to the Kalmiopsis Wilderness and its adjacent wildlands, which encompass the unparalleled Illinois River. This region, known as the North Kalmiopsis, has been the site of many classic conservation battles. For the past decade or so numerous incidents of civil disobedience have occurred, including tree sitting, tree spiking and several protests. ONRC and others have filed several lawsuits in efforts to stop illegal logging and roadbuilding. Today, many conservation, sportsmen and business organizations are working together to establish a Siskiyou National Park, which would include the North Kalmiopsis and a large portion of the Siskiyou National Forest, along with some BLM and other public lands.

Don't forget your Siskiyou National Forest recreation map.

1. World's Largest Port-Orford-Cedar

Port-Orford-cedar is found only in northwest California and southwest Oregon. Continued logging and the spread of an associated root disease jeopardize survival of the species.

Powers Ranger District
USGS 7.5' CHINA FLAT (1986)

ABOUT THE AREA

A day use picnic area is located near the record tree, as well as some large incense-cedar and Douglas-fir. The record Port-Orford-cedar is 219' high and just under 12' in diameter. Unfortunately, Forest Service clearcuts have rendered the nearby landscape a little exposed.

Logging has already wiped out vast areas of Port-Orford-cedar. However, the greatest threat to the tree is not the chainsaw but rather an introduced root rot, *Phytophthora lateralis*. The spores of this fungus can spread through an entire watershed when logging trucks carrying contaminated mud enter a formerly pristine, unroaded forest valley. Given the scarcity of Port-Orford-cedar and the serious threats it faces, ONRC and several local conservation and other citizens' organizations are actively seeking protection for all remaining undisturbed groves.

For more information on the ecology of this remarkable forest type, write the Pacific Northwest Forest and Range Experiment Station, PO Box 3890, Portland, Oregon 97208 and request a copy of Report PNW-184, *Ecology, Pathology and Management of Port-Orford-Cedar*, September 1985.

Port-Orford-cedar is one of the few tree species now being clearcut and legally exported as raw logs from National Forest lands. An exception to the usual ban on raw log exports from federal lands is granted for Port-Orford-cedar because of limited domestic demand for its aromatic, high-quality wood. Nearly all Port-Orford-cedar trees now cut are shipped to Japan, where they serve as an excellent substitute for the traditional *hinoki* cedar which is protected in that country because its forests have been overcut.

GETTING THERE
From Powers, drive south on Coos County Road 219, which becomes FS Road 33 (3300), for six miles to FS Road 3358. Bear east (left) and continue 4.25 miles, turning right at a sign for Big Tree Picnic Area. It's an eye-opening trip and paved all the way.

RECOMMENDED
In addition to the record tree, other large Port-Orford-cedar and some impressive Douglas-fir live in this small grove. As well, the upper trailhead for Elk Creek Falls Trail #1150 is near the big tree. This steep trail rolls downhill for one mile to the South Fork of the Coquille River and FS Road 33. Unfortunately, although the trail passes by many old growth trees, it is blemished by a poorly buffered clearcut which has spoiled the site's beauty. (The "falls" are on a side trail off the lower trailhead, 100 yards beyond Elk Creek and 0.3 mile south of the junction of FS Roads 3358 and 33.)

2. Johnson Creek Trail

This narrow canyon trail, carved from a serpentine rock hillside, actually follows Sucker Creek, beginning near Johnson Creek.

Powers Ranger District
USGS 7.5' CHINA FLAT (1986)
USGS 15' AGNESS (1954)

ABOUT THE AREA
Johnson Creek Trail #1256 is a miner's trail along and above the riparian ancient forest in Sucker Creek Canyon. Where it traverses rocky areas, the trail provides good views of the steep, open chasm. Although past logging is occasionally visible across the canyon, this little

mountain trail remains truly charming.

GETTING THERE
From Oregon Highway 42 between Coos Bay and Roseburg, take Coos County Road 219 south to the town of Powers. Continue south on Route 219, which becomes FS Road 33 (3300), for 11 miles to China Flat. Then turn right, cross a bridge over the South Fork of the Coquille River, and bear left for FS Road 3353 which, while still heading south, is west of FS Road 33. Stay on FS Road 3353, now gravel, for three miles. Turn left on one-lane FS Road 5591 after the three-mile post, opposite a sign for "Powers 14 miles." Drive one and a half miles on FS Road 5591 and, immediately after the Johnson Creek bridge, turn right at a sign for Johnson Creek Trail #1256, into an undeveloped campsite on Sucker Creek.

RECOMMENDED
Johnson Creek Trail #1256 follows Sucker Creek upstream for its first 100 yards, then jumps the creek. Rocks and logs permit easy crossing in summer. Look for a ribbon and small bench marking the trail on the other bank. During the first half-mile of trail, you'll encounter large Douglas-fir and good-sized Port-Orford-cedar on a shaded but rocky site. After crossing several small tributaries, you'll come to more big Douglas-fir in another mile. The entire trail is 2.5 miles long. It ends on a spur road, FS Road 260, which runs east off FS Road 3353 about nine miles from where you turned onto FS Road 5591.

3. Coquille River Falls Research Natural Area

Old growth Port-Orford-cedar, hemlock and Douglas-fir, with a series of waterfalls along a fairly steep trail.

Powers Ranger District
USGS 15' AGNESS (1954)

ABOUT THE AREA
This steep, wet Research Natural Area (RNA) harbors a dense cathedral forest with nary a clearcut in sight. It is one of the nicest ancient forest groves on the Powers Ranger District, and quite close to the northern entrance of the proposed Siskiyou National Park. Towering cliffs along the South Fork Coquille River make for a pleasant drive from Powers.

GETTING THERE
Drive 15 miles south of Powers on FS Road 33 along the South Fork Coquille River. Once you cross a bridge over the river, make the first left turn (east) on FS Road 3348. Drive 1.5 miles to a pull-off on the left, a quarter-mile before FS Road 5520 on the right.

RECOMMENDED
The trail switchbacks for a half-mile through virgin forest before coming to the falls. On the way to the river, you may notice numerous game trails; the RNA is heavily used by elk seeking cover in this undisturbed portion of an intensively logged watershed.

4. Lobster Creek Botanical Area

Giant Douglas-fir and the largest known Oregon-myrtle at the western gateway to the proposed Siskiyou National Park.

Gold Beach Ranger District
USGS 7.5' BRUSHY BALD MTN. (1986)

ABOUT THE AREA

The 445-acre Lobster Creek Botanical Area includes enormous Douglas-fir and Port-Orford-cedar, with some trees approaching eight feet in diameter. This hillside is north of the Rogue River on the west side of the otherwise logged-off Lobster Creek drainage. Although this remnant grove represents only a tiny fraction of the great forests that once covered river valleys along the southern Oregon coast, these surviving giants may be peeled into plywood if some in Congress and the Forest Service have their way.

GETTING THERE

From US Highway 101 in Gold Beach, drive east on Jerry's Flat Road (FS Road 33) toward Agness along the south shore of the Rogue River. In 9.5 miles, immediately after entering the Siskiyou National Forest, turn left on FS Road 3310, cross a bridge over the Rogue River, and take the first right on Silver Creek Road (FS Road 3533). Proceed exactly a quarter-mile and park at a small turn-out on the right. The steep riverside slope becomes a nearly flat bench covered with large Douglas-fir trees by the turn-out. (You may also be able to recognize the

The world's largest myrtlewood tree can be found along the Rogue River, in the proposed Siskiyou National Park.

turn-out by a small mound of serpentine rock and dirt dumped on the right-hand side of the road.)

RECOMMENDED
On the left (uphill) a light scar reveals a faint trail. You will see some large Oregon-myrtle as soon as you are 50' into the

forest. Proceed uphill about 600', holding slightly to the left. When you come to the outstanding Oregon-myrtle, you will know you have found it. Three large trunks extend high above a naturally hollow 13'-diameter base. Complete with a small ground-level opening, the living mound looks like a massive wooden wickiup.

5. Lower Rogue River Trail

A tremendous Douglas-fir 8' in diameter along the dramatic Rogue River, at the western gateway to the proposed Siskiyou National Park.

Gold Beach Ranger District
USGS 15' AGNESS (1954)

ABOUT THE AREA
This diverse trail follows the river's steep rocky canyon across wooden footbridges to abundant wildflowers, enticing side canyons and lush springs. On the way in, FS Road 3533 passes through an almost continuous grove of large Douglas-fir, as well as big tanoak and Oregon-myrtle at the springs. Although the Rogue's banks are steep, various cross-country routes through big trees down to the river are possible along the way. Watch out for poison oak!

GETTING THERE
For the downstream trailhead, follow the directions in the preceding entry to Lobster Grove Botanical Area, but drive another 6.25 miles on Silver Creek Road (FS Road 3533) and follow signs for Lower Rogue River Trail.

To reach the upstream (eastern) trailhead to the Lower Rogue River Trail, take FS Road 33 (Jerry's Flat Road) from Gold Beach for 30 miles, and cross the Rogue River bridge at Agness. Turn left on Curry County Road 375, drive

four miles, and turn right on Cougar Lane after the Agness Store.

RECOMMENDED
From its downstream (western) trailhead, the Lower Rogue River Trail winds along the north bank 12 miles upstream to Agness. (The trail is well buffered from the road on the south bank.) On the western end, the biggest trees are along the first mile of trail. On the eastern end, the trail passes through private (but nice) land with few big trees for the first two miles, and old growth forest only downstream on National Forest lands. Near the east end, large old growth Douglas-fir can be found from above Tom East Creek to Copper Canyon.

6. Pine Grove Trail

Old growth Jeffrey pine and a beautiful serpentine mountain meadow, with a few large Douglas-fir and Port-Orford-cedar.

Gold Beach Ranger District
USGS 15' AGNESS (1954)

ABOUT THE AREA

This area displays exceptional botanical diversity because of its serpentine (high magnesium content) subsoils. Serpentine sites create harsh conditions for plant growth, and in the Kalmiopsis region are occupied by many rare and endemic species.

The Forest Service has attempted to discourage off-road vehicle traffic on Pine Grove Trail #1170, and has posted a sign calling users' attention to fragile soils. However, they've offered no apologies for the huge, soil-destroying clearcuts all along the road and next to the pine grove. High-impact logging has continued despite the fact that reforestation failure rates have been extremely high, leaving many of the old cutting units as unforested brushfields.

Along with numerous other economic and environmental considerations, this sort of mismanagement has led to public calls for the designation of a million-acre plus Siskiyou National Park. Conservationists view the National Park Service as a worthy steward of the region's remaining pristine lands, the sensitive management of which is essential to Oregon's ecological and economic future.

GETTING THERE

From US Highway 101 in Gold Beach drive east on Jerry's Flat Road (FS Road 33) toward Agness, along the south shore of the Rogue River. About 0.1 mile after the 18-mile post, turn south (right) on FS Road 3318, which immediately turns to gravel and climbs sharply. Continue exactly 5.75 miles to a sign for Pine Grove Trail #1170, where three other roads intersect FS Road 3318 on the left. Take the middle road, FS Road 120.

RECOMMENDED

The trail, an old jeep road, starts immediately on the left. Old Jeffrey pine, some up to three feet in diameter, are immediately visible from the trail on a hill to the left. In a half-mile the trail comes to the north end of an attractive little meadow, surrounded by western azaleas and a small Port-Orford-cedar grove on the south. Bearing to the left, the jeep road continues up a steep incline through a nice 10 to 15-acre stand of Jeffrey pine, which feels very much like the open old growth ponderosa pine groves of eastern Oregon.

7. Illinois River Trail

The largest unprotected ancient forest on the Siskiyou National Forest.

Galice Ranger District
USGS 15' AGNESS (1954)
COLLIER BUTTE (1954)

ABOUT THE AREA

If you have the time, walk the entire 27-mile Illinois River Trail. Besides spectacular old growth forest, you'll see some of the wildest and most scenic country anywhere, and experience for yourself the site of one of the oldest and most controversial wilderness battles in the United States. The Forest Service continues to clearcut large areas of ancient forest in the remaining roadless lands of the North Kalmiopsis.

Since 1982, conservationist and philosopher Lou Gold has maintained a summer vigil near the Bald Mountain Lookout along the Illinois River Trail. Lou's winter trips across the nation have brought national attention to this unique and threatened area, which conservationists have proposed be added to the Kalmiopsis Wilderness and included in the proposed Siskiyou National Park. (See the Upper Briggs Creek and Onion Creek Trail entries which follow for nearby ancient forest sites.)

GETTING THERE

From the west: At Gold Beach on US Highway 101, drive up the Rogue River Road, FS Road 33, almost to Agness. Cross the Illinois River bridge just below the confluence of the Rogue and Illinois Rivers, and note the difference in water quality between the unlogged Illinois River and the disturbed Rogue River. Turn right on County Road 450 and then drive three miles to the trailhead at Oak Flat.

From the east: From US Highway 199 at Selma, drive west on the Illinois River Road, County Route 5070, which turns into FS Road 4103 and ends at Briggs Creek Campground. The last few miles of this road are steep and rough, suitable only for high clearance vehicles. Plan to walk that part.

RECOMMENDED

The best examples of old growth forest, including extensive stands of ancient Douglas-fir, are along the first part of the northern end of the trail. Hike all the way through or just spend the day wandering four miles into Indigo Flat, and another

Ancient firs, pines and broadleaf evergreen trees blanket the Illinois River Trail.

two miles up to the the rolling wild-flower-filled meadows of Silver Prairie. While the famous Silver Fire burned portions of this area in 1987, most of the

large pine, cedar and fir survived, insulated by thick, centuries-old bark adapted to such fires. Only the young plantations from former clearcuts were destroyed.

8. Upper Briggs Creek

A streamside trail through spectacular old growth Douglas-fir with a tall vine maple understory.

Galice Ranger District
USGS 15' SELMA (1954)

ABOUT THE AREA
This roadless area contains some of the most impressive old growth forests on the Galice Ranger District, including a grove of ancient Port-Orford-cedar. If you visit the area in early spring or late fall, you're better off coming from the north end of FS Road 25 and the Merlin-Galice Road, as the southern road from US Highway 199 climbs through snow at over 3600' before descending to the 2200' Briggs Valley. (See also entries for Illinois River Trail and Onion Creek Trail in this chapter.)

GETTING THERE
From I-5 take the Wolf Creek exit (from the north) or the Merlin exit (from the south). From Wolf Creek turn west on Front Street, drive under a train trestle and bear left, continuing 15 miles on a mostly paved road to the Grave Creek bridge over the Rogue River. Drive south on the Merlin-Galice Road along the Rogue for ten miles, and turn right on FS Road 25 opposite a sign for "Galice 3 miles" and "Merlin 8 miles."

From the Merlin exit on I-5 drive 12.5

These ancient firs in the proposed Siskiyou National Park act like a giant sponge, holding huge volumes of water in their systems and drawing on this reservoir during summer heat and forest fires.

miles up the Rogue River on the Merlin-Galice Road to FS Road 25 on the left. Either way, drive 15.4 miles on unpaved FS Road 25 to Secret Creek.

RECOMMENDED
Just after the bridge, turn right on FS Road 139 and drive or walk a half-mile through a big ugly clearcut, bearing right to the lower landing. At the very end of the landing an unmarked trail leads 50 yards downhill to a jeep road along Briggs Creek. Follow the jeep trail to the left (downstream) and enter the virgin forest. This jeep road crosses the creek in a half-mile at Elkhorn Mine. As Briggs Creek Trail #1132 is on the other side of the creek, cross the stream at your first opportunity and walk up- or downstream on the trail.

Upstream you will find a small grove of old growth Port-Orford-cedar and pass some big Douglas-fir. From here Briggs Creek Trail #1132 used to continue another 1.5 miles to Sam Brown Camp-

ground, but Forest Service clearcutting has spoiled it just beyond the cedar grove. The new trailhead begins from a spur to the south of FS Road 2512.

The longest stretch of pristine trail is downstream, with five stream crossings; the first is in one mile. The junction with the Onion Creek old growth trail is one mile downstream; roughly two and a half miles past Onion Creek, Briggs Creek Trail #1132 intersects Red Dog Creek Trail #1143 in Section 3 (T37S 9RW). Although it's not on the Siskiyou National Forest recreation map, the Illinois Valley Ranger District fireman's map shows a jeep road that runs west from this trail junction near Soldier Creek to the Illinois River Road a quarter-mile before its end at the southern and eastern terminus of the Illinois River Trail, in the mutual corners of Sections 5, 6, 7 and 8. It is approximately eight miles from Secret Creek to the Illinois River on Briggs Creek Trail #1132.

9. Onion Creek Trail

Streamside ancient forest trail leading to the Briggs Creek Trail and Illinois River Trail.

Galice Ranger District
USGS 15' SELMA (1954)

ABOUT THE AREA
This trail, although not shown on any map, is a well-developed miner's trail—complete with footbridges—which follows Onion Creek through a forest of old growth Douglas-fir (some five feet in diameter) and large Port-Orford-cedar, with a tall understory of maple, flowering dogwood, tanoak and giant Pacific yew. (See also the preceding entries in this chapter for Illinois River Trail and

Upper Briggs Creek, noting especially the warning about off-season access to Briggs Valley.)

GETTING THERE
From Grants Pass on Highway 199 turn right on FS Road 25 three miles past the 16-mile post (or four miles before Selma) for Onion Mountain Lookout. Drive 9.5 miles and turn left on FS Road 224, about 0.2 mile past the 24-mile post.

Continue down this well-graded but narrow gravel road for five miles to Onion Creek and signs for Lot-o-Luck Mine. You can also reach Onion Creek from the Secret Creek-Briggs Creek trailhead by driving eight miles further on FS Road 25 from its junction with FS Road 224; see the previous Upper Briggs Creek entry in this chapter.

RECOMMENDED
The trail starts on the left, along the north side of the stream, from an unmarked trailhead about 35 yards past the auto bridge, just before a sign for FS Road 655. In a little more than two miles you will come to Briggs Creek Trail #1132, about two miles below the trailhead near Secret Creek.

10. Eightdollar Mountain Botanical Area

A different kind of older forest: mature Jeffrey pine and insectivorous pitcher plants (Darlingtonia), *along the scenic Illinois River.*

Illinois Valley Ranger District
USGS 15' SELMA (1954)

ABOUT THE AREA
The dominant species here, Jeffrey pine, closely resembles ponderosa pine. It is most easily distinguished by the size of its cones (5-9" in length), which are otherwise similar to those of ponderosa (3-5" in length). These particular trees have not grown very large because of the site's fire history and serpentine soils. Much of the southern Kalmiopsis is covered by little-disturbed Jeffrey pine forests—a habitat type which, acre for acre, includes more species of wildflowers and rare plants than any other in the Northwest. ONRC and other conservation and civic organizations have proposed a Siskiyou National Park, in part to protect the unique and irreplaceable botanical values of one of North America's oldest and most diverse regions: the million-acre plus core of Oregon's Siskiyou-Klamath Mountains.

GETTING THERE
From Grants Pass take Highway 199 south. Turn east (right) on the Illinois River Road at the Selma Post Office,
south of the 20-mile post. This road, County Route 5070, becomes FS Road 4103. Follow it for three and a half miles and watch closely for FS Road 011 on the left, just before the road begins to climb steeply.

RECOMMENDED
Park and follow FS Road 011 (a dead-end jeep trail) downhill to Deer Creek at the base of Eightdollar Mountain. This stream flows down past azalea-lined bogs and eventually empties into the Illinois River.

118

Jeffrey pine, in the south Kalmiopsis; while not extremely large, these trees grow to be 400 years and older.

11. Babyfoot Lake, Kalmiopsis Wilderness

Ancient Brewer spruce, Port-Orford-cedar, pine and fir line a cool mountain trail to Babyfoot Lake—a jewel on the east side of the Kalmiopsis Wilderness.

Illinois Valley Ranger District
USGS 15' CHETCO PEAK (1954)

ABOUT THE AREA

The trail to Babyfoot Lake passes by rock outcroppings that offer magnificent views over the Kalmiopsis Wilderness and adjoining roadless lands. Old growth Brewer (or weeping) spruce—found only in the Siskiyou-Klamath Mountains—grow here to their greatest size. Look for grey, flaky, puzzle-piece bark and feel for sharp-tipped needles to identify this tree.

Like most of Oregon's forested Wilderness Areas, the big trees were left out when Congress drew the Wilderness boundaries. Few places are more striking in this respect than the Babyfoot Lake

area, where the lake is protected as Wilderness but the trail to the lake is not. Timber sales are planned for the next few years which will further define the Wilderness Area's boundary at the expense of this ancient forest. In addition, recreation pressure here is heavy; access is too easy, so be careful and lightfooted.

GETTING THERE

From Highway 199, take the Eightdollar Road-Kalmiopsis Wilderness Area turn-off 24 miles southwest of Grants Pass (and four miles northeast of Cave Junction), and drive 15 miles on what becomes FS Road 4201. At a sign for

Babyfoot Lake, turn left on FS Road 140 and drive 0.7 mile to the parking area.

RECOMMENDED

Babyfoot Lake: The lake is an easy 1.25-mile hike. Huge cedar and fir can be found behind and downhill from the lake, below the outlet.

Babyfoot Lake is an increasingly popular destination, perhaps best not visited on early summer weekends. In any event, please do not camp along the lakeshore, but explore other inviting trails in the area for spots where your campsite won't have so great an impact.

Fiddler Gulch Trail: While you're in the Babyfoot Lake area, consider taking a short, moderately steep hike on the recently recovered Fiddler Gulch Trail to see ancient Jeffrey and sugar pine forests in roadless areas that are proposed addi-tions to the Kalmiopsis Wilderness. Fiddler Gulch Trail begins on the high, un-named ridge which runs southeast from Hungry Hill, above and between Fiddler Gulch (to the northeast) and Canyon Creek (to the southwest). See the Siskiyou National Forest recreation map for details: Hungry Hill is in Section 32 of T38S R9W.

To reach the Fiddler Gulch trailhead, drive another half-mile past the parking area for Babyfoot Lake to the end of the logging spur road (FS Road 140). Walk straight down the ridge into the roadless area, following a crude trail marked by occasional blue ribbons and rock cairns. (Until local conservationists pointed it out to agency personnel, the Forest Service was not aware of the Fiddler Gulch Trail's existence. Many such public lands trails have similarly been "lost.")

Ancient Port-Orford-cedar, as well as Brewer spruce and other species of pine and fir, are found along the trail to and around Babyfoot Lake.

The first part of the primitive trail, along the backbone of the ridge, leads through beautiful serpentine-associated ancient Jeffrey pine trees, with the splendid backdrop of Tennesse Mountain to the east. (This unique forest is fascinating!) After about a quarter-mile, the trail swings to the left and descends first to a flat bench with big sugar pine and impressive rock outcrops, and then down to Josephine Creek in Fiddler Gulch far below. Keep a careful eye on the cairns and don't get too carried away with the scenery, or you'll miss the bend to the left.

At the end of FS Road 140, one of the three clearcut units of the infamous 1985 Hungry Timber Sale now dominates much of the upper watershed of Fiddler Gulch. Considering the scars left by the Hungry Sale clearcuts, and the ongoing reforestation failures both here and in clearcuts elsewhere in the area—where steep slopes, poor soils, and hot, dry summers create harsh conditions for the agency's tree farms—it seems incredible that the Forest Service is still planning more clearcuts in the old growth groves in the steep headwaters of Fiddler Gulch and Canyon Creek.

12. Sucker Creek, Red Buttes Wilderness

A scenic wilderness trail which rises from a lush low-elevation ancient forest to higher wildflower meadows surrounded by giant incense-cedars.

Illinois Valley Ranger District
USGS 15' OREGON CAVES (1954)

ABOUT THE AREA

Most of the 20,323-acre Red Buttes Wilderness is in California. For the Oregon side of the line, the House of Representatives passed a 25,895-acre bill in 1983, only to have it reduced to 3821 acres by Senator Hatfield in the final version. The area surrounding the Oregon portion of the Red Buttes Wilderness is included in the 150,000-acre Oregon Caves Unit of the proposed Siskiyou National Park. This area's high alpine ecosystems would complement and round out the biological diversity of the proposed park.

As you look north down Sucker Creek Canyon from the meadows above, you will see Swan Mountain (6269') and most of the ridge east of the canyon, both currently excluded from this beautiful Wilderness Area. (See also the Red Buttes Wilderness entry in the Rogue River National Forest chapter for suggested routes into the area's eastern portion.)

GETTING THERE

From US Highway 199 take Highway 46 from Cave Junction for Oregon Caves National Monument. Turn south (right) at a hairpin turn on FS Road 4612, about 13 miles from Cave Junction and six miles before Oregon Caves. Drive ten miles on FS Road 4612, then bear left on FS Road 098, heading south along Sucker Creek and above the Wilderness to the west. The pavement ends after the first two miles, but the road is good all the way to the trailhead.

RECOMMENDED

The recommended trail (FS Trail #1237) is 2.5 miles long. It follows Sucker Creek through some exceptionally large old growth white fir and Douglas-fir, sugar pine and Port-Orford-cedar, to the Sucker Creek shelter. (Elevation gains make this a challenging route, particularly the last mile, when FS Trail #1237 climbs from 3800' to 5200'.) The best car camping location on the way is at a bridge across Sucker Creek, just past the 11-mile post.

There are two trailheads for FS Trail #1237 on FS Road 098. The first, on the right 3.5 miles from the fork on FS Road 098 (or a half-mile after the 13-mile post), leads to the easiest part of the trail and the most impressive ancient forest. The second trailhead is 1.5 miles further, at the end of FS Road 098. It leads to the shortest route (down connector FS Trail #1237A to FS Trail #1237) to the big incense-cedars and wildflower meadows.

When you reach the meadows, about two miles from the first trailhead, bear to the left. Near the top of the first meadow, to

the left, is Fosters Temple, a monster old growth incense-cedar hollow on one side. Centuries ago some process—probably a lightning strike—transformed the hollowed base of this grand old tree. If modern "forest management" had existed then, this tree would most likely have been "salvaged." But with no one to fell it, it just kept on living.

More big cedars can be found in another scenic meadow on the way to the Forest Service shelter. Continue uphill bearing left, and pick up the trail again to the next meadow. In this nearly flat meadow, bear left again (heading east) and then cross its center, where you will again pick up the trail which now leads to some grand old cedars. From this meadow and the Sucker Creek shelter, you can make a loop by following the high, open ridge above to the west, along FS Trail #1207 and down the Fehley Gulch Trail (FS Trail #1243 to FS Trail #1231) back to Sucker Creek, about three-quarters of a mile from the first trailhead on FS Road 098.

13. Page Mountain Ancient Forest Grove

Cathedral forest grove of Port-Orford-cedar and Douglas-fir next to a two-lane paved road.

Illinois Valley Ranger District
USGS 15' CAVE JUNCTION (1954)

ABOUT THE AREA

The Page Mountain Botanical Area, near the border of the Klamath and Siskiyou National Forests, includes trees as large as 90" in diameter on 128 relatively undisturbed acres. A wet, east-facing site harbors a temperate rainforest which contrasts starkly to the other forests in the

Illinois Valley Ranger District. There are no trails through this cathedral forest grove, but it is relatively easy to explore and well worth seeing. Only 23 miles from Cave Junction, the Page Mountain grove borders the Oregon Caves Unit of the proposed Siskiyou National Park.

GETTING THERE

Eight miles south of Cave Junction on Highway 199, turn east on Waldo Road (or O'Brien Road—which joins Waldo Road in 0.75 mile). Drive about 15.5 miles on Waldo Road, following signs first for Takilma, then for Bolan Lake and Happy Camp. Once in the Siskiyou National Forest on FS Road 48, you climb through an impressive Jeffrey pine forest to an elevation of 4500'.

RECOMMENDED

The super old growth grove is on your left (east) three-quarters of a mile after the ten-mile post on FS Road 48, opposite the junction with FS Road 4810. Locate the sign for "Cave Junction 23 miles" and "Happy Camp 17 miles" immediately above a one-acre clearing, where the very top of the stand was clearcut in 1987. Drive just past the clearcut to a pull-out on the left. The grove continues down the hill for about 700 vertical feet. Several benches and little undergrowth make for fairly good cross-country hiking despite the slope, and the trees are big.

14. Oregon's Ancient Redwoods

A very special and very threatened area.

Chetco Ranger District
USGS 15' MOUNT EMILY (1954)

ABOUT THE AREA

While coast redwoods (*Sequoia sempervirens*) reach their greatest size along California's northern coast, Oregon also contains magnificent redwoods. They are found in Curry County, on public lands managed primarily by the Siskiyou National Forest.

Today, few ancient redwoods remain outside those groves protected in state or federal reserves. The tallest trees on Earth, sometimes living more than 2000 years, redwoods are properly characterized as the "ultimate" old growth trees. With increased public awareness of ancient forest values, and after two decades of national battles to save the remaining redwood forests, most people assume that public lands managers would neither clearcut old growth redwoods nor regard the logging of these unique giants as "harvesting a crop." But the Siskiyou National Forest only recently postponed its plans to log many of its last ancient redwoods. Oregon is the only state in the country where redwoods on public lands are still being cut.

Most of the remaining unprotected ancient redwood groves in Oregon are in the Peavine Ridge, Bear Ridge and Bridge Creek areas of southern Curry County, on the Chetco Ranger District of the Siskiyou National Forest. The northernmost, administratively protected stand is located near the top of Little Redwood Creek in the Siskiyou Forest's Snake Tooth Redwood Botanical Area. This old growth redwood preserve is only 21 acres in size, as most of the original grove has already been logged.

Presently, only two redwood stands are formally protected in Oregon: the 334-acre Wheeler Creek Research Natural Area, and a 50-acre grove along the Chetco River at Alfred A. Loeb State

Once blanketing two million acres of the Pacific Coastal Region, only 1350 acres of ancient redwoods remain today in isolated groves in southwest Oregon.

Park. (See the following Redwood Tree Nature Trail entry in this chapter.) Including some small, isolated groves, no more than 1350 acres of ancient redwoods remain standing in Oregon. Less than half of that total is now protected by policy or law. The rest could still be logged. For example, any administrative protection now afforded redwoods in the Siskiyou National Forest Plan is subject to change, at least every decade or whenever the Forest Service chooses to change their plan. Only protection by Congress really counts.

According to the Siskiyou National Forest, "some of the best examples of old growth redwood on the District" are on Peavine Ridge, the area described below. Half the conifer trees in this mixed-evergreen forest are redwoods, with an average diameter of approxi-

mately four feet. Other species include Douglas-fir, western hemlock, tanoak, Oregon-myrtle, red alder and Pacific dogwood. The largest known redwood tree in the Peavine Ridge grove is 11' in diameter; the second largest is nine feet. (You may find bigger ones!)

GETTING THERE

From US Highway 101 one mile north of the California border, turn east on the Winchuck River Road, drive 1.5 miles, and turn right across a concrete bridge over the Winchuck River. Continue for 3.6 miles on what becomes FS Road 1101 to the junction with FS Road 170 on the left.

RECOMMENDED

From this junction, three old growth redwood walks are recommended:

Big trees: Bear right at the junction with FS Road 170, staying on FS Road 1101, and continue 0.2 mile to where a surveyor's trail drops gradually downhill. This quarter-mile trail ends among small groves of redwood trees five to six feet in diameter. (Until recently, these trees were scheduled for clearcutting.)

Bigger trees: Bear left on FS Road 170, which ends 0.4 mile after a scenic overlook of the Pacific Ocean and the lower Winchuck River. A surveyor's trail (for a proposed logging road) continues straight ahead (north, between two medium-large redwoods) where the road turns 90 degrees to the left just before it ends. Follow this almost flat trail along the ridgetop through scattered redwood groves containing trees five to six feet in diameter. One very large redwood, easily twice the diameter of the other great trees, lives along this trail.

Biggest trees: Walk cross-country downhill off the north (left) side of FS Road 1101 immediately *before* the junction with FS Road 170. A little over 100 yards downhill you will first pass a nine-foot tree and then come to an ancient, fire-scarred redwood 11' in diameter. (This particular grove, though not currently scheduled for logging, is protected only in the Siskiyou Forest Plan, which can be changed administratively.)

15. Redwood Tree Nature Trail

Largest easily accessible coast redwoods in Oregon.

Chetco Ranger District
USGS 15' MOUNT EMILY (1954)

ABOUT THE AREA
The majestic redwoods along this trail range from 300 to 800 years in age. In favorable conditions, they could easily grow for another thousand years. While you're in the area, see the grove of big Oregon-myrtle protected at nearby Alfred A. Loeb State Park.

GETTING THERE
Take North Bank Road (off Highway 101 just south of Brookings) for eight miles along the Chetco River to the trailhead, a half-mile beyond Alfred A. Loeb State Park.

RECOMMENDED
This well-maintained nature trail forms a mile-long loop with a few steep sections.

Oregon still has some very big redwoods.

125

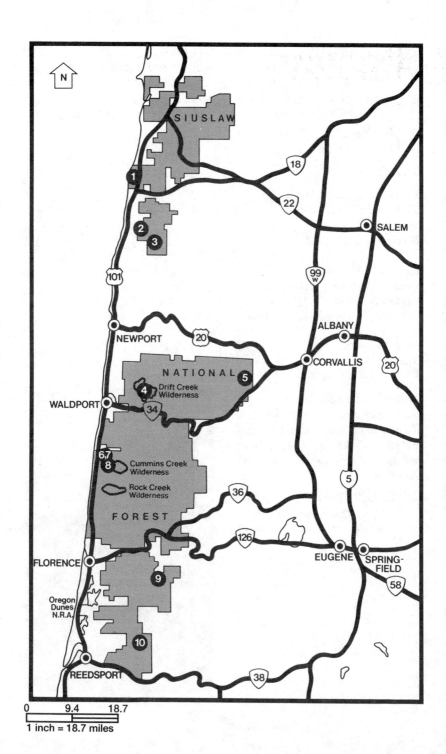

N

SIUSLAW

1

2
3

101

18
22

SALEM

99
W

NEWPORT
20

ALBANY

CORVALLIS

20

NATIONAL

4
Drift Creek
Wilderness

5

WALDPORT
34

6,7
8
Cummins Creek
Wilderness

Rock Creek
Wilderness

36

FOREST

126
EUGENE
SPRING-
FIELD

FLORENCE

9

58

Oregon
Dunes
N.R.A.

5

10

REEDSPORT

38

0   9.4   18.7

1 inch = 18.7 miles

Siuslaw National Forest

Spanning the Oregon Coast Range, the 625,000-acre Siuslaw is the smallest and the most heavily cutover National Forest in Oregon. But for a few thousand acres of classic old growth, most of the "mature and overmature" forest that remains is slated for logging in the 1990 Siuslaw Forest Plan.

The Coast Range originally contained the largest ancient trees in the state. The narrow band of Sitka spruce rainforest of the coastal fog belt was one of the most impressive forest ecosystems in the world. Unfortunately, private lands north of the Siuslaw National Forest were liquidated early in the century, and even public (National Forest, BLM, state and county) lands have been intensively managed almost exclusively for wood production. Today, roughly one percent of the Oregon Coast Range remains in an old growth forest condition!

Still, a few impressive pockets of ancient forest have survived, and deserve immediate protection. A first step was taken in 1984, when the Drift Creek, Cummins Creek and Rock Creek Wilderness Areas were established by Congress. Now the fate of the remaining unprotected groves is at stake.

The Siuslaw National Forest includes five ranger districts. The supervisor's office is in Corvallis.

Don't forget your Siuslaw National Forest recreation map.

1. Cascade Head

Scattered stands of ancient Sitka spruce forest along a steep trail to a rocky coastal headland.

Hebo Ranger District
USGS 7.5' NESKOWIN (1985)

ABOUT THE AREA
This trail through old growth Sitka spruce forest to Harts Cove on Cascade Head leads to other good hikes, including several cross-country routes. With the 1974 Cascade Head Scenic-Research Area Act, Congress established a 9670-acre management area unique in the nation to protect this well-known landmark. Under its terms, the Siuslaw National Forest continues to acquire ownership of and conservation easements on private lands in the Scenic-Research Area, which is roughly those lands west of Highway 101 between the Neskowin Crest Research Natural Area (RNA) on the north, and the Salmon River Estuary on the south. A particular focus of the Forest

Service's work at Cascade Head is restoration of the Salmon River Estuary and associated wetlands (about 70 percent of which are now under public ownership) to a natural condition, by removal of dikes and other "improvements." The Cascade Head Scenic-Research Area encompasses the Neskowin Crest RNA, about 4500 acres (one-third) of the Cascade Head Experimental Forest, a 300-acre Nature Conservancy preserve in the fragile meadow on the promontory itself, and the YMCA's spectacular Camp Westwind, south of the mouth of the Salmon River.

GETTING THERE

Take US Highway 101 north from Lincoln City. Immediately before the summit of Cascade Head and a half-mile south of the 100-mile post, turn west on Cascade Head Road (FS Road 1861).

Follow the signs for four miles to Harts Cove Trail #1345 at the end of FS Road 1861.

RECOMMENDED

Harts Cove Trail #1345 is 2.7 miles long and extremely steep. It ends in a meadow with a breathtaking view over the coastline and Pacific Ocean. You come to the first old growth stands of Sitka spruce and a few western hemlock at Cliff Creek, after a half-mile of switchbacks.

The upper drainage of Cliff Creek, which contains the nicest old growth grove on Cascade Head, can be reached from the road above by hiking cross-country. About 0.6 mile from the Harts Cove trailhead on FS Road 1861 (or 0.4 mile west of the junction with FS Road 122), an interpretive sign on the north side of the road reads "A Spruce Hemlock For-

Large ancient Sitka spruce are found in scattered groves at Cascade Head, reachable by trail or cross-country travel. (Photo by Bob Harvey)

est Community." Park here and walk north past the sign and downhill. Bear slightly up the canyon. Although there is no trail, this route is fairly open and less steep than the first part of the Harts Cove Trail.

Another attractive cross-country trek offers more gradual terrain but fewer super old growth spruce. At the intersection of Cascade Head Road and Highway 101, turn east (instead of west) on FS Road 1867, drive 2.1 miles and park. Although big trees inhabit both sides of the road, the most extensive grove is to the north (left), between FS Roads 119 and 131,

which turn off FS Road 1867 to the north. This area is part of the Cascade Head Experimental Forest; unfortunately, logging old growth trees seems to be the big emphasis of the "experiment."

Less than another mile down FS Road 1867 is the old Neskowin Scenic Highway, FS Road 12. Although they are important to have and enjoy, these last few scenic corridors (which are now quietly but steadily being cut) provide but an illusion of the once-great Oregon Forest. Appropriately, an interpretive sign picturing a log truck marks the intersection with FS Road 1867.

2. Gordey Creek

Large old growth western red-cedar along a steep cross-country trail.

Hebo Ranger District
USGS 7.5' DEVILS LAKE (1984)

ABOUT THE AREA
Because its wood is so highly valued by many, western red-cedar has often been the first cut in the Pacific Northwest. In many areas throughout Oregon that seem otherwise little-disturbed, most or all of the ancient cedar are long gone. Gordey Creek is one of the best red-cedar groves left in the entire Coast Range, only 3.3 miles from the Coast Highway.

GETTING THERE
From US Highway 101 roughly a mile south of Lincoln City, and about 0.1 mile north of the Drift Creek bridge, turn east on Drift Creek Road, County Route 109. In two miles turn right, following the sign for Wapiti Park and Drift Creek. Turn left on FS Road 17 in 0.4 mile, before coming to a covered bridge. In 0.35 mile bear right on FS Road 19, and

continue another half-mile to Gordey Creek, which is not signed. Ancient forest on both sides of the canyon upstream can be seen from the road. (From the Gordey Creek bridge it is another 7.5 miles on FS Road 19 to Drift Creek Organization Camp—see the following Drift Creek entry.)

RECOMMENDED
Just before the bridge across Gordey Creek, a jeep trail parallels the river for the first 100 yards upstream, and then narrows for another 100 yards before ending. Where the jeep trail narrows, and at the very end of the trail, poorly defined trails cut sharply up the hill on the left. Hike the steep and primitive trail from the end of the maintained trail further up the canyon to a gorgeous grove of old Douglas-fir and western red-cedar.

3. Drift Creek

Strikingly large ancient Sitka spruce and Douglas-fir on benches along a coastal salmon stream.

Hebo Ranger District
USGS 7.5' DEVILS LAKE (1984)

ABOUT THE AREA
This area is one of the more impressive scraps of ancient forest remaining on the heavily cutover Hebo Ranger District, on the heavily cutover Siuslaw National Forest. (Don't confuse it with the Drift Creek *Wilderness*, described in the next entry, which is about 30 miles to the south on the Waldport Ranger District.) Four different walks in the area are described here, two beginning inside the Drift Creek Organization Camp, and two from outside.

GETTING THERE
From Lincoln City, drive south on US Highway 101 about 1.7 miles past the Schooner Creek bridge just south of town. Turn east on Highway 229 at the Kernville-Siletz River junction, and drive 5.6 miles up the river to FS Road 19.

From the south, take Highway 20 to Toledo, roughly 6.5 miles east of Newport (and Highway 101). Turn north on Highway 229 at Toledo, drive about 16 miles north of Siletz, and turn right on FS Road 19 after the six-mile post.

Either way, drive east on FS Road 19 for a total of 5.4 miles from the paved highway. Be sure to bear left, staying on FS Road 19 at the junction where FS Road 1980 comes in on the right.

RECOMMENDED
Turn off at Drift Creek Organization Camp. Proceed 0.3 mile to the parking area, past the camp buildings. (Note: Although this is public land, you will want to identify yourself to camp caretakers.) An easy hiking trail leads through old growth Sitka spruce around the periphery of the camp; some of these trees are ten feet in diameter. In October and November, large fall Chinook salmon

Sitka spruce are generally confined to a narrow band along the Pacific Northwest Coast. Rarely do they extend more than five to ten miles inland, except, as at Drift Creek, where they range up river valleys.

can be seen spawning in Drift Creek adjacent to the grounds. Just before the main three-story A-frame lodge, a small sign labeled Inspiration Point and Narrows points the way to a trail up a ridge with views of the river lined with old growth trees. It soon steepens sharply but leads to large Douglas-fir on the ridge above.

For the third trail, drive 0.4 mile past Drift Creek Camp and turn off at a sign on the left describing North Creek Fish Weirs. (You can park just before the bridge, at a turn-off for an undesignated camping area to the left.) Just before the North Creek bridge on FS Road 19, an unmarked trail leads to the right up the canyon. In 250 yards the trail crosses the stream on a log. In another 200 yards

hold to the right at a "Y" in the trail, to make a loop past several large old growth Douglas-fir and an amazing down tree. If you go straight ahead (or to the left at the "Y") you will come to additional old growth trees. Since this trail is privately maintained, it is occasionally difficult to follow; you might even bring some clippers to cut a few salmonberry branches along the way.

The fourth option is 0.8 mile beyond Drift Creek Camp. Turn left on FS Road 1900-112. Drive a half-mile to the end of this road and park. Several short trails lead through the old growth Sitka spruce forest down to Drift Creek. The nicest groves are on your left as you drive in, on a level bench between the river bends.

4. Drift Creek Wilderness

The largest protected block of ancient forest in the Oregon Coast Range.

Waldport Ranger District
USGS 7.5' TIDEWATER (1984)

ABOUT THE AREA
Although it is far from exclusively an old growth reserve, the Drift Creek Wilderness Area includes some of the best old growth forest habitat in the Siuslaw National Forest and the Oregon Coast Range. The steep, densely forested slopes of the Drift Creek Wilderness support mostly younger forests with a thick understory, including quite a lot of salmonberry and alder on natural earth slumps. Most of the ancient forest here grows along the stream bottoms, where there are also a few small meadows on the lower sections of Drift Creek. Besides Douglas-fir, the forest includes red alder, bigleaf maple, and some large western red-cedar. Many trees are more than 40"

in diameter and 200' tall. Congress protected only 5839 acres as Wilderness in 1984, but another 6000 contiguous acres of intact forest remain unprotected and should be added to the Drift Creek Wilderness Area.

(Note: *This* Drift Creek flows into the Alsea River just east of Alsea Bay. The Siuslaw National Forest contains *another* ancient forest area on a different Drift Creek, which flows into Siletz Bay 30 miles to the north, on the Hebo Ranger District. It is described in the preceding entry in this chapter, for Drift Creek.)

GETTING THERE
Take US Highway 101 to the 149-mile post, about eight miles south of Newport

and seven miles north of Waldport. Opposite Ona Beach State Park, turn east at a sign for the Lincoln Grange. This is County Route 602—North Beaver Creek Road. Drive almost four miles (past Ona) and turn right on Elkhorn Road, just before North Beaver Creek Road narrows. Continue 6.2 miles on Elkhorn Road, which becomes FS Road 51. At the junction of FS Roads 51 and 50, bear left on FS Road 50. Follow it for 1.3 miles and turn right on (gravel) FS Road 5087, opposite a sign for Horse Creek Trail.

RECOMMENDED

The trailhead for Horse Creek Trail #1362 into the Wilderness is on the left in three and a half miles. It is steep going—three miles of trail climb about 1200'. After a quarter-mile you come to stands of large old growth Douglas-fir and western hemlock. The trail then winds through younger Douglas-fir down to the stream.

Large individual Douglas-fir are scattered along the trail and throughout the forest. About two and a half miles down the trail, an unmarked spur trail descends the slope to Drift Creek itself. A nice meadow can be found just upstream from this point.

For a truly wild experience, drop cross-country into the Trout Creek drainage. From the Horse Creek trailhead drive another one and a half miles to just before the end of FS Road 5087, and follow a spur road to the right across a clearcut and then downhill into the older forest. Trout Creek is not yet protected as Wilderness, and its incorporation into the designated Wilderness Area is a high priority for conservationists. Consult Sullivan (*Exploring Oregon's Wild Areas*—see Suggested Reading, beginning page 305) for more information about trails into Drift Creek Wilderness.

Ancient forest camping is becoming more and more popular, as increased public awareness of this special resource results from growing regional and national attention. (Photo by Diane Kelsay)

5. Marys Peak Watershed

The most significant stand of old growth forest left in the Coast Range.

Alsea Ranger District
USGS 7.5' MARYS PEAK (1984)

ABOUT THE AREA

This area east of Marys Peak in the central Coast Range is classic western Oregon old growth Douglas-fir forest, a community dominated by large Douglas-fir with some big western hemlock and western red-cedar, and an understory of bigleaf maple, alder and swordfern. In 1986 the Oregon Department of Fish and Wildlife described the value of the Marys Peak area to the northern spotted owl with characteristic understatement: "In the Coast Range, the Marys Peak Watershed now has the largest contiguous suitable habitat north of the Umpqua River. Thus, we consider the suitable habitat remaining in the watershed important to the survival of the spotted owl in the Coast Range." Nonetheless, this area is not off-limits to clearcutting.

This site's accessibility from the central coast and Willamette Valley, and a loop road which has not been extensively logged, together make it ideal for school field trips or other educational group tours. Several areas are described below which can serve either as starting points for forays into the forest, or as interpretive stations for group tours. Per usual, there are abundant opportunities to see "modern forest management" and young tree regeneration among the stumps along FS Road 3405 on your way into the designated watershed.

Marys Peak is the municipal watershed for the City of Corvallis. To enter it (regardless of whether you walk or drive), you must first obtain a permit and a key to pass through a locked gate. Keys and permits may be obtained weekdays from the Alsea Ranger Station (487-5811), or at the Utilities and Transportation Office at Corvallis City Hall (757-6941). Although Forest Service logging threatens to reduce both the area's water quality and quantity, public access is restricted to reduce the risk of human-caused fire and water contamination. Please avoid immediate contact with all major watercourses in the area.

GETTING THERE

From Corvallis, take US Highway 20 west and bear left (south) on Oregon Highway 34 west of Philomath at a sign for Marys Peak. Continue four miles and turn right on Rock Creek Road at a sign for Corvallis Watershed, just before the highway crosses Rock Creek. In 0.15 mile bear right for the locked gate and continue on FS Road 3405 for four miles (with Rock Creek on your right) to the junction of FS Roads 3405 and 3409. Cross a bridge over the South Fork of Rock Creek and FS Road 3405 bears left, providing good views of a typically nice old growth riparian zone. FS Roads 3405 and 3409 join again in the upper drainage, creating a six-mile loop through mostly mature and old growth forests.

RECOMMENDED

There are at least five good walks on the FS Road 3405–FS Road 3409 loop. They are described below in order from the lower junction, starting on FS Road 3409 (on the right):

0.9 mile - Lower Rock Creek (above City of Corvallis Reservoir): Bear right on FS Road 3409 and pull off on the right in 0.9 mile. Look for an overgrown spur road on the right, just before FS Road 3409 makes a hairpin turn to the left. The first 100 yards are easy, but walking becomes more difficult as you descend cross-country and up the canyon above the creek. Here you enter the cathedral forest and pass large Douglas-fir and western red-cedar.

1.25 miles - Connection Creek #1: This stream enters the South Fork of Rock Creek just above the lower junction of the loop, but it is difficult to reach from the very bottom. Instead drive 1.25 miles up FS Road 3409. Past the first stop you will drive through a younger forest. Park on the left just after you round a turn to the right and see old growth ahead on the left. A poorly defined, overgrown spur road veers to the left about 200' beyond the pull-out, and heads gradually downhill parallel to the main road to a superb old growth bench. Some of the big trees and most of the down woody material, both ecologically important components of intact old growth forests, have been removed.

1.5 miles - Connection Creek #2: This grove is less disturbed than the first and has more down logs and snags. There is a fairly flat place to park on the left, 1.5 miles from the beginning of the loop, which is about a quarter-mile from the last stop.

2.25+ miles - Upper Rock Creek: This is the most extensive and undisturbed ancient forest grove in the watershed, and requires considerable cross-country hiking across steep terrain. But it's worth the effort; it exudes the feeling of forest primeval. After 2.25 miles on FS Road 3409, bear right on FS Road 115, which continues downhill another mile. The last 100 yards are not gravelled; it would be easy to get stuck here when it's wet, so park before the gravel ends. Walk to the end of the road and continue downhill into the ancient forest just above Rock Creek. Big western red-cedar can be found just above the stream bottom. [No bus turnaround]

4+ miles - Upper Connection Creek: This outstanding old growth grove lies in a basin between the South Fork and the Main Fork of Rock Creek. From the junction of FS Roads 3405 and 3409, turn left and drive two miles up FS Road 3405. Bear right on FS Road 117 (left if you're coming from FS Road 3409). The nicest grove is more than a mile down, at the end of the road. Be careful not to get stuck here, either. [No bus turnaround]

6. Cape Creek

One of the largest Sitka spruce trees left in Oregon.

Waldport Ranger District
USGS 7.5' YACHATS (1984)

ABOUT THE AREA
Once trees like this were common in the Oregon Coast Range. Seeing this sole survivor, and driving through the extensively clearcut upper Cape Creek drainage, one is struck by how much of our national heritage has been destroyed in the last few decades.

GETTING THERE
Turn east off US Highway 101 just north of the Cape Perpetua Visitor Center on FS Road 55, and then immediately to the right into Cape Perpetua Campground.

RECOMMENDED
At the end and near the middle of the campground, footbridges cross Cape Creek to an easy hiking trail which ends at the incredible Sitka spruce tree.

Between Labor Day and Memorial Day Weekend, the campground is closed and the road providing easy driving access to the giant spruce is gated near the highway turn-off. To see the giant tree, either bicycle one mile up this almost level paved road, or walk up the trail beginning at an unmarked trailhead at Highway 101 on the south side of Cape Creek. There is a dirt (sand) pull-out on the ocean side along Highway 101. This is a beautiful streamside trail, but unfortunately the only really large trees are at the end.

7. Gwynn Creek

Seven-mile loop trail through old growth and younger coastal forests.

Waldport Ranger District
USGS 7.5' YACHATS (1984)

ABOUT THE AREA
A pamphlet available at the Cape Perpetua Visitor Center includes a trail map and identifies interesting points along Gwynn Creek Loop Trail. (The northeast portion of the loop contains no ancient forest.) If you wish, you can reach Gwynn Creek Trail from the eastern end of the drainage. This route passes through devastating Forest Service clearcuts not generally visible from Highway 101 on upper Cape Creek, before reaching the ridgetop above the Gwynn Creek drainage. Several years ago, Gwynn Creek was of victim of a massive series of landslides and debris torrents caused by logging the sensitive headwalls at the top of the watershed. Evidence of the severe damage to the stream channel is still visible.

GETTING THERE
On the west, Gwynn Creek Trail can be reached from the Cape Perpetua Visitor Center or from just south of the visitor center on US Highway 101, where Gwynn Creek enters the sea. For the highway access point, there's a parking area immediately opposite on the ocean side of Highway 101.

To reach the Gwynn Creek Trail from the

east side, take Highway 101 immediately north of the visitor center and turn east on FS Road 55. Drive roughly four miles, then turn west (right) on FS Road 5599 and drive about a mile to the trailhead at the end of the road.

RECOMMENDED
A nice old grove, with Sitka spruce up to

five feet in diameter, can be found about one mile up Gwynn Creek. In the southeast end of the loop you'll encounter old growth Douglas-fir and western hemlock. If you begin this loop trail in a clockwise direction from the visitor center, you will come to some large old growth Sitka spruce 1.5 miles up the steepest part of the trail, just beyond Riggin Slinger Loop.

8. Cummins Creek Wilderness

The only entirely intact ancient forest watershed on the Oregon Coast, where old growth Sitka spruce and Douglas-fir meet the sea.

Waldport Ranger District
USGS 7.5' YACHATS (1984)

ABOUT THE AREA
The Cummins Creek Wilderness Area is just east of Highway 101 and just south of Gwynn Creek (see above), about four miles south of the Yachats River bridge and ten miles north of Sea Lions Caves. Cummins Creek and Little Cummins Creek flow west through this 9300-acre Wilderness and meet near Highway 101, just before they reach the Pacific Ocean. Recommended below are trails up both streams into old growth Sitka spruce forest. Despite this great unique ecological and economic contribution, the Forest Service, as usual, vehemently opposed its protection as a congressionally classified Wilderness.

GETTING THERE
Cummins Creek Trail: Just north of the Highway 101 Cummins Creek bridge (and one mile south of the Cape Perpetua Visitors Center), take FS Road 1050 east at a sign for "Cummins Creek Trailhead 1/4 mile" and park at the barricade.

Little Cummins Creek Trail: Just south

of the Highway 101 Cummins Creek bridge, park on the west side of the highway at Neptune State Park.

RECOMMENDED
Cummins Creek Trail: Hike up FS Road 1050 a bit more than 200 yards and take an old, unmarked spur road downhill to the right, along the north side of Cummins Creek and through stunning ancient Sitka spruce. In a little less than a mile the trail ends at the stream's edge. You can continue another half-mile upstream on elk trails among tall sword ferns by crossing the stream over a fallen log and continuing up the south side. You will soon come to a bench and more old growth, with one huge spruce approximately 12' in diameter.

If instead you continue up the barricaded road, you will soon discover a trail that reaches the Cape Perpetua Visitor Center (via portions of the Gwynn Creek Trail—see preceding entry) in eight miles. A nice stand of old Douglas-fir can be found at the eastern end of this trail. Ironically,

Cecilia Ostrow, songwriter and performer, reposes by her favorite ancient Sitka spruce in the Cummins Creek Wilderness Area. (Photo by Ed Meyerowitz)

the Siuslaw National Forest, which recently constructed these trails, argued against designation of this area as Wilderness partly on the basis that it would be impossible to maintain a trail through it. (Logging roads would have been no problem.)

Little Cummins Creek Trail: Walk 50 yards south (carefully) along the shoulder of Highway 101, and enter the forest where several white concrete posts are set on the east side of the highway. Behind this barricade take the trail to the right. (The trail to the left dead-ends at the creek.) The first 100 yards are easy, with moderately large Sitka spruce, but the next quarter-mile is fairly steep and the trail quickly becomes overgrown. After descending to the creek, the trail rises steeply, then levels off midway up a ridge, finally disappearing. Cross-country travel is necessary to proceed further among the big trees, but it's worth it!

Another option is a cross-country trek down from the top of the drainage. From Neptune State Park drive a half-mile

south on Highway 101, and turn east on FS Road 1051 at the 169-mile post by a sign for "Cummins Ridge Trail 2 1/2 miles." Take FS Road 1051 to its terminus, where the road is barricaded and continues as a trail. Instead of walking down this old road, follow a logging road that takes off to the north (left). In a quarter-mile bear downhill to the left when the road forks, and continue to its end through a dense stand of alder saplings. Here you enter the old growth forest and a classic park-like bench of large Sitka spruce. For a wild experience, follow the ridge cross-country downstream to Highway 101. Consider carrying brush clippers, as the salal and salmonberries are thick in places. If you intend to return the way you came, note carefully where you enter the forest.

9. Kentucky Falls

A short trail through mature and ancient forests to the base of three 80' to 90' waterfalls, on the headwaters of the North Fork Smith River.

Mapleton Ranger District
USGS 7.5' BALDY MOUNTAIN (1984)

ABOUT THE AREA

The two-mile section of North Fork Smith River Trail #1351 along Kentucky Creek down to Kentucky Falls and North Fork Falls is steep, but the strenuous walk has not dimmed visitors' enthusiasm for this magnificent forest and spectacular falls. In fact, the area is receiving so many visitors these days that the Mapleton Ranger District is considering placing portable toilets at the trailhead!Eventually the Forest Service plans to extend the trail along the upper Smith River for more ancient forest hiking enjoyment.

Because of the maze of logging roads and clearcuts on the way to the trail, it is important to consult a Siuslaw National Forest map. Use a recreation map or, since the most recent Siuslaw recreation map was issued in 1982, call the forest supervisor's office in Corvallis (750-7000) and request an up-to-date transportation map for the south half of the Mapleton Ranger District.

Call the Mapleton Ranger District (268-4473) for more information and to receive their one-page description of the area.

GETTING THERE

In winter, snow and ice may be a problem on Roman Nose coming from Oregon Highway 126. In all seasons, be careful on FS Road 919 to the trailhead, as it is a steep and narrow gravel logging road.

From Eugene, drive west on Highway 126 and turn south (left) on Whittaker Creek Road (FS Road 23), a quarter-mile west of the 27-mile marker, at a sign for "Whittaker Rec. Area 2 miles." In two miles turn right at a sign for "Kentucky Falls 16 miles" on BLM Road 8-8-21 (which becomes FS Road 23). Continue eight miles to Roman Nose Mountain and another five miles on FS Road 2300 to FS Road 919. Turn right on FS Road 919 and drive three miles to the Kentucky Creek Falls trailhead in Section 17 of T19S R9W. (See the Siuslaw National Forest recreation map.)

From Reedsport, take the Smith River Road (County Route 48) up the North Fork Smith River. When Route 48 turns left and away from the river, follow the river and turn east on FS Road 23. It's less than ten paved miles to FS Road 919 on the left. If you cross the National Forest boundary, you've gone too far.

RECOMMENDED

Kentucky Falls Trail #1351 begins on the left side of FS Road 919 where the road crosses Kentucky Creek, near the very top of Section 17 (T19S R9W). You should recognize the trailhead without much trouble, given the signs on the way in and a pull-out large enough for about five cars on the right, across from the trailhead.

Facing page: The Kentucky Falls Trail is well worth the walk. (Photo by Don DeFazio)

10. Wassen Creek Wilderness (proposed)

The wildest area in this guide.

Mapleton Ranger District
USGS 7.5' SCOTTSBURG (1985)
DEER HEAD PEAK (1985)

ABOUT THE AREA

The proposed 12,000-acre Wassen Creek Wilderness was close to being enacted into law; it cleared the House of Representatives in 1984, but tragically was nixed in the Senate. This area is 12 miles east of Reedsport, on the divide between the lower Smith and Umpqua Rivers, on lands administered by both the Siuslaw National Forest and the Coos Bay District of the Bureau of Land Management (BLM). Wassen Creek flows for 17 miles from its source at Wassen Lake to the Smith River, through steep forested slopes without a single trail. While this means few people ever see this spectacular forest, the challenges and difficulties it offers are a great part of Wassen Creek's appeal to many. The area remains a high priority for protection among Oregon conservationists.

Wassen Creek is included here because it is an ancient forest in jeopardy, unmatched for beauty and wildness but threatened by the same forces which have despoiled countless similar places. (For another approach to the proposed Wassen Creek Wilderness, see the Wassen Lake entry in the BLM Forestlands chapter, under Coos Bay District.)

The Forest Service will soon build a new trail which will contour along the steep canyon, but agency plans are to maintain only half the area in a roadless condition.

The route described below takes you down a half-mile of primitive trail into some of the finer ancient forest along the southern boundary of the proposed Wilderness, roughly above the sharp bend in Wassen Creek at Devil's Staircase in the southern end of Section 16 (T21S R10W). Devil's Staircase is a series of huge rock steps over which Wassen Creek cascades. There are potholes of all sizes in the steps—some of them plenty big enough to swim in—filled with cold water with a clear, green cast. Be forewarned: the topography between the end of the trail and Devil's Staircase is almost vertical. The staircase does not appear to be accessible from the upper part of the canyon described below.

The only known way to see the heart of Wassen Creek is to climb down into the canyon from above and walk in the stream (carefully, please!). The going is rough; walking downstream from Wassen Lake to Devil's Staircase can easily take more than a day. For more information about Wassen Creek, consult Sullivan's *Exploring Oregon's Wild Areas*.

GETTING THERE

From I-5 (Highway 38): From the lower Willamette Valley, take I-5 south to Oregon Highway 99 at Anlauf, south of Cottage Grove. Take Oregon 99 from Anlauf to Drain, then turn west (right) on Highway 38. From southern Oregon, take Highway 138 west from I-5 near Sutherlin to its junction with Highway 38 at Elkton, and continue west along the Umpqua River on Oregon 38.

Take Highway 38 about 1.7 miles east of Scottsburg (and 0.3 mile west of the 19-mile post and Wells Creek bridge), and turn north off Highway 38 on Wells Creek Road. In 2.2 miles bear left for Ferntop (Mountain—elevation 1896') on BLM Road 21-9-32.0, then left again in 0.8 mile on FS Road 41 at a sign for "Highway 101 24 miles." Bear right at an unmarked fork in 0.2 mile; drive a total of 8.25 miles on FS Road 41. Turn right on FS Road 144. This turn is obscured by a big rock from this direction. (Again, be sure to check the Wassen Lake entry under the Coos Bay District portion of the BLM Forestlands chapter while you're in the vicinity.)

From Highway 101: A half-mile north of Reedsport, turn east on Smith River Road (Douglas County Route 48). In 3.25 miles turn right on Southside Road (Douglas County Route 195), which crosses over the Smith River. Follow this road along the south bank of the Smith River for 2.1 miles, cross Otter Slough, and turn right on Otter Slough Road (Douglas County Route 119). Drive 0.7 mile and bear right across Otter Creek, following a sign for "Scottsburg 21 miles." This road becomes FS Road 41. From Otter Creek it is 9.4 miles to FS Road 144 on the left.

RECOMMENDED
After one half-mile, FS Road 144 ends and a primitive trail marked with pink ribbons begins. (Hand clippers are useful here.) Follow this poorly defined trail north about a quarter-mile along the top of the ridge. There is an old clearcut on your left. The trail shortly turns to the east (right) and then breaks out of the huckle-berries, salal and rhododendrons. It ends above an ancient forest stand of big Douglas-fir and hemlock with an interesting sword fern understory. Be careful to keep track of your position if you continue ahead cross-country, as it is dangerously easy to become disoriented in the thick forests and rugged topography of the area.

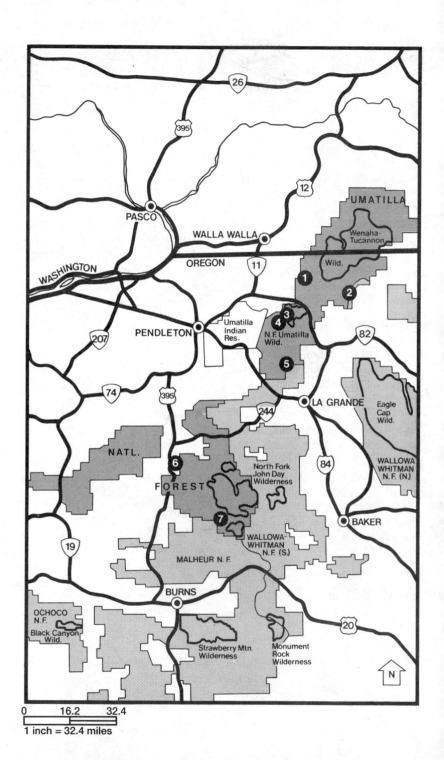

Umatilla National Forest

Named after the Umatilla Indian Nation, the vast Umatilla National Forest extends from northeast Oregon into southeast Washington. It contains several major drainages, including the North Fork John Day, Umatilla, Walla Walla, Grande Ronde, Wenaha and Tucannon Rivers. The 1.5–million acre forest is divided into four ranger districts and headquartered in Pendleton.

The Umatilla is not a well-known forest; it contains many unique and unspoiled places, but also has a history of more clearcutting and roadbuilding than many other eastern Oregon National Forests. Among the areas conservationists have successfully protected are the Wenaha-Tucannon Wilderness (with the densest population of Rocky Mountain elk in the world), the North Fork Umatilla Wilderness, and the heart of the unparalleled North Fork John Day Wilderness.

Don't forget your Umatilla National Forest recreation map.

1. Walla Walla Watershed Wilderness (proposed)

Follow the North or South Fork of the Walla Walla River into 34,500 acres of wildlands.

Walla Walla Ranger District
USGS 7.5' BIG MEADOWS (1983)
TOLLGATE (1983)

ABOUT THE AREA
The proposed Walla Walla Watershed Wilderness consists of the roadless lands on the western side of the Umatilla National Forest east of Milton-Freewater and west of the Wenaha-Tucannon Wilderness, roughly between the National Forest border (on the west), FS Road 6511 (on the north), and FS Road 64 (on the south and east), or Townships 4 and 5N, Ranges 38 and 39E. This is rugged, mountainous country, ranging in elevation from 2200' to 5000'. Its steep slopes and canyons are deeply incised by the North and South Forks of the Walla

Walla River, which flow west out of the proposed Wilderness. (The North and South Forks of the Walla Walla River do not meet until just east of Milton-Freewater, and should be considered completely separate rivers here.) There are a variety of ways to reach the trails which follow both river canyons, but in general the lower trailheads are along the North and South Forks, at the end of roads coming from Milton-Freewater; the upper trailheads are on FS Road 65.

About one-third of the proposed Wilderness is old growth forest. North aspects provide the best conditions for dense forests, primarily white fir, giving way to subalpine fir at higher elevations. Forests on southern slopes are usually stringers of ponderosa pine and other conifers, including fir and western larch. The longest continuous groves of ancient forest are along North Fork Trail #3222, although the upper reaches of both the North and South Fork canyons shelter fine old trees.

GETTING THERE
The fastest route to Milton-Freewater from western Oregon is on I-84 up the Columbia Gorge to Pendleton, but the drive along US Highway 26 to Mount Vernon and up US Highway 395 is much more interesting. From Pendleton, take Oregon Highway 11 north to Milton-Freewater. If you're heading for the lower trailheads to either river, drive into Milton-Freewater. Otherwise, you'll either want to leave Oregon Highway 11 near the town of Weston and drive east on County Route 204, which becomes FS Road 64, or continue up Highway 11 past Milton-Freewater into Walla Walla.

From FS Road 64 (Skyline Drive, a north-south route with spectacular sunset views of the Columbia River Valley and Cascade peaks 150 miles to the west), there are a few trails, described below, which lead into the South Fork Walla Walla River drainage.

To reach the upper trailheads from Walla Walla, take US Highway 12 a couple of miles east to a road (clearly marked on the Umatilla National Forest recreation map but not identified) which leads east and south through the villages of Tracy, Thomas and Kooskooskie. Just before

the road ends in Kooskooskie, turn left on FS Road 65, which reaches the upper trailheads before connecting to FS Road 64 past Deduck Spring Campground in about 20 miles.

To reach the lower trailheads, drive 14 miles east of Milton-Freewater (and about two miles above Umatilla County's Harris Park) along the South Fork Walla Walla River to Elbow Creek at the end of the road.

RECOMMENDED
It's two and a half miles up South Fork Trail #3225 to the National Forest boundary (through a public right-of-way across private land), where the old growth mixed-conifer forest begins in lush but scattered groves along the canyon bottom. South Fork Trail #3225 ends at the 18.2-mile post, near Deduck Spring and FS Road 65, which returns along Tiger Canyon and Mill Creek to Walla Walla, or connects with FS Road 64–Skyline Drive (see above).

South Fork Trail #3225 may also be reached from two trails off FS Road 64, along the southern edge of the proposed Walla Walla Watershed Wilderness. The first is Burnt Cabin Trail #3226, which runs down Burnt Cabin Gulch to the South Fork from the end of FS Road 6401, near the campground at Target Meadows. The second is Rough Fork Trail #3227, which leads down from FS Road 6403 just north of the turn-off to Mottet Campground (past Jubilee Lake). While these connector trails are both impressive, the big old trees along each are scattered among rocky outcrops. Of the two, Burnt Cabin Trail #3226 is the more densely forested.

Canyon bottoms on the Umatilla National Forest provide rainforest-like groves of huge ancient trees. (Photo by Chuck Swanson)

About 0.7 mile east of the National Forest boundary on South Fork Trail #3225, a total of 3.2 miles from Elbow Creek, is the Forest Service's Bear Creek Station; from this point Bear Creek Trail #3224 climbs over the ridge into the North Fork Walla Walla drainage to meet North Fork Trail #3222 in approximately three miles. North Fork Trail #3222, which can also be reached from a jeep trail along the North Fork Walla Walla River, follows the forest-lined North Fork to its upper headwaters and trailhead a few miles west on FS Road 65 from the South Fork Trail #3225 trailhead.

145

2. Grande Ronde Canyon Wilderness (proposed)

Float down a federal Wild and Scenic River and state Scenic Waterway past big, old ponderosa pine, fir and western larch in a roadless canyon little altered by civilization.

Walla Walla Ranger District
USGS 7.5' DEEP CREEK (1983)
FRY MEADOW (1983)

ABOUT THE AREA

The Grande Ronde River rises in the Elkhorn Mountains' Anthony Lakes area and flows through the northeast corner of Oregon, joining the Snake River just inside Washington. Along the eastern edge of the Umatilla National Forest, the Grande Ronde cuts a rugged, sparsely vegetated canyon deep into a conifer-covered plateau. About 1.5 miles below Rondowa, where the Grande Ronde merges with the Wallowa River, the river enters a 17-mile canyon in a 30,000-acre roadless area known as the "Eyebrow," a long-standing Wilderness proposal bisected by a river which already enjoys both state and federal waterway protection. This roadless area is sandwiched between the Umatilla (to the west and north) and Wallowa-Whitman (to the east and south) National Forests.

Although there are trails to the river, some still maintained on the Wallowa-Whitman side, the steep canyon walls make boating down the river the easiest and most popular way to enjoy the area. Snow melt in the Grande Ronde's high mountain source often allows river trips into July. It is a relatively easy float, rated between Classes II and III on the international scale of difficulty.

Roughly the lower two-thirds of the roadless area serves as winter range for big game, and about eight percent of the roadless area is ancient forest wildlife habitat. This fraction, concentrated in the canyon bottoms, provides critical seasonal habitat for the area's abundant mule deer, whitetail deer, Rocky Mountain elk, Rocky Mountain bighorn sheep, cougar and black bear. Rainbow trout, whitefish and Dolly Varden are the dominant resident fish species, but anadromous steelhead and salmon are also present. More than a thousand acres of roadless land have been lost in the last decade to logging in the upper canyon.

GETTING THERE

Take I-84 to La Grande, and then follow Oregon Highway 82 north and east. You will first pass the Grande Ronde River just south of Elgin, but the best places to put in are further down. The most accessible boat launch is just off Oregon Highway 82 at the state park two miles north of Minam: this puts you on the Wallowa River about ten miles south (upstream) of its confluence with the Grande Ronde at Rondowa. Later in the season, you may have to put in at Rondowa, which requires a little more driving.

RECOMMENDED

The usual float is from Minam to Troy, a distance of 44 miles, with only four major rapids. The ancient ponderosa pine in the river canyon really begins at the National Forest boundary. From Minam the trip through the Grande Ronde's nicest old growth canyons takes approximately four hours, but it is almost a full day to Troy. (Boaters also drift the 45-mile section from Troy to the Grande

Ronde's confluence with the Snake River. Downstream from Troy, the river valley is much broader and the slopes support fewer trees and more grass.)

3. North Fork Umatilla Wilderness

Two wilderness trailheads near old growth white fir, grand fir and black cottonwood along river benches, with some big Douglas-fir, ponderosa pine and western larch on the mid-slopes above.

Walla Walla Ranger District
USGS 7.5' BINGHAM SPRINGS (1983)
ANDIES PRAIRIE (1983)

ABOUT THE AREA

The North Fork Umatilla Wilderness Area includes about 18,000 acres of steep, rugged canyons carved by the North Fork Umatilla River, Buck Creek and many side drainages which finger up to a plateau at 5000'. (The relatively flat highlands, long since roaded and logged, are not in the Wilderness Area.) The North Fork Umatilla Wilderness is fairly typical of northeast Oregon canyon country: cooler, moister north slopes are heavily forested with pine and fir; warmer, drier south slopes support a combination of grasslands and ponderosa pine, and the really big old trees are concentrated in the canyon bottoms. A herd of more than 400 elk winters in the canyons, and the North Fork Umatilla River supports both steelhead and Dolly Varden trout. The trails recommended below follow the river and Buck Creek, and climb Nine Mile Ridge between them. Some of the biggest trees in the area are not far from the trailhead on Buck Creek Trail #3073.

GETTING THERE

From Pendleton and US Highway 30, take the Umatilla River Road east along the river, through the small communities of Mission, Thornhollow and Gibbon. Drive approximately 33 miles to the head of North Fork Umatilla Trail #6143, a half-mile inside the Umatilla National Forest. Buck Creek Trail #3073 starts 0.3 mile beyond the first turn-off for North Fork Umatilla Trail #6143.

From Elgin, take Oregon Highway 204 towards Tollgate for 13.5 miles, and turn left on Summit Road (FS Road 31). Follow this two-lane highway for just under ten miles to Ruckle Junction, where the pavement ends. Take a hard right for Pendleton on FS Road 32 and drive ten miles to a sign for Buck Creek Trail, or 10.3 miles to the North Fork Umatilla.

RECOMMENDED

North Fork Umatilla Trail #6143 provides a good look at the Wilderness' varying habitats as it climbs from 2400' to 5000' in 8.6 miles. For the first 4.5 miles, the trail follows the river through old growth black cottonwood, then groves of ancient white and Douglas-fir in the canyon bottom, with big old yellow belly ponderosa pine on the slopes above.

In the first mile, the river is dotted with tranquil beaver ponds. After the trail leaves the river, it climbs north up a ridge to rimrock which affords extensive views of the entire North Fork Umatilla Wilderness drainage, then grades out through ponderosa pine and open grasslands. The north trailhead for North Fork Trail #6143 is at the end of FS Road 3719-040, which meanders out Coyote Ridge (past Forest Service clearcuts) to Highway 204 near the town of Tollgate.

If you can't leave a vehicle at each end of North Fork Trail #6143 but want a really diverse hike, you might consider a moderately difficult loop hike, partly cross-country, on Nine Mile Ridge Trail #3072 and North Fork Trail #6143. Because it climbs its namesake ridge, Nine Mile Ridge Trail #3072 doesn't pass many big trees, but does provide dramatic views of the entire area. By following Nine Mile Ridge several miles to the northernmost saddle (in Section 24, nearest the North

Fork River), you can drop down one of the streams to the river and take North Fork Trail #6143 back to your rig. This is probably the best way to see the ancient fir forests on the area's north slopes.

As noted above, some of the biggest trees in the North Fork Umatilla Wilderness Area are close to the lower trailhead for Buck Creek Trail #3073. This exciting trail follows Buck Creek for three and a half miles, with numerous stream crossings; it then meets Lake Creek Trail #3079, which climbs the south canyon southerly for four miles to FS Road 3150 and 4500' Buck Mountain. (Elevations on Buck Creek Trail #3073 range from 2400' to 3200'.)

4. South Fork Umatilla River, Hellhole Wilderness (proposed)

Nice older groves of white fir along river benches.

Walla Walla Ranger District
USGS 7.5' BINGHAM SPRINGS (1983)

ABOUT THE AREA

Although not yet protected as formal Wilderness, this primitive trail along the South Fork Umatilla River is a true wilderness trail, with no fewer than five stream crossings the first half-mile. Needless to say, this trail is difficult, if not hazardous, except during low water in late summer. The South Fork Umatilla River is the biggest stream in the proposed 62,500-acre Hellhole Wilderness, and the primary drainage in the area's northern portion. The other major watercourse in the area is Shimmiehorn Creek, but the only streamside trail in the northern part of Hellhole is along the South Fork Umatilla River.

The bottom of the South Fork Umatilla River Canyon supports a great variety of deciduous shrubs and trees, which provide excellent wildlife habitat, especially for birds. Ancient forest along the canyon bottoms serves as important summer range for mule deer, Rocky Mountain elk, black bear and cougar. Only about a third of Hellhole is heavily forested, but the entire area could soon be rendered unfit for Wilderness designation under the Forest Service's plan to road and log its heart.

GETTING THERE

Follow the directions in the preceding entry for North Fork Umatilla Wilderness, but drive 3.25 miles past the North Fork Umatilla trailhead on FS Road 32. South Fork Trail #3076 begins across from South Fork Campground, near the FS Road 32 bridge over the South Fork at the river's confluence with Thomas Creek.

RECOMMENDED

The maintained trail along the South Fork Umatilla River passes the mouth of

Shimmiehorn Creek in a little over a mile and ends after 2.2 miles, near a large hunting camp. Here South Fork Trail #3076 joins the old Goodman Trail #3076, which climbs Goodman Ridge toward the center of the proposed Hellhole Wilderness Area. Continuing along the South Fork Umatilla River from the hunting camp, the trail becomes ever more primitive until it is finally lost upstream.

5. Bear Creek Trail, Hellhole Wilderness (proposed)

One of the area's most heavily forested trails, leading to a clear canyon stream.

Walla Walla Ranger District
USGS 7.5' DRUMHILL RIDGE (1984)
THIMBLEBERRY MTN. (1983)

ABOUT THE AREA

Some of the nicest and most accessible ancient forest in the proposed Hellhole Wilderness is near the area's southern edge, along Bear Creek Trail #3087 in the North Fork Meacham Creek drainage. The trail is a demanding one, but the forests along the bottoms of Bear Creek and North Fork Meacham Creek are easily worth the effort.

The Forest Service named this large (62,500 acres) backcountry tract Hellhole—a great name for a Wilderness Area, but one which misrepresents the area's lovely canyon scenery. Nearly half the roadless area is grassland, with old growth forest (primarily white fir) comprising only 11 percent of the total area. (Past logging has removed many big trees in the roadless area's center.) This 11 percent, however, is critically important as thermal cover for wintering populations of Rocky Mountain elk and mule deer, as well as habitat for many

In much of the Blue Mountains of northeast Oregon, as along Bear Creek Trail, old growth forests are confined largely to "stringers" along north-facing slopes and spring-fed canyons.

other mammals, birds and herptiles (reptiles and amphibians).

GETTING THERE

From I-84, take Exit 243 for Mt. Emily about 33 miles east of Pendleton. Follow Summit Road, FS Road 31, northeast for 12.5 miles to the junction with FS Road 3113. Turn left on FS Road 3113 and drive 0.8 mile to FS Road 014 (not shown on the Umatilla National Forest recreation map), across the road from the Summit Guard Station.

RECOMMENDED

Bear Creek Trail #3087 starts at an elevation of 4700' near Summit Guard Station, drops to 2800' at North Fork Meacham Creek, and climbs again to 5400' on Thimbleberry Mountain, a total distance of about 11 miles. The unmarked but prominent trailhead is to the left of FS Road 014, about 30' before a gate. The trail traverses a side canyon down to Bear Creek, then follows the stream through a cool old growth forest to meet FS Trail #3082 at the pristine North Fork Meacham Creek, a total of 6.2 miles.

FS Trail #3082 down Meacham Creek (west) leads to private land closed to the public, so follow FS Trail #3082 about 2.1 miles up North Fork Meacham Creek (east) to a grassy campsite at Pot Creek, where several primitive trails meet. One of these is Thimbleberry Mountain Trail #3088, which climbs a steep rocky ridge to flat-topped Thimbleberry Mountain, then runs along the mountain's south side to primitive FS Road 3100-155 (also not on the recreation map), about two and a half miles from Pot Creek. FS Road 3100-155 leads back to Summit Road/ FS Road 31, the same one you took from the Interstate.

6. Umatilla Ancient Forest Auto Tours, Bridge Creek Wildlife Management Area

Driving tours through stately groves of ancient ponderosa pine, Douglas-fir and western larch.

North Fork John Day Ranger District
USGS 7.5' BRIDGE CREEK (1983)

ABOUT THE AREA

Listed below are four easy car trips to fine ancient groves in or near the Umatilla National Forest. While this is really not the best way to experience the older forest community, people with limited mobility can take advantage of some of the many roads that already exist. If possible, stop your car often and walk through the trees.

Some of the nicest stands of old forest in this part of northeast Oregon are not on the Umatilla National Forest at all, but rather in the adjacent Oregon Department of Fish and Wildlife's Bridge Creek Wildlife Management Area. The Bridge Creek area includes a 12-mile corridor along US Highway 395 and Camas Creek, beginning on the north at the state-owned Ukiah-Dale Forest Wayside, about 2.5 miles west of Ukiah, and reaching south to the North Fork John Day River, one mile north of Dale. These ancient trees are important wildlife habitat components.

GETTING THERE

To find this stretch of US Highway 395 from western Oregon, take I-84 east from Portland or US Highway 26 east from Bend. Leave I-84 in Pendleton and take Highway 395 south, or take Highway 395 north from Highway 26 at Mount Vernon.

RECOMMENDED

Besides the Bridge Creek Wildlife Management Area described above, other easy-to-reach ancient forest sites in the area include:

Above Bridge Creek Canyon: From Ukiah, turn south off Main Street (Highway 244) at a sign for Granite on paved FS Road 52. Soon you'll notice the impressive vistas to the north, above the Ukiah Valley. After about 14 miles, to the south and southwest, are panoramic views of huge cliffs and rock formations in the canyons of the Upper and Middle Forks of Bridge Creek. Beside the road to the south, grand old stands of big ponderosa pine descend the ridges into the canyon below. The clearcut immediately north of the road at the 13-mile post was logged in 1988, and the Forest Service is preparing more timber sales in the area.

North Fork John Day River: One mile north of Dale on Highway 395, turn east on FS Road 55 at a bridge across the North Fork John Day River. Take FS Road 55 (gravel) 5.5 miles to Trough Creek Campground, at the junction with FS Road 5505. (FS Road 55 follows the North Fork John Day River through a stunning gorge and scattered groves of big trees.) At Trough Campground, cross the FS Road 5505 bridge and explore the riverside old growth grove of big pine, fir and larch.

Lane Creek and Bear Wallow Campgrounds: These two campgrounds, 11 miles east of Ukiah on the north side of Oregon Highway 244, are also good places to stay while you explore the region's ancient forest. At either site, you can explore canyons and forested benches above the campground, and sleep under big ponderosa pine, western larch and Douglas-fir.

Open park-like stands of ancient ponderosa pine have historically been maintained by periodic low-burning fires and an absence of chainsaws.

151

7. South Fork Desolation Creek

A streamside ancient forest trail beginning in a cathedral grove of Engelmann spruce.

North Fork John Day Ranger District
USGS 15' BATES (1951)
DESOLATION BUTTE (1951)

ABOUT THE AREA

This trail along the South Fork of Desolation Creek leads into the 25,600-acre Vinegar Hill-Indian Rock Scenic Area. The ancient Engelmann spruce near the bottom of the trail are large, up to 32" in diameter, which is quite exceptional for this region. As a bonus, a 15' waterfall, pools and a small beach are located about two and a half miles upstream.

GETTING THERE

The easiest access is from US Highway 395, one mile north of Dale or 16 miles south of Ukiah. Turn east on FS Road 55 just north of the bridge over the North Fork John Day River at a sign for "Olive Lake 28 miles-Granite 36 miles." In three quarters of a mile turn south (right) on FS Road 10, still following signs to Olive Lake. Between the 12 and 14-mile posts on FS Road 10, along Desolation Creek, is a nice grove of spruce, fir, pine and larch. Also, a good camping area can be found a little further up at its junction with FS Road 140 (not shown on map), just past the 14-mile post. About 0.1 mile past the 21-mile post, near a sign for "Olive Lake 6 miles," turn right on FS Road 45, and continue for one mile to the sign on the left for South Fork Trail #3001.

You can also reach the trailhead from the south, via Highway 26, Highway 7, and Grant County Route 20 to FS Road 45. See the Umatilla National Forest recreation map for details.

RECOMMENDED

South Fork Trail #3001 is *not* shown on the latest Umatilla National Forest recreation map, but the stream which it follows is indicated. In addition to the Engelmann spruce grove noted above, South Fork Trail #3001 passes through two other groves of old growth spruce, scattered large western larch, and some ponderosa pine and fir. From the trailhead at Desolation Creek, it is about eight miles upstream to the abandoned Portland Mine. When the streamside trail stops, continue beside the creek to the end of a large meadow, and follow the left fork of Desolation Creek up the hill (due east) to an old wagon road. This abandoned road leads to the mine and past it to Blue Mountain Trail #6141. If you reach the mine, you can loop back along the ridge east of Desolation Creek, walking mostly north on 6.1-mile Blue Mountain Trail #6141.

Driving in on FS Road 45, you may notice a turn-off for Blue Mountain Trail #6141 before reaching the Desolation Creek trailhead. However, this trailhead is not recommended, as the Forest Service has roaded and logged the first two miles of what used to be trail and has now gated the road part way in, claiming a need to "reduce road maintenance costs." So, to return to the South Fork Desolation Creek trailhead from the Portland Mine, either return the way you came on South Fork Desolation Creek Trail #3001, or follow Blue Mountain Trail #6141 most of the way back north (toward the ruined trailhead), and then bushwhack downhill to the west to South Fork Desolation Creek Trail #3001 once you see some logged areas.

Two other attractive spots in the vicinity are Olive Lake and Indian Rock Lookout. Take FS Road 140 to Olive Lake, as described above. The lookout is seven and a half miles south of the South Fork Desolation Creek trailhead on FS Road 45, along the western edge of the roadless area. One-third mile south of the ten-mile post on FS Road 45, turn east on FS Road 537 at a sign for "Indian Rock LO 2 miles" and "Squaw Rock Trail 251."

At 7353', Indian Rock Lookout provides a 360-degree view over much of the Umatilla and Malheur National Forests. To the northeast is the South Fork Desolation Creek Canyon in the middle ground, with the jagged Elkhorns in the background. FS Road 537, the steep side road to the lookout, is often slippery and impassable until late July. In any season, stop at the small campground at the base of the lookout and don't try to drive the very rough last half-mile, where there is little or no room to park. Finally, another mile down FS Road 45, past FS Road 537, an old growth white fir grove can be found around some meadows, visible below the road.

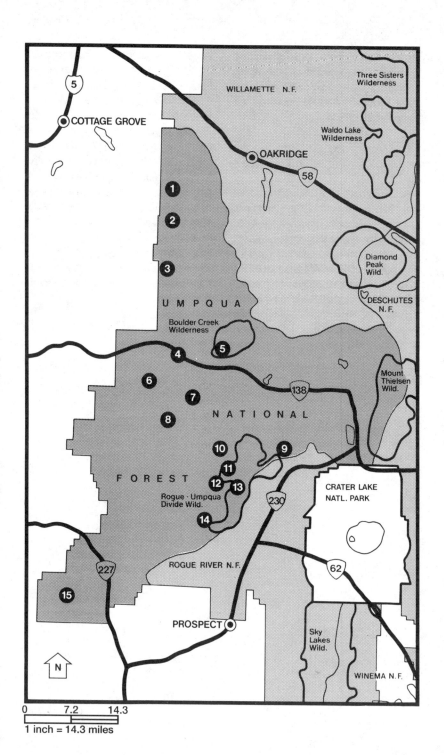

Three Sisters
Wilderness

WILLAMETTE N.F.

⑤

⦿ COTTAGE GROVE

Waldo Lake
Wilderness

⦿ OAKRIDGE

58

❶

❷

Diamond
Peak
Wild.

❸

U M P Q U A

DESCHUTES
N. F.

Boulder Creek
Wilderness

❺

❹

138

Mount
Thielsen
Wild.

❻

❼

N A T I O N A L

❽

⑩

⑨

⑪

F O R E S T

⑫

⑬

CRATER LAKE
NATL. PARK

Rogue · Umpqua
Divide Wild.

⑭

230

227

ROGUE RIVER N.F.

62

⑮

PROSPECT ⦿

Sky
Lakes
Wild.

⬆
N

WINEMA N.F.

0   7.2   14.3

1 inch = 14.3 miles

Umpqua National Forest

The Umpqua National Forest is named for the Umpqua Indians who once inhabited much of southwest Oregon. Its million acres encompass some of the most magnificent forestlands in Oregon, with outstanding wildlife and fish habitat, recreational opportunities and archeological sites. Based in Roseburg, it is managed on the ground through four ranger districts.

The Umpqua Forest harbors one of Oregon's most renowned river systems. The North Umpqua is both a federal Wild and Scenic River and a State Scenic Waterway, while the South Umpqua is increasingly valued for its role in fisheries, recreation and water production. The South Umpqua drainage has been logged intensively, and this has resulted in many watershed problems.

Along with the Willamette Forest to the north, the Umpqua contains more ancient forest than any other National Forest in the state. Although logging levels have been extraordinarily high for many years, many of the large blocks of unfragmented old growth forest can be found here, due partly to the relative protection that has been accorded roadless areas as a result of decades of battles over wilderness. Although three Wilderness Areas have been established on the Umpqua National Forest, only one (Boulder Creek) contains the extensive stands of lower elevation ancient forest that is so threatened. Many of Oregon's most significant groves of unprotected old growth forest remain here, awaiting their fate.

As you venture into these exciting places, don't forget your Umpqua National Forest recreation map.

1. Brice Creek

A recently constructed, nearly level 5.5-mile streamside trail for easy, year-round access to superlative groves of old growth Douglas-fir in rocky canyons.

Cottage Grove Ranger District
USGS 7.5' ROSE HILL (1986)

ABOUT THE AREA
Although Brice Creek Trail #1403 and FS Road 2470 parallel one another on opposite sides of the stream, the trail is well-buffered except for one mile south of (upstream from) Cedar Creek Campground. In the same stretch, small falls with deep pools easily reached from the trail are popular with swimmers on warm summer weekends.

GETTING THERE

From I-5, take Exit 174 for Cottage Grove and Dorena Lake. Turn east at the light and take Row River Road (which becomes Government Road in four miles) to just beyond the 19-mile post. Turn right on Brice Creek Road, which becomes FS Road 2470, and drive 3.3 miles to the first (furthest downstream) trailhead, just before the highway bridge across Brice Creek.

RECOMMENDED

Brice Creek Trail #1430 runs along the north bank of Brice Creek. The next two trailheads are at Cedar Creek Campground and Lund Park, 1.5 and four trail miles upstream respectively, from the lowest trailhead. To reach the trail from either site, you must cross the river on a 100-foot span, laminated beam (no longer dependent on old growth!) footbridge.

To walk the longest stretch of secluded ancient forest trail, drive five miles beyond the first trailhead to the southern-most (upstream) trailhead, where FS Road 2470 once again crosses the stream. Find the sign for "Brice Creek Trail No. 1403" and walk downstream. In a half-mile you cross Trestle Creek, where the Forest Service is planning a spur trail to more old trees and a waterfall. Shortly after Trestle Creek you'll enter a beautiful cathedral-like grove on a bench above the river. Another outstanding grove is located just downstream from Lund Park.

If you want to hike still further, a much steeper trail rises above Brice Creek from near the last (furthest upstream) Brice Creek trailhead. Just before crossing Brice Creek, turn right on FS Road 2473 for Champion Creek and watch for Noon Day Trail #1405 immediately on the left.

2. Fairview Peak Wilderness (proposed)

Gradual but primitive trail in the only remaining roadless area on the Cottage Grove Ranger District.

Cottage Grove Ranger District
USGS 7.5' FAIRVIEW PEAK (1986)

ABOUT THE AREA

This low-elevation miners' trail follows a pretty rushing stream (Fairview Creek) along canyon bottoms between steep hillsides lined with old growth Douglas-fir three to four feet in diameter. Fairview Creek is the main watercourse from 5933' Fairview Peak.

GETTING THERE

From I-5, take Exit 174 for Cottage Grove and Dorena Lake. Turn east at the light and take Row River Road (which becomes Government Road in four miles) to just beyond the 16-mile marker. Turn right on Sharps Creek Road. After the 10-

mile post turn left, continuing on Sharps Creek Road (FS Road 2460 on the map) at its junction with Martin Creek Road (FS Road 23). This is a gravel road, and a sign for the turn reads "Bohemia Mines 8 miles." Continue for 1.75 miles until you cross Fairview Creek.

RECOMMENDED

The unmarked trailhead is by a red outhouse on the left, opposite Mineral Campground on the right. The trail requires one stream crossing in 100 yards; in a quarter-mile it becomes less defined. Should there be too much water to cross easily, begin hiking upstream from the

Ancient trees and snags provide homes for scores of insects, salamanders, birds and small mammals, and anchor the soil on downhill slopes and streams.

auto bridge before crossing Fairview Creek, and you'll soon pick up the trail.

At one time this trail led east all the way to the Fairview Peak rim, from which

views of the entire drainage can be enjoyed. These days, after about 1.5 miles (which brings you to an old homestead at Cinge Creek), it is nearly impossible to find the grown-over trail.

3. Canton Creek Roadless Area

A primitive trail up Canton Creek to its falls, nestled between steep canyon walls forested with large Douglas-fir and western red-cedar.

Diamond Lake Ranger District
USGS 7.5' FAIRVIEW PEAK (1986)
USGS 15' ILLAHEE ROCK (1955)

ABOUT THE AREA

Canton Creek Trail #1537 meanders back and forth across Canton Creek. The six stream crossings before the falls (which are about 50' high) make rubber boots desirable. All but the last half-mile of road to the 2400' trailhead is paved.

Although Canton Creek Trail #1537 is not presently maintained by the Forest Service, it's possible to follow the trail from Canton Point down to the (lower) trailhead described below. This route takes you through some very fine ancient forest.

GETTING THERE

From I-5 at Roseburg, drive east on the North Umpqua Highway (Oregon Highway 138) to Steamboat, about 22 miles past Glide, and turn left on FS Road 38 before the Steamboat Creek bridge. In a half-mile turn left on Canton Creek Road at the sign for "Cottage Grove 49 miles." Continue nine and a half miles on the paved road, then turn right on Upper Canton Creek Road (BLM Road 24-1-26.0). Cross Canton Creek, drive 2.6 miles, cross a second bridge, continue 0.35 mile and turn right on unpaved FS Road 600.

Fallen logs along Canton Creek are essential to its health, filtering debris and providing shelter for a vast array of aquatic life.

RECOMMENDED

In a half-mile a trailhead sign on the right reads "Canton Creek Trail #1537 Falls 1.5 mi." The first quarter-mile of the trail leads through a clearcut, and then you enter a pleasant rainforest canyon.

Beyond the falls, the trail is not well-maintained, but the forest is just great. Climb the falls on the right, cross the stream, and then follow the creek on the left until you pick up a primitive trail. As you continue up Canton Creek, you'll come to a large logjam across both Canton Creek and a small eastern tributary. Skirt the fallen trees on the west, then cross Canton Creek above the logjam to find the trail, which soon leaves the creek and climbs to Canton Point. If you follow it up another mile or so, you'll come to a bench which may still be marked with a 1930's era sign for Coyote Flat. For a longer, downhill hike, take Canton Creek Trail #1537 from the top down. The upper trailhead is in Section 33 of T23S R1E.

4. North Umpqua River Trail, Upper Segments

A nice walk through the big trees, on a National Recreational Trail along the North Umpqua River.

North Umpqua Ranger District
USGS 15' ILLAHEE ROCK (1955)
MACE MTN. (1955)

ABOUT THE AREA

This trail leads through old growth fir, cedar, and some big sugar pine along portions of the river. At 1200', the elevation is relatively low. For over ten years ONRC and other conservation organizations worked for inclusion of the North Umpqua in the National Wild and Scenic Rivers System, which finally occurred in 1988. In 1984, at ONRC's insistence, Congress had designated the North Umpqua (including Steamboat Creek) a Study River, providing it full protection prior to the anticipated final congressional designation.

GETTING THERE

From Roseburg, take Oregon Highway 138 east up the North Umpqua River in the Oregon Cascades. It is roughly 35 miles from Roseburg to the nearest trailhead discussed below, at Wright Creek Road (FS Road 4711).

RECOMMENDED

Below are three access points to more than 26 miles of great trail along and above the south side of the North Umpqua River. They are (from west to east) Wright Creek Road, Steamboat Creek and Apple Creek Campground (FS Road 4714).

Western section—Mott Trail: After the "Entering the Umpqua National Forest" sign and just before the 34-mile marker, take the next possible right turn across the bridge to Wright Creek Road (FS Road 4711). The trailhead for the newest section of trail (heading downstream) is on the right, immediately after a small parking area. This segment extends approximately 14 miles downstream to Swiftwater County Park, four miles east of Glide on Oregon Highway 138. (Also see the North Umpqua River Trail, Lower Segments entry in the Roseburg District section of the BLM Forestlands chapter.) The trail upstream to Steamboat is another quarter-mile ahead on the left.

It is five miles on Mott Trail #1530 from Wright Creek to Steamboat. This portion of the trail follows the river most of the way. A long natural rock garden wall, dripping with moss and wildflowers, can be found about two-thirds of a mile upstream. The most easily reached old growth grove along the entire trail also begins at this trailhead. But overall, this is an open, riverside trail, rather than a true old growth forest trail. The recently constructed two-mile section of trail, heading west and downstream, rises into a mixed-age forest above the river.

Middle section—Steamboat: Drive 22.25 miles east of the North Umpqua Ranger District Office on Oregon Highway 138, past Steamboat Inn and Steamboat Creek. Turn right over the bridge across the North Umpqua River at a sign for a State of Oregon Department of Transportation Maintenance Station. The Panther section of North Umpqua Trail #1414 is immediately across the bridge on the left. Just ahead on the right is a parking area and the trailhead for Mott Trail #1530 (downstream). If you begin the Panther section (upstream) here, you will also pass along another lovely rock wall covered with mosses and flowers before entering the deeper forest in a couple of miles.

Ancient trees often reach their largest sizes on sheltered river benches, such as this one along the North Umpqua River Trail.

Panther Trail #1414 provides the most seclusion from the North Umpqua Highway. This portion of the trail rises high above the river and cuts back into a few dark, old growth forest canyons. Watch for occasional giant sugar pine. It is five and a half miles from Steamboat Creek to Apple Creek.

Eastern section—Apple Creek Campground: Drive five miles past Steamboat on Oregon Highway 138 and turn right on FS Road 4714 just before the Apple Creek Campground. The trailhead is on your right just after the bridge. This trail is recommended as the finest cathedral forest experience found along the river. When the North Umpqua River Trail is completed, it will span seventy-seven miles and tie into the Pacific Crest Trail near this manificent river's headwaters.

5. Pine Bench, Boulder Creek Wilderness

Two-mile hike to a special 140-acre stand of ancient ponderosa pine in the Boulder Creek Wilderness, generally accessible year-round.

Diamond Lake Ranger District
USGS 15' ILLAHEE ROCK (1955)

ABOUT THE AREA

The Boulder Creek Wilderness' outstanding ancient forest includes a unique stand of giant old growth ponderosa pine on the flats of Pine Bench, high above the North Umpqua River. This is the northernmost extension of this forest type (familiar east of the Cascade Crest) into the western Cascades. It is a sacred place to conservationists, who fought courageously (and successfully) for many years to protect the entire Boulder Creek Watershed. It was also used heavily by Native Americans.

GETTING THERE

Drive east on Oregon Highway 138 (the North Umpqua Highway) from Roseburg. About seven miles past the Dry Creek Store, turn left on poorly marked Medicine Creek Road (FS Road 2686). Immediately turn left again on FS Road 2661. In a mile FS Road 2661 crosses a narrow bridge downriver from Soda Springs Dam, and comes to a parking area for the Boulder Creek and Soda Springs trailheads.

RECOMMENDED

Soda Springs Stub Trail #1493 begins at a footbridge that crosses under a flume pipe. In a quarter-mile bear left on Bradley Trail #1491. The prevalence of ponderosa pine and grassy openings gradually increases until Bradley Trail #1491 meets Boulder Creek Trail #1552 in the heart of the ancient pines. After you cross Pine Bench, head a short distance north, past a shelter. Veer to your left and climb out on the rocks for a spectacular view of Boulder Creek Canyon and adjacent portions of the Wilderness Area. To make a loop back to Soda Springs Trailhead, continue south down Boulder Creek Trail #1552. After many switchbacks you will come to a primitive spur road on the left. Follow this (east) for another mile back to the trailhead.

6. President Taft Grove

"Super" old growth forest: the biggest trees left in the North Umpqua drainage.

North Umpqua Ranger District
USGS 15' RED BUTTE (1955)
MACE MTN (1955)

ABOUT THE AREA

This large grove (about 1000 acres) is dominated by Douglas-fir six feet and western hemlock four feet in diameter. Nearby, surrounded by clearcuts, is the embarassingly small Emile Creek Botanical Area, which contains the 9'10"-diameter "Bill Taft" tree, a Douglas-fir named for the former US President and Chief Justice. About 23 miles from Glide, at an elevation of 3800', this area can be easily reached much of the year.

GETTING THERE

Take Oregon Highway 138 (the North Umpqua Highway) east from Roseburg towards Glide. A quarter-mile west of Glide, take Little River Road (County Route 17) south and east for fifteen and three-quarter miles, to its junction with Lookout Mountain Road (FS Road 2703) across from Coolwater Campground. Turn left on FS Road 2703 and follow it seven and a half miles to Wright Creek Road (FS Road 4711). Turn left again on FS Road 4711 and drive 0.3 mile to FS Road 750 on the right. Just 50 yards ahead on the left is a sign for "Giant Douglas Fir 400 ft.," and a short trail leading to the Bill Taft Tree.

RECOMMENDED

You may return as you came or continue north on FS Road 4711, which joins Highway 138 at the Wright Creek bridge on the North Umpqua River in 11 miles. If you return down FS Road 2703, take a side trip to Grotto Falls off FS Road 150

(a total of 6.3 miles from County Route 17). The trail starts uphill through an old clearcut. After one-third mile, you can walk behind these spectacular falls. Incredibly, the Forest Service chose to log within 100 yards of the falls, but it didn't improve the view.

Several cross-country hikes provide the best way to see some of the area's remaining ancient forest (in Sections 1, 2, 3 and 10 of T27S R1W and Section 35 of T26S R1W—see the Umpqua National Forest recreation map). They are:

Northern end of President Taft Grove: Follow FS Road 750 to the end of the grove and some of the area's largest trees. Turn right in one mile at a sign for "Willow Flats Fire Sump 1/4 mile," or continue 0.9 mile to a pull-out on the right. Here you can follow a short spur road up through a large clearcut to the forest on the west side of the grove. Another option is to drive further on FS Road 750, bear right and make a "U" loop into the northeast side of this grove (Section 35). Park and walk downhill among trees with massive, pillar-like trunks.

Emile Shelter and Taft Mountain: Drive another mile east on FS Road 2703 to Emile Shelter. The north slope of Taft Mountain will be on your right. This part of the grove (Sections 10 and 11) can be reached cross-country from FS Road 2703, or across a wet meadow just west of Emile Shelter.

Emile Creek: Continue another half-mile on FS Road 2703 past Emile Shelter to a pond on the left. Walk across the small dam and bear left to reach more big old growth (in Section 2) north of Emile Creek.

7. Twin Lakes, Calf Creek Wilderness (proposed)

One of the most beautiful areas on the North Umpqua Ranger District.

North Umpqua Ranger District
USGS 15' QUARTZ MTN. (1955)

ABOUT THE AREA

The Twin Lakes are turquoise ("Crater Lake blue") jewels surrounded by spectacular wildflower meadows and forests of mature Alaska yellow-cedar and large old growth fir. The ridges above provide stunning views of Mount Bailey and Mount Thielsen to the east, and Middle and South Sisters across the uncut Boulder Creek Wilderness to the northeast. At 5000', the area provides cross-country skiing in winter when the roads are clear. Despite its many graces, the pristine Twin Lakes-Calf Creek region (including the headwaters of Copeland Creek to the south) is presently slated for clearcutting by the Forest Service.

GETTING THERE

Take the North Umpqua Highway (Oregon 138) about 11 miles east of Steamboat. Turn right for the Marsters bridge a half-mile east of the 49-mile post. Then turn left on FS Road 4770 (Wilson Creek Road) and follow this main gravel road ten miles to the trailhead.

RECOMMENDED

Twin Lakes Trail #1500 leads 1.25 miles through small groves of large fir to the first and larger of the Twin Lakes. From Twin Lakes Basin, FS Trail #1500 leads to the left for Twin Lakes Mountain (elevation 5879') and the FS Road 2715-530 trailhead (off Little River Road - FS Road 27). This higher trail provides spectacular views of the Cascade Crest, the Calf Creek drainage, and Twin Lakes directly below.

There are two good ways to see the area's largest old growth trees. Past the junction with the upper trail and before a rustic shelter, an unmarked trail crosses a meadow to the right. This is Deception Trail #1510; it leads 2.5 miles downhill to the northeast, past big old trees and more wildflower meadows. (The lower trailhead for Deception Trail #1510 is near the end of FS Road 800 off FS Road 4750, which leaves Oregon Highway 138 just east of Horseshoe Bend. Don't try to reach it except in a high clearance vehicle.)

The second, more popular option is to proceed into the Twin Lakes Basin on a trail which loops around both lakes. Alaska yellow-cedar, uncommon south of Mount Jefferson, grows along the shores of both lakes. The largest grove is on the cool south shore of the upper lake. At the westernmost (furthest) end of the upper lake, head cross-country to the ridgetop into a stand of big ancient fir. You might also follow Calf Creek cross-country from the northwest side of the larger lake to see what's left of the roadless area in that drainage, which has been hammered by logging in recent years.

As along portions of Yellow Jacket Glade Trail, most ancient forest groves first reach the old growth stage after two centuries, developing fundamental characteristics of structure and appearance.

8. Yellow Jacket Glade Loop Trail

Ancient Shasta red fir, Pacific silver fir and Douglas-fir among breathtaking wet meadows high in the mountains.

North Umpqua Ranger District
USGS 15' QUARTZ MTN. (1955)

ABOUT THE AREA

Late July and August are the best wildflower months, and the ideal time to hike Yellow Jacket Glade Trail #1522. A few years ago, the Forest Service had to reroute the middle of the loop trail when it was obliterated by a large clearcut. It seemed humorous, therefore, to find a sign late one year near the trailhead reading "No Christmas tree cutting allowed."

Although cross-country ski trails are not marked, the gentle contours and variety of access points to this high-elevation forest make it a great place for cross-country skiing in early or late season, when snow levels are still relatively high.

GETTING THERE

Take Oregon Highway 138 (the North Umpqua Highway) east of Roseburg to Glide, and turn south onto Little River Road (County Route 17), which becomes FS Road 27 at the National Forest boundary. From the junction with Oregon 138, follow Little River Road (FS Road 27) for 30.5 miles (the first 19 of which are paved) to Hemlock Lake.

RECOMMENDED

Cross the dam (the "lake" is actually a reservoir) to Hemlock Lake Campground, where Yellow Jacket Glade Trail #1522 begins next to an open meadow. The west side of the 6.5-mile loop trail, which passes through a series of wet meadows, is the prettiest part. Walking counterclockwise around the loop, it is about a mile to some larger trees and a side trail to Flatrock Mountain, which is also an old growth trail you won't want to miss.

Other big trees, mostly Pacific silver fir, grow nearby in Section 26 (T27S R1E), close to Snowbird Shelter. FS Trail #1517 heads east to the shelter from FS Road 27, one mile past Hemlock Lake. This trail also passes through beautiful, wildflower-filled meadows. To get to the eastern end of FS Trail #1517, turn east from FS Road 27 to FS Road 2715 three miles north of Hemlock Lake. Drive six miles on FS Road 2715, following signs for Twin Lake Trail, and turn right on FS Road 100. The trailhead is on the right in 0.1 mile. From FS Road 100 it is 0.75 mile to Snowbird Shelter, and 3.75 miles to the southeast end of Yellow Jacket Glade Trail.

9. Incense-Cedar Grove

Open meadows within a 100-acre grove of some of the largest incense-cedar in the country.

Diamond Lake Ranger District
USGS 7.5' GARWOOD BUTTE (1985)
HAMAKER BUTTE (1985)

ABOUT THE AREA
While it is located on the Diamond Lake Ranger District of the Umpqua National Forest, this old growth cedar grove is most conveniently reached from the Rogue River National Forest side of the Rogue-Umpqua Divide. Due to its high elevation, this stand is easily accessible only in summer and early fall.

GETTING THERE
Oregon Highway 230, which follows the upper Rogue River southeast of Diamond Lake, is the most direct route to this impressive incense-cedar grove. From I-5, take either Oregon Highway 138 east from Roseburg, Oregon Highway 227 east from Canyonville, or (further south) Oregon Highway 62 north from Medford to Oregon 230. If you're coming from the east, take US Highway 97 to Oregon Highway 138 and drive west and north to Oregon Highway 230.

About 0.2 mile north of the 12-mile post on Oregon 230, turn north onto FS Road 6560 at a sign for Buck Canyon Trail, opposite the turn-off for Haymaker Campground and West Lake. After four miles on FS Road 6560, you'll reach the summit of the Rogue-Umpqua Divide between the Rogue and Umpqua National Forests, and the road you are following becomes FS Road 37.

RECOMMENDED
After passing Rogue-Umpqua Divide Trail #1470 in 0.1 mile (where you can hike through more wildflower meadows and some big cedars), continue 0.3 mile to FS Road 800 on the left, identified as the Incense Cedar Loop Road. Drive three miles to the junction with FS Road 870 on the left and park. An unmarked trail begins on the right—once you penetrate the brush immediately along the road—and leads back toward the meadow which you just drove past, to your right on the way in.

Another option is to take an unmarked trail which is on the left two and a half miles in on FS Road 800. This trail winds uphill past more huge cedars before fading into a large meadow. Continue uphill another quarter-mile to Rogue-Umpqua Divide Trail #1470, which leads into the Rogue-Umpqua Divide Wilderness. Note that none of the big trees between the main (lower) cedar grove and the (upper) Wilderness trail are yet protected.

10. Camp Comfort

An easy quarter-mile streamside trail through big firs and a few large sugar pine near Fish Lake.

Tiller Ranger District
USGS 15' QUARTZ MTN. (1955)

ABOUT THE AREA

The trail is very short, but this campground at the headwaters of the South Umpqua River is a nice place to sleep near the stream and big trees before hiking into Fish Lake. (See the next entry in this chapter.)

GETTING THERE

Take I-5 south of Roseburg to Exit 98 for Canyonville and Days Creek. From Canyonville take the South Umpqua Road (Oregon Highway 227) east for 22 miles to its junction with Oregon Highway 46 at Tiller. Turn left on Highway 46, which shortly becomes FS Road 28, and drive east for 25.5 miles along the South Umpqua River to Camp Comfort, about two miles past the end of the pavement.

RECOMMENDED

A short trail begins at a wooden shelter. It follows the South Umpqua River to its source, which is the confluence of Castle Rock Fork and Black Rock Fork in a rocky gorge. Rough fishing trails continue a short way up both streams, which are well worth exploring.

Taxol, extracted from the bark and needles of Pacific yew (Taxus brevifolia), is proving effective in the treatment of certain cancers. This species grows slowly in the shade of Northwest ancient forests; because of increasing scarcity, ONRC and others have petitioned for its listing as "threatened or endangered" under the Endangered Species Act. This would both protect yew trees and their old growth habitat, as well as ensure the availability of a natural taxol source for medical purposes in the future.

11. Fish Lake

Easy four-mile trail up Fish Lake Creek to Fish Lake, through medium-size old Douglas-fir and some large sugar pine.

Tiller Ranger District
USGS 15' QUARTZ MTN. (1955)
GARWOOD BUTTE (1956)

ABOUT THE AREA

Although Fish Lake itself and most of Fish Lake Trail #1570 are protected as part of the Rogue-Umpqua Divide Wilderness, the forest along the first 2.5 miles of this trail is not in the Wilderness Area. Not long ago, the Forest Service planned a salvage sale in it.

Luckily, the largest trees in this vicinity are in the Wilderness. They are about 1.5 miles beyond Fish Lake, on the *upper* Fish Lake Trail #1570, in Section 9 of T29S R3E. Old growth Douglas-fir trees here reach ten feet in diameter! In another mile, large incense-cedar surround a sweeping meadow near the junction with Rogue-Umpqua Divide Trail #1470.

GETTING THERE

Take I-5 south of Roseburg to Exit 98, for Canyonville and Days Creek. From Canyonville, take the South Umpqua Road (Oregon Highway 227) east for 22 miles to its junction with Highway 46 at Tiller. Turn left on Oregon Highway 46,

which shortly becomes FS Road 28, and drive east for 23.5 miles along the South Umpqua River towards Camp Comfort. Four miles after South Umpqua Falls, and just before the pavement ends on FS Road 28, turn right on paved FS Road 2823. Drive 2.3 miles on FS Road 2823 and turn right on unpaved FS Road 2830. Drive 1.7 miles and turn left onto FS Road 2840 at the sign for "Fish Lake Trail 1/2 mile."

RECOMMENDED

The trailhead is well marked. As noted above, it is about four miles to Fish Lake, then another four miles through the Wilderness on Fish Lake Trail #1570 beyond the lake to more magnificent ancient forest near its junction with Rogue-Umpqua Divide Trail #1470. (You can easily reach the southern end of Rogue-Umpqua Divide Trail #1470 from Acker Divide Trail #1437 east of Cripple Camp—see the following description for details.)

12. Acker Divide Trail

Nicest ancient forest trail in the Rogue-Umpqua Divide Wilderness.

Tiller Ranger District
USGS 15' QUARTZ MTN. (1955)
GARWOOD BUTTE (1956)

ABOUT THE AREA

Acker Divide Trail #1437 connects with several trails through the ancient forests of the Rogue-Umpqua Divide Wilderness Area. Either way you walk on this trail, you'll enjoy a mix of towering Douglas-fir, Shasta red fir and incense-cedar

that is arguably the most impressive in the area. About a half-mile east of the trailhead described below, Acker Divide Trail #1437 meets Grasshopper Trail #1574, which will take you to nearby Grasshopper Mountain. Geologically interesting itself, Grasshopper Mountain provides spectacular views of the surrounding Rogue-Umpqua Divide Wilderness from its summit. (See also the following entry for Triangle Lake, Cripple Creek, for directions to Hershberger Mountain Trail #1435, which is an eastern route to Acker Divide Trail #1437.)

GETTING THERE
Take I-5 south of Roseburg to Exit 98 for Canyonville and Days Creek. From Canyonville, take the South Umpqua Road (Oregon Highway 227) east for 22 miles to its junction with Oregon Highway 46 at Tiller. Turn left on Highway 46 (which becomes FS Road 28) and drive five miles northeast to Jackson Creek Road (FS Road 29). Turn right and drive up Jackson Creek to where FS Road 29 heads up the slope to the left. From there, follow FS Road 29 for 6.5 miles to FS Road 550. Turn right and drive another half-mile to the trailhead of Acker Divide Trail #1437. (You can also reach the same trailhead by taking FS Road 28 up the South Umpqua River from Tiller, and turning right on FS Road 29 one mile before South Umpqua Falls. FS Road 29 eventually leads to FS Road 550. Regardless of which route you choose, it is 30 miles from Tiller to the trailhead.)

Ancient incense-cedars more than 3 feet in diameter are often over 500 years old. Of Oregon's four "cedars," this species can tolerate the driest sites.

RECOMMENDED
The biggest old growth trees on the 7.6-mile Acker Divide Trail #1437 are near the trailhead to Grasshopper Meadows and around the Cripple Camp shelter area. (Remember to consult the Triangle Lake, Cripple Camp entry which follows.)

13. Triangle Lake, Cripple Camp

Some of the largest trees on the Umpqua National Forest.

Tiller Ranger District
USGS 15' GARWOOD BUTTE (1956)

ABOUT THE AREA
Hikes on maintained trails or cross-country through the forest bring you to a Forest Service shelter and three pretty little mountain lakes, nestled among some of the biggest trees you'll ever see.

GETTING THERE
Take I-5 south of Roseburg to Exit 98 for Canyonville and Days Creek. From Canyonville, take the South Umpqua Road (Oregon Highway 227) east for 22 miles to its junction with Oregon High-

way 46 at Tiller. Turn left on Highway 46 (which becomes FS Road 28) and drive five miles northeast to Jackson Creek Road (FS Road 29). Turn right on FS Road 29 and drive 21 miles up Jackson Creek, staying next to the stream on FS Road 2947 when FS Road 29 turns left. Continue along Jackson Creek up FS Road 2947 as it becomes FS Road 2947-400 after two miles, following signs for Hershberger Mountain Trail #1435. It is seven and a half miles from the start of FS Road 2947-400 to the trailhead for Hershberger Mountain Trail #1435, marked Cripple Camp.

RECOMMENDED

Take FS Trail #1435 three-quarters of a mile up to Acker Divide Trail #1437. The trail to the left leads to Grasshopper Mountain (see the previous Acker Divide Trail entry for a description), although large trees are abundant in both directions. But to see some of the biggest trees, go right on Acker Divide Trail #1437. The Cripple Camp shelter is just ahead, beside a Douglas-fir eight feet in diameter. Below the shelter a meadow

slopes downhill. At the bottom of the meadow, a way-trail leads first to Toad Lake, then to Triangle Lake and some of the grandest trees on the Umpqua National Forest.

If you lose the faint trail to Triangle Lake from the Cripple Camp shelter, or if you want to get there more directly, another unmarked trail leads to Triangle Lake from a point to the right of the established Hershberger Mountain trailhead. This unnamed trail was constructed without Forest Service sanction years before designation of the Rogue-Umpqua Divide Wilderness Area, and is not maintained by the agency. From FS Road 2947-400, it meanders through an old clearcut and into the forest to Triangle Lake. If you find this trail, it's possible to make a loop by Triangle Lake and Cripple Camp back down the maintained trails to your vehicle. Once you find Triangle Lake, you can also head cross-country down Jackson Creek Canyon to Poole Lake and big incense-cedar. Further still is a beaver marsh, and generally very nice native forest all around.

14. Cougar Butte Trail

Ancient incense-cedar among mountain meadows.

Tiller Ranger District
USGS 15' ABBOTT BUTTE (1944)

ABOUT THE AREA

About four miles from the trailhead you enter the Rogue-Umpqua Divide Wilderness Area. (You'll notice Congress has not yet chosen to protect the area west of Cougar Butte from logging.) If you have time, continue two miles past the Wilderness boundary through more meadows and groves of large incense-cedar. An excellent campsite is tucked

alongside a perennial stream below Abbott Butte at the end of the trail.

GETTING THERE

From I-5 south of Roseburg, take Exit 98 for Canyonville and Days Creek. Drive to Canyonville and take the South Umpqua Road (Oregon Highway 227) east for 22 miles to its junction with Oregon Highway 46 at Tiller. Turn left on

Highway 46 (which becomes FS Road 28) and drive five miles northeast to Jackson Creek Road (FS Road 29). Turn right on FS Road 29 and drive approximately 12 miles to FS Road 30, a mile past Cover Camp. Turn right on FS Road 30 and drive seven miles to the junction with FS Road 500. The marked trailhead for Cougar Butte Trail #1432 is on your left, but start looking for it just after unmaintained FS Road 500 takes off to the north.

RECOMMENDED

The first mile of Cougar Butte Trail #1432 is rather steep, dry and cutover. But past that, you enter beautiful groves of in-cense-cedar, mountain ash, and quaking aspen rubbed bare by elk.

While you're in the area, take a short trip to see the "World's Largest Sugar Pine." About nine miles from Oregon Highway 46/FS Road 28 on FS Road 29 (or three miles before the turn-off for Cougar Butte), a sign calls attention to the record tree. Turn right on FS Road 2995, then left on FS Road 2950. The big tree is on your left, exactly 0.9 mile from FS Road 29. A few other large sugar pine occur along this road for the next half-mile, between the clearcuts. Take a look at the big stumps and imagine what this area was once like.

15. Upper Cow Creek Trail

Huge old trees along a low-elevation stream (2300').

Tiller Ranger District
USGS 15' TILLER (1944)

ABOUT THE AREA

This streamside trail through a lush, low-elevation rainforest of cedar, fir, maple and yew is exactly the kind of forest that's becoming so rare.

GETTING THERE

From I-5, turn off at Azalea (between Canyonville and Wolf Creek) and drive 19 miles east on Douglas County Road 36 to its junction with FS Road 3232. The trailhead for Cow Creek Trail #1424 is on the right one mile up FS Road 3232. Parking is best just beyond the trailhead on the right.

RECOMMENDED

You must cross the stream several times near the beginning of Cow Creek Trail #1424, and again occasionally along its seven-mile length. A fallen tree 100' up-stream provides the best opportunity for the first crossing. The next four miles of trail lead through a magnificent ancient forest, but the largest trees occur in the first mile.

A nearby point of interest is Cow Creek Gorge. A short trail starting across from Devil's Flat Campground (two miles before the junction of County Road 36 and FS Road 3232) leads to a deep bedrock gorge. A nearby historic forest ranger's cabin can be explored.

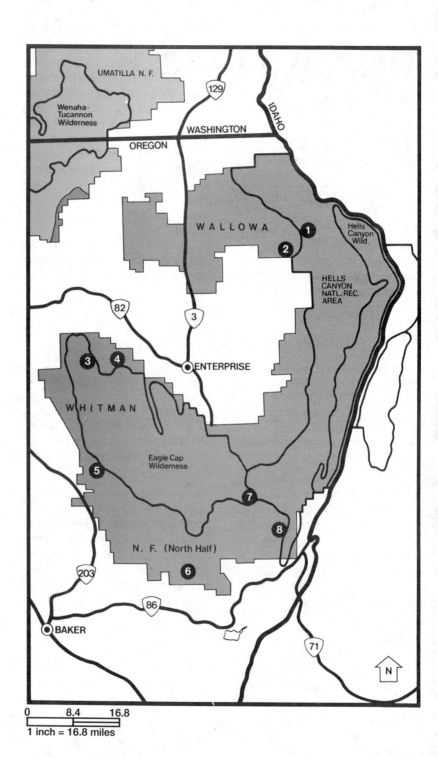

UMATILLA N. F.

Wenaha-
Tucannon
Wilderness

129

WASHINGTON
OREGON

IDAHO

W A L L O W A

Hells
Canyon
Wild.

1

2

HELLS
CANYON
NATL. REC.
AREA

82

3

ENTERPRISE

3

4

W H I T M A N

Eagle Cap
Wilderness

5

7

8

N. F. (North Half)

6

203

86

BAKER

71

N

0   8.4   16.8

1 inch = 16.8 miles

Wallowa-Whitman National Forest (North Half)

The 2.3-million acre Wallowa-Whitman National Forest is Oregon's largest. Technically it is two separate forests, the Wallowa and Whitman, which were administratively combined in 1954. This National Forest covers much of the northeast corner of the state, with its headquarters in Baker. The Wallowa-Whitman Forest contains seven ranger districts, five of which are found in the north half. It is one of Oregon's most popular public forests.

The north half of the Wallowa-Whitman National Forest is home to some of Oregon's finest ancient forest groves. It includes the renowned Wallowa Mountains and Eagle Cap Wilderness, the Snake River and Hells Canyon (the deepest gorge on Earth), Joseph Canyon, the lower Grande Ronde Canyon, the Imnaha River, the Cornucopia mining district, and many other lesser-known but very special places. Its old growth ponderosa pine forests are legend, but some of Oregon's largest larch and spruce trees are found here as well.

The northern half of the Wallowa-Whitman Forest includes all the *original* Wallowa National Forest (everything from the Minam River and the crest of the Wallowa Mountains north) as well as the northern part of the *original* Whitman Forest. (The south half of the Wallowa-Whitman Forest, which is really south and west, contains the remainder of the original Whitman Forest—see the following chapter.)

A good portion of the north half of the Wallowa-Whitman National Forest (including the existing Eagle Cap Wilderness, Hells Canyon Wilderness and National Recreation Area, along with adjacent unprotected lands) is proposed as Oregon's portion of the tri-state Hells Canyon National Park and Preserve. Many citizens want to name it the Chief Joseph National Park, after the famous leader of the local Nez Perce Indian band that inhabited the Wallowa Valley a little over a century ago.

Don't forget your Wallowa-Whitman National Forest (North Half) recreation map.

171

1. Hells Canyon National Recreation Area

Hells Canyon—the deepest gorge on Earth—drops nearly 8000' from the top of Seven Devils Mountains in Idaho to the Snake River in the canyon bottom.

Hells Canyon NRA Ranger District
USGS 7.5' DEADHORSE RIDGE (1963)

ABOUT THE AREA

The two areas described below contain dramatic vistas through stands of big ponderosa pine over the Imnaha River, from the west rim of Hells Canyon. Corral Creek Trail #1678 is a steep eight-mile pitch down Corral Creek from the top of Hells Canyon's western rim into the lower Imnaha River Canyon. Buckhorn Springs, the site of a campground and lookout, boasts one of the most magnificent viewpoints in the National Recreation Area (NRA). It is a great place for a fairly level hike along Hells Canyon's western rim. As well, the Buckhorn Springs area includes the proposed Mountain Sheep additions to the Hells Canyon Wilderness. (See also the following description for the Thomason Meadow, Chesnimnus Creek entry in this chapter for other nearby old growth forests, and the Imnaha River entry for a look at the upper end of the river.)

The Forest Service contends that most logging in the National Recreation Area is necessary to salvage dead or hazardous trees. But far more timber cutting occurs than conservationists believe is allowed by the 1975 Hells Canyon NRA Act, which is a relatively restrictive law. The agency's behavior is driven by congressionally mandated timber quotas, but it also reflects the Forest Service's policy of ignoring the important wildlife habitat that snags (dead, standing trees) and other "deformities" represent in the

living old growth forest. The National Recreation Area Act clearly states that protection of wildlife, scenery and natural ecological values are to take precedence over timber management, but the Forest Service has continued a timber sale-as-usual approach. When challenged, agency foresters argue that timber management *improves* these other values.

In the summer of 1988, the Tepee Butte Fire burned much of Hells Canyon north of Buckhorn Lookout. While the natural fire was burning in the lower canyon, Forest Service firefighters set backfires along the western rim of Hells Canyon. Many of the big trees, both living and dead, were subsequently salvaged by overzealous forest managers. Scenic trails from Buckhorn Lookout nevertheless provide an interesting post-fire interpretive experience for visitors to the NRA. They can learn how forest fires burn accumulated ground vegetation and woody material, recycling nutrients, creating new meadows and natural clearings, serving finally to rejuvenate—not destroy—the processes that are the life of the natural forest ecosystem. Fires of the magnitude and severity as those at Yellowstone National Park in 1989 will likely be repeated throughout the West until rational and ecologically sound fire management policies are adopted, including prescribed burning and "let-burn" strategies for most areas.

GETTING THERE

From La Grande, take Oregon Highway 82 three miles east of Enterprise (and 2.6 miles north of Joseph). Turn north on Crow Creek Road at a sign for "Buckhorn Sprs. 35 miles." In five miles, bear right on Zumwalt Road (FS Road 46), following signs for Zumwalt. At Thomason Meadows and the Forest Service guard station near the junction of Zumwalt Road and FS Road 4690, continue on what is now FS Road 46 for another 2.5 miles to FS Road 975 (for the Corral Creek Trail), or another 5.3 miles to Buckhorn Lookout and Campground. (Note: The Wallowa-Whitman National Forest recreation map shows FS Road 975 as being 1.3 miles *before* the Guard Station, not 2.5 miles after it. The map is wrong. Follow these directions.)

RECOMMENDED

Corral Creek: The trailhead, marked by a short post supported by rocks, is on the south side of FS Road 46, just north of (past) the junction with FS Road 975, and 2.8 miles before the Buckhorn turn-off. Despite the post, the start of the trail, like many in eastern Oregon, isn't immediately evident. After locating the trailhead post, look for a dense grove of trees running down a draw, beginning about 100 yards to the south. This is the headwaters of the Dry Lake Fork of Corral Creek. Walk along the east side of the draw, and pick up the trail on the outside edge of the old pine and fir trees in the ravine.

Another option is to take FS Road 975 to a glorious bench of ancient ponderosa pine with views over the massive Imnaha River Canyon. Walk or drive 1.4 miles south on FS Road 975 (low clearance

Trees peeled (but not killed) by Native Americans near Corral Creek in the Hells Canyon National Recreation Area.

vehicles not recommended) through a barbed wire fence gate in 0.9 mile, to FS Road 983, which is not shown on the Wallowa-Whitman National Forest recreation map. About 75 yards down FS Road 983 are two large "peeler" trees on the right side of the road. These are old ponderosa pine partially peeled of their bark, perhaps over a century ago, by Native Americans gathering the trees' cambium for food. This inner bark is reported to taste like cantaloupe. Observe that earlier Oregonians took care not to kill the big old guys.

Beyond the junction with FS Road 983, walk another 0.1 mile out of the forest into a dry open meadow. Follow the tire track trail to the left, then immediately left again (east), toward the canyon rim, to reach the ancient forest bench and some spectacular views.

The smaller canyon to the north is Corral Creek. From it you can pick up the steep trail down to the Imnaha River.

Buckhorn Springs (Campground and Lookout): The canyon below the lookout was carved by the Imnaha River; the Snake River flows at the very bottom of this immense gorge. The Snake can be seen from the viewpoint described below.

At FS Road 780, which leads to the lookout hut and viewpoint, bear left and follow a single-lane road 0.9 mile to a barbed wire fence and gate. Park here and walk generally north along Cemetery Ridge. A healthy grove of big pine trees can be found down along Cherry Creek, now on your left. An old wagon road soon forks right and drops down to the Snake River at Eureka Bar. If you head up the ridge between the two forks of the road, you can get an eagle's eye view of the Snake in the bottom of Hells Canyon.

2. Thomason Meadows, Chesnimnus Creek

Three easily reached old growth areas on the way to Buckhorn Springs and Hells Canyon.

Wallowa Valley Ranger District
USGS 15' IMNAHA (1954)

ABOUT THE AREA

On your way to Buckhorn Lookout, stop and hike through pleasant groves of ponderosa pine, Engelmann spruce and other big trees at Vance Creek, Thomason Meadows or Chesnimnus Creek. (See also the preceding Hells Canyon National Recreation Area description in this chapter.)

The edge of Zumwalt Prairie and the great ponderosa pine forest along the Hells Canyon rim were major food-gathering areas for the Nez Perce Tribe, who made their summer home in the upper Wallowa Valley and wintered in the Snake River Canyon. Centuries-old peeler trees—ponderosa pine whose bark the native people stripped a few feet up the trunk to expose the sweet inner cambium—can still be found living in these forests. In open scabland flats, biscuit root (*Lomatium* sp.) tubers could be collected without digging, by simply turning over rocks. In the right season and place, camas bulbs could easily be pulled from the ground. (Note: Casual visitors should *never* attempt to eat wild plants. For example, the nutritious camas and the deadly poisonous camas are often indistinguishable, and may even grow together. Their white and/or blue flowers are very pretty.)

Today, most of the big pine have been logged, and the survivors are being cut. The once-blue camas fields, which Lewis and Clark from a distance mistook for a lake, have been heavily thinned or eliminated by overgrazing. Yet the three forest remnants described below are still little-disturbed. With the rebirth of spring, and a respectful touch of imagination, you can still feel the spirit and presence of aboriginal peoples who for thousands of years found their sustenance among these sacred meadows and ancient woodlands.

GETTING THERE

From La Grande, take Oregon Highway 82 three miles east of Enterprise, about 2.6 miles north of Joseph. Turn north on Crow Creek Road at a sign for "Buckhorn Sprs. 35 miles." In five miles, bear right on Zumwalt Road (FS Road 46), following signs for Zumwalt. At the intersection with FS Road 4695 just before the National Forest boundary, a sign indicates it's ten miles to Buckhorn. For Vance Creek, continue a half-mile on what is now FS Road 46 and park on the left by a gate. Otherwise, continue on FS Road 46 for another three miles to the corral and Forest Service guard station on the right at Thomason Meadows.

RECOMMENDED

Vance Creek: Cross the fence on the left and head mostly north down a draw into the woods. This grove contains some very big ponderosa pine and Douglas-fir. Because of this site's old growth forest values, a few old peeler trees and other evidence of past Indian use, the Forest Service is planning to develop it as an interpretive area.

Thomason Meadows: Walk mostly south up the meadows to the left of the Forest Service guard station and corral. There are three park-like groves of large ponderosa pine between Sections 25 and 26 (T28N R47E).

South Fork Chesnimnus Creek: An old growth stringer, a classic example of ancient forests in the Blue Mountains, parallels the upper length of this creek. Like stringers in general, this particular grove has been identified by wildlife biologists as important thermal cover for the area's Rocky Mountain elk herds.

However, unlike most remaining old growth forest stringers, the slope here (which runs almost to the rim of Hells Canyon) is gradual.

A sign at Thomason Meadows reads "Buckhorn Springs six miles." Turn left here on FS Road 4690, at another sign for "Vigne Campround 12 miles." Drive exactly 0.7 mile on FS Road 4690, cross Chesnimnus Creek, turn right immediately on FS Road 015, and then turn right again in 0.1 mile on FS Road 020. (Neither FS Road 015 nor FS Road 020 are shown on the Wallowa-Whitman National Forest recreation map.) Drive another 0.1 mile and park. Walk down a gentle grade and find one of the elk trails to follow into the dense forest along the creek. The trees are primarily old growth Engelmann spruce, with some big ponderosa pine and western larch on the drier edges. If you continue up FS Road 020 you'll discover better views of the old growth stringer above a dry meadow, but the descent into the forest is steeper.

3. Minam River, Eagle Cap Wilderness

A relatively easy Wilderness trail along a ridge through ancient ponderosa pine into the Minam River Canyon.

Eagle Cap Ranger District
USGS 7.5' MINAM (1984)
MOUNT MORIAH (1984)

ABOUT THE AREA

Park-like groves of ponderosa pine along Cougar Ridge Trail #1668 open onto dramatic views of knife-edge ridges and the rock face of 5587' Mount Moriah on the opposite side of the canyon. If you have time for at least one overnight stop in the Eagle Cap Wilderness, Cougar Ridge Trail #1668 will take you to a number of great loop hikes. The upper Minam River is a true wilderness river, stunning in its beauty. (See also the Baker Canyon entry which follows.)

Loggers cut most of the lower Minam River's big trees long ago. A splash dam

On gentle ridges high above the Minam River, this grove of ponderosa pine is among the very few in Oregon that have received Wilderness protection by Congress.

on Trout Creek held logs which were flushed down the river to a long-abandoned mill at Minam. The upper Minam River was added to the Eagle Cap Wilderness in 1972, as newspaper headlines and bumper stickers urged "Save the Minam"—a cry which was finally heard in Washington, DC. Later that decade, as logging continued downstream, the lower Minam became the focus of another conservation campaign. In 1984, most (but not all) of the remaining wildlands of the lower Minam were added to the Eagle Cap Wilderness Area.

GETTING THERE

From La Grande, take Oregon Highway 82 about 1.2 miles east of Minam (or 11.5 miles west of Wallowa). Turn south on FS Road 8270 at a sign for Big Canyon Road and Bear Wallow Trailhead, near the 35-mile post. Drive 10.2 miles south on this well-graded one-lane road and bear right, staying on FS Road 8270 where FS Road 050 splits to the left, at a sign for "Bear Wallow Trailhead 6 miles." Continue up a steep, narrow dirt road which becomes FS Road 190 in another 3.5 miles. Approximately 1.4 miles further, FS Road 190 ends at a "Y" near the top of Cougar Ridge. (This road is not shown on the Wallowa-Whitman National Forest recreation map.)

RECOMMENDED

The connector trail, marked only by a weathered gray No motorized vehicles sign, heads north between the forks of the "Y" and climbs steeply for first half-mile through a younger forest of lodgepole pine, Douglas-fir and white fir. It then swings right around the top of the small gulch you've been skirting, and crosses the boundary of the Eagle Cap Wilderness. A bit further, the connector trail meets Cougar Ridge Trail #1668 proper, where a sign on a pine tree reads Division Camp. From here you can see out over Trout Creek and the Minam River drainage for the first time. At this junction Cougar Ridge Trail becomes FS Trail #1649 to the north, but continues to the south as FS Trail #1668.

To see big trees, head north (right) on Cougar Ridge Trail #1649. It follows Cougar Ridge down gradually for five miles to the Minam River. You'll pass draws of old growth white fir and Douglas-fir, and about a mile north of Division Camp, enter open benches of big ponderosa pine. Cougar Ridge Trail #1649 joins Mimam River Trail #1673 just below Trout Creek. Walk upstream along the Minam River to see more big trees or to make one of the loop hikes discussed below.

From Division Camp, Cougar Ridge Trail #1668 (to the left, up the ridge to the south) leads to Standley Spring and eventually to the Wallowa Mountains' high-elevation lakes and peaks. From Standley Spring, you have a number of options for extended loop hikes in the Wilderness on one of the trails that follow watercourses and ridges north, back to the lower Minam River.

Conservationists continue to press Congress to add the unprotected roadless lands to the Eagle Cap Wilderness.

4. Baker Canyon, Huckleberry Mountain Additions to Eagle Cap Wilderness (proposed)

Spectacular ancient ponderosa pine in proposed expansions of the Eagle Cap Wilderness Area.

Eagle Cap Ranger District
USGS 7.5' FOX POINT (1984)

ABOUT THE AREA

Like most of Oregon's designated Wilderness Areas, the Eagle Cap, for all its size, is "old growth poor"—its boundaries were drawn to exclude the largest stands of big old trees. In this instance, the ancient ponderosa pine forest north of Huckleberry Mountain's Wilderness slopes are marked for cutting. They stand like a forest of silent prisoners, their massive trunks striped with blue paint—condemned innocents waiting quietly on death row.

A recent visitor to the forest was so impressed by the majesty of one such grove that he offered to pay the Forest Service the value of the timber if the agency would agree not to log it. "This, of course, isn't something we are able to do ... This particular individual did have the means to pay for it, too ..." commented a bemused Forest Service employee.

GETTING THERE
From La Grande, take Oregon Highway 82 to Wallowa. Turn west (right) as you enter town, and in about a quarter-mile turn south (left) on Bear Creek Road. Drive nine miles south on this road, which becomes FS Road 8250, to Boundary Campground.

RECOMMENDED
From the campground, walk 1.5 miles south on Bear Creek Trail #1653 to FS Trail #1667, which leads to a sensational grove of ancient ponderosa pine in two miles. FS Trail #1667 is officially abandoned, but it's easy to follow—once you find it from Bear Creek Trail #1653.

Coming south from the campground, watch closely for an old sign reading Baker Gulch. Cross the stream (which is labeled Baker Canyon on the Wallowa-Whitman National Forest recreation map) and walk to the top of the next rise on Bear Creek Trail #1653. From an unmarked trailhead at this spot, FS Trail #1667 leads to the east (left), to the Baker and Huckleberry summits on Huckleberry Mountain. Big trees are abundant throughout Bear Creek Canyon, but the most impressive grove of ponderosa pine is two miles up FS Trail #1667.

Another option is to make an 18-mile loop up Goat Creek to the southeast, back to the northwest along the extensive ridge of Huckleberry Mountain, returning to Bear Creek through the superb ponderosa pine grove noted above. The well-marked head of Goat Creek Trail #1665 is four miles south of Boundary Campground on Bear Creek Trail #1653. Three miles up Goat Creek, the trail leaves the stream and switchbacks up the steep south face of Huckleberry Mountain. (It is 6.7 miles from Bear Creek to the Huckleberry Mountain summit and its 360-degree view.) Follow the ridge to the point where FS Trail #1665 branches off the north face. Don't take this trail—continue northwest along the ridge on FS Trail #1667. After the Baker summit, it descends steeply to Baker Canyon through the ancient ponderosa pine grove. (For more information on this and 17 other hikes in the area, obtain a copy of *Hiking the High Wallowas and Hells Canyon*, by the Wallowa Resource Council, published by Pika Press in Enterprise, Oregon.)

5. Catherine Creek Additions to Eagle Cap Wilderness (proposed)

A streamside trail through a lovely old growth forest of spruce, ponderosa pine, Douglas-fir and black cottonwood.

La Grande Ranger District
USGS 7.5' CHINA CAP (1984)

ABOUT THE AREA
The campground and trails through the ancient mixed-conifer forests on Catherine Creek are popular gateways to the southwest Eagle Cap Wilderness. These lower reaches of Catherine Creek were included in the version of the Oregon Forest Wilderness bill passed by the House of Representatives in 1983. But Senator Hatfield, acting on behalf of the timber industry, substituted lands with no old growth trees for Catherine Creek in the final version of the bill.

GETTING THERE
From either La Grande or Baker, take Oregon Highway 203 to its junction with FS Road 7785, eight miles north of Medical Springs or 12 miles south of Union. Turn east on FS Road 7785 at a sign for Catherine Creek. Drive six miles along the North Fork of Catherine Creek to the end of the gravel road and the trailhead, just beyond the North Fork Catherine Creek Campground.

RECOMMENDED
Follow FS Trail #1905 five miles to Catherine Creek Meadow in the Eagle Cap Wilderness. If you wish to walk further, it is nine miles from the North Fork Catherine Creek Campground to the Minam River on one of the world's prettiest trails.

6. Eagle Creek

Six miles of trail along the lower reaches of a wide mountain stream, which flows clear and high even in late summer and early fall.

Pine Ranger District
USGS 15' SPARTA (1957)

ABOUT THE AREA
This six-mile canyon hike past massive rock outcrops and impressive ponderosa pine is about as nice as they come. A big pool below a small waterfall and rapids about two miles up the trail from the lower trailhead makes an easy destination for an even shorter hike. Eagle Creek flows from the south side of the high Wallowa Mountains in the Eagle Cap Wilderness, but this piece of trail is entirely outside the unprotected roadless lands contiguous with the Eagle Cap Wilderness.

GETTING THERE
From I-84 north of Baker, take Exit 302 for Richland and Hells Canyon. Drive east on Oregon Highway 86 along the Powder River to Richland. Turn north (left) on Sparta Road at the sign for New Bridge and Sparta just before the 41-mile post. Drive 2.4 miles on Sparta Road, then proceed straight ahead on Eagle Creek Road, following signs for Eagle Forks Campground. Take Eagle Creek Road (which becomes FS Road 7735) one mile past the National Forest boundary and turn left into Eagle Forks

An enchanting streamside trail through the ancient ponderosa pine forest closely parallels Eagle Creek, which originates clear and cold in the Eagle Cap Wilderness.

Campground. It is a total of ten miles from Richland and Highway 86 to the campground and lower trailhead.

To reach the upper trailhead (along a huge cliff) by road, drive north on FS Road 7735 for three and a half miles, and continue straight on FS Road 7720 for another 1.4 miles. Finally, bear left on FS Road 77 and drive 6.3 miles to a sign on the left for Upper Martin Bridge Trail.

RECOMMENDED

Martin Bridge Trail #1878 begins on the right before the campsites, where a footbridge crosses Little Eagle Creek above its confluence with Eagle Creek. This trail follows the east bank of Eagle Creek for six miles through a roadless parcel of National Forest to FS Road 77. Big ponderosa pine grow on this south-facing slope, while the opposite shore is forested with Douglas-fir and mixed species of pine.

At the upper trailhead, FS Road 77 joins Eagle Creek and follows it for 14 miles to the trailhead for the popular Boulder Park Trail #1922 into the Eagle Cap Wilderness. The forest corridor along FS Road 77 on the way to Boulder Park includes old growth Engelmann spruce, white fir, ponderosa pine and western larch, and a lot of nice places to camp.

7. Imnaha River

Benches of big ponderosa pine and dome-shaped rock outcrops along the Imnaha River.

Hells Canyon NRA Ranger District
USGS 15' CORNUCOPIA (1954)

ABOUT THE AREA

The Imnaha River flows east from the southeast side of the Wallowa Mountains in the Eagle Cap Wilderness, then turns north and runs almost the entire length of the Hells Canyon National Recreation Area (NRA) to its rendezvous with the Snake River some 50 miles to the north. The section of the Imnaha discussed below flows past Indian Crossing Campground, which is 33 miles north of Halfway and 38 miles south of Joseph. It lies just east of the southeast tip of the Eagle Cap Wilderness.

From the campground to the Wilderness boundary three miles away, Imnaha River Trail #1816 passes large ponderosa pine, black cottonwood, western larch, Engelmann spruce and Douglas-fir. On the way to Indian Crossing are several other campgrounds surrounded by stands of big ponderosa pine along the Imnaha River. In 1988, the Forest Service sold the Skook Timber Sale, west of Skookum Creek and above Coverdale Campground, destroying some of the National Recreation Area's most majestic ancient ponderosa pine. Fortunately, some very large pine survive near two small ponds in Section 22 (T8S R47E). This area can be reached from the west end of FS Road 3925 off FS Road 3960 above Coverdale Campground. If you walk too far into the forest you'll enter the clearcut.

After seeing the big trees along the upper Imnaha River, head for nearby McGraw Lookout for a grand view of the Snake River from the rim of Hells Canyon. From the junction of FS Roads 39 and 3960 at the Imnaha River, drive one mile south on FS Road 39 (toward Halfway). Turn east (left) on FS Road 3965 and drive nine miles to the lookout.

GETTING THERE
North access: Take Oregon Highway 82 from La Grande to the town of Joseph in the Wallowa Valley. From Joseph, take Oregon Highway 350 eight miles east, following signs for Imnaha. After the eight-mile post, turn south (right) on FS Road 39 at a sign for Halfway. Drive south, then east, to the Imnaha River. Rather than cross the river, continue south and west along the Imnaha's north bank on FS Road 3960 to Indian Crossing Campground.

South access: Take I-84 (or US Highway 26 and Oregon Highway 7) to Baker. Just north of Baker, take Exit 302 off I-84 and follow Oregon Highway 86 east for 63 miles, through Richland, Pine and Halfway. Ten miles east of Halfway (a half-mile after the 63-mile post), turn left on FS Road 39 at a sign for Imnaha River and Joseph at the Hells Canyon NRA boundary. Drive 23 miles north on FS Road 39 and cross the Imnaha River. Turn south and west (left) on FS Road 3960 at a sign for "Indian Crossing Campground 10 miles" (it's actually just under nine miles).

RECOMMENDED
Imnaha River Trail #1816 begins on the east end of Indian Crossing Campground at 4526'. It follows the Imnaha River along the north side of the canyon bottom through the forest for more than 16 miles, 13 of them in the Eagle Cap Wilderness. In 6.5 miles, FS Trail #1816 passes

The Forest Service's selective logging continues to reduce the size and number of really big ponderosa pine along the Imnaha River.

through some record-size western larch at the confluence of the North and South Forks of the Imnaha River. Here the trail crosses the North Fork (its only stream crossing) and follows the South Fork Imnaha River to its headwaters below Cusick Mountain. In its first significant elevation gain, FS Trail #1816 climbs

7800' Hawkins Pass to the lakes and peaks deep in the Wilderness Area.

About two and a half miles west of the campground trailhead, FS Trail #1874 leaves FS Trail #1816 to the south, crossing the Imnaha River at Blue Hole, a spectacular long and deep gorge.

8. Lake Fork Additions to Hells Canyon Wilderness (proposed)

Rocky Mountain elk travel here from miles around to enjoy the solitude and shelter of the undisturbed, roadless old growth forest.

Pine and Hells Canyon NRA Districts
USGS 15' HOMESTEAD (1957)

ABOUT THE AREA
The six-mile Lake Fork Trail #1876 to (seasonal) Horse Lake—the lowest elevation lake in the area—passes through big Engelmann spruce, white fir, Douglas-fir, western larch and black cottonwood. Other trails on south-facing slopes in the proposed Wilderness lead through broad benches of park-like ponderosa pine and large, scenic meadows. Horse Lake, at the center of the roadless area, is also accessible from Fish Lake Road to the north.

GETTING THERE
From I-84 north of Baker, take Exit 302 for Richland and Hells Canyon. Drive east on Oregon Highway 86 for 63 miles, to the entrance of the Hells Canyon National Recreation Area ten miles east of Halfway. A half-mile after the 63-mile post, turn north (left) onto FS Road 39 at a sign for Imnaha River and Joseph. Drive eight miles north on FS Road 39 to Lake Fork Campground, where you can camp by the stream under the big trees.

To reach the upper (western) trailheads for Horse Lake, drive 4.7 miles north on FS Road 39 beyond Lake Fork Campground. Just after the pavement ends, turn east (left) on FS Road 66 at a sign for "Fish Lake 16 miles." The marked head of Buck Crossing Trail #1866 is on the left in nine miles, a quarter-mile after the 21-mile post. The most direct route to Fish Lake from Halfway is to turn off Highway 86 at Halfway, and turn right on East Pine Road at a sign for Fish Lake immediately north of town.

RECOMMENDED
Lake Fork Trail #1876 follows Lake Fork Creek upstream to the west for 11 miles to its headwaters at Fish Lake, bisecting the middle of the roadless area proposed for congressional Wilderness protection. The clearly marked trailhead is on the west side of FS Road 39, just north of the bridge over Lake Fork Creek.

For the first couple of miles, Lake Fork Trail #1876 leads through dense old growth ponderosa pine and Douglas-fir, as well as large cottonwoods along the creek bottoms. The big trees are more scattered over the next two miles, and the trail passes a couple of small frog ponds in Section 21 (T6S R47E). Two miles further west is the junction with FS Trail #1866 to Horse Lake. Either walk north to the dry lake, or continue another five miles west on FS Trail #1876 to Fish Lake. If you hike Lake Fork Trail #1876 east from Fish Lake, you will descend from an alpine zone into the big trees after about two miles.

It is five miles from FS Road 39 south to Horse Lake on Buck Crossing Trail #1866. The trail first enters a mixed-conifer forest of mature lodgepole pine and white fir with a few scattered but giant old Douglas-fir, interrupted by a series of scenic meadows. From Aspen Creek down to Horse Lake, large ponderosa pine trees live close to the species' elevational limit.

Above Horse Lake, you can follow the ridge east on FS Trail #1873 (a jeep track that turns into a trail and then disappears), and then cut downhill cross-country by a marsh in Section 21 to the frog ponds and Lake Fork Trail #1876. This can make a nice loop trip, especially if you are hiking up and back from the Lake Fork Campground trailhead.

A diverse streamside trail in the Lake Fork roadless area wanders through ancient mixed-conifer groves and by impressive ponderosa pine trees.

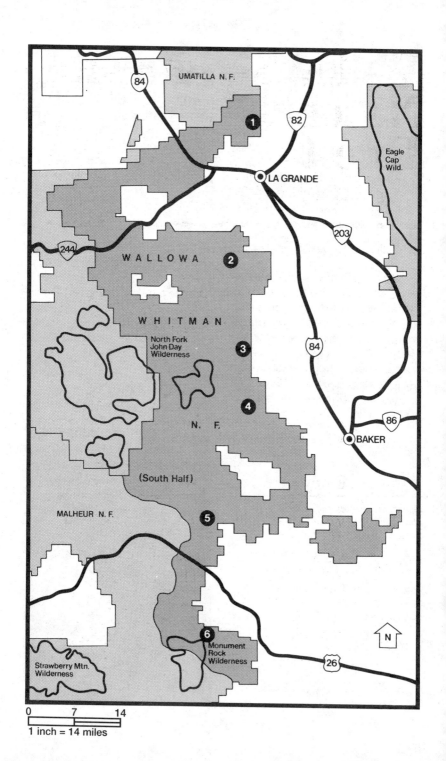

UMATILLA N. F.

84

82

LA GRANDE

203

W A L L O W A

Eagle
Cap
Wild.

244

W H I T M A N

North Fork
John Day
Wilderness

84

N. F.

BAKER

86

(South Half)

MALHEUR N. F.

Strawberry Mtn.
Wilderness

Monument
Rock
Wilderness

26

N

0   7   14
1 inch = 14 miles

Wallowa-Whitman National Forest (South Half)

The south half of the Wallowa-Whitman National Forest encompasses the majority of the original Whitman National Forest, and includes the portion of the Blue Mountains west of La Grande and the Elkhorns Range west of Baker. It is drained by the Grande Ronde, Powder and Burnt River Systems. The supervisor's office is in Baker, while on-the-ground management is implemented through three ranger districts.

The southern portion of this National Forest is not nearly as well-known or popular as the famous Wallowa Mountains in the north half, and solitude is easier to obtain. Some of northeast Oregon's most exciting old growth forests can be found here, from the backcountry of Mount Emily (due north of La Grande) to the Starkey Experimental Forest, and from the spectacular Elkhorns Range to the wilds of Bullrun Mountain (near Unity) at the edge of the desert.

Don't forget your Wallowa-Whitman National Forest (South Half) recreation map.

1. Mount Emily Lookout and Wilderness (proposed)

Dense, moist forests of ancient white fir and Engelmann spruce are summer range for elk and a paradise for hikers.

La Grande Ranger District
USGS 7.5' SUMMERVILLE (1984)

ABOUT THE AREA
Hike through this diverse 12,500-acre roadless area and see outstanding views of the Grande Ronde Valley from the lookout on 6042' Mount Emily. A nice grove of old growth white fir can be found south of the Mount Emily Lookout, just before the summit's edge.

Of the major drainages in the proposed Wilderness, the Emily Creek Watershed contains far more old growth than Five Points Creek Valley, which was railroad-logged years ago. In 1988 the Forest Service built a new road west into the roadless area and began clearcutting between Five Points Trail #1859 and the primitive Grandview Campground.

The proposed Mount Emily Wilderness may be reached from two points off I-84 near La Grande, making a loop tour of the area possible with a high clearance vehicle. The primary route into the Mount Emily area (and the only one recommended for conventional vehicles) is from the more northern of the I-84 access points on FS Road 31. This road winds around the west side of the proposed Wilderness, then circles to the north, ultimately taking you to the east side of the roadless area.

GETTING THERE

From the north—Upper Five Points Trail #1859 (east or west side of the proposed Wilderness): From I-84, take Exit 243 for Mt. Emily approximately 33 miles east of Pendleton, and drive north on Summit Road.

To reach Five Points Trail #1859 from the west, follow Summit Road (FS Road 31) northeast for 13.2 miles, about 0.6 mile past the junction with FS Road 3112. Watch for a sign on the right for "Upper Five Points Trail #1859 1 mile."

To enter the proposed Wilderness on Upper Five Points Trail from the east, drive 19 miles north from I-84 on FS Road 31 to its junction with FS Road 3120. Turn south on FS Road 3120 and continue four miles to Grandview Campground (on the right) or five miles to Mount Emily Lookout (left). The suggested eastside routes described below begin at Grandview Campground, 0.1 mile before the turn-off to the lookout.

From the south (east side of the proposed Wilderness; high clearance vehicles only): From I-84 at La Grande, take Exit 261 and turn west on four-lane Island Avenue. At the second light, turn right on Monroe and immediately right again on North Spruce. Turn left at signs for Mt. Emily and Fairgrounds in 1.2 miles. Turn right on Owsley Canyon Road in another 0.6 mile, still following signs for Mount Emily. When the road forks in three miles, bear left and drive 12.5 miles up a narrow, rough road. The turn-off on the right for Mount Emily is two and a half miles past the National Forest boundary, while Grandview Campground is another mile.

RECOMMENDED

West side: Five Points Trail #1859 begins as a jeep road to the right of FS Road 31, crosses private land, and in about one mile meets FS Trail #1843 at Five Points Creek. Bear left (upstream) on FS Trail #1843, and in about one-third mile look for Five Points Trail #1859 again on the right. Follow Five Points Trail #1859 as it crosses Five Points Creek and climbs Telephone Ridge, eventually leading to the Mount Emily Lookout.

East side: About 0.1 mile north of the Mount Emily turn-off, Five Points Trail #1859 departs to the left from an unmarked trailhead. It follows the ridge down to Five Points Creek and FS Trail #1843 in Section 22 (T1S R37E), a total of five miles. Another option is to drive one mile past this trailhead and turn left on FS Road 100 at Grandview Campground. Drive or walk 0.1 mile to the end of the campground, and continue hiking directly downhill and slightly to the left of the adjoining meadow. In a quarter-mile you will come to a big Engelmann spruce five feet in diameter at the upper edge of a large meadow. Keep following Emily Creek downhill into the Five Points Creek drainage to see more of the roadless area's old growth fir and spruce.

For a longer, partly cross-country loop hike, begin on Five Points Trail #1859 (just north of the Mount Emily Lookout turn-off) and pick up FS Trail #1843 along Five Points Creek at the bottom of the canyon. This trail crosses the Middle Fork and follows Mount Emily Creek upstream for a little over a mile. When the trail begins to veer sharply to the north (left), away from the stream, continue up Mount Emily Creek cross-country through some splendid big trees to Grandview Campground. (If you follow FS Trail #1843 instead, you'll eventually join FS Road 3120 just beyond Indian Rock—another spectacular viewpoint. The trailhead on FS Road 3120 for FS Trail #1843 is unmarked and difficult to locate.)

Other outstanding ancient forest groves of big pine and fir can be found on the south slope of Green Mountain (in Sections 15 and 22 of T1S R37E), approximately a mile north of the junction of FS Trail #1859 and FS Trail #1843. Here, slumps and bogs fed by numerous springs near the headwaters of Five Points Creek produce a diverse flora and ideal growth conditions for big trees, which are otherwise rare on hot, dry south aspects in northeast Oregon.

Bald eagles, flammulated owls, white-headed woodpeckers, pygmy nuthatches and dozens of other birds and wildlife species all need big ponderosa pine. Mount Emily contains many other impressive old growth trees, including white fir and Engelmann spruce.

2. La Grande Watershed

Some of the nicest old growth white fir on the Wallowa-Whitman National Forest, in a pristine area with a spectacular cliff and great views of the Elkhorns.

La Grande Ranger District
USGS 7.5' LA GRANDE RESERVOIR (1984)

ABOUT THE AREA

This is a cross-country hike through big Douglas-fir on unmaintained but nearly flat hunters' trails to Old Glory, an 800' precipice. The La Grande Watershed is a rare example of a forest still unroaded, unlogged and ungrazed by domestic livestock, although chainsaws are chipping away. Undisturbed stands of mixed Douglas-fir, white fir, ponderosa pine, western larch and the ever-present lodgepole pine, with all age classes represented for every species, make this area worth the effort.

GETTING THERE

Turn off I-84 at Exit 283 for Wolf Creek, 22 miles south of La Grande and 21 miles north of Baker. Head west on Wolf Creek Road (which becomes FS Road 4315), following signs for Wolf Creek Reservoir for 15 miles to a junction of five roads. Here take FS Road 43 to the left (southwest) for 1.2 miles. Turn right on FS Road 250 immediately beyond the 15-mile post. (This road is not marked on the Wallowa-Whitman National Forest recreation map.) Walk or bicycle (or drive, in a high clearance vehicle) 1.2 miles to

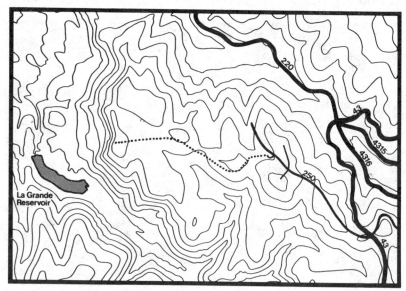

LA GRANDE WATERSHED. The hunters' trail is reached from FS Roads 4315, 43 and 250 (see text on this and facing page).

N

0   .43   .86
1 inch = .86 miles

the barricaded end of FS Road 250. A small spur road bends to the left, down into a hunters' camp and the unmarked trailhead.

RECOMMENDED
To the left of an outhouse a barely visible trail leads west. Walk through an ordinary lodgepole pine forest up a grade for just under a quarter-mile to the bottom of a small, open rocky meadow. Here the trail almost disappears. Bear left at an almost 90-degree angle, heading mostly south for 100 yards to the edge of a large meadow with an expansive view of the forest before the Elkhorn Mountains. Follow the upper edge of this meadow, generally continuing west.

At the far end of the meadow, a hunter-built trail climbs a rise, following the ridge due west. In about a mile you'll begin seeing big old white fir along the east side of the flat ridgetop and down the gradual north-facing slope to the right. Walk into this delightfully "decadent" forest. (The biggest white fir are on the northeast side of Section 9, T5S R37E.) Continue west along the ridge and in another mile you'll come to Old Glory Rim—an 800' drop—and another incredible view, this time over the Beaver Creek drainage and the La Grande Watershed reservoir directly below. Still heading west along the ridge, the trail passes through a series of small meadows surrounded by big old firs. Most of the meadows are cigar-shaped, running east to west. At the end of each meadow the trail picks up again, through the next grove of trees.

3. Dutch Flat Creek Additions to the Elkhorns Unit, North Fork John Day Wilderness (proposed)

A trail which starts low in the valley, along a stream full of brook trout, and climbs high into the Elkhorn Mountains.

Baker Ranger District
USGS 7.5' ANTHONY LAKES (1984)

ABOUT THE AREA
The Elkhorns, a unique granitic mountain range which towers over Baker, contain the headwaters of the Grande Ronde, North Fork John Day and North Powder Rivers. The western portion of the range is part of the North Fork John Day Wilderness, while the eastern face and forest is not yet protected. Rather, this region of the Elkhorns is exposed, threatened by roadbuilding, logging and mining. The hike described below provides an intimate look at the heart of this special place.

"Diverse" describes both the landscape and the forest along Dutch Flat Creek

Trail #1607. The trail follows Dutch Flat Creek to Dutch Flat Meadow and Lake through intermittent streamside groves of old growth Engelmann spruce and many other tree species. In mid-to-late October, the brilliant yellow-gold needles of the deciduous western larch light up the middle slopes along Dutch Flat Creek like fire.

A good low-elevation camping spot can be found on the way to the trailhead, along Antone Creek on a small disjunct piece of Forest Service land. Watch for FS Road 010 heading left down to the stream, a half-mile west of the first National Forest boundary sign and 1.7 miles before the turn-off on FS Road 7307.

GETTING THERE

From I-84 take Exit 285 for North Powder and Anthony Lakes, and follow signs for Anthony Lakes. Drive 12 miles on County Route 411 and FS Road 73. About 0.8 mile after the second Wallowa-Whitman National Forest boundary sign and another for Antone Creek, turn left on FS Road 7307. A sign reads "This road is not recommended for passenger cars," but the author had no problem driving the remaining 1.2 miles to the trailhead for Dutch Flat Creek Trail #1607.

RECOMMENDED

Dutch Flat Creek Trail #1607 begins with a steep half-mile climb through old growth ponderosa pine and white fir, and then reaches an open, boulder-strewn gorge. Here it turns and follows Dutch

Flat Creek Canyon upstream for a mile or so through young lodgepole pine and western larch, with big ponderosa pine on the hill above. Most of the way you can hear the rushing stream, even if you can't see it. Once the trail enters a shaded older forest, begin looking for places to climb down to the old growth Engelmann spruce along the stream.

From the trailhead on FS Road 7307, it is 7.5 miles to Dutch Flat Meadow, and another mile through an older Engelmann spruce forest to Dutch Flat Lake. A steep mile of switchbacks takes you to Dutch Flat Saddle and Elkhorn Crest Trail #164, with magnificent views over the lake, meadow, forested canyon and Baker Valley below. You can also reach this alpine viewpoint by walking 3.3 miles south on Elkhorn Crest Trail #164 from Anthony Lakes. (Your map may show Elkhorn Crest Trail as FS Trail #1164.)

4. Rock Creek Additions to the Elkhorns Unit, North Fork John Day Wilderness (proposed)

Overnight pack trip into the northern Elkhorns.

Baker Ranger District
USGS 7.5' BOURNE (1984)
ELKHORN PEAK (1984)

ABOUT THE AREA

Isolated groves of old growth Engelmann spruce, western larch and fir are intermixed with lush meadows, mountain lakes and spectacular rock cliffs. This relatively remote area is a great place to spend a few days in the proposed Wilderness additions, learning about trees.

GETTING THERE

From I-84 take Exit 285 for North Powder and Anthony Lakes, and drive eight miles south on Oregon Highway 237 to

Haines. On Front Street in Haines turn west (right) on Fourth Street at a sign for Anthony Lakes. In 1.6 miles turn left at a sign for Rock Creek. Bear right in another 0.3 mile on FS Road 5220.

About 7.5 miles from Haines, park near a sign for "Killamacue Trail #1617 2 miles" and "Rock Creek Trail #1626 4 miles" (it's really 4.5 miles). If you have a high clearance vehicle you may continue another mile to the Forest Service boundary. Beyond that it is best to walk,

Rocky Mountain elk in northeast Oregon's Elkhorn Range want Rock Creek protected as Wilderness. (Photo by Diane Kelsay)

as the road is limited to four-wheel drives, and a difficult and unsafe bridge crossing awaits you near the first large meadow.

RECOMMENDED

There are several opportunities to see big trees and outstanding scenery in the Rock Creek area.

Cougar Basin: Halfway to the trailhead for Rock Creek Trail #1626 you'll pass through Eilertson Meadow. Follow an old jeep road (FS Road 090 — not shown on the Wallowa-Whitman National Forest recreation map) south to the abandoned, picturesque Highland and Baisley Elkhorn Mines. To get to Cougar Basin, keep walking south cross-country along a stream above Highland Mine through a forest of mixed conifers 24" to 36" in diameter.

Rock Creek Lake: A small spur road (FS Road 250) takes off to the left at the clearly marked trailhead for Rock Creek (Lake) Trail #1626. The trail crosses two streams at the beginning (no bridges, but fairly easy fords) and climbs the slope

east of Rock Creek for about four miles to Rock Creek Lake. A steep section of trail above the lake climbs from 5800' to 7800' and provides great views of the upper Rock Creek drainage and the granitic Elkhorn Crest, including Rock Creek Butte, the highest point in the Elkhorns at 9100'.

Water is abundant along the trail, and at several places it's easy to drop down into the extensive meadows along the creek (see below). Good campsites are located both at the lower end of the meadows and at the lake.

Rock Creek Lake itself has a dam for irrigation purposes (complete with an underwater tunnel), so the water level fluctuates throughout the summer. Little Rock Creek Lake sits just below it, and you can bushwhack up the south slope to the nearby Bucket Lake Basin.

Abandoned trail: Although you'll want to take in all the sights on the way to Rock Creek Lake, the best ancient forest is along an old trail that crosses Rock Creek

Trail #1626 in the first mile. This trail crosses Rock Creek and climbs along its west bank for about two miles to the meadow described above. A fine grove of old growth Engelmann spruce can be found above this meadow.

North Fork Rock Creek Basin: The final option is to continue another mile up the jeep road beyond Rock Creek Lake Trail #1626 to some large old growth western larch in the North Fork Rock Creek Basin.

5. North Fork Burnt River

Some of the most accessible groves of ancient western larch in eastern Oregon.

Unity Ranger District
USGS 7.5' UNITY RESERVOIR (1984)
POGUE POINT (1984)
WHITNEY (1984)

ABOUT THE AREA
Big, old ponderosa pine live in the lower, less-logged portions of this river canyon. Along with the premier yellow-bellies, western larch trees reach impressive dimensions and dominate the landscape. In most of eastern Oregon, the deciduous

western larch achieves its most magnificent yellow-gold brilliance around the middle of October. Along the North Fork of the Burnt River, most trees usually change to their autumn colors by October 1.

A sign at the semi-ghost town of Whitney explains: "In 1911 loggers 'daylighted' (let the daylight into) the (once) giant stands of yellow pine nearby, as logging railroads were built in all directions." With the big trees felled, the good times ended in 1947, when the railroads were abandoned and "the town closed down." Fortunately, a few big pines were spared, but only in the river bottoms. Amazingly, even here the Forest Service has been gradually removing the last remaining ancient trees.

GETTING THERE
From I-84, take Oregon Highway 7 west and south from Baker, 13 miles past Sumpter to the town of Whitney. From Highway 26, it is 16 miles east on Highway 7 to Whitney. At Whitney, turn south on County Road 507 (unsigned, but it's the only road).

Loggers in the early part of the century "daylighted" the big pine all through the North Fork Burnt River Valley. But some stunning ancient ponderosa pine and western larch still remain in this scenic river canyon.

RECOMMENDED

Continue two miles on this gravel road past the Forest Service's Antlers Guard Station and enter the forested river corridor. For the next six miles you'll pass beautiful big pine and larch with numerous cross-country hiking opportunities on both sides of the river.

Approximately two and a half miles past the guard station pull into the (unsigned) Fourth Creek Campground. While there are no trails as such, single-lane dirt roads meander along the old growth-lined river bottom to numerous camping sites sheltered by the big trees.

6. Bull Run Creek Additions to Monument Rock Wilderness (proposed)

Ancient ponderosa pine and western larch along a low-elevation trail into the east side of Monument Rock Wilderness.

Unity Ranger District
USGS 7.5' BULLRUN ROCK (1983)

ABOUT THE AREA

Bull Run Creek Canyon seems like a secret passage into another world as it enters the Blue Mountains, high above a sagebrush plain. Recent wildfires have emphasized the fact that it's an ever-changing place. Unfortunately, the non-Wilderness part of the area has suffered from salvage logging.

There are some very large old trees in Koski Basin (between Sections 12 and 13, T14S R36E). From here you can continue onto 7873' Bullrun Rock and 7736' Monument Rock in the middle of Monument Rock Wilderness. (See also the Monument Rock Wilderness entry in the Malheur National Forest chapter.)

GETTING THERE

From Unity take paved County Route 600 due west of town for the State Hatchery and "Elk Center G.S." In exactly one mile turn south on a gravel road at a sign for Bull Run Creek. Following signs for Bull Run Trail #1961, bear right at the first major fork in four miles. Drive a total of 4.5 miles.

RECOMMENDED

Park at the abandoned Record Mine and hike up the jeep road beside Bull Run Creek. In a mile and a half the primitive road crosses the stream and continues as a trail.

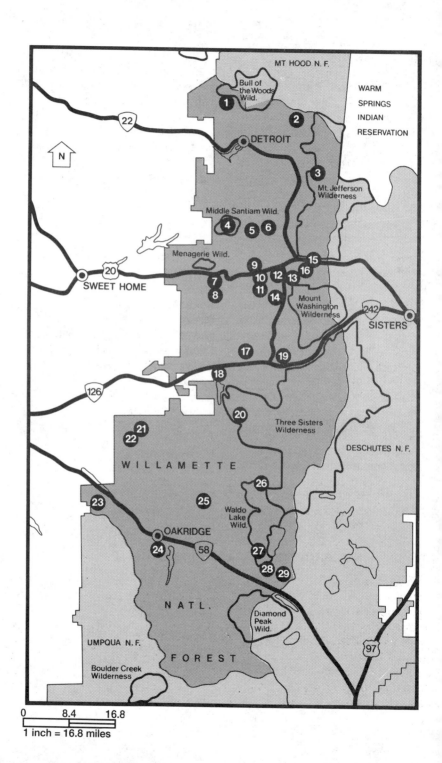

Willamette National Forest

The Willamette is the flagship of the National Forest System. It not only contains more old growth than any other National Forest in the nation (outside of Alaska), but it also cuts more timber. Consequently, the Willamette Forest is at the vortex of the ancient forest issue. It has been the focus of research and planning for years, and often serves as the prototype model for management plans. The bottom line, unfortunately, is that more ancient forest is logged here than anywhere else. Due to the extreme significance of its remaining old growth stands, and because of its tradition, the future of the Willamette in many ways symbolizes the fate of ancient forests throughout the Northwest and elsewhere.

The 1.7-million acre Willamette National Forest spans the western Cascades, stretching for 110 miles from Mount Jefferson to Diamond Peak. Its supervisor's office is located in Eugene, and seven ranger districts are responsible for daily management activities. This predominately Douglas-fir/western hemlock region contains vast stands of classic ancient forest, in both large, intact blocks as well as scattered, fragmented groves across the landscape. The Willamette is home to the H.J. Andrews Experimental Forest, site of much of the old growth research conducted over the last two decades.

Although the Willamette Forest is of utmost importance in its entirety, and provides opportunities to practice ecosystem management in already entered areas, it also contains a treasurehouse of special places which have become hallowed to conservationists. You'll hear epic stories of efforts to protect these irreplaceable groves and drainages, including Opal Creek, Breitenbush, the Millennium Grove, Middle Santiam, Old Cascades, the McKenzie Valley, the Waldo Country, Hardesty Mountain, and the Calapooya Divide, to mention but a few.

Readers will note this is the most extensive chapter in the *Walking Guide*, and it could easily have been much longer. However, once on the ground, you will find it difficult to ignore how fast these places are disappearing.

Don't forget your Willamette National Forest recreation map.

1. Opal Creek Additions to Bull-of-the-Woods Wilderness (proposed)

One of the finest ancient forest valleys in the Oregon Cascades, home to black bear, Roosevelt elk and spotted owls.

Detroit Ranger District
USGS 7.5' BATTLE AX (1985)

ABOUT THE AREA

Take an all-day hike into the proposed Opal Creek Wilderness, 36 miles east of Salem. The 31,000-acre watershed, which is contiguous with the Bull-of-the-Woods Wilderness, contains classic ancient forest with trees up to 250' high and 1000 years old. One of Oregon's few remaining unlogged old growth forest drainages and a key part of the largest intact stand of ancient forest in the western Cascades, the Opal Creek Valley includes 50 waterfalls (among them the 250'-high Opal Falls), five lakes, and 29 miles of hiking and equestrian trails. The area has become a major battleground and symbol of the conflict between conservationists and the timber industry over the fate of Oregon's remaining ancient forest. The wood products industry and some in the Forest Service have vowed to see Opal Creek cut, but conservationists are even more committed to protecting it. Forest Service plans still call for building a road up Opal Creek and clearcutting large areas of the forest. Eighteen timber sales are currently scheduled.

Jawbone Flat, the picturesque old mining town at the bottom of Opal Creek (which flows into the Little North Fork Santiam River), is the home of the Shiny Rock Mining Company's environmentally sensitive operations. The owners and managers of the mine have worked for decades, to protect Opal Creek from logging. They deserve everyone's gratitude. Please respect their property, don't enter any mine shafts, and perhaps thank them for their commitment to Opal Creek's survival. Ask them how you might help.

GETTING THERE

From I-5 at Salem, take the North Santiam Highway (Oregon Highway 22) approximately 25 miles east, to just west of Mehama. Following a sign for the Elkhorn Recreation Area, turn north on Little North Fork Road at a flashing yellow light between the State Forestry Department building on the north side of Oregon Highway 22 and the Swiss Village Restaurant across the road. (This is 0.2 mile before the 23-mile post, on the west side of Mehama.) Drive 21 miles up the Little North Fork Santiam River. In 15 miles you'll cross the national forest boundary, and Little North Fork Road becomes FS Road 2207. At the only major fork in the road, bear left (it's almost straight ahead) on FS Road 2209. Park at the locked gate at the end of the road.

RECOMMENDED

Continue down the jeep road on foot or bicycle for three miles to Jawbone Flat. (If you do bring a bicycle, make it a clunker or a mountain bike.) Almost immediately you will pass some scattered 800-year-old trees in an area that was selectively logged many decades ago. In 1.5 miles you will enter a beautiful and undisturbed old growth grove above the Little North Fork. The forest on your left, to the north, is protected in the Bull-of-the-Woods Wilderness Area. But the trees and stream on your right (the Little North Fork Santiam River), like Opal Creek ahead, are not protected.

Walk through Jawbone Flat on the jeep road, cross the bridge over Battle Ax Creek, turn right and walk down the road to the south past the rest of the mining camp's buildings. Walk about a quarter-mile to the third major switchback, and look to the south (right) for the white plastic water pipe (for the mining operation's hydroelectric generator) which marks the Opal Creek Trail. Follow the trail into the forest alongside the water line. Before the first switchback, look for a sign on the right directing you to the exquisite and appropriately named Opal Pool. Just below Opal Pool, Opal Creek and Battle Ax Creek converge to form the Little North Fork Santiam River.

Back on Opal Creek Trail, you encounter older trees again in about 150 yards. Within another quarter-mile, the primitive trail leads down to the edge of a small boulder-lined creek. Cross the stream before reaching the end of the water line and follow the trail up a ridge for some

sweeping views over much of the Opal Creek area. The trail then enters the Opal Creek drainage proper, passes a waterfall, and follows the east side of the creek another two miles upstream.

The next major tributary in your path is the East Fork of Opal Creek. The trail continues another quarter-mile beyond it to an impressive grove of western redcedar, with some trees seven feet in diameter. The distance from the gate to the cedar grove is about six and a half miles. Making progress upstream, toward Opal Lake at the upper end of the valley, becomes increasingly difficult as the trail gradually fades, requiring cross-country travel through thick forest on steep terrain. The bears who built this unofficial trail (a local rumor; the Forest Service opposed its construction) seem to think the best way to reach Opal Lake is to descend from the top of the valley. The ridge is best reached on FS Trail #3358, or you can cheat and drive in on FS Road 2207 at the top of the drainage (see the Willamette National Forest recreation map). An "official" trail from Jawbone Flat to Opal Lake along Opal Creek is planned.

2. Breitenbush Spotted Owl Trail

A trail through young stands, clearcuts, and some really beautiful virgin forest.

Detroit Ranger District
USGS 15' BREITENBUSH HOT SPRINGS

ABOUT THE AREA
The Spotted Owl Trail was built by the staff of the nearby Breitenbush Hot Springs Retreat and Conference Center and Friends of the Breitenbush Cascades in 1986. It offers an excellent four-mile loop hike through varied terrain and both natural and "managed" forest.

A word about Breitenbush Hot Springs. This rustic resort caters primarily to group events (including occasional ONRC conferences and workshops), but they often have space available for day use of the hot springs and gourmet vegetarian meals. If you haven't been to Brietenbush, you're missing something special! Day use is $5-10 for all day, and meals are $5. Overnight stays can also be arranged: rates for a cabin and three meals range around $40 per person. Always call ahead at 854-3314, as reservations are required. Please support this business, which has been instrumental in focusing attention on the ancient forests of this area.

GETTING THERE

Take Oregon Highway 22 to Detroit, about 35 miles east of Salem. On the west end of town, just east of the bridge, turn north on FS Road 46. Drive ten miles to Cleator Bend Campground. Just past the campground, turn right on FS Road 2231, cross the bridge over the Breitenbush River and turn left, staying on FS Road 2231. At 0.6 mile past the bridge, take the left fork (FS Road 890) and drive another 0.6 mile to the Breitenbush Hot Springs sign.

RECOMMENDED

Across from the Breitenbush Hot Springs sign is a small (6-acre) clearcut. Park along the road next to it. The trail begins in the eastern part of the clearcut, near the corner.

The well-signed trail runs along the east edge of the clearcut, meanders through a selectively cut area, and emerges at another small clearcut, where there are stumps with more than 650 rings. After another half-mile of winding through selectively cut ancient forest, the trail crosses a footbridge over Devil's Creek and follows the east bank downstream for a quarter-mile. It then heads uphill into still-pristine ancient forest. (About a quarter-mile in is a fork in the trail and a clear sign indicating the Tree Trail and Cliff Trail. You can walk either way and follow the loop back to this spot.)

Near Breitenbush Hot Springs, many western red-cedars grow along the area's trails. Trees over 40 inches in diameter may be more than half a millennium old.

The Tree Trail soon crosses a ravine with a magnificent multi-layered canopy of fir, cedar, hemlock and yew. This is also a nesting area for a pair of spotted owls, who have produced offspring in three of the last four years. It is very important to travel this area gently and not disturb the owls, who often roost low in the branches with their owlets.

After the ravine the trail continues upward for a half-mile, then descends into a wet basin, where a perennial creek flows from a bog fed by springs on its eastern end, which in turn flow from below some giant western red-cedars. In this basin, the Spotted Owl Trail joins the old Devil's Ridge Trail, which crosses a saddle and makes a short, steep climb to the Cliff Trail part of the loop.

If you take the left fork, following the Devil's Ridge Trail, it is another half-mile to "Management Outlook" where, on a clear day, you can see more than a hundred clearcuts in the Breitenbush Watershed. The Devil's Ridge Trail continues on to 4529' Devil's Peak and the Mount Jefferson Wilderness Area.

Still following the loop, the trail (now the Cliff Trail) enters an area where many large trees show a distinctive bend at their base, acquired when they were young trees struggling against heavy snows on this west-facing slope. The trail drops down to another junction with the Devil's Ridge Trail on the left (which would be the way up to Management Outlook for folks foolish enough to walk the trail backwards). Less than one-quarter mile further, a spur trail goes out a short distance to the "cliffs" for which the trail was named, and to Manzanita Lookout, where you can gaze over the ancient forest from above—and peruse a series of clearcuts and tree farms along Devil's Creek. It's another half-mile from this spur down to the junction with the Tree Trail.

3. Pamelia Lake Trail, Mount Jefferson Wilderness

A popular Wilderness trail through a classic western Oregon ancient forest along a rushing stream.

Detroit Ranger District
USGS 15' MOUNT JEFFERSON (1961)

ABOUT THE AREA

The 2.4-mile trail to Pamelia Lake in the Mount Jefferson Wilderness is one of the most popular in the Cascades. While no one believed the Forest Service would ever try to log the big trees at the head of Pamelia Lake Trail, in 1986 ONRC successfully appealed a Forest Service decision to do just that. Unfortunately, the Forest Service persisted and logged two other units, one near the Highway 22

junction, the other at Milk Creek—only one mile from the head of Pamelia Lake Trail.

Pamelia Creek was named by Marion County road surveyor John Minto for Pamelia Ann Berry, a young woman who cooked for the survey crew. Pamelia Lake was later named after the stream by Judge John B. Waldo. Regarded as "Oregon's John Muir," Judge Waldo wrote eloquently a century ago of the Cascades' wilderness beauty and was one of the earliest advocates for forest protection. He penned some great stories about the big old solitary grizzlies that once roamed the entirety of the Oregon Cascades.

GETTING THERE
Take Oregon Highway 22 approximately 12 miles east and south of Detroit (or 19 miles north of the US Highway 20 junction). Turn east on Pamelia Lake Road (FS Road 2248), about 0.3 mile south of the 62-mile post. Drive 3.6 miles east to the trailhead.

RECOMMENDED
The first half-mile of the trail is through a beautiful old forest, but the trees get smaller after you reach the Wilderness boundary in a quarter-mile. Another option is hiking on to 5799' Grizzly Peak.

Fallen logs help ancient forest streams retain most nutrients and debris. Of the organic material that falls or slides into small streams each year, less than 35 percent is lost downstream.
(Photo by Diane Kelsay)

4. Gordon Peak Trail

Another spectacular big tree trail at the northeast edge of the Middle Santiam Wilderness.

Sweet Home Ranger District
USGS 7.5' CHIMNEY PEAK (1984)

ABOUT THE AREA

The Middle Santiam Wilderness and its adjacent but unprotected wildlands contain the biggest—and probably the oldest—trees in Oregon. The area's topography varies widely, from high forested peaks and ridges to gentler slopes and benches. Like many other undeveloped areas, the Middle Santiam is still roadless for good reason. It is a highly unstable region, where the likelihood of erosion and loss of fish habitat as a result of logging is very high. Elevations range from about 2000' along the Middle Santiam River to 5022' on Scar Mountain, just east of the the upper trailhead. Gordon Peak (or Swamp Creek) Trail #3387 begins near Gordon Peak in the northeast corner of the drainage, and leads down to the impressive valley floor below, ending in the Middle Santiam Wilderness, just past a clearcut and a log spur road. Follow the directions carefully, as a specific trailhead is no longer clearly defined.

This route requires driving on only two and a half miles of winding gravel logging roads, in contrast to the route described in the following entry in this chapter for Middle Santiam Wilderness and Pyramid Creek.

GETTING THERE

Take Oregon Highway 22 about 19 miles south and east of Detroit. Turn west at a sign for Straight Creek Road (FS Road 11). Continue on paved FS Road 11 for 10.5 miles. Just beyond the end of the

pavement turn left on FS Road 1152. Continue 2.2 miles and turn left on FS Road 660. This road dead-ends in 0.3 mile at the top of a clearcut.

RECOMMENDED

Park about 0.1 mile before the end of the road and walk cross-country, perpendicular to the road and toward the ridge, into the forest. In approximately 100 yards you will come to the trail; follow it to the right. (To the left the trail ends in the southwest corner of the last clearcut you passed, 0.1 mile before you turned onto FS Road 660. You may also follow the western edge of this clearcut to the top and locate the trail.)

The very lower end of Gordon Peak Trail #3387 joins Chimney Peak Trail #3382 in the Middle Santiam Wilderness. You may begin the lower Gordon Peak Trail #3387 approximately one mile up the Chimney Peak Trail #3382. (See the description for the Middle Santiam Wilderness and Pyramid Creek entry which follows in this chapter for details.)

*Pyramid Creek from
the end of Pyramid
Creek Trail.*

5. Middle Santiam Wilderness and Pyramid Creek

*Ridge after ridge of ancient forest, includ-
ing what are probably the finest and largest
trees in Oregon.*

Sweet Home Ranger District
USGS 7.5' CHIMNEY PEAK (1984)

ABOUT THE AREA

This old growth forest is comprised of
the classic cathedral stands once common throughout Oregon. The upper
Middle Santiam drainage contains both
the greatest concentration and the largest
contiguous area of really big, ancient trees
left in the state. Unfortunately, the Forest
Service has been intensively roading and
logging the area for the past decade, and
only a third of the remaining old growth
forest is protected from these depredations. The Oregon Forest Wilderness Act
of 1984 designated 8553 acres for the
Middle Santiam Wilderness, leaving over
16,000 adjacent ancient forest acres unprotected. Although roads and clearcuts
have destroyed some of this area, the
virgin forest which remains is a top priority for protection.

GETTING THERE

Take US Highway 20 approximately 22
miles east of the Sweet Home Ranger
District office, and turn north on Soda
Fork Road, just west of Mountain House
Restaurant. Within a mile the road forks;
bear left on FS Road 2041. Continue on
FS Road 2041 the rest of the way, carefully noting intersections. (Confusion is
contagious in this maze of logging roads.)
Once you've driven over the ridge to the
north and descended into the Middle
Santiam Valley, you'll pass a large landslide to the right, around which the road
has been routed. In another half-mile
cross the Middle Santiam River bridge.

RECOMMENDED

The recommended option is to drive a
mile and a half past the Middle Santiam
bridge up the road to the head of Chimney Peak Trail #3382, which leads to
Donaca Lake (2.7 miles) in the Middle
Santiam Wilderness. (It is 8.8 miles to the
western end of the Wilderness Area on

Chimney Peak Trail #3382.) Continue 1.3 miles on FS Road 2041, across the Pyramid Creek bridge to the signed trailhead on the left.

Pyramid Creek has been the scene of several blockades by protesters who, after exhausting all legal means, used civil disobedience to try to stop clearcutting in these old growth forests. ONRC is deeply involved in efforts to protect—through education, legislation and litigation—as much of Oregon's ancient and native forests as possible. The Council does not condone unlawful action on anyone's part, whether it be civil disobedience or illegal logging by the Forest Service.

The more adventurous alternative is to drive only 200-300' past the Middle Santiam bridge and pull over at a large gravel quarry on your right. Hike to the top of the pit and find a small but conspicuous trail which leads into the forest up the hill, originating near the highest point of the open, disturbed area. (Occasional red plastic and paper strips mark the trail.) After about 100 yards (going straight up) and past a huge sugar pine, the trail makes a "Y." The right trail follows the north side of the Middle Santiam River, and the left fork leads up Pyramid Creek and crosses at a huge log about a mile upstream. These "user-made" trails should not be attempted by those averse to cross-country hiking. None of the immediate area is protected from logging. You'll find the trees here "treemendous."

6. Pyramids Unit, Old Cascades Wilderness (proposed)

Sensational stands of ancient noble and Pacific silver fir, interspersed with rock cliffs and wildflower-filled mountain meadows.

Sweet Home Ranger District
USGS 7.5' COFFIN MTN. (1984)
USGS 15' ECHO MTN. (1955)

ABOUT THE AREA
The Pyramids Unit of the proposed Old Cascades Wilderness lies to the east of the Middle Santiam Wilderness. It includes three peaks: the North, Middle and South Pyramids. A trail on the east side of the area leads to the Middle Pyramid.

Other units of the proposed Old Cascades Wilderness described in this guide (both north and south of the South Santiam Highway, US Highway 20) include Browder Ridge, Gordon Meadows, Pyramid Creek, and Echo Mountain-Iron Mountain. (If this Wilderness complex were established, the existing Menagerie Wilderness would be incorporated as a unit of the Old Cascades Wilderness.)

GETTING THERE
From the junction of Highways 22 and 126, drive north on Highway 22 for five miles and turn west on Lava Lake Meadow Road (FS Road 2067) a quarter-mile north of the 77-mile post. Continue two miles on FS Road 2067, cross the Parks Creek bridge, and bear right on FS Road 560. Continue about three and a half miles to a sign on the left for Pyramids Trail #3380.

RECOMMENDED
The trailhead is a half-mile beyond the

junction of FS Road 572 with FS Road 560, before a hairpin right turn.

The three-mile Pyramids Trail, which is adjacent to the small gorge of the North Fork Parks Creek, winds among noble fir four to five feet thick with a beautiful green herbaceous groundcover. In the upper elevations—often not accessible before the middle of June—Alaska yellow-cedar, subalpine fir and dwarf juniper grow. Higher still, rocky crags are covered with many species of alpine cushion and rock plants, which bloom in abundance every July. The Old Cascades contain remarkable botanical diversity.

New age druids try communicating with a giant sugar pine tree through its cones.

7. House Rock Loop

Accessible, easy trail with giant trees.

Sweet Home Ranger District
USGS 7.5' HARTER MTN. (1984)

ABOUT THE AREA
House Rock is an overhanging boulder that once sheltered snow-bound pioneers. Cross the footbridge over the South Fork Santiam River at the campground and picnic area below the confluence of Sheep and Squaw Creeks, and enter the multi-layered canopy of big old western hemlock and Douglas-fir.

GETTING THERE
Take US Highway 20 about 24 miles east of the Sweet Home Ranger District and two miles east of the Mountain House Restaurant. Turn south on Squaw Creek Road (FS Road 2044) at the House Rock Campground turn-off. Drive 0.2 mile to FS Road 202, which is the entrance to House Rock Campground.

Drive or walk (if the campground is closed for the winter) about 400 yards down FS Road 202. The trailhead for House Rock Trail #3406 is on the right, before the bridge over Sheep Creek. In 100 yards, the trail leads to a footbridge over the South Santiam River, and then to a picnic area.

RECOMMENDED
The 0.8-mile loop trail winds past House Rock and a fantastic view of a scenic waterfall. The trail soon intersects the Old Santiam Wagon Road. Follow the signs and return to House Rock on the historic wagon road, the predecessor of US Highway 20.

8. Millennium Grove, Gordon Lakes Unit, Old Cascades Wilderness (proposed)

The oldest known trees in Oregon, along a pleasant trail to Gordon Lakes.

Sweet Home Ranger District
USGS 15' ECHO MTN. (1955)
CASCADIA (1955)

ABOUT THE AREA
At 750-1000 years old, the trees in Millennium Grove constitute the largest stand of the oldest known Douglas-fir trees left in Oregon. However, because of the elevation at which they live, these trees are no bigger (up to six feet in diameter) than many trees half their age. Although much of the original grove has been fragmented by clearcut logging which you will experience on your way in, some uncut ancient trees remain in the proposed Gordon Meadows Unit of the Old Cascades Wilderness. For all its stature, the Millennium Grove is not classic "cathedral" forest, as most of the trees are scattered throughout a forest of much younger ones.

There are no trails through most of this area. The largest groves of ancient trees lie below Gordon Lakes, along the east and west forks of Three Creek. Most of the ground is fairly steep and even a downhill route is difficult hiking. The worst of the brushy understory can be avoided by staying out of stream bottoms. The easiest trip is to observe the many old broken-top trees from your car, and then

hike this gentle trail into Gordon Lakes.

GETTING THERE
Take US Highway 20 approximately 24 miles east of the Sweet Home Ranger District office and two miles east of the Mountain House Restaurant. At the House Rock Campground turn-off, turn south on Squaw Creek Road (FS Road 2044), and follow it a total of 5.4 miles to FS Road 230.

En route, you will cross the lower two forks of Three Creek. About 4.7 miles south of Highway 20, FS Road 2046 bears right, into the heart of the Millennium Grove and the infamous clearcuts that Willamette Industries created in 1986, despite public knowledge of the trees' incredible age. (After a long, protracted public squabble over the fate of these very old trees, the company agreed to a court hearing, and tree-sitting protesters came down at the judge's request. Willamette Industries then immediately cut the trees, and when Monday's court hearing began only stumps remained. As the judge explained, there was nothing he could do to make those trees stand up again.)

To reach Gordon Lakes, turn right on FS Road 230 and follow it 2.7 miles to the clearly marked trailhead at the road's end. Bands of ancient trees are easily seen from the road at several points: from

"They are felling Oregon's glory, trunk by trunk. The majestic old trees six feet thick and soaring 200 feet into the blue northern sky, have stood on these mountains since the discovery of America. Now they are crashing down in record numbers ... disappearing at an equivalent of 86 football fields a day ..."
The Times of London, November 1988

the junction with FS Road 2044; from the east side of FS Road 230 about 0.8 mile down the road; at 1.1 miles, where the ancient forest along Three Creek is visible; and at 1.4 miles, where there is a good spot to pull off and view the Three Creek forest.

RECOMMENDED

The two Gordon Lakes are in a basin just beyond the trailhead. Several big old Douglas-fir live at the first lake, in the western end of Millennium Grove. A secondary trail, which forks to the left just 100' beyond the trailhead, passes through very large noble fir on this upper lake's south side, and then rejoins the main trail.

Follow the main trail to the lower lake. (Here a fork to the left leads another three miles to Gordon Meadows in the middle of the proposed Wilderness.) At the lower lake's outlet, Three Creek, walk downhill to a small grove of ancient trees among devil's club and other shade-loving plants. Below this point the contours are steep. If you can arrange a car shuttle to pick you up below, walk cross-country a mile and a half down to the first stream you crossed coming in on FS Road 2044.

9. Echo Mountain - Iron Mountain Unit, Old Cascades Wilderness (proposed)

Some of the largest and most easily reached Alaska yellow-cedar in Oregon.

Sweet Home Ranger District
USGS 15' ECHO MTN. (1955)

ABOUT THE AREA

Most of the proposed Old Cascades Wilderness is high rocky peaks with isolated pockets of ancient forest. The proposed Echo Mountain-Iron Mountain Unit contains beautiful meadows along two

ridges, with forested slopes below. It is noted for the popular Iron and Crescent Mountain Trails, which climb through diverse topography and some of the finest wildflower meadows and rocky outcrops in the Cascades.

Crescent Mountain, a long, curving ridge with dry meadows on south-facing slopes, dominates the north side of the area, above the densely forested Maude and Cougar Creek Valleys. On the south side of the area, the five-peaked ridge of Echo Mountain rises between the valleys and US Highway 20. The westernmost peak, Iron Mountain, is flanked by a high red spire. To the east, Cone Peak features smooth cinder south slopes and a long, 20'-high dike on the north side. The ridge continues to South Peak, Echo Mountain and North Peak.

Alaska yellow-cedar are not common south of Mount Jefferson, and even there tend to be smaller, higher elevation trees. The small grove described here is exceptional: some trees are over four feet thick at breast height. In order to have reached such impressive size these cedars must be very old (500-600 years), as this species grows slowly.

Consider visiting both the stand described below and the nearby Hackleman Creek

Ancient Forest Grove (see the next entry). The short trails at both areas would nicely balance a day of hiking.

GETTING THERE
Take US Highway 20 east from Tombstone Prairie, and turn north on Echo Creek Road (FS Road 055) approximately 0.6 mile east of the 66-mile post. Drive two miles and watch for the trailhead on the right at the second crossing over Echo Creek.

RECOMMENDED
The trailhead is marked by a broken sign that once read "Echo Basin Old Growth Grove Trail." The first, moderately steep half-mile runs just above the creek at the bottom of an old clearcut. The trail then makes a loop, crossing a wet meadow high in the basin. You can climb cross-country from the top of the meadow to the summit of Echo Mountain. After the meadow crossing, you pass more big cedars and firs and return to the trail at the edge of the clearcut. Total mileage around the loop is about a mile and a half.

Small natural openings, which enhance forest diversity, are a common component of the ancient forest. (Photo by Diane Kelsay)

207

10. Hackleman Creek Ancient Forest Grove

A streamside trail leads through old growth fir and western hemlock, and offers snowshoeing possibilities when snow accumulates below 4000'.

Sweet Home Ranger District
USGS 15' ECHO MTN. (1955)

ABOUT THE AREA

Scattered Forest Service clearcuts and resulting blowdown have begun to spoil this grove's integrity. But because it is a level, easy-to-reach area, it remains a good place to see fine old growth western hemlock and Engelmann spruce, as well as the ubiquitous Douglas-fir.

GETTING THERE

Take US Highway 20 east of Tombstone Prairie, and turn south one-third mile east of the 66-mile post (a quarter-mile west of Echo Creek Road) on FS Road 066. You'll have to watch for this intersection carefully, as it is not obvious along the road or on the Willamette National Forest recreation map.

RECOMMENDED

Follow the marked trail or spur road to the west into the ancient forest along Hackleman Creek.

Parking at the FS Road 066 turn-off when there is snow on the ground is difficult, if not impossible. In winter, drive a half-mile east to the snow parking area at Lost Prairie Campground, on the south side of US Highway 20. You will have to walk or ski one-third mile back (west) along the road before cutting south and west into the forest, as several stream crossings prevent your walking directly up the canyon from the snow park.

11. Browder Ridge Unit, Old Cascades Wilderness (proposed)

Impressive ancient forest in a proposed Wilderness Area four miles from US Highway 20.

Sweet Home Ranger District
USGS 15' ECHO MTN. (1955)

ABOUT THE AREA

The ancient trees in the Browder Ridge area, estimated by Forest Service ecologists to be between 700-1000 years old, are threatened by planned roads and clearcuts. ONRC has proposed that the 4600-acre roadless area be protected as part of the Old Cascades Wilderness.

The first route described below takes you into the east side of the proposed Browder Ridge Unit of the Old Cascades Wilderness, on Gate Creek Trail #3412. Al-

though it is a longer hike to see the biggest trees, you can take Browder Ridge Trail #3409 from the west side of the roadless area to where it meets Gate Creek Trail #3412 between Sections 9 and 10 on top of Browder Ridge. To walk the eight miles of trail across the proposed Wilderness, leave a car at the Browder Ridge trailhead on the west side and begin on the east side (at Gate Creek).

From Browder Ridge you can also follow Heart Lake Trail #3407 north through the roadless area. Because this trail is very steep, it is recommended that you begin at Gate Creek and park a second car below Heart Lake.

GETTING THERE

Drive US Highway 20 approximately 38 miles east from Sweet Home, about two miles west of the Highway 126 intersection. Take Hackleman Creek Road (FS Road 2672) to the south. In roughly two miles, turn right (heading south) on FS Road 1598, and drive about two and a half miles south and west to a hairpin turn at Gate Creek. Just after the stream crossing, look for the Gate Creek trailhead on the right.

To reach the western trailhead for Browder Ridge Trail #3409, which joins Gate Creek Trail #3412, take US Highway 20 approximately 33 miles east of Sweet Home, or seven miles west of Oregon Highway 126. Just east of the 63-mile post, turn south on Deer Creek Road (FS Road 15), and follow it 2.5 miles to FS Road 080 on the left. Make the turn and drive 0.2 mile, just past Browder Creek. The trailhead is on the left.

To reach the Heart Lake trailhead, take Highway 20 to Tombstone Pass, and turn south on Heart Lake Road (FS Road 060). About three and a half miles south of the highway and one mile south of Indian Creek and FS Road 061, Heart Lake Trail #3407 starts (or ends) in a clearcut. From the bottom follow a fire trail around the western edge of the clearcut until you find the trail.

RECOMMENDED

From the east side of the roadless area: The first half-mile of Gate Creek Trail #3412 contains steep switchbacks through a younger forest. Once you reach the top of the ridge, your efforts will be rewarded by a gentle trail and some exceptionally nice stands of Douglas-fir and true fir. Many trees have diameters of six feet and more. It is two and a half miles to Browder Ridge Trail #3409.

From the west: Browder Ridge Trail #3409 passes through old growth noble and Pacific silver fir along wet meadows of wildflowers before coming to the groves of ancient forest on the ridge. The first half-mile of the trail is gradual, but it then rises steeply though open meadows for the next mile. Once on top of Browder Ridge the terrain becomes more civilized. Browder Ridge Trail #3409 meets Gate Creek Trail #3412 in 5.5 miles, then continues another two miles along the ridge to an unmarked, unmaintained trailhead near the end of FS Road 410, off FS Road 2672. (This eastern portion of Browder Ridge Trail #3409 is not recommended, as it is in poor condition and the terrain is rough.)

Heart Lake Trail #3407 drops off Browder Ridge in a stand of western white pine, and then winds through old growth noble fir, an alpine meadow, the edge of a flat, and down to Heart Lake.

12. Fish Lake

Easy cross-country skiing through big trees.

McKenzie Ranger District
USGS 15' ECHO MTN. (1955)

ABOUT THE AREA

Just west of the Santiam Pass lava fields, a lovely grove of large old growth Douglas-fir reach to the sky near the species' upper elevational limit. Seasonal Fish Lake—it becomes a wet meadow in late summer—flows down to Clear Lake, the source of the McKenzie River.

GETTING THERE

Fish Lake is just west of Fish Lake Work Center and Fish Lake Campground. The ancient forest is west of Oregon Highway 126, south of US Highway 20, and east of FS Road 2672, and can be reached cross-country from any of these roads in the summer.

In winter, parking is often difficult because of roadside snowbanks. Your best bet is to drive on Highway 20 approximately 0.6 mile west from its intersection with Highway 126, and look for a spur road to the south which parallels High-

way 126. If snow still complicates parking, try the opposite side of the highway at FS Road 2067. (The area up FS Road 2067 would have been a good ancient forest ski area, but is now riddled with clearcuts.)

RECOMMENDED

Ski down the unmarked spur road to the south. In less than a mile this road joins Highway 126. Here, look for an entry into the forest to the west (right) and continue cross-country in a southerly direction 0.2 mile; you will come out on FS Road 780. This quarter-mile road leads to the historic Forest Service Fish Lake Pack Station (closed in winter). From here you can ski west up the edge of Fish Lake Valley. The other option is to continue south along Highway 126, cross the highway at the beginning of the McKenzie River Trail, and ski south through more big old growth trees along the Old Santiam Wagon Road.

13. Upper McKenzie River Trail (North)

A beautiful big tree trail north of Clear Lake along Fish Lake Creek.

McKenzie Ranger District
USGS 15' ECHO MTN. (1955)
THREE FINGERED JACK (1959)

ABOUT THE AREA

When it doesn't flow directly along Highway 126, the 26.5-mile McKenzie River Trail #3507 provides many opportunities for forest solitude. On the lower portions of the trail, true ancient forest stands tend to be somewhat scattered, as much of this area has been selectively logged and salvaged over the years. (Al-

though McKenzie River Trail #3507 is a designated National Recreational Trail, it is still not protected from logging.) Some fine ancient forest areas remain along this extreme northern end of the trail.

Like the trail south of Clear Lake (see the following entry in this chapter), this sec-

We cannot have either a sustainable yield or a sustainable habitat without a sustainable forest."
—*Chris Maser*

tion of McKenzie River Trail #3507 is a striking place to hike in fall, rivalling even the forests of New England for autumn color. When the snow line drops below 3500', intermediate-ability skiers can enjoy a number of cross-country skiing opportunities.

GETTING THERE

Take Oregon Highway 126 east and north from Springfield until you're 17.5 miles north of the intersection with Oregon Highway 242, and just under two miles south of the junction with US Highway 20. A large sign on the east side of the road clearly identifies the trailhead for McKenzie River Trail #3507. Pull in at the trailhead if it's not too muddy or covered with snow. Otherwise, use the parking area just north of the trailhead on the east side of the highway.

RECOMMENDED

From the parking area north of the trailhead, McKenzie River Trail #3507 crosses a footbridge.

Take the signed trail, which leads south and crosses FS Road 2676 (yet another

place to park—see, all those logging roads do promote "multiple use"). From here you'll pass groves of large Douglas-fir and some sizeable western white pine along a small lake and a stream crossed by rustic footbridges. (The stream flows only in winter, as water rapidly drains through the porous lava after the spring snowmelt.)

In 1.5 miles McKenzie River Trail #3507 leads to an arm on the northeast side of Clear Lake, where large trees grow through openings in a lava flow. This end of the trail, as well as the old wagon road, can also be reached on cross-country skis after a heavy snowfall below 4000'.

The other option is to walk south (staying on the parking area side of the creek) along the historic Old Santiam Wagon Road, which leads a half-mile through a forest of old growth Douglas-fir with a vine maple understory growing among lava flows. The vine maple, in full autumn color by late September, provides excellent photo opportunities against the black lava.

It is usually difficult to park at the described trailheads when there is snow on the ground. If so, drive two miles south on Highway 126 and park at Ikenick Snow Park across from the Clear Lake Resort turn-off. Ski down the spur road toward Clear Lake and follow the hiking trail north. Cross the first footbridge.

When you reach the second bridge don't cross, but continue north along Fish Lake Creek through more big trees. (Caution: Do not attempt to ski around the east side of Clear Lake north of Cold Water Cove Campground, as three extensive and virtually impassable lava fields block your way.)

14. Upper McKenzie River Trail (South)

For great scenery—big trees, lava outcrops, rushing streams, log footbridges, waterfalls, cliffs and river gorges—this 7.5-mile stretch is one of the best on the Willamette National Forest.

McKenzie Ranger District
USGS 15' ECHO MTN. (1955)

ABOUT THE AREA
The scenery on this trail south of Clear Lake is always beautiful, but in September the contrast of red vine maple leaves,

The Upper McKenzie River Trail provides exceptional views of Sahalie Falls.
(Photo by Diane Kelsay)

black lava and green Douglas-fir makes for an especially colorful hike. The easiest way to enjoy this trail is to arrange a car shuttle and walk downhill. (Also see the previous description for the Upper McKenzie River Trail-North entry.)

GETTING THERE
Take Oregon Highway 126 to approximately five miles south of its junction with US Highway 20. McKenzie River Trail #3507 crosses Highway 126 just south of the turn-off to Coldwater Campground. (You may also get on McKenzie River Trail #3507 at Carmen Reservoir from Highway 126.)

The only parking at this trailhead is along the narrow shoulder of Highway 126. If you'd rather park in a safer place, drive south of the Coldwater Campground turn-off. Watch for a poorly marked road which leads to the west exactly 0.2 mile south of the campground turn-off and 50 yards north of a sign for "Sahalie Falls Jct. 1/4 mile." Follow this road about 0.1 mile to a footbridge over the McKenzie River. Park and cross the footbridge.

The lower end of the 7.5-mile hike discussed below is on FS Road 655. Turn west at a sign for EWEB Powerhouse and Smith River Reservoir a quarter-mile north of the 11-mile post on Highway 126. Cross the river and bear right on FS Road 655. Drive 0.4 mile to the "McKenzie River Trail No. 3507" sign.

RECOMMENDED
Heading south from the upper trailhead, you will pass Sahalie and Koosha Falls and then arrive at Carmen Reservoir in two miles. Below Carmen Reservoir walk through the geologically interesting Tamolitch Valley and enter some stately ancient forest groves. While McKenzie River Trail #3507 follows the

McKenzie River to Carmen Reservoir, the river is absent for the next 3.5 miles, except during heavy winter run-off. This is partly due to the porous nature of the volcanic soils, but mostly because of man: Carmen Reservoir diverts water from the McKenzie River two miles underground to Smith Reservoir.

The river emerges again at crystal blue Tamolitch Pool, roughly two miles before the end of this 7.5-mile section of trail (counting from the upper trailhead). After following the river again through an impressive lava gorge and back into a deep old growth forest, McKenzie River Trail #3507 crosses FS Road 655 just above Trail Bridge Reservoir.

15. Lost Lake

Opportunities for cross-country skiing to an ancient forest grove in winter, or a steep shortcut to the Pacific Crest Trail in summer.

McKenzie Ranger District
USGS 15' THREE FINGERED JACK (1959)

ABOUT THE AREA
Big old growth Douglas-fir, Engelmann spruce and black cottonwood grow at their upper elevational limit on a ridge east of Lost Lake. This ancient forest stand is fairly small and the terrain is rugged. The best way to locate the grove is to hike in on the steep trail described below. A one-mile road (FS Road 835) dead-ends at Lost Lake across from the ancient forest grove. It can serve as a pleasant beginner's ski route, but it is difficult to reach in winter if the turn-off is not plowed to make parking space.

GETTING THERE
Take US Highway 20 to about two miles east of its junction with Oregon Highway 22. The turn-off for Lost Lake Camp-

ground (FS Road 835) is on the north, just west of the lake itself. In summer drive to the end of FS Road 835.

RECOMMENDED
Hike up a precipitous fishermen's trail which begins near the outhouses and follows a cascading stream. It passes through big trees and leads to a small unnamed lake in the southwest corner of Section 15 (T13S R7½E). If you choose to continue walking north and west, in another mile you'll come to Craig Lake, and finally intersect the Pacific Crest Trail near the Cascade Crest.

16. Hash Brown Loop Ski Tour

A cross-country ski tour through ancient Douglas-fir near the Santiam Pass Summit.

McKenzie Ranger District
USGS 15' THREE FINGERED JACK (1959)

ABOUT THE AREA

The Hash Brown ski trail makes a four-mile loop through some nice ancient forest, although much is either clearcut or else comprised of extensive lodgepole pine thickets. This is an intermediate-level ski tour through old growth Douglas-fir, growing near its upper elevational limit, to a western viewpoint. In winter snow almost always can be found here, even when there is none at lower elevations.

GETTING THERE

Take US Highway 20 east of its junction with Oregon Highway 22 to just before Lost Lake, four miles west of the turn-off to Hoodoo Ski Bowl. Turn south on Jack Pine Road (FS Road 830) at the Potato Hill Snow Park.

RECOMMENDED

To enjoy the biggest trees bear right in one-third mile, at the beginning of the loop. Continue down this hill for 0.2 mile and then take the next possible right on FS Road 892. This road dead-ends at a clearcut in 0.7 mile, with views of the Cascades and the Willamette Valley to the west. The Forest Service is planning to develop additional nordic ski trails in this area in the near future.

Ancient Douglas-fir trees live along portions of this ski tour at their upper elevational limits, assuring good cross-country skiing among big trees most of the season.

17. H. J. Andrews Experimental Forest

One of the largest concentrations of old growth left on the Willamette Forest, including a unique area dominated by ancient cedars.

Blue River Ranger District
USGS 15' MCKENZIE BRIDGE (1955)

ABOUT THE AREA

If you enjoy big old western red-cedar, you should plan a visit to the H. J. Andrews Experimental Forest. A great deal of important research into the structure, function and general ecology of old growth forests has been and is still conducted in this reserve. (Unfortunately, much of the research has been the grand "experiment" of converting ancient forests into tree farms.) To protect the "less intensive" research projects, public vehicle access is discouraged by numerous locked gates. Of course, those gates won't impede you if you're on foot, or riding a mountain bike on all the logging roads. If you decide to make an unsanctioned visit to the area, please be careful not to disturb ongoing research sites, plots and/or flagging. There may never be an opportunity to replicate much of the excellent and enlightening research now being conducted in the Andrews Forest.

Interested organizations and individuals are encouraged to write or call the Blue River Ranger District to inquire about guided interpretive tours through the H. J. Andrews Experimental Forest (Blue River Ranger District, Blue River, Oregon 97413, 822-3317).

GETTING THERE

The H. J. Andrews Experimental Forest is north of the town of McKenzie Bridge on Oregon Highway 126, east of Blue River. The best way into the area is from the Blue River Reservoir off FS Road 15.

Numerous roads lead into the area from the top of the reservoir.

RECOMMENDED

As this guide went to press, the Forest Service and Oregon State University were working to re-open an old growth trail around the base of Lookout Mountain that had not been maintained for several years. The trailhead for the Lookout Creek Old Growth Trail is almost exactly ten miles up (ungated) FS Road 1506 from its junction with FS Road 15, at a pull-out marked with a trail sign on the west (right) side of FS Road 1506.

For its three-mile length, the Lookout Creek Old Growth Trail meanders through superlative old growth forest, beginning in the transition zone between the higher altitude true firs and the more familiar Douglas-fir forest, then leading gradually down across the slope into a forest dominated by huge cedars. It is very unusual to find the moisture-loving cedars so widely established over such a relatively large area. The trail ends in the cedar grove, at least until the Forest Service establishes a second trailhead off FS Road 1506.

215

18. Delta Grove

A Willamette National Forest showcase nature trail, through a spectacular old growth grove with year-round access.

McKenzie Ranger District
USGS 15' BLUE RIVER (1955)

ABOUT THE AREA

This flat, easy trail passes a small riparian area where giant bigleaf maple grow. It crosses a long, single-log footbridge, and winds through huge, centuries-old trees near the confluence of the South and Main Forks of the McKenzie River. Delta Grove is famous locally and cherished by citizens throughout the McKenzie Valley.

GETTING THERE

Take Highway 126 four miles east of the town of Blue River. Turn south on FS Road 19 (Aufderheide Forest Drive) for Cougar Reservoir. Cross the Main Fork of the McKenzie River and turn right on FS Road 400 for Delta Campground.

RECOMMENDED

The short nature trail is at the west (far)

end of Delta Campground, 1.25 miles from FS Road 19. Exactly 0.75 mile from the FS Road 19 turn-off, an abandoned jeep road—blocked by a mound of dirt—turns south (to the left). Follow this trail to a nice grove of large incense-cedar.

Other large old trees live both up and downstream on the south side of the Main Fork McKenzie River. To go upstream take King Road (FS Road 2639) east from Cougar Lake Road (FS Road 19). Immediately south of the road and north of Castle Rock (between Sections 20 and 21) is a nice grove, but some cross-country hiking is required to reach it. Look for snag-top trees as you drive east to plan a point of entry. Continue east to Horse Creek Campground.

Older trees, like older people, have much to teach us.

19. Lost Creek Grove

Outstanding examples of old growth cedar and fir among beautiful springs and pools, connected by a primitive but fairly easy trail.

ABOUT THE AREA

The large trees growing at about 1800' elevation near Lost Creek and its tributary, White Branch Creek, are accessible year-round. A series of seeps, springs, waterfalls, and emerald and turquoise pools provide an unusual and attractive setting for this ancient forest hike.

GETTING THERE

Take Oregon Highway 126 a little over two miles east of the McKenzie Bridge Ranger District Office. Turn right on Oregon Highway 242 (McKenzie Pass Highway). Drive three and a half miles

and pull off just after the 59-mile post, by an open meadow on the left.

RECOMMENDED

At the north end of the one-acre meadow, an unmarked trail leads into the forest, perpendicular to Highway 242. The biggest trees are north on this trail. Another unmarked trail leads west, parallel to White Branch Creek and Highway 242.

20. French Pete Creek, Three Sisters Wilderness

Scattered groves of ancient and mature Douglas-fir along a scenic streamside trail beckon you to walk further than you intended into one of Oregon's most stunning Wilderness Areas.

ABOUT THE AREA

The Three Sisters Wilderness is one of the few places in Oregon where you can walk through a range of western Cascades ecosystem types, from low-elevation forest to alpine communities, in a pristine Wilderness Area.

Because of its outstanding wildlife habitat, the Three Sisters Wilderness is also one of the last strongholds in the Oregon Cascades for the fisher and wolverine. It is likely the most promising place to reintroduce the timber wolf

(present in the Cascades as late as 1962, relic populations of which may still survive). In recognition of its ecological significance, the Three Sisters Wilderness has been designated a World Biosphere Reserve.

The French Pete Trail enters a broad U-shaped valley and follows French Pete Creek most of the way in, which is nice because most of the biggest trees are along the stream bottom. French Pete Trail is relatively easy, climbing gradually through grove after grove of gor-

French Pete Creek, a classic example of an ancient forest stream providing the Northwest's purest water. (Photo by Diane Kelsay and Bob Harvey)

geous old growth Douglas-fir and western red-cedar. The whole experience is so enticing that, on a recent visit, my wife and I walked eight miles when we had planned to go only two.

The battle to save French Pete ended in one of the landmark conservation victories of the 1970's, when the valley was returned to its rightful place in the Three Sisters Wilderness in 1978. All had seemed lost—the Forest Service had planned miles of logging roads with multiple clearcuts throughout the entire drainage, all administrative appeals had been denied, and Senator Mark Hatfield refused to budge. But the pressure continued. People from all over Oregon (and the nation) wrote letters to Congress demanding that this forest community be forever protected as Wilderness. A mock congressional hearing was held in Eugene, where people marched in the streets. In the end, thanks to the dedication of so many who refused to accept defeat, the impossible was accomplished and French Pete was saved. To all of those—many no longer living—whose personal sacrifices made this victory possible, and to conservationists working desperately to save the Northwest's remaining ancient forests, French Pete is far more than just another protected, pretty place. Come and enjoy its solitude and inspiration—it is our church in the Wilderness.

French Pete Creek Trail #3311 begins beside the paved highway (FS Road 19) along the South Fork McKenzie River, and closely follows the cascading creek up a broad, U-shaped canyon to higher elevations in the Three Sisters Wilderness. If you can arrange a car shuttle, you might want to consider a 10.75-mile one-way ancient forest hike on French Pete Creek Trail #3311, beginning at the upper (FS Road 1993) trailhead and ending on FS Road 19.

GETTING THERE

Take Oregon Highway 126 four miles east of Blue River. Turn south on FS Road 19 (Aufderheide Forest Drive), and drive 11 miles south (two miles south of Cougar Reservoir). The trailhead for French Pete Creek Trail #3311 is on the east side of the road, opposite French Pete Campground along the South Fork of the McKenzie River.

To locate the upper trailhead to French Pete Creek, turn south on FS Road 19 off Highway 26, and drive four miles to Cougar Dam. Cross the dam impoundment and turn east on FS Road 1993. Drive 14 miles east to the Pat Saddle trailhead. Here, Olallie Trail #3529 crosses the road and heads north (out of the Wilderness) for 13 miles, through the Lamb Butte Scenic Area and Olallie Ridge Research Natural Area (RNA). While this is an extraordinarily scenic trail, the really big trees, including Douglas-fir more than six feet in diameter, grow only along the first half-mile. French Pete Creek Trail #3311 and Olallie Ridge Trail #3530 climb into the Three Sisters Wilderness from the south side of FS Road 1993. To head for French Pete Creek, look for a small, inconspicuous sign for Pat Creek Trail #3319 beside a large signboard. This trailhead is obscured by the sign and a small campsite on the trailhead, but it is to the right of the Olallie Ridge Trail #3530 trailhead.

To return to Highway 126 from Pat Saddle, consider a loop drive by continuing on FS Road 1993, which turns north and west after Pat Saddle and returns to Highway 126 at McKenzie Bridge. This route is four miles longer than returning the way you came, but FS Road 1993 is paved from five miles after the trailhead, and provides great views of the Cascade Crest from the Three Sisters to Mount Hood. (Driving north on FS Road 1993 also takes you to trailheads, just after the nine-mile post and just after the three-mile post, for the northern portion of Olallie Trail #3529.) Either route you pick, you will notice how clearcutting is rapidly defining the northern boundary of the French Pete portion of the Three Sisters Wilderness.

RECOMMENDED

French Pete Creek Trail #3311 varies from an easy walk to a hike of moderate difficulty. From the trailhead on FS Road 19, the trail follows the stream for the first five miles, crossing two log bridges. If you wander this far, don't stop! The trail traverses above the stream (though you can still hear it), and then returns to the creek and an outstanding grove of super old growth in French Pete Valley, just before the eight-mile trail mark. It is another 2.75 miles, through more amazing ancient forest along Pat Creek, to FS Road 1993 and Olallie Trail #3529.

21. Towering Trees Ancient Forest Grove

A half-mile trail to a small basin containing the tallest known Douglas-fir tree; can be combined with a trip to Fall Creek.

Lowell Ranger District
USGS 7.5' SADDLEBLANKET MTN. (1986)
USGS 15' LEABURG (1951)

ABOUT THE AREA

This canyon contains some classic western Cascades mid-elevation ancient forest, including some of the most impressive individual Douglas-fir trees in the world. The designated 150-acre Towering Trees Ancient Forest Grove contains 500-year-old trees which range from 270' to 310' in height, with the very tallest tree estimated at 322'. Unfortunately, this magnificent stand of trees is only a fragment of the great forest which once blanketed the Little Fall Creek drainage.

While you're in the area you might want to visit Fall Creek, the next drainage to the south. The 5.8-mile Jones Creek Trail

#3472, which begins only a few miles south of the tall trees grove, follows the divide between Fall Creek and Little Fall Creek. The trailhead is on the south side of FS Road 1817, in the middle of Section 10 (T18S R2E; see the Willamette National Forest recreation map). Also see the following entry for Fall Creek Corridor in this chapter.

GETTING THERE

South of Eugene off I-5, take Oregon Highway 58 about 13.5 miles south and east to the Lowell turn-off. Turn north and drive through Lowell. Turn west (left) on North Shore Drive, and then after 0.2 mile turn north (right) on the Jasper-Lowell Road. In two miles you'll drive across a covered bridge. Take the second right, 2.4 miles after the covered bridge, on Little Fall Creek Road. Follow it along the stream for 17 miles to where FS Road 1806 veers to the right, just before a sign which reads "Entering Private Lands." Take FS Road 1806 uphill for 1.5 miles, bear right on FS Road 427, and drive another half-mile to the trailhead for the Towering Trees.

RECOMMENDED

The trail to the tallest trees enters an almost bowl-shaped canyon, providing an excellent location to photographically capture the grove. The trail ends after crossing the stream in the canyon bottom. The Forest Service plans to make this trail wheelchair accessible.

It takes many arms to fully embrace one of nature's pillars. (Photo by Phillip Renault)

22. Fall Creek Corridor

Classic old growth Douglas-fir forest, visible from the road or several easy trail segments totalling 14 miles.

Lowell Ranger District
USGS 7.5' SADDLEBLANKET MTN. (1986)

ABOUT THE AREA

Fall Creek is as densely blanketed with fine old forest as Little Fall Creek to the north is deforested. The low-elevation forests like those which used to stand in the Little Fall Creek drainage once yielded five times as much timber per acre as the steeper, higher elevation areas now being "intensively managed" in the same national forest—which should tell you something about the Forest Service's so-called "sustained yield" policies. While the Willamette National Forest has shown remarkable restraint in the Fall Creek area, creating a showpiece of multiple use management, much of the credit must go to some extraordinary local citizens who convinced the agency to administratively protect much of the remaining pristine canyon bottoms and tributaries.

At an elevation range of only 960' to 1385', the Fall Creek corridor is accessible year-round. The scenic Fall Creek Trail #3455 meanders through ancient forests for 14 miles. Along the stream, you will pass many deep pools, a little whitewater, bold rock outcrops, and beautiful tributary streams lined with wildflowers in the spring. There are numerous opportunities to stop for a cold but refreshing dip during hot summer months, or to angle for cutthroat or rainbow trout. In May, the flowering dogwoods are a special treat. Many magnificent groves of the "Big Three" ancient forest trees (Douglas-fir, western hemlock and western red-cedar) in this area range from 300 to 500 years in age.

Fall Creek Trail #3455 is the focus here, but the Fall Creek corridor is also one of the few ancient forests that can be appreciated from a car on a paved road, in this case FS Road 18. There are also a couple of good, short nature trails along this road which make the Fall Creek corridor accessible to all. These include Clark Creek Nature Trail, a 1.1-mile loop east of Clark Creek Organization Camp, and Johnny Creek Nature Trail, a paved, wheelchair accessible half-mile loop off FS Road 1821, which passes several 500-year-old trees.

Fallen logs provide important travelways (and benches) for forest dwellers. (Photo by Phillip Renault)

GETTING THERE

South of Eugene off I-5, take Oregon Highway 58 (the Willamette Pass Highway) about 13.5 miles south and east to the Lowell turn-off. Turn north and drive through Lowell. Turn west (left) on North Shore Drive, then north (right) onto Jasper-Lowell Road in 0.2 mile. After two miles turn right before a covered bridge on Big Fall Creek Road, following the sign for Fall Creek Dam. Continue on this road along the north shore of Fall Creek Reservoir. Big Fall Creek Road becomes FS Road 18 at the Willamette National Forest boundary. Continuing east on FS Road 18, you will enter a specially managed ancient forest corridor. (If you think it's typical of the Lowell Ranger District, just take any side road!)

RECOMMENDED

The biggest old trees are along the eastern end (the last five miles) of Fall Creek Trail #3455. From west to east on Fall Creek Trail #3455 are five major trailheads. The first (at 0.0 trail miles) is on the south side of Fall Creek, just west of Dolly Varden Picnic Area; the second (at 3.5 trail miles) is where Fall Creek Trail #3455 crosses FS Road 18, just west of Johnny Creek Nature Trail and the junction with FS Road 1821; the third (at 5.2 trail miles) is north of FS Road 18, at Bedrock Campground; the fourth (at 9.3 trail miles) is where Fall Creek Trail #3455 crosses FS Road 18, near the junction with FS Road 1828; and the eastern trailhead (at 14 trail miles) is where Fall Creek Trail #3455 ends on the south side of FS Road 18.

23. Hardesty Mountain Wilderness (proposed)

Low-elevation ancient forest only 25 miles east of Eugene and Springfield.

Lowell Ranger District
USGS 7.5' MOUNT JUNE (1986)

ABOUT THE AREA

The pristine slopes of Hardesty Mountain and Mount June are home to spotted owls, bald eagle and cougar. It's a great place to hike and camp. This area merits the Wilderness protection it has so far been denied. As noted above, the Lowell Ranger District is extensively cutover, but thanks to its steep slopes and ardent citizen defenders, the proposed Hardesty Mountain Wilderness remains an island of wild forest in a sea of clearcuts and tree plantations. The greatest concentration of big trees is along South Willamette Trail #3465. At about 1000', this is one of the lowest of the few relatively intact ancient forest areas in the Willamette Valley. You may wish to obtain a copy of

the pamphlet *Hiking the Hardesty Wilderness*, published in 1981 by the Hardesty Mountain Study Group, and available through ONRC.

GETTING THERE

From I-5 south of Eugene, drive east on the Willamette Pass Highway (Oregon Highway 58). Shortly after the 21-mile marker, make the first possible right turn on Crale Creek Road (FS Road 5835). Park on the right at your first opportunity.

RECOMMENDED

The trailhead for South Willamette Trail #3465 is 0.15 mile past the turn-off on the right side of FS Road 5835. Take the trail to the right (downhill). After a challenging mile and a half, the trail to the left (uphill) enters a fine ancient forest, which is best reached from Eula Ridge Trail #3463 (see below).

South Willamette Trail #3465 to Hardesty Mountain Trail #3469: There are three stream crossings in the first half-mile of the trail, which runs through large old growth Douglas-fir, impressive bigleaf maple, western hemlock and incense-cedar. After the third footbridge, South Willamette Trail #3465 leaves the creek and follows the lower portion of a 1984 Forest Service salvage cut, which degraded the proposed Wilderness somewhat.

South Willamette Trail #3465 leads west for another mile and ends at Hardesty Mountain Trail #3469, approximately 0.6 mile above its trailhead and 3.5 miles below the 4273' summit of Hardesty Mountain. (Hardesty Mountain Trail #3469 starts from Oregon Highway 58, three-quarters of a mile west of FS Road 5835. It is five miles from the trailhead to the summit and the old fire lookout.) For an incomplete two-mile loop, walk down Hardesty Mountain Trail #3469 to High-

way 58 and back to your vehicle on FS Road 5835.

South Willamette Trail #3465 from Eula Ridge Trail #3463: Another three-mile segment of South Willamette Trail #3465 starts a quarter-mile up Eula Ridge Trail #3463 and leads to the trailhead on FS Road 5835. To reach the trailhead for Eula Ridge Trail #3463, continue on Highway 58 to just after the 24-mile post and park by a sign for Eula Ridge Trail #3463. (Eula Ridge Trail #3463 ends at Hardesty Mountain Trail #3469, a half-mile from the top of Hardesty Mountain.)

At the first fork in the trail, hold to the right and you'll soon enter fine stands of ancient forest. Continue at least a mile and a half to the third bridge, where the trail descends into a bowl-shaped canyon full of ancient Douglas-fir and western red-cedar. You may return as you came or keep walking west another 1.5 miles to the trailhead at FS Road 5385. Unfortunately, this half of the trail leaves the ancient forest and skirts the edge of two glaring clearcuts.

24. Larison Creek and Larison Rock Trails

Nice low-elevation old growth forest near Oakridge.

Rigdon Ranger District
USGS 7.5' OAKRIDGE (1986)

ABOUT THE AREA

These are the best low-elevation ancient forest trails on the north end of the Rigdon Ranger District. Most of the upper drainage of the Middle Fork Willamette River has been heavily logged, and the largest trees went first, so remaining scraps of ancient forest are on the younger end of the functional old growth spectrum.

While this area contains some very big trees, old growth trees on the Rigdon District average only 29" in diameter. Much larger trees and snags are visible along these two trails. Larison Rock Trail #3623 climbs steeply from the Middle Fork Willamette River to the top of 3607' Larison Rock. Larison Creek Trail #3646 is a more gradual route along the unlogged lower reaches of Larison Creek, which flows east from the mountains around Holland Point to Hills Creek Reservoir.

ONRC has recommended to the Forest Service that these areas be maintained in their present natural condition as administratively designated Backcountry Areas. A trail connecting Larison Creek Trail #3646 and Larison Rock Trail #3623, as well as a footbridge at Greenwater City Park, have been recommended to improve hikers' access.

GETTING THERE

Take Oregon Highway 58 east from I-5 south of Eugene or west from US Highway 97. Just east of Oakridge, turn south off Highway 58 near the 37-mile post, at a sign for Hills Creek Dam. Drive a half-mile south and bear right on FS Road 21 at the first intersection.

For the lower trailhead for Larison Rock Trail #3623, drive one-third mile on FS Road 21, cross the Middle Fork Willamette River, and immediately turn right on FS Road 5852. The trailhead is on the left in 1.6 miles. This lower trailhead is just west of Oakridge's

Greenwater City Park on Highway 58, but it's across the river. To reach the upper trailhead for Larison Rock Trail #3623 by car, turn south (left) to stay on FS Road 21 after the Middle Fork Willamette River bridge. Take the next right on FS Road 2102 at a sign for "Larison Rock 4 miles." The trailhead is on the right.

To get to Larison Creek Trail #3646, drive three miles south of the Middle Fork Willamette River bridge on FS Road 21. Turn right before the first bridge across an arm of Hills Creek Reservoir, just before a sign for Junction 2106.

RECOMMENDED

Larison Rock Trail #3623: In its four-mile length, the trail climbs from 1300' to 3600'. Along with big Douglas-fir and western red-cedar, several large sugar pine stand in the trail corridor.

Larison Creek Trail #3646: This 6.3-mile, gradual trail follows Larison Creek for the first 5.2 miles. Unfortunately, the first mile or so of the stream is drowned under the reservoir. But the next mile and a half bring you to the largest trees and nicest forest.

25. Warm Springs

Easily accessible old growth trail nine miles from Oakridge.

Oakridge Ranger District
USGS 7.5' HUCKLEBERRY MTN. (1986)

ABOUT THE AREA

A large bathtub-warm (not hot) spring awaits you at the end of a quarter-mile streamside trail. This is a special place: please bring a litter bag and help clean up, if necessary, for less considerate users. (Also see the description for the Lillian Falls entry which follows.)

GETTING THERE

Take Oregon Highway 58 east from I-5 south of Eugene or west from US Highway 97 to Oakridge. Turn north at the only signal in town. Drive over the railroad tracks and turn east (right) on East First Street, which becomes Salmon Creek Road (FS Road 24). Eight miles after re-entering the Willamette National Forest, turn left on FS Road 1934 at a sign for "Blair Lake 8 miles." Drive a half-mile to a pull-out on the left at a sharp hairpin turn (between Sections 26 and 27 in T20S R4E).

RECOMMENDED
A log set across three small cement pillars marks the trailhead.

26. Shale Ridge Trail

Probably the finest old growth Douglas-fir and western red-cedar on the southern portion of the Willamette National Forest.

Oakridge Ranger District
USGS 7.5' WALDO MTN. (1986)
CHUCKSNEY MTN. (1986)

ABOUT THE AREA
Shale Ridge Trail #3567 follows the federally designated Wild and Scenic North Fork of the Middle Fork Willamette River many miles up a magnificent U-shaped canyon, connecting with other trails to the river's headwaters at mile-high Waldo Lake. Along the first two miles of trail—to Skookum Creek—the forest is protected as Wilderness only west of the river, and the old growth trees on either side of the trail and east face of the canyon could be logged at the Forest Service's discretion.

GETTING THERE
Take Oregon Highway 58 east from I-5 south of Eugene or west from US Highway 97 to the Westfir turn-off, just west of Oakridge. This will put you on FS Road 19, which follows the North Fork of the Middle Fork Willamette River approximately 30 miles to the road's easternmost point, which is a hairpin turn to the north just before the 30-mile post. Shale Ridge Trail #3567 heads south from FS Road 19 on the outside (right side) of this turn, five miles east of FS Road 1944.

As in this cedar grove, down trees protect the forest's riparian edge and create local environments of quiet water where fine sediments and organic debris are deposited during high flows. (Photo by Phillip Renault)

RECOMMENDED
The 4.7-mile Shale Ridge Trail #3567 leads almost due south along the east side of the river. The forest is fantastic from the start, but some of the largest trees are about two miles in, past a large marsh.

27. Lillian Falls, Waldo Wilderness

An exciting trail which winds through one of the few low-elevation old growth forests in the Waldo Wilderness, to a 100' waterfall.

Oakridge Ranger District
USGS 7.5' WALDO LAKE (1986)

ABOUT THE AREA
This upper trail affords spectacular views of Black Creek Canyon and, eventually, Waldo Lake. While the ancient forest along the first mile of Black Creek Trail is protected, forests along the road where you drove in are threatened by Forest Service timber sales. Logging roads have already significantly reduced the forests on this western side of the Waldo Wilderness.

Before winter snows reach lower elevations—into late November—the trail to Lillian Falls is usually open. Heat held in by the insulating ancient forest canopy keeps the forest floor unfrozen—even studded with emerging mushrooms—while surrounding clearcuts are frosted with a white glaze. At such times, these forests provide important thermal cover for small animals as well as deer and elk. In the summer, they play the same regulating role, and provide equally important shelter from extremely high temperatures.

GETTING THERE
Take Oregon Highway 58 east from I-5 south of Eugene, or west from US Highway 97, to Oakridge. Turn north at the only signal in town. Continue beyond the railroad tracks and turn east (right) on East First Street, which becomes Salmon Creek Road (FS Road 24). Drive 13 miles into the Willamette National Forest, following signs for Black Creek Trail #3551, to the end of FS Road 24. Bear left over Black Creek on FS Road 2422, then bear right on FS Road 2421. Drive eight miles to the end of FS Road 2421 and the trailhead for Black Creek Trail #3551.

As at Lillian Falls, fallen trees and other large pieces of wood significantly shape energy flow, nutrient cycling and structural characteristics—all positively affecting the many lifeforms in and along the stream.
(Photo by Phillip Renault)

RECOMMENDED

Black Creek Trail #3551 begins in an old clearcut (next to a new clearcut), but it soon enters the Waldo Wilderness at 3400'. Lillian Falls is a mile and a half up the trail. On the way, drop off the trail for better views of the canyon and old growth western red-cedar. After Lillian Falls, Black Creek Trail #3551 switchbacks up a steep grade through smaller trees to Waldo Lake at 5400'. It is a total of 3.8 miles from the trailhead to Waldo Lake.

28. Mount Ray - Fuji Mountain Additions to Waldo Wilderness (proposed)

Superb stands of high-elevation old growth mountain hemlock forest in an unprotected area adjacent to the Waldo Wilderness.

Oakridge Ranger District
USGS 7.5' WALDO LAKE (1986)

ABOUT THE AREA

The Waldo Country offers some of the best examples of old growth mountain hemlock forest in Oregon. This species doesn't grow as large as noble fir, Douglas-fir or other familiar ancient forest trees, but the denizens along the fascinating Fuji Mountain Trail #3674 are quite impressive. They are an excellent example of this relatively rare forest type.

The roadless area which contains these trees is called the Mount Ray–Fuji Mountain Additions to the Waldo Wilderness. It is known for its botanical variety and the ecological diversity it contributes to the Waldo Country, and is proposed by local citizens to be added to the Three Sisters Wilderness.

Stop at the Oakridge Ranger District to pick up a large-scale trail map for the Waldo Country, which shows topographic contours and points of interest.

GETTING THERE

Take Oregon Highway 58 east from I-5 south of Eugene, or west from US Highway 97. Turn north on Waldo Lake Road (FS Road 5897) at the sign for Waldo Lake, just west of the 59-mile post.

RECOMMENDED

The trailhead for Fuji Mountain Trail #3674 is on the left near the two-mile post on FS Road 5897, across from the head of Gold Lake Trail #3677. Fuji Mountain Trail #3674 passes through and by a series of pleasant meadows and small lakes. It is two and a half miles to the junction with South Waldo Trail #3586. Walk north and east on South Waldo Trail #3586 for 2.8 miles to Mount Ray Trail #3682. From that junction, it is two miles east to the Mount Ray Trail #3682 trailhead on FS Road 5897.

The Mount Ray trailhead is 3.75 miles north of the junction with Oregon Highway 58. Begin here if you wish to walk less uphill than downhill, or else leave a bicycle at this upper trailhead and ride back down to the Fuji Mountain trailhead. If you incorporate Gold Lake Trail #3677 (see the description for the Gold Lake Bog Engelmann Spruce entry which follows in this chapter), you can take a nine and a half mile loop hike, beginning and ending at this trailhead.

29. Gold Lake Bog Engelmann Spruce

An outstanding Engelmann spruce grove for a scenic summer hike or winter cross-country ski tour.

Oakridge Ranger District
USGS 7.5' WILLAMETTE PASS (1986)
WALDO LAKE (1986)

ABOUT THE AREA

This gentle trail (Gold Lake Trail #3677) along the northwest shore of Gold Lake leads to spectacular mountain views, a Research Natural Area mountain bog, lush meadows of wildflowers, and a forest of ten different conifer species. Since this locale is just under 5000', only a few of the elderly trees are really large.

But west of Gold Lake Bog, Gold Lake Trail #3677 passes through lovely meadows surrounded by an outstanding grove of Engelmann spruce. Some of the trees in this scattered stand are more than three feet thick—quite large for this species—and perhaps 400 to 500 years old. This grove is one mile northeast of the Gold Lake Campground, in the southwest corner of the proposed Maiden Peak Wilderness Area. Engelmann spruce, seldom widespread, are often found along the edge of watercourses and wet meadows. They are easily identified by their very sharp needles, flaky grey bark, and distinctive shingle-scaled cones.

GETTING THERE

Take Oregon Highway 58 to Waldo Lake Road (FS Road 5897), approximately 0.4 mile east of the 61-mile post and a few miles west of Willamette Pass. Turn

north and drive to the trailheads for Gold Lake Trail #3677. The first is on the right, just before the two-mile post, opposite the trailhead for Fuji Mountain Trail #3674. The second is 3.75 miles from the junction with Highway 58, on the right opposite Mount Ray Trail #3682.

Alternately, from Highway 58 just west of the Willamette Pass summit, a one-lane gravel road (FS Road 500) leads two miles to Gold Lake Campground, on the southwest end of Gold Lake. A snow park area is located on the south side of Highway 58, just east of FS Road 500.

RECOMMENDED

The spruce grove is about midway between the northern and southern trailheads of Gold Lake Trail #3677 on FS Road 5897. Gold Lake is perfect for canoes, and restricted to fly-fishing. If you drove to Gold Lake, walk across the bridge by the boat launch and bear right on Gold Lake Trail #3677. Walk along the north shore of Gold Lake and a quarter-mile north of a sign for Gold Lake Bog to where the big old spruce begin. Leave the trail to explore these groves and the surrounding meadows. Don't forget this is a Research Natural Area, so walk carefully.

Facing page: The Waldo Country contains the Cascades' largest contiguous groves of ancient mountain hemlock, Tsuga mertensiana. Even on good sites, trees only 18 to 20 inches in diameter are from 180 to 250 years old. (Photo by Diane Kelsay)

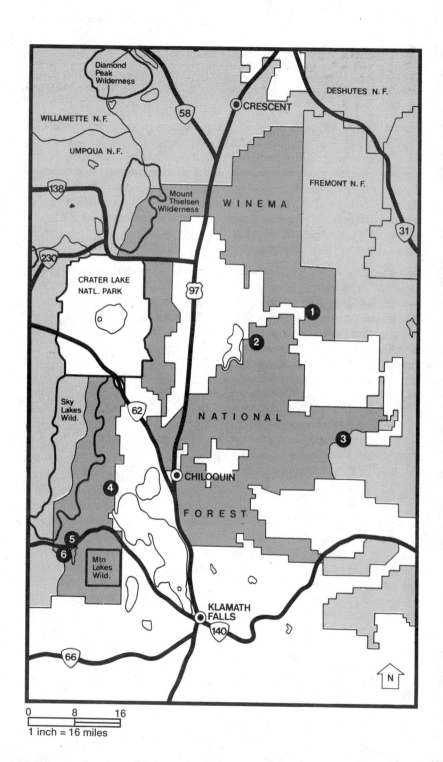

Diamond
Peak
Wilderness

WILLAMETTE N. F.

DESHUTES N. F.

58   CRESCENT

UMPQUA N. F.

FREMONT N. F.

138

Mount
Thielsen
Wilderness

WINEMA

31

230

CRATER LAKE
NATL. PARK

97

1

2

Sky
Lakes
Wild.

NATIONAL

62

3

CHILOQUIN

4

FOREST

5

6

Mtn
Lakes
Wild.

KLAMATH
FALLS

140

66

N

0   8   16
1 inch = 16 miles

Winema National Forest

The Winema National Forest in south-central Oregon is named for the woman who betrayed her uncle, Captain Jack, during the Modoc Indian War. Along with the nearby Fremont Forest, the Winema is a relatively unknown national forest perceived by some as a "stepchild" in Forest Service Region 6 (Oregon and Washington). It is a unique forest; about half its lands were once part of the Klamath Indian Reservation.

The Winema National Forest contains 1.1 million acres, and is based in Klamath Falls. It is managed through three ranger districts. Because of its particular history, much of the ancient forest on old Tribal lands (as well as the original National Forest Reserve) has been cut. However, the Winema Forest harbors many outstanding examples of older forest communities. From Mount Thielsen south to Upper Klamath Lake, from the Cascade Crest east to Yamsay Mountain, and from the edge of Crater Lake National Park to the Klamath Marsh, ancient forest groves await you.

Don't forget your Winema National Forest recreation map.

1. Jackson Creek, Yamsay Mountain Wilderness (proposed)

Ancient forest at the base of the mountain the Klamath Indians know as Yamsah, "Home of the North Wind."

Chiloquin Ranger District
USGS 15' YAMSAY MTN. (1960)

ABOUT THE AREA
ONRC and other conservation and sportsmen organizations have proposed that 21,000 acres of wild, roadless lands straddling the border of the Winema and Fremont National Forests, now managed by the Forest Service as the Yamsay Mountain Dispersed Recreation Area, be permanently protected by Congress as Wilderness. The Jackson Creek area, on the northwest side of the proposed Yamsay Mountain Wilderness, includes some of the most accessible old growth ponderosa pine along lovely perennial streams on the Winema National Forest. Outside the roadless area, the Forest Service is logging almost all of the big pine and fir; in general, undisturbed forests remain only in riparian (streamside) areas. (See also the description for the Buck Creek entry in the Fremont National Forest chapter, which will take you

to the northeast side of the proposed Yamsay Mountain Wilderness.)

Described below are two possible routes: a cross-country hike up Jackson Creek from Jackson Creek Campground (outside the roadless area), and a walk up a trail to the top of the Yamsay Mountain caldera in the proposed Wilderness Area. (The latter route has fewer big old trees but better views.)

GETTING THERE

Take US Highway 97 approximately 26 miles south of Chemult and 48 miles north of Klamath Falls. At a sign for Klamath Forest National Wildlife Refuge, 0.2 mile north of the 228-mile post, turn east on Silver Lake Road (County Route 676). Drive through the refuge, and follow Route 676 north about one-third mile east of the 26-mile post. Turn right on FS Road 49 and continue 4.5 miles to Jackson Creek Campground.

If you want to walk to the top of Yamsay Mountain, continue south from Jackson Creek Campground on FS Road 49 for another 0.4 mile and turn left on FS Road 4972. Drive a mile and a half, turn left again on FS Road 4973, and follow it four miles to its end.

RECOMMENDED

From the campground, hike cross-country upstream along small meadows past some big ponderosa pine. Dramatic rock outcrops add to the beauty of this small canyon.

If you choose to continue up FS Road 4973 for the "summit" trail, the head of the trail (which is a closed jeep road) is on the left at the end of FS Road 4973. Although most of the area you drive through en route to the trailhead has been selectively logged, many big ponderosa pine remain on the west (especially the southwest) slopes of Yamsay Mountain. Unfortunately, the big ponderosa are displaced by smaller lodgepole pine and mountain hemlock near the beginning of the trail, about where you enter the Dispersed Recreation Area.

Big ponderosa pine along a pleasant canyon stream above Jackson Creek Campground.

Undisturbed ponderosa pine forests are uncommon on the Winema National Forest, since most stands have already been entered at least twice. Blue Jay Springs is truly an oasis in a "managed" forest.

2. Blue Jay Springs Research Natural Area

A small spring surrounded by aspen, eight miles east of the Klamath Forest National Wildlife Refuge.

Chiloquin Ranger District
USGS 15' KLAMATH MARSH (1957)

ABOUT THE AREA

Blue Jay Springs is the only source of water for several miles, so it is an excellent place to watch songbirds and other forest wildlife among the snags and big trees of this rare, undisturbed, unmanaged ponderosa pine forest.

Abraham Flat, a large meadow east of the main highway and west of Blue Jay Springs Research Natural Area (RNA), was recently added to the Klamath Forest National Wildlife Refuge, along with 20,000 acres of rangeland. Conservationists have asked that some of the area's forestlands also be added to the refuge to better protect their old growth values for bald eagles and other ancient forest-dependent wildlife species.

GETTING THERE

Take US Highway 97 about 26 miles south of Chemult and 48 miles north of Klamath Falls. At a sign for Klamath Forest National Wildlife Refuge, 0.2 mile north of the 228-mile post, turn east on Silver Lake Road (County Route 676). A quarter-mile east of the 13-mile post, turn right on FS Road 7640. In a half-mile turn left on FS Road 7642. Drive 2.2 miles, then turn left back on FS Road 7640 and drive another mile. Finally, turn left on FS Road 440 and drive a quarter-mile to a parking area by the spring.

RECOMMENDED

Beside Blue Jay Springs is an undeveloped camping area with an outhouse but no tables or firepits. An old jeep trail leads from the parking area into the Research Natural Area, providing easy hiking through these impressive groves of big ponderosa pine. Be sure to bring your binoculars.

3. Sycan River Gorge

Magnificent ponderosa pine along a rimrock river gorge, accessible by foot or canoe.

Chiloquin Ranger District
USGS 15' FUEGO MTN. (1960)

ABOUT THE AREA

Most of the Chiloquin Ranger District—indeed, much of the Winema National Forest—was once part of the now-dissolved Klamath Indian Reservation. These lands were managed by the Bureau of Indian Affairs and then held in trust by US National Bank for the Klamath Tribe. During this period, virtually the entire forest was logged, and many areas have been partially cut three or more times. As usual, the biggest trees were the first to go. But a few near-pristine groves still stand along a sixteen-mile stretch of the Sycan River Gorge, on the boundary between the Fremont and Winema National Forests.

The trees were not the only natural resource to suffer in the plundering of the Klamath Indian Reservation. The Klamath short-nosed sucker, once a major food source for local peoples, is now a federally listed species under the Endangered Species Act. And populations of mule deer, another important food source for the Klamath Tribe, have been decimated by the destruction of old growth forest habitat throughout the Winema National Forest and other public and private forestlands. Alarmed at the decline in mule deer numbers, and much to their credit, the Klamath Indian Tribe is now demanding better resource management of the Forest Service, and has become a significant and respected voice in the many decision-making processes affecting old growth forests.

The ancient forest in the Sycan River Gorge is one of the least disturbed areas on the eastern portion of the Winema National Forest, but it is not the only attraction in the gorge. The Sycan River, now part of the National Wild and Scenic Rivers System, is a Class I stream (the easiest rating) for rafting, canoeing and floating during the snow melts of April and May. Even in high water, the few rapids are small and shallow. By June, flows are too low to float the river.

You can walk the length of the gorge along the stream's banks in any season (except in Teddy Powers Meadow—see below). Spring is the best time for 8–14" rainbow trout. The riparian corridor also provides habitat for deer, beaver, great blue heron, mallard and merganser ducks, white-headed woodpeckers and many other wildlife. Unfortunately, the Forest Service also expects you to tolerate the ubiquitous cow, never far from sight in eastern Oregon. (This has been the case for so long that some people believe cows are a native species.)

GETTING THERE

Take US Highway 97 south from Bend or north from Klamath Falls to Chiloquin. In downtown Chiloquin, cross the railroad tracks heading east and turn north (left) for the Sprague River on North First Avenue, which becomes the Sprague River Road (County Route 858). Continue for five miles on Route 858 and turn north (left) on Williamson River Road (County Road 600). Drive 25 miles to the end of the pavement. The gravel road continuing east becomes FS Road 46.

RECOMMENDED

From FS Road 46 are several options for reaching the Sycan River Gorge. Dispersed camping is possible at each access point listed below, as well as elsewhere throughout the Winema National Forest. The only (semi-developed) campground in the area is Head of the River Campground, a mile north of FS Road 46 on FS Road 4648. (FS Road 4648 bears north just after the beginning of FS Road 46.)

Sycan Ford is the most easily reached scenic hike in the gorge. Sycan Gorge Headwaters and Teddy Powers Meadow are both recommended as put-ins and take-outs for watercraft.

Sycan Gorge Headwaters: Continue 12.5 miles east on FS Road 46 and turn south (right) on FS Road 27. Drive one mile to the river. This furthest upstream put-in is above the gorge in a lodgepole pine forest.

Sycan Ford: Continue 3.4 miles east on FS Road 46 and turn south (right) on FS Road 4650. Drive 4.5 miles to the Sycan River, then follow the river a half-mile upstream (north) to where the road fords the stream. Park before the crossing and hike upstream on the northwest side of the river canyon. In about two and a half miles, you will come to Torrent Spring, a rushing gush of icy water which emerges from the yellow monkey-flower-covered rimrock of the southeast side of the gorge.

Teddy Powers Meadow: Continue 0.4 mile east on FS Road 46 and turn south (right) on FS Road 44. Drive six miles to the 19-mile post and the junction with FS Road 4483 on the right. Continuing on FS Road 44, drive exactly 1.35 miles past the junction, turn left on an unmarked road, and follow it to the river. This access point is just downstream from the Meadow (cow pasture), which is private land. Please note that walking along the stream through Teddy Powers Meadow—on either bank—is trespassing. So while this is a good take-out point for floaters, it is not an appropriate place to start hiking upstream.

4. Malone Springs and Pelican Butte Additions to Sky Lakes Wilderness (proposed)

Outstanding views of ancient mixed-conifer forests on Pelican Butte, from the teeming marshes of the Upper Klamath National Wildlife Refuge.

Klamath Ranger District
USGS 7.5' CRYSTAL SPRING (1985)
PELICAN BUTTE (1985)

ABOUT THE AREA

Mature and old growth forests on 8036' Pelican Butte adjoin both the Sky Lakes Wilderness Area and one of Oregon's largest natural marshes, the Upper Klamath National Wildlife Refuge. The resulting habitat produces a rich display of diverse and abundant wildlife. In addition to bald eagles nesting and roosting in big old ponderosa pine, Pelican Butte's extensive ancient forests support eight pairs of northern spotted owls. This is one of the densest concentrations of the rare bird outside of western Oregon, which says a lot about the quality of this south-central Oregon Cascades forest habitat.

Bald eagle nests in the Northwest are usually located in uneven-aged (multi-storied) old growth forest stands, near water bodies which support adequate food supplies. (Photo by Frank Isaacs)

Despite its great scenic, recreational and wildlife values, most of Pelican Butte is not protected from Forest Service-sanctioned roading and logging. To make matters worse, developers and the City of Klamath Falls want to build a huge ski resort and "winter sports area" (snowmobile park) in the heart of Pelican Butte's pristine forests. Conservationists have proposed that most of Pelican Butte be protected as part of the Sky Lakes Wilderness, and that already roaded national forest lands be added to the adjacent Upper Klamath National Wildlife Refuge.

It is of some interest that Lake Natasha, a small high mountain lake within the contiguous Wilderness Area, is considered by scientists to be the purest lake in the world, more pristine than Waldo Lake, Crater Lake or even Lake Baikal. Lake Natasha is four miles north of and directly downstream from the proposed Pelican Butte ski development.

GETTING THERE

From Klamath Falls, take Oregon Highway 140 north and west to Rocky Point, about 25 miles. From Medford, take Highway 140 east and north to Rocky Point, which is roughly 45 miles. At the Rocky Point junction, near the northwest edge of Upper Klamath Lake (east of Lake of the Woods and the Cascade summit), turn north on County Route 531 (Westside Road) for Crater Lake and Fort Klamath. Drive three miles to a sign for Rocky Point Resort (where you can rent a canoe), then another three miles north, past the 11-mile post, and turn right for Malone Springs. From the boat launch at Malone Springs, a two-mile stretch of the road along the marsh (FS Road 3459) has been closed to vehicles to protect nesting bald eagles. You can also put in at the boat launch at Rocky Point Resort and paddle three miles north to Malone Springs.

RECOMMENDED

While you can walk (or cross-country ski in winter) along FS Road 3459 and enjoy nice views of the marsh and wildlife associated with large quaking aspen, fir and ponderosa pine, a canoe trip through the marsh is even better. A few hours of easy rowing or paddling provide intimate, close-up views of black terns, yellow-headed blackbirds, beaver lodges and many species of waterfowl in the marsh. (The "noise" can be incredible!) In spring, young bald eagles may be seen testing their wings in nests constructed in old growth pines high above the shore.

To hike through more ancient white fir, ponderosa pine and Engelmann spruce

into the Sky Lakes Wilderness, take County Route 531 a quarter-mile north of the six-mile post and turn west on FS Road 3450, at a sign for "Cherry Creek Trail–2 miles." Cherry Creek Trail #3708 follows Cherry Creek for about a half-mile before it enters the Wilderness where, six miles from the trailhead, it meets the Pacific Crest Trail. Occasional forest openings provide impressive views of 6623' Cherry Peak. Most of the biggest trees are along the north side of Cherry Creek, but the astute naturalist will note a remarkable variety of Cascade tree species in this pretty little canyon, including some nice spruce groves along the stream. Portions of the Cherry Creek drainage comprised a key expansion of the Sky Lakes Wilderness in 1984, although not all deserving roadless and undeveloped lands were protected..

5. Lake of the Woods

Large Douglas-fir growing near the upper limit of the species' range.

Klamath Ranger District
USGS 7.5' LAKE OF THE WOODS
(NORTH) (1985)

ABOUT THE AREA

Little of the original old growth cathedral forest remains in the southern Cascades. Some remnant stands of large Douglas-fir can be seen along the two short hikes described below, near the summer home areas on the east and west shores of Lake of the Woods, and just north of the lake and Oregon Highway 140. Unfortunately, even these visual corridors (and those along the highway west of Fish Lake) are increasingly threatened by logging. (See the Rye Springs and Fish Lake entries in the Rogue River National Forest chapter for more information about ancient forest areas west of Lake of the Woods.)

GETTING THERE

Take Oregon Highway 140 approximately 40 miles east of Medford (or about 30 miles west of Klamath Falls) to Lake of the Woods.

RECOMMENDED

One of the nicest groves near Lake of the Woods is above the east shore, off Dead Indian Road, between Sunset Campground and Low Echo (Girl Scout) Camp. For a short hike into this grove, drive exactly 0.9 mile south of the turn-off for Sunset Campground (or 0.3 mile north of Low Echo Campground) and look for an unmarked trail on the uphill (east) side of

Dead Indian Road. You're probably in the right place if you can see a yellow "Curve" highway sign on the east side of the road. The trail runs south, parallel to the road for about a quarter-mile, and into a beautiful draw uphill from Low Echo Camp. Unlike most of the area, snags, down logs and other important old growth components of this forest are still largely intact.

Another option is Billy Creek Nature Trail #3735, north of Lake of the Woods. Just west of the junction of Highway 140 and FS Road 3704, this short loop trail leads from the north (uphill) side of Highway 140 from a trailhead it shares with Rye Spur Trail #3771. Park 0.1 mile east of the 36-mile post on Highway 140 and look for a sign for "Rye Spur Trail

#3771," set back from but facing the main highway. Walk a quarter-mile to Billy Creek Nature Trail #3735. It features two small footbridges across Billy Creek, and passes by large Shasta red fir, western white pine, a few large Douglas-fir, and a nice grove of Engelmann spruce along the creek. This quarter-mile loop trail is far enough back from the road to avoid traffic noise, but passes within view of some minimally buffered clearcuts in what used to be old growth forest.

The Forest Service's Rye Spur Trail #3771, which continues uphill from the junction with the nature trail, winds six miles to Four Mile Lake, but the area beyond the "Potemkin Forest" facade of Highway 140's scenic corridor has been devastated by clearcut logging.

6. Brown Mountain Wilderness (proposed)

A forest of ancient Shasta red fir, western white pine and a few large Douglas-fir, on the flanks of a caldera just west of Lake of the Woods.

Klamath Ranger District
USGS 7.5' LAKE OF THE WOODS (NORTH) (1985)
USGS 15' MT. MCLAUGHLIN (1955)

ABOUT THE AREA

The proposed Brown Mountain Wilderness includes approximately 8000 acres on the Klamath Ranger District of the Winema National Forest and the Butte Falls Ranger District of the Rogue River National Forest. This roadless area used to extend to the west shore of Lake of the Woods, but as one Forest Service employee explained, FS Road 3640 was constructed "...to get the big trees out." The 7311' mountain is prominent from the north shore of Fish Lake and the east shore of Lake of the Woods.

Brown Mountain contains an oval

cinder cone 328' long and 33' deep, and is covered with huge lava flows of a blocky, fine-grained basaltic andesite, except on its east flank, which is correspondingly the best place to walk cross-country to its summit. While there are no trails to the top, the Pacific Crest Trail (PCT) countours around its west side, and Brown Mountain Trail #3724 traverses it to the south and east. Both trails lead through large trees, meadows, streams and lava flows, but the biggest trees live along Brown Mountain Trail #3724, which begins on the east side of the roadless area above Lake of the Woods, and crosses the PCT on the area's south side. The PCT then runs north, meeting Oregon Highway 140 about 0.1 mile east of the 32-mile post, which makes a long near-loop walk around the mountain possible.

GETTING THERE

To hike on the east side of Brown Mountain, turn south off the Lake of the Woods Highway (Oregon Highway 140) at a sign for Westside Summer Homes and Camp McLoughlin about 0.6 mile west of the 36-mile post, onto paved FS Road 3601.

RECOMMENDED

Brown Mountain Trail #3724 showcases nine species of conifers, including some huge Douglas-fir and western white pine. There are two trailheads for Brown Mountain Trail #3724 on the east side of roadless area. The lowest is a half-mile south of Oregon Highway 140 on FS Road 3601, just north of the Boy Scouts' Camp McLoughlin. To reach another, slightly higher trailhead at the edge of the roadless area, drive about 0.15 mile south on FS Road 3601 and turn right on gravel FS Road 3640. In 0.6 mile, Brown Mountain Trail #3724 crosses FS Road 3640 nearly a quarter-mile above the lower trailhead. There's a good camping spot down the trail on the left. The largest trees, which grow around Ichabod Springs, begin about a quarter-mile inside the roadless area.

Another option is to drive a total of 2.9 miles south on FS Road 3640 to the trailhead for North Brown Mountain Trail #950A, on the west side of the road. The first 0.7 mile of this trail is blighted by a large shelterwood cut that has become the roadless area's southeast boundary. You can also reach this trailhead from Dead Indian Road on the east side of the lake. From the west, the junction with FS Road 3640 is opposite a yellow "Hill" road sign. The trailhead for North Brown Mountain Trail #950A is 3.1 miles to the north.

Big Douglas-fir and true fir on the lower eastern slopes of Brown Mountain.

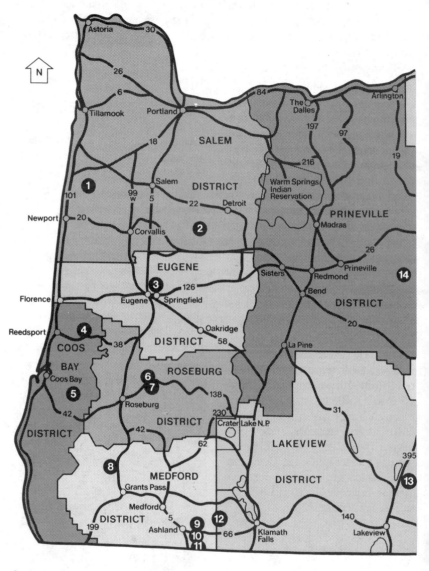

N

Astoria   30

26

6

Tillamook   Portland

18

101   Salem   SALEM   DISTRICT

99w   5   22   Detroit   Warm Springs Indian Reservation   PRINEVILLE

Newport   20   Corvallis   2   Madras

Florence   EUGENE   Sisters   Prineville   14

Eugene   Springfield   126   Redmond   DISTRICT

3   Bend

Reedsport   4   Oakridge   58   DISTRICT   20

COOS   38   La Pine

BAY   ROSEBURG

Coos Bay   6

5   7   138   31

Roseburg   230

42   Crater Lake N.P.

DISTRICT   LAKEVIEW

42   62

8   DISTRICT   395

MEDFORD   13

Grants Pass

Medford   140

DISTRICT   5   9   12

199   Ashland   10   66   Klamath   Lakeview
                    11   Falls

The Dalles   197   97   19   Arlington

84   216

0   28.1   56.2
1 inch = 56.2 miles

Bureau of Land Management Forestlands

The Bureau of Land Management (BLM) is the nation's largest land-managing agency, yet is also the least known or understood. Indeed, of the four major land-managing entities of the federal government of most concern to conservationists (BLM, Forest Service, National Park Service and Fish and Wildlife Service), it is the only agency still classified as a bureau, rather than a service. (We're conveniently ignoring the Department of Defense, Bureau of Indian Affairs and a few others for purposes of simplicity.) However, as part of the Department of Interior, and as mandated by the 1976 Federal Lands Policy and Management Act, BLM is a full-fledged multiple use agency with stewardship responsibilities to all Americans.

Throughout the West, BLM is generally perceived as a grazing agency for arid, unforested public domain lands. In fact, the Bureau contains some of America's most valuable forestlands, albeit significantly less than the National Forest System. This is especially true in western Oregon, where BLM manages almost 2.5 million acres. (This includes most of the "O & C" lands, revested forestlands once ceded to the Oregon and California Railroad, which were recovered by the federal government in the 1930s when the railroad defaulted on its contract to construct a north-south line.) The management and revenue-sharing history for BLM forests is complex and not the subject of this guidebook, but readers should note that BLM forest policy issues are especially complicated and controversial.

Some of Oregon's most treasured ancient forest groves are found on BLM lands. Two legendary examples are Valley of the Giants and Crabtree Valley, both featured herein. This chapter includes samples of these unique old growth stands listed by District, on all five western Oregon BLM Districts and two of four eastern Oregon Districts. (A BLM District is analogous to a National Forest; each BLM District contains Resource Areas, which are very roughly analogous to National Forest Ranger Districts.)

In western Oregon, BLM lands are generally lower in elevation than adjacent National Forests, providing rare opportunities for protection of the few low-elevation ancient forest groves still standing. In eastern Oregon, BLM forests often comprise the transition lands between National Forest and high desert lands. Consequently, these unique forestlands are the interface between two distinct physiographic regions, and their role in terms of wildlife and fish habitat (among others) is critical. As timber producers, they would be marginal at best.

Enjoy your visits to these very special

ancient forests, and remember that BLM forestlands are among the most threatened in Oregon.

Don't forget your Bureau of Land Management visitors recreation map.

Salem District BLM

1. Valley of the Giants

One of the last remaining stands of giant old growth trees in the northern Oregon Coast Range.

Yamhill Resource Area
USGS 7.5' WARNICKE CREEK (1974)

ABOUT THE AREA
This 47-acre tract, 60 miles (two and a half hours) west of Salem, was designated an Outstanding Natural Area (ONA) by BLM in 1976—one of the most protective administrative classifications available, short of statutory designations. The stark, stump- and debris-laden landscape around Valsetz (val-sets´) Lake gives this remaining stand of huge trees an oasis-like quality which makes it all the more spectacular.

The grove contains over a dozen trees 8' to 11' in diameter, and possibly the largest Douglas-fir in Oregon. In 1981, wind toppled a previous record tree known as Big Guy, which was 35.5' in circumference and 230' tall. Even fallen, this tree is extremely impressive. Several of Oregon's record trees have blown over after adjacent trees which had provided protective buffers for centuries were logged.

Snow sometimes blocks the road as late as mid-April. Call the Salem District BLM at 399-5646 to check conditions.

GETTING THERE
The trip to Valley of the Giants requires

an arduous drive over 28 miles of bumpy, poorly marked gravel roads. From Salem drive 27 miles west on Oregon Highway 22 to Falls City. Drive southwest out of Falls City, bearing left at the intersection at the outskirts of town. In about 1.5 miles the road becomes gravel. Approximately 14.7 miles past the intersection, bear left around the south end of Valsetz "Lake" (a former log pond, now partially drained and full of debris which makes it unsafe for swimming). Some maps still show a road along the lake's east side, through the town of Valsetz, but the road is now blocked by a gate. This Boise Cascade company town was abandoned and razed in 1983, when the timber that was supposed to last forever ran out.

Drive two miles around the former Valsetz Lake. (As you drive north, it will be on your right.) Continue north beyond the lake for 3.8 miles and cross a log bridge. Approximately 0.3 mile beyond the bridge, bear right (uphill) on North Fork Siletz Road. Stay on this main road for 6.4 miles. The Siletz River can be seen on the left until you cross a second bridge, five miles beyond the log bridge. Continue another 1.2 miles and bear right on Carter Creek Road (BLM Road 7-8-32). Drive another half-mile to a small parking lot on the right, which may or may not be marked with a small, handwritten sign saying "V of G."

RECOMMENDED

An old logging road leads down to the North Fork of the Siletz River. The short (0.8-mile) loop trail, flagged with pink ribbons, begins at a log footbridge over the river.

2. Crabtree Valley

Although much of the surrounding forest has been destroyed by clearcutting, 750 to 800-year-old trees, among the oldest in Oregon, still stand in this basin.

Santiam Resource Area
USGS 7.5' YELLOWSTONE MTN. (1985)

ABOUT THE AREA

These ancient groves of Douglas-fir, western red-cedar and western hemlock are a fine example of a Cascades forest community spared from major fires and chainsaws over the centuries. After years of efforts by conservationists to protect the area from its owners, BLM acquired Section 16 (T11S R3E)

of Crabtree Valley from Willamette Industries, who to their credit became willing and eager sellers. (For a sad counterpoint, see the description for the Millennium Grove entry in the Willamette National Forest chapter.) Before BLM acquired Section 16, the agency designated 260 adjoining acres as Carolyn's Crown Research Natural

Old growth forests have been virtually eliminated on private lands, and are almost gone from even the public forests. Overall, only a small fraction, about one tenth of our ancient forest legacy, remains.

Area (RNA). It is now time for the Bureau to expand this protection to the remaining forest giants in Section 16. Use the Willamette National Forest recreation map or the BLM Santiam Resource Area transportation map for exploring this area.

GETTING THERE
Turn north off US Highway 20 four miles east of the Sweet Home Ranger Station on the Middle Santiam River Road (County Road 912), at a sign for Green Peter Dam and Quartzville. Continue 20.5 miles east on what becomes the Quartzville Access Road, along the north side of Green Peter Reservoir. Approximately three miles beyond (east of) the reservoir, turn north (left) on Yellowstone Access Road (BLM Road 11-3E-35.1). Stay on the paved road for 6.75 miles. When the pavement ends, bear left, following the sign for Snow Peak Camp.

The last three miles are on narrow gravel roads. In 0.8 mile bear left (don't take BLM Road 11-3E-18.1, which rises steeply to the right). In another 0.3 mile, the road bears right and drops directly into Crabtree Valley. Crabtree Lake and a beaver pond (further north) are visible below on your left. At the bottom of the hill (one mile from the top) make the first possible left turn.

RECOMMENDED
Three hikes into the old growth forest, each requiring some cross-country travel, begin from this final road.

Option 1: In a quarter-mile look for an old jeep road to the left, perpendicular to the road. This crosses a small stream and winds among the big trees north of the beaver pond.

Option 2: In 0.4 mile make the first possible right turn. About 0.1 mile further, a fallen tree partially blocks the road. Enter the forest here for a cross-country hike through the area's most continuous old growth grove.

Option 3: In three-quarters of a mile (past the beaver pond) walk across a small logjam at the outlet of Crabtree Lake. An old jeep road continues a short way around the back side of the lake, past some very big trees.

Eugene District BLM

3. Mohawk Research Natural Area and McGowen Creek Outdoor Education Area

Small stand of low-elevation old growth Douglas-fir, close to Eugene.

McKenzie Resource Area
USGS 15' MARCOLA (1950)

ABOUT THE AREA
This lush ancient forest is low enough in elevation to be accessible year-round. It is divided into two administrative units by the road; of the two, the Mohawk Research Natural Area (RNA) is consid-erably larger, but the McGowen Creek Outdoor Education Area is far more accessible. The forest here is dense and "decadent," with down trees all over the forest floor, so it is difficult to get very far into the trailless 293 acres of the Mohawk

RNA. Although they are becoming overgrown, several trails do exist through the 40-acre Outdoor Education Area.

As a Research Natural Area, the Mohawk grove is now protected from the clearcuts that have devastated BLM's once-extensive holdings of ancient forest in western Oregon. Unfortunately, several areas in the RNA, including a large portion in its center, were clearcut before the RNA was designated. (The Mohawk RNA has also been identified by BLM as an Area of Critical Environmental Concern, which sounds impressive but mandates little real protection.) Unfortunately the Outdoor Education Area is still included by BLM's Eugene District in its timber base calculation, which means the area will someday be clearcut—or that the "sustainable" cut level for the rest of the Eugene District's timberlands is inflated.

Please bring a litter bag and help pick up trash left by less considerate visitors.

GETTING THERE

From I-5 near Eugene and Springfield, take Exit 194A onto Highway 126 East. Drive four miles to the third exit (for 42nd Street and Jasper), turn left at the light, go under the overpass, and drive 0.7 mile to a stop sign at Marcola Road. Turn right and drive 6.5 miles to the *second* junction with Sunderman Road. (Sunderman Road loops south of Marcola Road. This can be a bit confusing, so watch your mileage for the second junction.) Turn left on Sunderman Road, drive 0.1 mile, and turn right on Donna Road in front of the Mohawk General Store. Drive 0.6 mile on Donna Road to McGowen Creek Road and turn left. Drive 3.5 miles on this paved road, and turn left on a gravel road just before a

"Ancient forests may hold the answers to questions we have not yet thought to ask."
—David Brower

yellow road sign that cautions "Winding Road next 2 1/2 miles." This is BLM Road 16-2-20, but the sign is not visible until after the turn and has been shot up anyway. Drive another half-mile and park at a turn-out on the right, where a jeep road leads down the hill.

RECOMMENDED

The Outdoor Education Area is on your right, across McGowen Creek, but ironically is not marked at all. Follow the jeep track downhill, across the small stream. Several trails lead into the Outdoor Education Area from this point.

From the turn-out on the right, the Research Natural Area is just ahead on the left side of the road. Because there are no signs marking its borders, it is not clear where the RNA begins. As noted above, there are no trails into the heavy old growth.

This lack of trails is common in RNAs, and usually a good thing, as RNAs are established for baseline research purposes, not recreation. Even though they are not large areas, RNAs are great places to discover big trees, if you're willing to walk softly in the forest.

Coos Bay District BLM

4. Wassen Lake

On the eastern side of the proposed Wassen Creek Wilderness, Wassen Lake offers some big trees, a skunk cabbage marsh, and the only real "flat" ground in the area.

Umpqua Resource Area
USGS 7.5' SMITH RIVER FALLS (1984)

ABOUT THE AREA

Wassen Lake is a natural, spring-fed slump lake which supports a diverse botanical community at the head of Wassen Creek. The shallow lake provides some fishing, but is most noted for its abundance of newts. Particularly during their mating season in early spring, newts are virtually everywhere on the ground and in the water.

Massive red alders surround the lake, but the biggest trees (Douglas-fir and western red-cedar) grow on the north side of the lake and down Wassen Creek to the west. Wassen Creek flows for 17 miles between canyon walls lined with steep old growth forest. The area's dense virgin forest and forbidding terrain distinguish it as the wildest and most rugged site for a wilderness experience in Oregon's Coast Range. Wassen Creek is probably the most impassable place described in this book. It is one of the few areas for which ONRC has requested the construction of a trail, both to provide

The snags still standing in Wassen Lake indicate a "recent" landslide across Wassen Creek formed this rare lake.

access into this exciting area and to protect the stream from heavy-booted hikers. While the Forest Service has agreed to this concept, BLM, whose holdings comprise the east side of the roadless area, needs more prompting. (See also the Wassen Creek entry in the Siuslaw National Forest chapter.)

GETTING THERE
The road to Wassen Lake is a winding one, but paved all the way. Take Oregon Highway 38 from I-5 south of Cottage Grove (or US Highway 101 at Reedsport). About 0.3 mile west of the 19-mile post and the Wells Creek bridge, and 1.7 miles east of Scottsburg, turn north on Wells Creek Road. In 2.2 miles bear left for Ferntop (Mountain—elevation 1896') on BLM Road 21-9-32.0, and in 3.3 miles bear right on Wassen Lake Road (BLM Road 21-9-10). Stop at a pull-out and a

jeep road on the left in another 3.7 miles.

RECOMMENDED
Walk down this dirt road 100 yards to the southeast side of Wassen Lake. From the north side of the lake, head uphill to an old growth forest bench above the west end of the lake, and follow this contour downstream above Wassen Creek to get the flavor of the canyon. There are no formal trails in Wassen Creek, but a cross-country hike around the lake and down Wassen Creek is rewarding. Although there are logs across the creek and most wet areas, rubber shoes or boots are recommended, as the easiest going in the Wassen Creek drainage is in the streambed itself. Even in the creek it is very difficult to travel more than about five miles a day. Be gentle (and in good shape) if you choose to explore this special place.

5. Cherry Creek Research Natural Area and Vaughns Creek

Some of the nicest old growth forest remaining on BLM's Coos Bay District.

Tioga Resource Area
USGS 15' SITKUM (1955)

ABOUT THE AREA
The small grove in the Cherry Creek RNA contains some very large Douglas-fir, exemplary of the forests which once covered this region. At nearby Vaughns Creek is another small but striking remnant grove of ancient Douglas-fir. On the way to both sites is a stand of old growth Oregon-myrtle worth seeing.

Road numbers below correspond to the Coos Bay District, Tioga Resource Area Transportation Map #3, available from the BLM office in Coos Bay.

GETTING THERE
Enjoy a scenic drive on Oregon Highway 42 to Coquille, turn left just past the high school, and take the Coquille-Fairview Road (BLM Road 73009) for nine miles to Fairview. Turn right at the four-way stop sign on the Coos Bay Wagon Road (BLM Road 72080) and drive 6.5 miles, following signs for Dora. Across from Cherry Creek Park, turn left on Cherry Creek County Road (BLM Road 71062) and drive north and east for 5.5 miles. (Do not turn on Cherry Creek Ridge Road.)

RECOMMENDED

The Cherry Creek Research Natural Area is north of BLM Road 71062, in Sections 18 and 19 (T27S R10W). You will come to a small parking area and a wooden signpost that used to hold a good-sized sign. There are five picnic tables, a pit toilet, and a short trail leading to the "Big Tree." A sign at Big Tree provides its vital statistics: 600 years old, 282' tall, 9.7' diameter at breast height. A short (quarter-mile) trail loops through the impressive old forest.

The ancient forest along Vaughns Creek is one section to the northeast of the Cherry Creek RNA, in Section 8 (T27S R10W). To get to Vaughns Creek from the Cherry Creek RNA, continue east on Cherry Creek Road past the RNA and take the next left on North Fork Cherry Creek Road (BLM Road 27-10-18.0). Turn north on BLM Road 27-10-0.3, then right on Vaughns Creek Road (BLM Road 27-10-6.1).

To go directly to the Vaughns Creek grove, drive a little more than four miles past Fairview on the Coos Bay Wagon Road (BLM Road 72080), then turn north (left) on Middle Creek Road (BLM Road 27-11-20.0). After eight miles, turn right on Vaughns Creek Road (BLM Road 27-10-6.1). Drive to the end of the road; the Cherry Creek old growth trees will be on your right. Although the Vaughns Creek area is steeper than Cherry Creek and there is no trail, it is not difficult to explore.

Another nearby point of interest is La Verne County Park, which contains one of the area's nicest old growth Oregon-myrtle groves and a few ancient Douglas-firs. The park and developed campground are five miles north of Fairview (or 14 miles north of Coquille) on Coos County Route 9. Wade the North Fork of the Coquille River to a small but more secluded myrtle grove opposite campsite #61.

Roseburg District BLM

6. North Umpqua River Trail, Tioga Segment

Western end of the North Umpqua River Trail.

North Umpqua Resource Area
USGS 15' MACE MTN. (1955)
GLIDE (1954)

ABOUT THE AREA

The Tioga segment of the North Umpqua Trail provides some initial solitude from the traffic along Oregon Highway 138, which is sometimes a little too visible and audible from the river's edge. Beginning four miles east of Glide and heading upstream, this trail joins and continues as

FS Trail #1414 in eleven miles. The entire length of this trail parallels the south shore of the North Umpqua River, now part of the National Wild and Scenic River System.

GETTING THERE

East of Roseburg and Glide on the North

Umpqua Highway (Oregon Highway 138), turn south between the 22 and 23-mile markers at the turn-off for Douglas County's Swiftwater Park, and cross the bridge over the river.

RECOMMENDED
Immediately after the bridge, a trail leads to the left (upstream). The first mile goes through a pleasant forest of old growth Douglas-fir and a few large sugar pine. The next upstream trailhead is on the Umpqua National Forest across the Wright Creek bridge.

(Also see the description for the North Umpqua River Trail, Upper Segments entry in the Umpqua National Forest chapter.)

"Old growth forests are not cellulose cemeteries, despite what the (timber) industry says." —Dr. Jerry Franklin

7. Wolf Creek Falls

An easy hike along an old growth riparian area to spectacular waterfalls.

North Umpqua Resource Area
USGS 15' RED BUTTE (1955)

ABOUT THE AREA
This one-mile trail through a canyon to upper and lower Wolf Creek Falls leads through a lush lowland rainforest of ancient Douglas-fir and western red–cedar—a forest type now all too rare in Oregon.

GETTING THERE
From Highway 138 a quarter-mile west of Glide, turn south on Little River Road and follow it (as County Route 17) up the Little River for 10.5 miles. (You'll see signs for Civilian Conservation Center.) The trail leads up Wolf Creek, south of Little River and just west of the Umpqua National Forest boundary.

RECOMMENDED
The trail begins over an arched foot-bridge south of County Route 17. A parking area is located just east of the trailhead on the north side of the road. In a quarter-mile, after a second, smaller footbridge, a steep trail leads to the right. It rejoins the main trail after passing through some of the area's larger trees, with breathtaking views of the canyon below.

Medford District BLM

8. London Peak

*The most accessible ancient forest trail
along Interstate 5.*

Glendale Resource Area
USGS 7.5' GLENDALE (1986)

ABOUT THE AREA

While the really big trees are widely
scattered, this beautiful and diverse old
growth forest includes madrone, chinquapin, Douglas-fir, incense-cedar, a few
large pines, tanoak, canyon live oak and
Pacific yew. The trail is quite steep—it
rises 1500' in two miles. A large rock at
the 2848' summit, named for author Jack
London, provides excellent views above
the older forest to the east. After visiting
the peak, you may wish to stop in at the
historic Wolf Creek Inn, see the small
room upstairs where London reportedly
stayed, and enjoy an outstanding meal or
refreshments.

GETTING THERE

From I-5 take Exit 76 for Wolf Creek.
Just above the Wolf Creek Inn turn north
(right) on First Street, then west (left) on
Main for a half-mile to Wolf Creek Park.

RECOMMENDED

The trailhead for London Peak is at a
footbridge near camp space #10 at Wolf
Creek Park. The nicest forest stands are
after the first half-mile. Local residents
are building a new trail, which begins
from the lower London Peak Trail and
follows Wolf Creek to the west.

*Named for Jack London, who once stayed at the
nearby historic Wolf Creek Tavern, London
Peak offers a steep trail to its summit. You may
also want to visit the restored inn at its base.*

9. Chinquapin Mountain Grove, Pacific Crest Trail

Hiking and cross-country skiing on and near the Pacific Crest Trail north of "Route 66."

Ashland Resource Area
USGS 15' HYATT RESERVOIR (1955)

ABOUT THE AREA

See the following Hobart Bluff Grove entry in this chapter for remarks about BLM resource management along the Pacific Crest Trail (PCT), comments which are generally applicable here. The old forest north of Highway 66 and south of Hyatt Reservoir is scattered over Sections 15, 22, 20, 19 and 30 (from east to west) in T39S R3E. (See the Pacific Crest National Scenic Trail—Oregon Southern Portion map.) The PCT travels through these ancient forest groves as it passes south and east of Hyatt Reservoir. You can also walk or ski cross-country from Chinquapin Road into more ancient forest groves on the east side of Chinquapin Mountain.

GETTING THERE

Take Highway 66 to the Green Springs Inn (a great place to eat), east of the Green Springs summit between mileposts 17 and 18. Turn north here, on East Hyatt Lake Road.

RECOMMENDED

To ski or walk cross-country through the ancient forest around Chinquapin Mountain, watch for Chinquapin Road (BLM Road 39-3E-27) on the right in 1.4 miles. Take this gravel road for approximately one mile, and then choose a cross-country route to explore the west face of the mountain.

To hike on the Pacific Crest Trail, drive another 1.5 miles and bear right where Hyatt Prairie Road angles off to the left.

Big pine and fir along the Pacific Crest Trail at Chinquapin Mountain are threatened by BLM's proposed clearcuts.

Continue two more miles and park where a spur road (BLM Road 39-3E-15) turns to the right, 0.1 mile after the Hyatt Lake overflow camping area on the left. Look for the PCT, which crosses BLM Road 39-3E-15 in about 100 yards. Follow the trail to the west (right). Once you pass a recent BLM clearcut, the trail leads through a half-mile of beautiful old growth forest. You can also get on the PCT at the junction of East Hyatt Lake and Hyatt Prairie Roads, from where it is 1.5 miles to some very nice ancient forest east of Little Hyatt Lake, in Sections 20, 19 and 30 of T39S R3E. (See the following entry for Hobart Bluff Grove, Pacific Crest Trail.)

10. Hobart Bluff Grove, Pacific Crest Trail

Ancient pine and fir along the Pacific Crest Trail south of "Route 66."

Ashland Resource Area
USGS 15' HYATT RESERVOIR (1955)

ABOUT THE AREA

Federal law requires the Bureau of Land Management to provide for wildlife and fisheries, watersheds and recreation resources as well as wood, but the dominance of timber in BLM's policies is soon apparent to anyone who spends even a little time on western Oregon BLM lands. Nowhere have established recreational values been more abused than by BLM along the Pacific Crest Trail (PCT) in this area. (The Pacific Crest National Scenic Trail—Oregon Southern Portion map has been made obsolete by the many new miles of roads and clearcuts BLM has carved out along the scenic trail.) While sigificant old growth groves can still be found, most of the biggest trees have been selectively logged, and now BLM is beginning to clearcut what remains.

Still, these areas are well worth exploring. The Hobart Bluff ancient forest grove (Section 9, T40S R3E) is a large meadow surrounded by big old ponderosa pine which, a quarter-mile to the south, transitions into even larger virgin Douglas-fir. It remains one of the most diverse and pristine areas on the BLM-managed portion of the Pacific Crest Trail. Two routes to this very special place are described below.

While you are in the area, you may wish to visit similar sites north of Oregon Highway 66; for example, see the preceding Chinquapin Mountain Grove entry in this chapter.

A timber sale in this grove was recently cancelled as a result of public pressure to protect the area.

GETTING THERE

Take Highway 66 to the summit of Green Springs Mountain (elevation 4551'). For a shortcut to the Hobart Bluff grove, turn south (right) just before the Green Springs summit on Soda Mountain Road (BLM Road 39-3E-32.3), 15.6 miles east of Ashland and 0.8 mile east of Tyler Creek Road. Drive exactly one mile south on Soda Mountain Road from the junction with Highway 66.

RECOMMENDED

The PCT crosses Highway 66 at the Green Springs summit, then travels south along the northwestern edge of the proposed Soda Mountain Wilderness to Soda Mountain (seven miles) and beyond. (See the Dutch Oven and Scotch Creek descriptions in the following Soda Mountain Wilderness proposal entry in this chapter.) About a mile and a half south of Highway 66, the trail enters the meadow

and big ponderosa pine.

If you're taking the shortcut, park a mile down Soda Mountain Road. Walk uphill about 100 yards to where the PCT comes closest to the road (which it parallels, and then crosses in another 2.8 miles). When you come to the trail go south (right) for a half-mile to the meadow and big trees.

Another way to reach the PCT is to drive to Little Hyatt Lake. From the Green Springs summit and Highway 66, head north on an unmarked BLM dirt road for 2.8 miles to the PCT at Little Hyatt Lake. Take the PCT to the west by crossing a wooden bridge over the creek below the dam. Some of the area's finest pristine forest grows here, north of the trail and west of the reservoir. As the PCT turns south in the next couple of miles, you pass more undisturbed forest and come to a fantastic view of the Ashland Valley and the Siskiyou Mountains beyond.

11. Soda Mountain Wilderness (proposed)

Enchanting little pools and varied topography along magical streams in steep, forested canyons.

Ashland Resource Area
USGS 7.5' SISKIYOU PASS (1983)
SODA MOUNTAIN (1988)
USGS 15' HYATT RESERVOIR (1955)

ABOUT THE AREA

The ancient forest areas described here, on the northern and southern edges of the proposed Soda Mountain Wilderness, reflect some of the great beauty and diversity of the area. These are the most pristine and secluded ancient forests remaining on BLM's Medford District. The glaciers of Mount Shasta greet you from the ridgetops on clear days. From monolithic Pilot Rock near I-5, the proposed Soda Mountain Wilderness stretches in two units to Jenny Creek at the eastern end of Keene Creek Ridge.

From the Pacific Crest Trail (PCT) just north of Soda Mountain (6091'), the area plunges down and southward into critical deer winter range in northern California's oak-grassland country (around 2300'). Snow usually covers access roads and the PCT from December through March or longer.

Together, both units of this roadless area comprise 32,000 acres, but BLM has seen fit to study and recommend only 5640 acres in the area's central core for possible designation as federal Wilder-

Pockets of ancient forest are distributed along the Pacific Crest Trail and the upper canyons of the proposed Soda Mountain Wilderness Area.

ness. Even so, the Soda Mountain Wilderness Study Area is the only significantly forested BLM Wilderness Study Area in the entire state.

The descriptions below are divided into two broad categories for northwestern and north central approaches to Soda Mountain, each of which can be treated as a separate area for purposes of this guidebook. Additional maps of the area that may be helpful include the Pacific Crest National Scenic Trail Map—Oregon Southern Portion (available from either the Forest Service or BLM), and the BLM Medford District transportation map for the Ashland Resource Area, 1"/mile (1989).

Northwest Access, Scotch Creek Headwaters and Pilot Rock

ABOUT THE AREA
Short hikes on the Pacific Crest Trail offer big old trees, tremendous views of Mount Shasta, and impressive up-close looks at Pilot Rock. Those without acrophobia will enjoy the climb to Pilot Rock's summit.

GETTING THERE
Drive nine miles south of Ashland on I-5. Take Exit 5 for Mount Ashland and go straight ahead (south), following signs for Siskiyou Summit. Continue 1.4 miles (over the summit), and turn left on Pilot Rock Road (BLM Road 40-2E-33).

Continue two miles to a gravel pit where the road forks. Take the fork to the right to begin hiking on the PCT at Pilot Rock. (This road is badly rutted and not suited for low clearance vehicles.) The trailhead is on the left at the top of the ridge in 0.8 mile. Drive another 0.2 mile past the PCT trailhead for an outstanding view of Pilot Rock above a meadow surrounded by ancient forest. This is also a very enjoyable cross-country ski route in winter.

To reach the PCT east of Pilot Rock, on the edge of the proposed Soda Mountain

Wilderness, take the fork to the left and drive a total of 1.7 miles, bearing right when BLM Road 40-2E-35 heads right. Park at a fence next to a sign that reads "Highway 99 3.5 miles," just past a large BLM clearcut on the left.

RECOMMENDED
Continue on foot through the fence straight down the road. Immediately beyond the fence the PCT crosses the road. Following the trail to the left (predominantly east) will take you through some big Douglas-fir, grand fir and incense-cedar along the northwest boundary of the proposed Soda Mountain Wilderness.

This piece of wilderness trail can be reached from the northeast by the following directions for the PCT under *North Central Access.* The trail to the right heads west above the headwaters of the west fork of Scotch Creek (corner of Section 35), leading you through big trees, a few meadows, and finally to the old firs which still carpet Pilot Rock's north ridge. In about two miles, the trail reaches the westernmost Pilot Rock trailhead described above.

By continuing straight down the road rather than taking the PCT in either direction, in less than a mile you'll arrive at a beautiful meadow surrounded by more big trees.

If you wish to climb Pilot Rock, follow the PCT from either direction to the west side of the rock, where you can best make the ascent. Even on the west side, though, it's a Class 3 (hand and foot hold) climb. From the top you'll get a bird's eye view of the western half of the proposed Soda Mountain Wilderness and spectacular views of Mount Shasta.

North Central Access, Dutch Oven and Camp Creeks (cross-country)

ABOUT THE AREA
This area shelters dense, "dripping wet" rainforest groves interspersed with meadows and oak woodlands.

GETTING THERE
From I-5 take Exit 14 in Ashland to Oregon Highway 66 and drive east toward Klamath Falls. Less than one mile west of the summit of Green Springs Mountain (and 0.8 mile east of the 14-mile post) on Highway 66, turn south on Tyler Creek Road. Proceed 1.5 miles and turn south (left) on Baldy Creek Road (40-3E-5). Continue on Baldy Creek Road for exactly six miles, then turn left on BLM Road 40-3E-29, which crosses a cattle guard in 100' (before a sign for the Pacific Crest Trail on the left) and then forks. If you're heading for Dutch Oven Creek, park before the fork (it's easy to get stuck below).

To travel deeper into the proposed Soda Mountain Wilderness, take the left fork (BLM Road 40-E3-29). Bear left at the next fork (passing a spur road that dead-ends to the right). About 1.7 miles beyond this fork, the road turns south and forks again into two jeep trails on the divide between Dutch Oven and Camp Creeks. Stop at this fork.

RECOMMENDED
Dutch Oven Creek: Again, stop at the first fork after the cattle guard, then walk

down the right fork about 0.3 mile to the headwaters of Dutch Oven Creek. (The Wilderness Study Area boundary is just below a recent clearcut above the stream.) Walk downstream along Dutch Oven Creek through a magnificent old growth forest of fir, cedar and pine. If you continue to where this (west) fork enters the main stem of Dutch Oven Creek, you will be in Section 5, which contains some of the area's nicest old growth forest. BLM declined to review this area for Wilderness consideration.

Camp Creek: From the third fork, walk due east to explore the headwaters and depths of the Camp Creek drainage below the summit of Soda Mountain. This fork of Camp Creek is one of the few remaining uncut drainages in the proposed Wilderness. Again, the big trees in the headwaters were excluded by BLM from its Wilderness Study Area and are scheduled for logging.

Another option (about a ten-minute hike) is to follow the Dutch Oven-Camp Creek Divide (known locally as Juniper Ridge) south to 5770' Boccard Point. Take the fork to the right and then bear to the left. From this promontory, named by conservationists for the late Bruce Boccard (former ONRC staff member and founder of the Soda Mountain Wilderness Council), you can plot trips into Soda Mountain's ancient forest, limited only by your imagination, energy and time.

Lakeview District BLM

12. Surveyor Campground

Large western white pine and Douglas-fir five feet thick along an alder and aspen-lined marsh.

Klamath Resource Area
USGS 7.5' SURVEYOR MTN. (1985)
LAKE OF THE WOODS (SOUTH) (1985)

ABOUT THE AREA
Small pools along the trail and a number of big snags make this area an excellent place for wildlife observation. The route below is a loop drive through some fine big trees. Use the Rogue River National Forest recreation map for this area.

GETTING THERE
From Highway 66, turn north on Dead Indian Road for Lake-of-the-Woods. About 0.3 mile past the 27-mile post, turn south on BLM Road 38-5E-21.1. Drive 4.1 miles south to the junction with the main BLM road east of (and accessible from) Howard Prairie Reservoir. Turn east (left) and drive 0.8 mile to Surveyor Campground on your right (in Section 21 of T38S R5E). When you leave the campground, turn left and follow this road back to Dead Indian Road on the way to Howard Prairie Reservoir, approximately 12 miles. Large ponderosa pine, western white pine and Douglas-fir, as well as alder and aspen, dominate the landscape.

RECOMMENDED
From Surveyor Campground, follow the primitive (unmarked) trail west, past a fenced spring along the edge of the marsh. The big trees are everywhere!

13. Abert Rim Wilderness Study Area

An isolated but beautiful ponderosa pine grove, remnant of a moister era, which rises from the sagebrush steppe high on Abert Rim.

Lakeview Resource Area
USGS 7.5' LAKE ABERT SOUTH (1968)

ABOUT THE AREA
The Bureau of Land Management's Abert Rim Wilderness Study Area (WSA) includes 23,760 acres east of US Highway 395 and Lake Abert. The long, narrow WSA follows the west-facing Abert Rim—the largest continuous fault scarp in North America, rising more than 2000' above Lake Abert—about 21 miles from north to south. Conservationists' proposal for protection of eastern Oregon's wildlands includes designation of 79,200 acres of Wilderness in the Abert Rim area, including some nearby lands on the Fremont National Forest.

Though several intermittent springs, creeks and ponds can be found within the WSA, this is generally dry country. The sloping plateaus east of the rim are dominated by open sagebrush and bunchgrass plant communities, with stringers of mountain mahogany, juniper, and aspen in occasional wet areas. Both the rim and the WSA uplands provide habitat for many wildlife species, including California bighorn sheep, pronghorn antelope, mule deer, prairie falcons, great horned owls and golden eagles.

Beyond the rim itself, perhaps the most exceptional feature of the Abert Rim WSA is a 600-acre grove of old growth ponderosa pine known as the Colvin Timbers, found in the southeast part of the WSA. This lovely stand is the northernmost ponderosa pine in the Warner Mountains, and one of the most eastern

outposts of old growth ponderosa pine in Oregon's Great Basin country. Portions of the Colvin Timbers grove were once selectively logged, but it still contains many trees several feet thick. Stringers of ponderosa pine and aspen extend north of the grove, and other small stands thrive in canyons to the east.

GETTING THERE
As the crow flies, Abert Rim WSA is 26 miles north of Lakeview and three miles northeast of Valley Falls (the junction of Highways 31 and 395). The easiest way into Colvin Timbers is to drive from the south—but this route requires a high

Ponderosa pine thrive on the edge of the high desert at Colvin Timbers.

257

clearance vehicle. If you don't have one, the best way to reach the top of Abert Rim is probably the two-hour walk from US Highway 395 on the east side of Lake Abert up Poison Creek Trail, which rises 1700' in two miles; this still leaves you several miles north of the Colvin Timbers grove. (See William L. Sullivan's *Exploring Oregon's Wild Areas* for more details.)

If your rig can handle it: From Lakeview, drive 4.5 miles north of town on Highway 395, then turn east on Highway 140 for Adel. After 8.5 miles on Highway 140, turn north (left) on North Wagner Road (FS Road 3615) and drive for 28.5 miles to Colvin Timbers. North Wagner Road is paved for the first 16.25 miles, and except for the first four miles, the paved portion of the road through National Forest land is especially scenic, passing many big ponderosa pine, large meadows, and spectacular quaking aspen groves. Unfortunately, Forest Service clearcut logging is rapidly compromising this beauty.

When the pavement ends, bear right, staying on FS Road 3615, and continue another 7.5 miles to a cattle guard. Here the Forest Service land ends and the road gets significantly worse. For the next 5.5 miles, the road—now the east border of the WSA—makes a better trail than a road. Again, high clearance vehicles only!

RECOMMENDED

Park before the forest and follow the "road" into the Colvin Timbers grove. As you drive or walk north, this stand looks like a green blanket surrounded by a sea of sagebrush. To the east are great views over Coyote and Rabbit Hills, with the scarps of Hart Mountain and Poker Jim Ridge appearing far off across the Warner Valley.

Other features beckon above Abert Rim. Roughly a half-mile south of Colvin Timbers, a jeep track forks to the left toward a sizeable aspen grove. This is the shortest way to the rim on this route. The shallow, several-acre Colvin Lake is a bit more than a mile to the east of Colvin Timbers.

If you're looking for a good camping spot in the area, try Mud Creek Campground, 6.8 miles up FS Road 3615 from Highway 140. The creek—which is actually clear—feeds Bull Prairie, a large meadow surrounded by big pine.

There are several fantastic viewpoints on top of Abert Rim, even if you don't go all the way into Colvin Timbers. For an incredibly scenic view on the south end of the rim, turn west (left) a quarter-mile north of the 21-mile post on FS Road 032, a 1.5-mile loop road passable for all vehicles.

A half-mile north of Mud Creek Campground (about 7.25 miles up FS Road 3615 from Highway 140), turn right on FS Road 019 and drive five miles to a fire lookout with views of the Drake-McDowell roadless area to the northeast, Crane Mountain and its roadless area to the south, and Hart Mountain and the Warner Valley to the east. This viewpoint presents some great cross-country opportunities for the truly hardy. The Drake-McDowell roadless area—forested with big old ponderosa pine on its north slopes—can be reached only from here, as private land owners do not permit entry on the lower elevation east side.

From the fire lookout, continue north to the top of Light Peak and then due east down a saddle toward 8402' Drake Peak. Descend this forest slope (losing 1500' in about three quarters of a mile) into the Twelve Mile Creek drainage to the north.

Another impressive destination from North Warner Road (FS Road 3415) is North Warner Viewpoint, which faces west. Look for a sign once you've passed FS Road 019.

Prineville District BLM

14. North Fork Wilderness Study Area

A diverse canyon wilderness, adjacent to roadless lands on the Ochoco National Forest.

Central Oregon Resource Area
USGS 7.5' COMMITTEE CREEK (1983)
RABBIT VALLEY (1982)

ABOUT THE AREA

Seven miles of the North Fork Crooked River wind through a canyon 800-900' deep in this 10,800-acre Wilderness Study Area (WSA), one of the few on eastern Oregon BLM lands with ancient ponderosa pine. There are also mature and older Douglas-fir on north exposures and along the draws. Rainbow trout, smallmouth bass and other fish lurk in the Crooked River's deep pools. Elk and deer are common, and antelope, as well as bald and golden eagles, visit the canyon. The author spotted a mature bald eagle and several common mergansers with their ducklings during one July visit.

The North Fork Wilderness Study Area is contiguous with another 1100 acres of roadless lands on the Ochoco National Forest, which adds to its importance as habitat. (Also see the North Fork Crooked River entry in the Ochoco National Forest chapter.) Despite the rarity of forestlands (other than juniper forests) on BLM's holdings in eastern Oregon, the agency has not recommended Wilderness protection for the North Fork WSA.

BLM has decided instead that the 1257 acres of the WSA which have been identified as "commercial forest" shall be allocated to logging rather than Wilderness protection. The eight million board feet BLM thinks it could log every year is about the same volume as one timber sale on the Willamette National Forest. Incredible as it seems, BLM claims that if this dry, remote area were managed for timber it could produce a paltry five to ten board feet per acre per year.

One particularly attractive spot in the North Fork WSA is Lost Falls, where the Crooked River roars through a narrow basalt canyon over falls 15 feet high. About four miles inside the WSA (a mile down into the Crooked River Canyon and three miles up the river), Lost Falls (in Section 12 of T16S R21E) is a tempting and reasonable destination for a long day hike. It is also one of the finest swimming holes in the Ochocos, although you should check for obstructions before jumping through the falls.

The last two and a half miles before the falls require a lot of boulder-hopping and stream crossings, but they also include most of the big ponderosa pine. It takes a minimum of three hours each way to reach the falls, but you will doubtless want to take more. The best time to walk (and wade) the canyon is from July to early fall, when temperatures are warm and the river level low. Be sure to carry water (or purifying tablets at least—there are a lot of cows and campgrounds upstream). In the last mile before the falls, a couple of springs trickle down among the red-osier dogwood on the north side of the canyon.

The only way to enter the Wilderness Study Area is by hiking cross-country. The route described below should be considered a moderately difficult hike.

Teaters Ranch lies at the mouth of the canyon and provides the easiest access. However, it is private property, so permission must be obtained before crossing the ranch. (There is a locked gate a mile before the ranch.) The directions below describe how to enter the canyon entirely on BLM lands, from a gradual slope high above the river. The area is shown on both the Ochoco National Forest's and the BLM's Central Oregon Public Lands recreation maps, although neither map depicts the WSA boundaries.

GETTING THERE

From US Highway 26 on the east end of Prineville, turn south a quarter-mile west of the 20-mile post, at a sign for Paulina and Prineville Reservoir. Bear left at the next major junction (toward Post and Paulina, not Prineville Reservoir). Con-

Big ponderosa pine hug the canyon bottoms, while juniper forests predominate over most of the WSA.

tinue on the Crooked River Highway about 35 miles east of Prineville (or 21 miles west of Paulina), and turn north on a gravel road at a sign for Teaters Road west of the 35-mile post. In 4.5 miles Teaters Road forks. The right fork leads to Teaters Ranch, so bear left and stay on BLM Road 6578 all the way in. In another 1.4 miles bear right where BLM Road 6578A forks to the left, drive another 1.8 miles, and bear right again where BLM Road 6579 goes left. Drive another half-mile to a large Wilderness Study Area sign on the right. At this sign there is a box for visitor maps to the area, but don't count on there being any maps in it. If you don't have a high clearance vehicle, park here. Otherwise bear right at the sign and proceed downhill on an unmarked and unimproved dirt road. (There are some pretty meadows on the right.) Take the next major junction to the left in 1.8 miles, drive another half-mile and park. The entire route in requires opening (and closing, please) three barbed-wire fence gates.

RECOMMENDED
Committee Creek, which enters the North Fork Crooked River just upsteam from the Teaters Ranch, flows through the canyon just ahead of you. When you reach the crest of the hill (in the last half-mile), follow the ridge to your right (heading south) through a forest of western juniper. Contour downhill to Committee Creek, and then follow it downstream. In about a mile you will come to a narrow dirt road on the north bank of the Crooked River. Follow this road upstream along a small irrigation canal, as it turns into a trail and ends where the canyon narrows in a little over a half-mile. From here on the canyon walls

grow steep and lovely. Leave your hiking boots behind one of the big pines and don your old stream-wading tennis shoes. (Unless you go in very late summer, you're practically certain to get your feet wet.) It's another boulder-hopping 2.5 miles to Lost Falls along a little-disturbed riparian zone with benches of big ponderosa pine at most every bend. The long, deep canyon basin below Lost Falls is one of the best swimming holes around, and a good place to watch golden eagles while sunning on the rocks across from the waterfall. Do your swimming in mid-afternoon unless you like your baths colder than most.

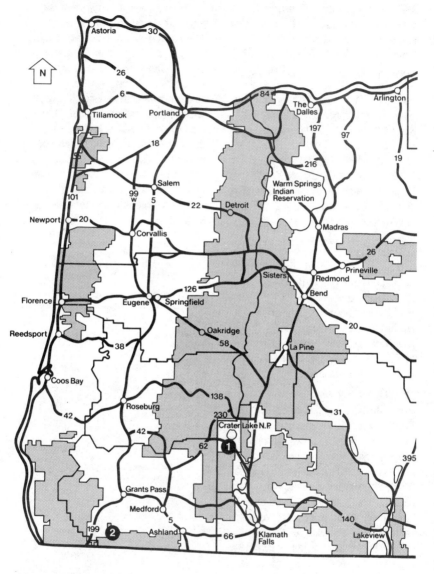

N

Astoria — 30

26

6

Tillamook — Portland

18

Salem
99 W — 5 — 22 — Detroit

Newport — 20

101

Corvallis

Florence — Eugene — Springfield — 126

Reedsport — 38

Oakridge

58

Coos Bay

Roseburg

42

42 — 138

230
Crater Lake N.P.

62

Grants Pass

Medford — 5

199 — Ashland — 66

84 — The Dalles — Arlington

197 — 97 — 19

216

Warm Springs
Indian
Reservation

Madras — 26

Prineville

Sisters — Redmond
Bend

20

La Pine

31

395

140

Klamath
Falls — Lakeview

0   28.1   56.2
1 inch = 56.2 miles

National Parks & Monuments

Oregon has not been blessed with the National Park and National Monument designations most other western states enjoy. (Our only National Park, Crater Lake, apparently had to be the eighth wonder of the world in order to qualify.) Oregon has one National Park, two Park Service National Monuments (Oregon Caves and John Day Fossil Beds), and Newberry National Volcanic Monument.

National Park Service-managed lands are administered within the Department of Interior. Newberry National Volcanic Monument, Oregon's newest monument, is Forest Service-managed and therefore part of the Department of Agriculture, which includes National Forests. The reason for so few National Park Service-managed lands is politics.

Regardless, outstanding examples of ancient forest groves can be found in these areas. In this brief chapter only two stands are identified, but future editions of the *Walking Guide* will undoubtedly contain more. Also, Oregon conservationists are working together with civic, business and community leaders, sportsmens' organizations and others to increase Oregon's National Park holdings. The Siskiyou–Klamath Mountains, Hells Canyon, Steens Mountain, Owyhee Canyonlands, Mount Hood and Newberry Crater are examples of landforms needing more protection that might best be provided by some kind of National Park designation. These decisions are being made today. And undoubtedly there will be an effort to expand Crater Lake National Park to the Greater Mount Mazama Ecosystem National Park.

Three National Forest recreation maps will make the following directions easier to follow: Rogue River and Winema (for Crater Lake) and Siskiyou (for Oregon Caves). Of course, Crater Lake National Park and Oregon Caves National Monument maps are available from the National Park Service (see Selected Agency Addresses & Phone Numbers, beginning on page 299) and will complement your trips nicely.

1. Crater Lake National Park

Drive through big ponderosa pine on the way to hike or ski through a cathedral grove of ancient mountain hemlocks.

Klamath County
USGS 7.5' CRATER LAKE WEST (1985)
UNION PEAK (1985)

ABOUT THE AREA
Oregon's only National Park contains relatively few examples of the state's famous ancient forests, as most of Mount Mazama—the great volcano which holds Crater Lake—is blanketed with high-elevation lodgepole pine forest. Stands of really big trees occur mostly at lower

elevations around the margins of the park, which underlines conservationists' contention that Crater Lake National Park, left alone in a sea of clearcuts, could not maintain a healthy and viable forest ecosystem. Still, the park contains several ancient forest groves worth visiting.

For more information about the park, including access to backcountry areas and seasonal conditions, contact the superintendent's office at 594-2211.

GETTING THERE

There are many routes to Crater Lake National Park, but you must enter the park on either Oregon Highway 62 (west and south entrances) or Oregon Highway 209 (north entrance).

RECOMMENDED

The finest, easily accessible old growth forest in the park is on the Pacific Crest Trail (PCT) south of Highway 62. The PCT crosses the highway 0.8 mile west of the turn-off to park headquarters. Walk south along the trail, which begins in lodgepole pine but quickly enters a two-mile long cathedral stand of mountain hemlock, with many trees three to four feet in diameter. If you have all day continue south to the Union Peak Trail, which leads to the top of that 7709' promontory and provides panoramic views from the southwest corner of the park. Please note that this section of the PCT is often snowbound well into summer. In some years you can ski it as late as May.

Along the Crater Lake rim, popular ski trails pass some massive mountain hemlocks and a lot of spectacular scenery. Below the rim of Mount Mazama, a few large old growth Shasta red fir and moun-

tain hemlock grow along Godfrey Glen Trail and Castle Crest Wildflower Trail (both short loops).

Stunning groves of ancient ponderosa pine and white fir inhabit the region near the south entrance to the park, which can be reached by short cross-country walks or on skis in winter. Two turn-outs on the east side of Highway 62 overlook Annie Creek Canyon in the area known as the Panhandle. One is about four and a half miles north of the south entrance, while the other is only a half-mile from the entrance. Stop at either turn-out and hike cross-county into the old growth forest on the west side of Highway 62 (in Sections 13 and 24 of T32S R6E). For cross-country skiing opportunities, look for a pull-out on the east side of Highway 62 approximately 2.5 miles north of the south entrance. A spur road across from this pull-out leads to large ponderosa pine and spectacular white fir.

The most extensive ancient forests in Crater Lake National Park are the ponderosa pine groves in the seldom-visited backcountry areas north of Mount Scott, on the extreme east side of the park. At Desert Creek (Section 34, T29S R6E), a cigar-shaped meadow surrounded by big ponderosa pine provides an exciting cross-country trek off FS Road 2308 (on the Winema National Forest).

2. Oregon Caves National Monument

Ancient mixed-evergreen forest along three scenic loop trails.

Josephine County
USGS 7.5' OREGON CAVES (1986)

ABOUT THE AREA

The forest along the trails recommended below includes Douglas-fir and white fir trees three to six feet in diameter.

Be forewarned: Beyond the National Monument boundary, Forest Service clearcuts along the trails are only minimally buffered. Call Oregon Caves National Monument (592-2100) for maps, information about hiking, and weather conditions in the area.

GETTING THERE

Take US Highway 199 to Cave Junction; then follow Oregon Highway 46 approximately 20 miles southeast to Oregon Caves National Monument and the parking area.

RECOMMENDED

The monument's nicest ancient forest is along the 3.3-mile Big Tree Loop Trail, which passes a Douglas-fir 13' 1" in diameter near its halfway point. This tree is estimated to be between 1200 and 1500 years old, and many believe it's the largest Douglas-fir in Oregon (see also page 242). Other old conifers on the Big Tree Trail include white fir, Port-Orford-cedar and incense-cedar.

Begin the trail above the Chalet (gift shop) and take the loop trail to the right (two miles to Big Tree) to enter the older forest. This trail begins at 4000' and switchbacks up a moderately steep grade, but to compensate it also passes through wildflower-filled meadows. A half-mile before Big Tree is a trail to the right for Mount Elijah and Bigelow Lakes. It is

2.4 miles to Mount Elijah, but only a mile and a half to a nice grove of ancient Port-Orford-cedar on the west side of the smaller Bigelow Lake. (This is east of the trail, on the east side of Section 14, T40S R6W. Consult the Siskiyou National Forest recreation map.)

Fine examples of the area's diverse mixed-evergreen old growth forests can also be seen along Cliff, No Name and Caves Creek Trails, all of which start from the monument headquarters.

This big Douglas-fir tree, located at Oregon Caves National Monument, measures over 13 feet in diameter and may be the largest in the state.

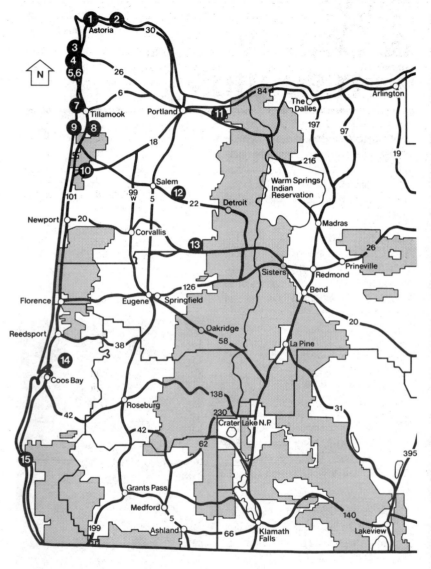

N

1 Astoria   2   30

3
4
5,6   26

6
7 Tillamook   Portland   11   84   The Dalles   Arlington
9 8   197   97   19

18   216

10   Salem   12   Warm Springs
101   99   5   22   Detroit   Indian
w   Reservation
Newport   20   Madras
Corvallis   13   26
Sisters   Redmond   Prineville
126   Bend
Florence   Eugene   Springfield
20
Reedsport   Oakridge   58   La Pine
38
14
Coos Bay
138   31
42   Roseburg   230
Crater Lake N.P.
42   62   395
15
Grants Pass
Medford   140
5   Klamath   Lakeview
199   Ashland   66   Falls

0   28.1   56.2
1 inch = 56.2 miles

State & County Forestlands

Although most of Oregon's public lands are federally managed, some of its most valuable public forestlands are in state or county ownership. Often these are parks or other special lands which have long been recognized for their unique or outstanding characteristics, such as their big, old trees.

County and state government, as well as municipalities, need to be encouraged to protect these areas, and to be congratulated for such efforts. (It can be particularly effective to point out to local politicians and civic leaders the economic benefits of protecting old trees or groves.) Often it is easy to ignore or otherwise take for granted these more localized treasures. And yet, more threatened ancient forests on state, county and city lands that need to be identified by local citizens and rescued from the chainsaw.

The astute reader will notice that a few examples of old growth forests on state lands are included in earlier "federal" chapters. This is because of their proximity to those lands and convenience for the visitor. In particular, please see the Deschutes National Forest (Oregon's Biggest Ponderosa Pine entry) and Umatilla National Forest (Umatilla Ancient Forest Auto Tours, Bridge Creek Wildlife Management Area entry) chapters.

Your Oregon state highway map will provide all the information necessary for directions to the following entries' locations.

1. City of Astoria, Urban Forest City Park (proposed)

A 700-acre grove containing 250-year-old western hemlock and a few 650-year-old Sitka spruce.

Clatsop County
USGS 7.5' ASTORIA (1984)

ABOUT THE AREA
Together with a few small forest groves further south, the surviving big old trees in this "Museum Grove" directly above downtown Astoria provide vital diversity in one of the most heavily clearcut counties in western Oregon. Some of these rare timber stands outside Astoria provide critical nesting and roosting areas for bald eagles of the lower Columbia River. After Astoria conservationists collected 700 local citizens' signatures opposing the logging of this and nearby old growth groves, the city council orga-

A few Sitka spruce were somehow spared in the frenzy to supply raw materials for airplane construction during World War I.

nized a citizens' committee to devise management recommendations for these relic ancient forest stands. At this writing, the fate of the groves is still undecided, as the city now wants to salvage trees which fell during a recent windstorm, following logging on adjacent state lands. (Salvage logging is an insidious threat to ancient forest ecosystem health.) See also the description for the Tongue Point entry which follows in this chapter.

GETTING THERE
Take US Highway 30 or US Highway 101 to Astoria. Follow the main street of town (Marine Drive) to 16th Street, and turn south at a sign for Clatsop Community College. Proceed uphill for several blocks and turn left on Irving Street. Drive three-quarters of a mile east and

park at a pull-off on the left, two houses west of (before) the sign for 28th Street on the right. From the street sign, an otherwise unmarked trail follows a water pipe up the hill to the biggest spruce trees. The pipe is wide enough to serve as a bridge over some of the smaller rivulets.

RECOMMENDED
Follow the trail uphill about a quarter-mile to the Cathedral Tree, an enormous old Sitka spruce quite popular locally. The giant has a passage through its base, evidence of the long-decayed nurse log on which its life began.

After seeing this grove you may want to follow signs up the hill to the Astoria Column. Constructed in 1926, the 164-step column commemorates "the winning of the West" and the "settlement and civilization of the Sunset Empire." Of course, Clatsop County's biggest and best monuments of spruce, cedar and Douglas-fir were all cut as the West was "won." The column of concrete proudly towers over a headland with a commanding view of today's "managed forest," as well as the Columbia River, Pacific Ocean and coast mountains beyond.

While on the subject of settlement and civilization, you might also be interested in the Fort Clatsop National Memorial, east of Astoria. The National Park Service's very worthwhile exhibit presents the early 19th century history of the north coast in a near-natural setting along the Lewis and Clark River, among a few large Sitka spruce. Fort Clatsop includes a visitor center, a replica of the original fort, and nature trails with signs identifying the area's common tree and plant species.

2. Tongue Point

Oregon's northernmost ancient forest grove, which provides critical habitat for bald eagles and other sensitive species.

Clatsop County
USGS 7.5' ASTORIA (1984)

ABOUT THE AREA

Tongue Point is a 150-acre peninsula in the Columbia River just east of Astoria, presently owned by the Job Corps (US Department of Labor), which occupies an old Naval station on the Point's southern end. The little-developed northern end of Tongue Point, which harbors ancient Sitka spruce, Douglas-fir, western hemlock and bigleaf maple, has been proposed for transfer to the US Fish and Wildlife Service because of the critical habitat this remnant old growth forest provides for wintering and nesting bald eagles. Because of the area's special biological values, public access to the area is understandably restricted. Organized groups will probably have better luck receiving permission to visit Tongue Point than will individuals. To obtain permission to enter the area, contact the Director of the Job Corps Center at Tongue Point (325-2131).

GETTING THERE

Turn north off Highway 30 near the 95-mile post and a flashing yellow light at a sign for Tongue Point. Proceed 0.4 mile to the Job Corp Center security entrance. A half-mile past the security station, bear right at a fork and immediately turn left on Tongue Point Street, beside "Residence 3." Park at the end of the paved road in 0.2 mile.

RECOMMENDED

An old military road, now a wide trail, continues north around the point and leads to old growth-topped rock cliffs on the northwest end of Tongue Point. While the area is essentially natural, abandoned military bunkers are common everywhere. The Navy managed to build these installations with little effect on most of the Point's old growth eagle trees.

To reach the heart of the grove, bear left after walking the first 100 yards of the trail. A road leads uphill, switchbacking past bunkers to the top of the cliff. When you arrive at an enormous spruce tree on the right, head directly uphill to the ridgeline and the top of the cliff face.

Where guns and other military fortifications protected us from an ocean invasion during World War II, a few big firs and spruce still stand guard at Tongue Point near the mouth of the Columbia River. Bleached white stumps with spring holes as eyes, scattered over the landscape of Clatsop County, appear like little white crosses in a military cemetery as memorials to their fallen brethren.

3. Tillamook Head

A 7.5-mile trail along headlands from   *Clatsop County*
Seaside to Cannon Beach.   USGS 7.5' TILLAMOOK HEAD (1973)

ABOUT THE AREA

This strip of ancient coastal forest is known as the Elmer Feldenheimer Forest Preserve. The inscription on a plaque at the trailhead laments the loss of the area's ancient forests, as the preserve was dedicated to "... the return of Tillamook Head to its pristine state, as it was when so richly endowed by Lewis and Clark with our nation's history." Indeed, the trail to the 1130' summit of Tillamook Head follows the route taken in January 1806 by members of the Lewis and Clark Expedition en route to Cannon Beach for oil and blubber from a beached whale. The big spruce trees along the trail not only predate that expedition, but are also among the few of their kind remaining in all of Clatsop County. (See also the Ecola State Park entry which follows, for information about the southern end of the trail and the Feldenheimer Forest Preserve.)

GETTING THERE

Take US Highway 101 to the south end of Seaside. Turn west on Avenue U at a sign for "beach access," across from a Shell gas station. In a quarter-mile turn left on South Edgewood Road, which leads south along the beach as Sunset Boulevard. Drive to the trailhead in the parking area at the road's end.

RECOMMENDED

This trail is steep, so be sure to wear suitable boots or heavy shoes during the rainy season. Small groves of very large Sitka spruce and western hemlock are scattered along the first two miles of the trail. In a mile and a half you'll come to an old clearcut, but keep going; in another quarter-mile you will re-enter the old growth forest and encounter a scenic viewpoint overlooking the western tip of Tillamook Head.

Relatively close to Cannon Beach, at Klootchy Creek County Park, is an enormous Sitka spruce, billed as the "largest in the U.S." It is more than 52' in circumference. When you read the signs about the former Crown Zellerbach's graciousness in sparing this tree, remind yourself what they did to virtually the entire remaining ancient forest watershed of which this admittedly magnificent specimen was a part. Klootchy Creek County Park is just north of US Highway 26, one and a half miles east of the junction of Highway 26 and Highway 101.

4. Ecola State Park

*Scenic coastline hike passing several
big Sitka spruce.*

Clatsop County
USGS 7.5' TILLAMOOK HEAD (1973)

ABOUT THE AREA
Between Tillamook Head on the north
and Cannon Beach on the south, this
lovely and easily reached state park is
close to some prime specimens of our
temperate rainforest. This forest community, dominated by Sitka spruce,
western red-cedar and western hemlock,
blanketed the Pacific Northwest coast
from Brookings to Juneau a hundred and
fifty years ago.

GETTING THERE
Take US Highway 26 or US Highway
101 to Cannon Beach. On the north end
of the City of Cannon Beach, follow
signs for Ecola Creek State Park about
2.5 miles to the day use parking area,
bearing left where the right fork leads to
Indian Beach.

RECOMMENDED
At the east end of the parking area, walk
north across a mowed lawn to the trailhead
for the Pacific Coast Trail, which is
marked by a small sign for Indian Beach.
After half-mile, just over the first hill,
you enter a small but lovely grove of
large spruce, actually in Feldenheimer
State Park. It is 1.5 miles to Indian Beach
via the trail, but in summer you can also
take the road to Indian Beach (it's closed
in winter) to reach the old growth along
the trail. Another option is to walk through
the ancient forest along the road to the
parking area. A trail into the forest begins
at a gate on the left 0.7 mile from the
entrance.

If you want to take a longer hike, continue up the Pacific Coast Trail to
Tillamook Head (see the preceding entry
in this chapter). Most of the big trees are
at the northern end of the trail, near
Tillamook Head. Still, this southern part
of the trail is less steep at the start, and it
offers the best coastline views.

5. Oswald West State Park (North)

*A steep, 2.5-mile section of the Oregon
Coast Trail which winds among the only
ancient forest left in Clatsop County east
of Highway 101.*

Clatsop County
USGS 7.5' ARCH CAPE (1985)

ABOUT THE AREA
Though they were spared the chainsaw,
many of the old growth trees in this area
succumbed to a major windstorm in 1981.
While these fallen giants might have
served vital ecological functions on the
forest floor for another 500 years, Oregon
State Park officials chose to salvage them.
Besides leaving long-lasting scars on the
land, this logging is evidence that, even
in Oregon's state parks, surviving old
growth forests are not protected as ecosystems. (See also the following entry
for Oswald West State Park–South, for
information about the more heavily developed and visited portion of the park.)

GETTING THERE
Take US Highway 101 south from Cannon Beach or north from Manzanita.

RECOMMENDED
From the north: Just north of the Highway 101 tunnel at the community of Arch Cape, turn on Arch Cape Mill Road. Bear left (east) on Webb Avenue (unmarked) and drive a half-mile. The trailhead is marked by a small "trail" sign on a gray 8" x 8" post on the right. Park wherever you can. The trail begins in a private driveway, crosses a small suspension bridge which spans Cape Arch Creek, and then climbs to the forest above. For five miles, the trail traverses an old coastal rain forest of spruce and hemlock to Cape Falcon. This trail can be reached from other points to the south.

From the south: Drive to just north of the 37-mile marker on Highway 101 (also north of the Clatsop/Tillamook County line). Park on the east side of the highway near a black-and-white banded gate, across from a log skid road that marks the trailhead. Just south of and across Highway 101 from the gate, a gray 8" x 8" post marks the Oregon Coast Trail south to the beachfront portion of Oswald West State Park in Tillamook County.

You can reach the same trail from a bit further south and avoid the steep sections, though you'll miss some great ancient forest. Turn west off Highway 101 at a sign for Cove Beach and Falcon Cove onto a country road. The Oregon Coast Trail crosses this road 200 feet west of Highway 101. This crossing is not signed and there is barely parking for one car. Large trees are scattered along this part of the trail.

Rhododendrons provide a show of color in many of Oregon's ancient forests. (Photo by Diane Kelsay)

6. Oswald West State Park (South)

Super old growth spruce, hemlock and cedar
overlooking a breathtaking Pacific cove.

Tillamook County
USGS 7.5' ARCH CAPE (1985)

ABOUT THE AREA

In addition to spectacular cliffs and beaches, the southern section of Oswald West State Park contains one of the most magnificent ancient forest groves in northwest Oregon. It is a prime example of the original coastal rainforest, and a great place to take the kids for the day or an easy overnight stay.

GETTING THERE

Take US Highway 101 south from Cannon Beach or north from Manzanita. There are two parking areas on the west side of the highway.

RECOMMENDED

Half-mile paved trails lead to the beach from the parking areas and connect them.

A dramatic coastline trail continues north to Cape Falcon, Falcon Cove and beyond. (See the description for the preceding entry for Oswald West State Park–North.) To the south, the Oregon Coast Trail crosses a suspension bridge just before the beach. Follow the route of an old Indian trail along the coast and up the hill to Neahkahnie Punchbowl (in two miles). Legend has it Spanish treasure is buried nearby, and that strangely worked rocks point the way to this bounty. The trail crosses Highway 101 and passes through more alder and mature rainforest. About five miles from the suspension bridge this historic Indian trail rises to the top of 1700' Neahkanie Mountain for an awesome view of the Oregon Coast.

7. Cape Meares State Park

Giant old growth Sitka spruce grace this
promontory.

Tillamook County
USGS 7.5' NETARTS (1986)

ABOUT THE AREA

The once-extensive ancient forest west and south of Tillamook Bay has been reduced to a few tiny remnant stands, one of which keeps watch from the state park on Cape Meares. With the accelerated clearcutting (for export, and years ahead of schedule) of second growth "forests" on private lands in the Oregon Coast Range, this is not an easy area to visit. But the loop trail in the remaining forest on Cape Meares does have its highlights.

GETTING THERE

Drive to either Tillamook or Cloverdale.

A number of possible routes will take you to either town, which are both on US Highway 101. From Highway 101 in downtown Tillamook, turn west on Third Street, opposite Oregon Highway 6 (which leads east to Portland). Drive two miles, turn right on Bay Ocean Road, and follow the Cape Meares and Three Capes Scenic Route signs for another seven miles. Park in the lot at Cape Meares State Park.

From Highway 101 at Cloverdale, turn west for Pacific City and drive north, following signs for Three Capes Scenic

Route to the northernmost of the three capes.

RECOMMENDED

As you turn into the park, look for the trailhead immediately at the turn, beside a Cape Meares National Wildlife Refuge sign. The trail soon passes several enormous Sitka spruce. Walk a little further to "Big Spruce," one of the largest known examples of the species. Though its crown is broken, this primeval monarch still reigns over an ancient forest dominion as old and diminished as the British Empire. From the gigantic spruce, the trail soon loops north, then back south, arriving at the parking area. It then heads southeast to the "Octopus Tree." This unique spruce lacks a central trunk, but its limbs, three to five feet thick, branch out close to the ground.

Large ancient Sitka spruce, Picea sitchensis, *which once blanketed coastal forests to the edge of the sea, are now confined mostly to state parks west of US Highway 101.*

8. Munson Creek Falls County Park

Two quarter-mile trails to the highest waterfall in the Coast Range.

Tillamook County
USGS 7.5' BEAVER (1985)

ABOUT THE AREA

Upper and lower trails, beginning only 1.6 miles from US Highway 101, lead through a beautiful little box canyon lined with ancient fir and cedar to 266' Munson Creek Falls. Old growth red alders festooned with moss help give the Munson Creek trails a real feeling of the coastal rainforest.

GETTING THERE

Take US Highway 101 to about 6.5 miles south of Tillamook, just north of the 73-mile post. Turn east and follow the signs for Munson Creek Falls County Park.

RECOMMENDED

The upper trail includes a series of wooden stairs and boardwalks that allow you to traverse the steep canyon walls.

9. Cape Lookout State Park

Huge Sitka spruce and western hemlock below and along the cape.

Tillamook County
USGS 7.5' SAND LAKE (1985)

ABOUT THE AREA

Cape Lookout is the middle and longest of the three capes on the Three Capes Scenic Route. The ocean surrounds and the salt air shapes this ancient forest headland.

GETTING THERE

Drive to either Tillamook or Cloverdale. A number of possible routes will take you to either town, which are both on US Highway 101. From Highway 101 in downtown Tillamook, turn west on Third Street, opposite Oregon Highway 6 (which leads east to Portland). Drive two miles, turn right on Bay Ocean Road, and follow the Three Capes Scenic Route signs. Coming from the north, drive three miles south of the first turn-off for Cape Lookout State Park day use and camping area, as the trail to the big trees starts at Cape Lookout itself.

From Highway 101 at Cloverdale, turn west for Pacific City and drive north, following signs for Three Capes Scenic Route to Cape Lookout. From either direction, the turn-off for Cape Lookout is clearly marked at the top of a hill.

RECOMMENDED

Two trails, each about 2.5 miles long, start from the west end of the parking area. The left trail is more heavily used. It leads to the end of the cape and spectacular vistas of the coast. Several large spruce grow north of the trail in the lower, relatively sheltered areas.

Most of the big trees are on the upper portion (the section nearest the parking lot) of the trail to the right. This trail descends, steeply in places, to the beach and day use area.

10. Van Duzer State Park

A few big old trees along a narrow scenic highway corridor.

Lincoln County
USGS 7.5' DOLPH (1985)

ABOUT THE AREA

This is one small but beautiful island of ancient forest in a sea of clearcuts. It's a great place to stop and eat your lunch among the big trees, but the corridor is so narrow you can't escape the sounds of highway traffic. Try visiting on a weekday for a bit more seclusion.

GETTING THERE

The Van Duzer Forest Corridor Wayside is on Oregon Highway 18, roughly midway between Willamina and US

Highway 101. The picnic area is at the western end of the scenic corridor, 0.3 mile west of the 10-mile post on Highway 18.

RECOMMENDED

For a brief but pleasant taste of older forest, drive exactly one mile east of the Van Duzer State Park entrance and 0.4 mile east of the Lincoln/Tillamook County line. Park at a pull-out on the south side of the highway. A short trail leads to a swimming hole beneath big trees along the Salmon River.

Just across the road, another pull-out indicates the start of a short jeep trail. This track heads east and narrows in a

hundred yards, but leads through large old growth Douglas-fir. A pair of brush clippers will be of use if you wish to venture far.

11. Oxbow Park, Sandy River Gorge

Ancient forest close to the Portland metropolitan area.

Multnomah County
USGS 7.5' WASHOUGAL (WA) (1975)
SANDY (1985)

ABOUT THE AREA

The steep walls of the Sandy River Gorge protected one small part of the low-elevation ancient forest in the lower (northern) Willamette Valley from logging. This modest grove of fine old growth trees, on the south bank of the Sandy River in Multnomah County's Oxbow Park, is east to reach.

It is not quite so easy to reach the more spectacular ancient forest on portions of the 400-acre Sandy River Gorge Outstanding Natural Area (ONA), managed by the Salem District of the Bureau of Land Management. The ONA is upstream of Oxbow Park, below Dodge Park and across the river from (east of) Indian John Island. Some of the trees in the Sandy River Gorge ONA are more than 500 years old.

GETTING THERE

Take I-84 to Exit 16A for Wood Village and Gresham. Drive 2.6 miles south on the road which starts as NE 238th, becomes SE 242nd, then continues as NE Hagan. At the intersection of NE Hagan and Division, turn left on Division and drive seven miles east, out of Gresham, following signs for Oxbow Park.

RECOMMENDED

It will cost you $2 to drive into Oxbow Park, but no fee is required if you park at the entrance and bicycle or hike to the grove. The old growth trees are 1.3 miles inside the park on both sides of the main road. A trail to the grove parallels the road from the park entrance. (Obtain a map provided at the entrance to help with the following instructions.)

The trail through the old growth Douglas-fir, western red-cedar and bigleaf maple begins at Area D. Small trails to the right head steeply uphill into the heart of the grove. For an easy half-mile loop, walk south on the main trail to Area F, cross the road at the group picnic ground, and head back (north) upstream through more big trees along the Sandy River. An old jeep trail leads back into the woods.

One way to reach the Sandy River Gorge ONA is to raft or canoe the six-mile stretch between Dodge Park and Oxbow Park. This portion of the Sandy River is Class II (easy rapids). It can run at 1200 to 3000 cubic feet per second (cfs) during the winter and spring. To get to Dodge Park, drive to Powell Valley Road and follow signs to the park.

12. Silver Falls State Park

Several miles of trails through old growth Douglas-fir three to four feet in diameter, only 25 miles east of Salem.

Marion County
USGS 7.5' LYONS (1985)
STOUT MTN. (1985)

ABOUT THE AREA

Most of the ancient forest in Silver Falls State Park was "highgraded" (the biggest, best trees were removed) years ago, but the upper (southern) end of the park still contains extensive, open stands of large trees. Unfortunately, the big trees do not live along the popular North and South Falls–Silver Creek Canyon trail. Evidence of logging is apparent on the trails described below, but there is a positive side to it: the park's old logging roads lead you to fine examples of how much better managed and structurally diverse our public and private forests would be if they were selectively logged rather than clearcut. The trails listed below are between Silver Falls State Park and Howard Creek Camp, so directions to Howard Creek Camp are included.

GETTING THERE

From I-5 at Salem, take Oregon High-

way 22 east to Oregon Highway 214. Drive northeast on Highway 214, following signs for Silver Falls. If you're coming from further north on I-5, you can get on Highway 214 at Woodburn. Either way, turn east off Highway 214 at the 25-mile post and follow the conference center signs for a mile and a half.

RECOMMENDED

A trail into the old growth forest begins between the conference center's dining hall and meeting hall. After crossing a footbridge, the trail forks. The left fork ("Jogging Trail") is the southern end of a 3.1-mile loop running trail. It follows Smith Creek two miles to the north, past huge old growth Douglas-fir and western hemlock. You can also reach the jogging trail from the north at Howard Creek Camp.

The right fork after the bridge ("Equestrian Trail") leads to a system of un-

Although most of Silver Falls State Park's biggest trees are not found along trails passing the waterfalls, no seeker of Oregon's natural wonders should miss this experience. (Photo by Diane Kelsay)

groomed horse trails which weave beneath big trees along the ridges. You can make a loop on the horse trails through the less-visited portion of Silver Falls Park, and some of the biggest trees. Walk a steep half-mile, take a left at the first junction, and bear left at all major junctions. You will descend to the jogging trail just before some big old trees at Howard Creek Camp.

The turn-off for Howard Creek Camp is just a half-mile south of the Silver Falls State Park turn-off on Oregon Highway 214. Look for a Howard Creek sign and a road to the west. A closed gate may block the road in winter, but you can park at the gate and find the running trail. It runs parallel to the road and is covered with wood chips. The big trees are just ahead on this trail.

13. Cascadia State Park

A short trail to a lovely waterfall, through the lowest ancient forest grove left in the South Santiam River drainage.

Linn County
USGS 7.5' CASCADIA (1985)

ABOUT THE AREA
The attractions at Cascadia State Park include a pleasant picnic area, a campground and good river access, all beneath a canopy of old growth Douglas-fir. Lichen-covered Pacific yew and lush undergrowth hint at the temperate rainforest that once covered these low-elevation foothills of the Oregon Cascades.

GETTING THERE
Take US Highway 20 east of Sweet Home and west of Sisters. Note your mileage as you pass the Sweet Home Ranger Station; drive another 16.4 miles east, and turn north one-third mile east of the 41-mile post.

RECOMMENDED
Take the three-quarter-mile trail to Soda Creek Falls. This trail emerges above a rock headwall and follows the stream gradually up, past a few enormous Douglas-fir and some good-sized western red-cedar, western hemlock and bigleaf maple.

14. Gold and Silver Falls State Park

Old growth Douglas-fir, myrtlewood, bigleaf maple and red alder along trails to two dramatic waterfalls.

Coos County
USGS 15' IVERS PEAK (1955)

ABOUT THE AREA
The trees in this small state park are practically all that remains of the ancient forests which once blanketed this 25-mile-long valley. And were it not for two beautiful waterfalls at the headwaters of the Coos River, even these trees would long ago have been cut and sawed, chipped or peeled.

After countless generations of existence, the virgin coastal forest was destroyed in less than a human lifetime. As one example among many, this part of Oregon will never again be the "Timber Capital of the World." Instead, Oregon's economy must diversify, with emphasis on fisheries, tourism and other resources dependent on ancient forests.

GETTING THERE
Take US Highway 101 to the southern end of Coos Bay. Turn east at a sign for Coos River and Allegany on the Coos River Highway (County Route 48). Follow signs for Allegany for 15 miles, and then signs for Gold and Silver Falls for a total of 25 miles along the Coos River.

RECOMMENDED
The two lower trails are the shortest and easiest routes to the falls. They are, consequently, the more heavily traveled. But the upper trail leads to both falls and open rocky cliffs, and offers you an uncommon bird's-eye view of the older forest.

15. Humbug Mountain State Park

A three-mile hike to the top of 1756'
Humbug Mountain, where giant
Douglas-fir meet the sea.

Curry County
USGS 7.5' PORT ORFORD (1986)

ABOUT THE AREA
This is the last uncut old growth grove along a huge stretch of the Pacific Coast—from the Cummins Creek Wilderness north of Florence to the Redwood National Park south of Crescent City, California. In addition to Douglas-fir more than five feet in diameter, the Humbug Mountain Trail boasts small fern-lined creeks, large grand fir, old growth myrtlewood, tanoak, bigleaf maple, western hemlock, western red-cedar, madrone and rhododendron.

GETTING THERE
Take US Highway 101 six miles south of Port Orford and 21 miles north of Gold Beach. Watch for a sign for "Humbug Mt. Trail Parking" near a flashing yellow traffic light. The trailhead is on the west side of Highway 101.

RECOMMENDED
The first mile of this trail is the steepest: then it rises gradually for occasional ocean views. An opening at the summit faces west over a small rocky meadow.

Due to the abundance and diversity of broadleaf and coniferous tree and bush species, a walk up Humbug Mountain demonstrates why this is called a "mixed-evergreen" forest.

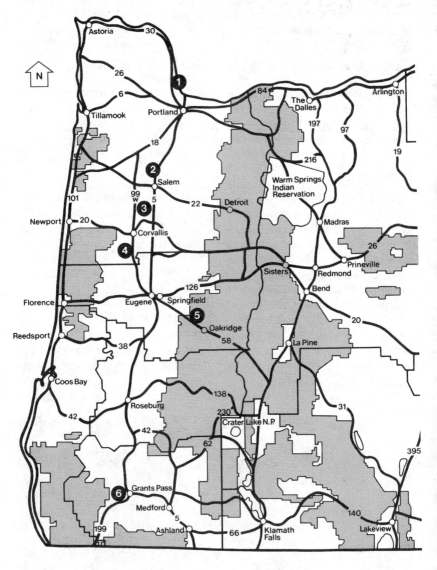

N

Astoria — 30
26
6
Tillamook
Portland ① 84 The Dalles Arlington
18 197 97
55 216 19
② Salem
99 22 Warm Springs
w 5 Detroit Indian Reservation
③ Madras
Newport — 20
Corvallis 26
④ Prineville
Sisters Redmond
101 Bend
Florence 126
Eugene Springfield 20
⑤ Oakridge
Reedsport 58 La Pine
38
138 31
Coos Bay 230
Roseburg Crater Lake N.P.
42 395
42 62
⑥ Grants Pass 140
Medford Lakeview
199 5
Ashland 66 Klamath
Falls

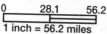

0   28.1   56.2
1 inch = 56.2 miles

Broadleaf Forests

This final chapter of the *Walking Guide* highlights several impressive examples of old growth broadleaf forest stands. The ancient forests controversy has centered almost exclusively on conifers, which is understandable given the majestic and vast evergreen forests which dominate the Pacific Northwest landscape. But while most ancient forest battles have and will continue to focus on conifers, Oregon contains some remarkable groves of old growth broadleaf trees you don't want to miss.

It is often difficult to draw that thin line between trees and shrubs, and the distinction is exacerbated when dealing with broadleaf trees. This chapter features several well-known deciduous species such as black cottonwood, quaking aspen, vine maple, red alder, madrone, white oak and others. These groves are found on federal, state and county lands. A list of common Oregon trees (19 broadleaf species and 29 conifers) referenced in the *Walking Guide* follows this chapter.

An Oregon highway map will provide the necessary information to locate these places. A map of the William L. Finley National Wildlife Refuge, available at the refuge headquarters and displayed on several bulletin boards, will enhance your trip there.

1. Sauvie Island Wildlife Management Area

Superb examples of old growth black cottonwood, Oregon ash and Oregon white oak, survivors of the unique lowland forests of the Willamette River Valley.

Columbia and Multnomah Counties
USGS 7.5' ST. HELENS (1970)

ABOUT THE AREA

Only ten miles from downtown Portland, Sauvie Island's forests, fields and wetlands shelter some 250 species of resident or visiting birds. During peak migrations, over 150,000 ducks and geese and several thousand sandhill cranes stop over on the island. The great blue heron is common year-round; more than 100 individuals have been counted feeding on Sturgeon Lake at one time.

Most of the northern half of the Sauvie Island Wildlife Management Area is publicly owned and managed by the Oregon Department of Fish and Wildlife (ODFW), which maintains an office on the island where maps, bird lists and general information are available. Two walks in the old growth broadleaf forests are recommended below, but perhaps the best way to see the unspoiled side of Sauvie Island's forests is by canoe. ODFW requires wildlife area parking permits for the trailheads noted below. Daily permits cost $2.50. Annual

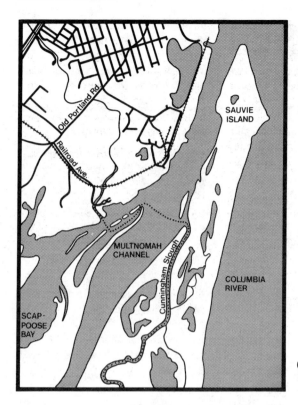

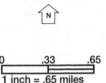

SAUVIE ISLAND.
Travel by boat for the best
way to see wildlife. Be
especially careful as you
cross the Multnomah
Channel (see text pages
283-284).

permits are $10. Both are available in Portland and from stores on the island. Call ODFW at 229-5403 for more information.

GETTING THERE

Take US Highway 30 west from Portland, following signs for Astoria and Saint Helens. Before the eleven-mile post, turn right across the Sauvie Island bridge over Multnomah Channel, and continue straight ahead (north) for two miles on Sauvie Island Road to Reeder Road. Turn right on Reeder Road. (The ODFW office is on Sauvie Island Road, just past the junction with Reeder Road.)

RECOMMENDED

Two ancient forest trails are especially nice.

Oak Island: Outstanding groves of Oregon white oak thrive along the west shore of Sturgeon Lake. Drive 1.25 miles east on Reeder Road. Turn left on Oak Island Road; drive three miles on pavement and another 0.9 mile on gravel over a dike to a "Y." To launch a boat in Sturgeon Lake, bear right at the "Y" and drive a half-mile to the lake. Otherwise, bear left at the "Y" and continue another 0.4 mile to a parking area. Take the middle trail (a jeep road closed to vehicles) leading north. In a quarter-mile, after a cattle guard, bear right and walk to the shore of Sturgeon Lake. Here you can circle the lakeshore or walk directly into a shaded and inviting oak forest. There are several connecting trails in the area, which allow up to a three-mile loop back to your vehicle. (Note: During hunting season—about mid-October to mid-January—Oak Island is closed to entry except by permit. Check with ODFW for details.)

Columbia River (north unit): A trail along the big river's shoreline winds through old growth black cottonwood, Oregon ash and willow on the extreme northern end of Sauvie Island. Drive 13 miles east on Reeder Road to the end of both the road and the island. (The last 2.25 miles of Reeder Road are gravel.)

Cross a cow pasture (one of the less pristine parts of the area) and walk north along the Columbia River's shore. It is 3.5 miles to the tip of the island. Unofficial trails wind to the left, past lakes, sloughs and more big broadleaf trees, implying the appearance Sauvie Island

might have had in the early years of white settlement, when Laurent Sauvé ran a dairy farm to supply milk to Fort Vancouver. Of course, "Sauvé's" island had been home for centuries to Native Americans, who lived in the largest permanent settlement discovered by Lewis and Clark in the Northwest.

Cunningham Slough (boat access): For one of the island's best "wilderness" experiences, paddle a canoe up Cunningham Slough, which is also in the Wildlife Management Area's North Unit. On US Highway 30 West, drive 17 miles west of the Sauvie Island bridge to Saint Helens. Take the first possible right turn after the city limits sign on Gable Road. Drive a half-mile, cross the railroad tracks and turn right on Railroad Avenue. Drive another half-mile and park off the road just before the bridge over a small slough, Milton Creek.

It's easy to launch a canoe on the upstream side of the bridge, among some industrial debris. Paddle downstream 0.1 mile to what may appear to be the river's

Oregon white oaks, Quercus garryana, with diameters of only 20 inches are easily 200 years old.

main channel. Cross it by steering directly perpendicular to the opposite shore, then slip between two islands into a more protected channel. Head north (downstream) for about a quarter-mile, to the end of Cathlacom Point (now the peninsula to your right). You now face the widest part of the Multnomah Channel. Keep an eye out for river traffic, especially speedboats, as you cross the river. Again, steer directly across (perpendicular to) the current. The east shore ahead is

Sauvie Island. A smaller island, Louse Island, hugs Sauvie Island's shore. The entrance to Cunningham Slough is just north of the southern tip of Louse Island (see map on page 282). This channel, several miles long, remains much the way Lewis and Clark first saw these forested and wildlife-filled wetlands, engulfed by big, overhanging ash trees—a startling contrast to the urban world just beyond.

2. Willamette Mission State Park

Forested sloughs of the Willamette River await discovery by canoe.

Marion County
USGS 7.5' MISSION BOTTOM

ABOUT THE AREA

About half of this park's 2000 acres are covered by a natural forest of large maples, cottonwoods, willows and ash. You can still see some of the old Willamette River's many channels among the forest, filbert orchards and grasslands. One deep channel now forms two long, slender lakes.

Willamette Mission Park is actually comprised of two units, one on each bank of the Willamette. They are discussed here as the "East Bank" and "West Bank" Units, even though the way the river bends they might just as well be called the "south" and "north" units. (This is going to seem a little complicated; the map on page 285 should help.) The Wheatland Ferry divides the park, with the East Bank Unit (upstream) to the south and the West Bank Unit (downstream) to the north. The East Bank Unit is developed and bounded on the south by Windsor Island Slough, while the

West Bank Unit is undeveloped and lies north of Lambert Slough. Wheatland Ferry and Spring Valley Access (which is a couple of miles upriver from the West Bank Unit) make the entire park area very accessible to the canoeist. Although Wheatland Ferry and Spring Valley Access are only a couple of highway miles apart, they provide several miles of easy slough and river paddling through one of the Willamette's nicest forested areas.

In the East Bank Unit, the largest black cottonwood in the world (155' tall and 26' 3" in circumference) towers over the stagnant shores of one old river channel. When the monarch was discovered to be a record tree, the State Parks Division laid a neat gravel trail to its base and planted a grassy lawn in its massive shadow. A being so symbolic of the once-wild valley forest could not be left undomesticated, even here.

WILLAMETTE MISSION.
The Willamette River
bisects Willamette Mission
State Park, and numerous
access points by land and
water await the adventurer
(see text, pages 284-287).

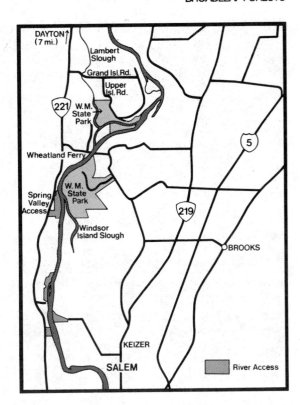

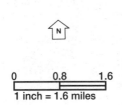

1 inch = 1.6 miles

To aid your exploration of this marvelous place, obtain a copy of the Willamette River Recreation Guide, which includes maps of the principal roads and river access points from the Oregon State Parks Division. Call 238-7491 (Portland), 378-6305 (Salem) or 343-7812 (Eugene).

GETTING THERE

East Bank Unit: From I-5 north of Salem, take Exit 263 for Brooks. Drive 1.75 miles west on Brooklake Road. Turn north on Wheatland Road and drive 2.5 miles to the park entrance on the left. Once in the park, drive two miles, bearing left at all junctions, to a parking area and trailhead to the river. You'll pass the

trailhead for the World's Largest Cottonwood Tree on the way.

Another route to the East Bank Unit begins in downtown Salem. Take Oregon Highway 22 west, toward the coast. Immediately after crossing the Willamette River, take the Dayton/Wallace Road turn-off for Oregon Highway 221, and drive nine miles north on Highway 221. If you're heading for Spring Valley River Access, turn right just north of the 12-mile post and just south of the Western Mennonite School. If you drive another three miles north on Wallace Road/Highway 221, you'll come to Wheatland Road, which leads to the Wheatland Ferry. (Of

The world's largest black cottonwood, Populus trichocarpa, *stands proudly at Willamette Mission State Park. Comparatively fast growing trees, cottonwoods from 2 to 3 feet in diameter range from 85 to 110 years old.*

course, you could also drive south on Highway 221, from Dayton.)

West Bank Unit: The best way to see the forest from the river is to put in at Spring Valley Access, noted above. Otherwise, follow the directions to Wheatland Ferry.

RECOMMENDED
If you wish to explore the park on foot, the East Bank Unit offers the only maintained trails. However, a tunnel-like riparian trail heads upstream from the boat landing at Spring Valley Access. You can put a boat in the river at Spring Valley Access, Wheatland Ferry, or at a spot on Lambert Slough described below.

If you prefer to walk the trails in the East Bank Unit, leave from the main parking area at the end of the road, follow a trail west along the south side of a filbert orchard, then head either up- or downstream along the river under big cottonwoods in a little-disturbed riparian zone. If you head upstream, the next two trails to the left (east) will loop back to the

parking area through more broadleaf woodlands.

To paddle up Windsor Island Slough (East Bank Unit), put in upstream at Spring Valley Access, across the river from Windsor Island Slough.

If you don't wish to paddle (or drift) downriver to Lambert Slough in the West Bank Unit, put in at the Wheatland Ferry. Watch for a channel to the left immediately after some old wooden pilings along the West Bank. There is a good pull-out on the left just before the channel returns to the main river (in almost exactly two miles). To leave a vehicle at this point, turn east off Highway 221 on Grand Island Road. Coming from the north, Grand Island Road is seven miles south of Dayton; coming from the south, it is the next right after the turn for Wheatland Ferry. From Grand Island Road, turn right on Upper Island Road and watch for an unmarked gravel road on the right, before Upper Island Road turns north along the Willamette River.

3. Luckiamute River

A lovely, intact forest of big black cotton-wood, bigleaf maple and very old willow.

Polk County
USGS 7.5' MONMOUTH (1986)

ABOUT THE AREA
The Luckiamute River enters the Willamette River from the west, just north of Albany, opposite the confluence of the Santiam and Willamette Rivers. For its last 2.5 miles, the Luckiamute meanders through a wonderful stretch of broadleaf ancient forest (see map, page 288). During low water it is easy to paddle up the Luckiamute River among some of the biggest trees in the area.

GETTING THERE
From Albany, take Highway 20 west over the Willamette River. Almost immediately turn right on Springhill Drive and drive almost six miles to Buena Vista Road. Turn north (right) on Buena Vista Road, and drive about one and a quarter miles to the Luckiamute River.

RECOMMENDED
The best place to launch a canoe is on the

north (downstream) side of the bridge. There is another fairly good launch a little more than 150 yards downstream, off a dirt road which runs along the north bank.

Another option, especially in late summer when water levels are low, is to put a canoe in on the Santiam River near the rest area off Interstate 5. It is six river miles to the Willamette and Luckiamute Rivers. The Santiam enters the Willamette by another big cottonwood-covered bar just upstream from and on the opposite bank from the Luckiamute.

Otherwise, follow the dirt road along the south bank (very muddy in the rainy season) another mile and a half, and park

where a cultivated field ends and the road enters a shady forest of maple, cottonwood, ash and willow. Following the road, it is a half-mile to the Willamette River.

Another quarter-mile downstream on the jeep road, the Santiam River joins the Willamette on the opposite shore. The mouth of the Luckiamute River is just ahead, but it takes some difficult cross-country hiking to get to it. The best way to penetrate the forest on foot is to follow a primitive trail that starts just 20 yards south of (upstream from) an outhouse and the Luckiamute Landing (and river mile 108) sign. Much of this area is flooded in the winter and early spring.

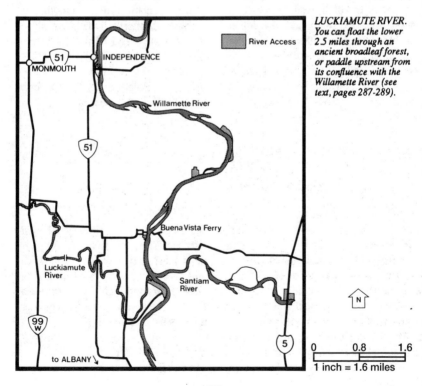

LUCKIAMUTE RIVER. You can float the lower 2.5 miles through an ancient broadleaf forest, or paddle upstream from its confluence with the Willamette River (see text, pages 287-289).

It is easy to miss the mouth of the Luckiamute River. When coming down the Willamette, watch for the channel along the west bank, just downstream from the mouth of the Santiam River on the Willamette's east bank. Look for a blue metal drum just upstream from a long white cliff. There is a good take-out at Buena Vista Ferry, another mile and a half down the Willamette.

If you stay on the Willamette River past Buena Vista Ferry, you'll almost imme-diately come to Wells Island. This is an undeveloped Polk County Park leased from the Bureau of Land Management; because of its important natural values it si also proposed for designation as an Area of Critical Environmental Concern (ACEC). This mile-long island is cov-ered with large old cottonwoods and willows. The easiest landing is on the east side, although the nicest canoe route is along the west side. Expect to encoun-ter deer and ruffed grouse under the island's big trees.

4. William L. Finley National Wildlife Refuge

Ancient Oregon white oak along the west side of the refuge and the north side of Pigeon Butte.

Benton County
USGS 7.5' GREENBERRY (1969)

ABOUT THE AREA

The William L. Finley National Wildlife Refuge was named for William Lovell Finley, a pioneer wildlife photographer and conservationist who worked for the (former) Oregon Fish and Game Com-mission for many years. The refuge was created primarily for wintering dusky Canada geese, and most of the refuge is intensively farmed to provide food crops for these game birds. The largest and most impressive Oregon white oak in Finley is on Pigeon Butte in the south-central part of the refuge, but it is not particularly easy to reach. Also, that portion of the refuge is closed from Oc-tober 1 to April 15 to protect nesting and foraging geese. However, there is a little-disturbed riparian zone (and Research Natural Area) along Muddy Creek through the middle of the refuge, and hiking trails meander among some of the refuge's stately old oak trees.

Maps of the area are available at the refuge headquarters, and are displayed on several informational bulletin boards.

GETTING THERE

Take Oregon Highway 99W eight miles north of Monroe or nine miles south of Corvallis. Turn west at the 93-mile post and drive a mile and a half down a gravel road. Turn left on Finley Refuge Road.

There is also a western entrance to the Finley National Wildlife Refuge. It is off Bellfountain Road, which runs parallel to Highway 99W, four miles north of the Bellfountain Market. It is only half a mile from the Bellfountain entrance to the Mill Hill Loop Trail mentioned below. When water sheets across the eastern (Highway 99W) entrance after heavy winter rains, the Bellfountain en-trance is the only way to reach the oak forest trails.

RECOMMENDED

Drive a few miles past the refuge headquarters to the first parking area on the right. Take the Woodpecker Loop Trail to the right and you will shortly come to a small but fine grove of old oaks.

Drive south on the gravel road to the next parking area, near a pond, red barn and house. This is the beginning of Mill Hill Loop Trail, which heads south for about 0.75 mile before forking at the beginning of the roughly two-mile loop. Either way you walk through some stupendous old oak groves and a second growth Douglas-fir forest. If you bear left where the loop begins, you will soon arrive at an active beaver marsh dominated by big cottonwoods, which are surrounded by younger Douglas-fir.

5. Middle Fork Willamette River Old Growth Riparian Area

Mature Douglas-fir and old black cottonwoods on a short, easy trail along a nice river bench.

Lane County
USGS 7.5' WESTFIR WEST (1986)

ABOUT THE AREA

This area is on the Lowell Ranger District of the Willamette National Forest, but is included in this chapter because it's an excellent example of a broadleaf riparian forest. Unfortunately, the sounds of Oregon Highway 58 and passing trains make it difficult to imagine yourself back in the days when such forests were common in western Oregon. The Willamette National Forest recreation map does not show the roads described below very well.

GETTING THERE

From I-5 south of Eugene, take Highway 58 east toward Oakridge. Just west of Oakridge, across from the Oakridge Ranger District Office (and 0.3 mile east of the 31-mile post), turn left at the sign for Westfir. (The Willamette National Forest's Rigdon Ranger District Office is in Oakridge proper.) Drive a half-mile, cross a bridge over the North Fork of the Middle Fork Willamette River, and turn left at a sign for Westfir and North Fork Road. After 0.8 mile, turn left on Winfrey Road. Cross another bridge, bear left (staying on Winfrey Road, which becomes FS Road 5828), and follow the river and signs for USFS Nursery. In two miles turn left at a sign for Buckhead Wildlife Area.

RECOMMENDED

In the Buckhead Wildlife Area, a Forest Service trail makes a short loop beside the Middle Fork Willamette River through mature Douglas-fir, a variety of hardwood species, and six habitat-types. While this trail provides the easiest access into this area, a "cross-country" route winds its way through large cottonwoods (some three feet in diameter) and mature and old growth Douglas-fir.

From the Buckhead Wildlife Area, drive another 0.2 mile west on FS Road 5828. Cross a railroad track and turn left on FS Road 5821. Continue west another mile, once again crossing the railroad track at Burnt Bridge Creek, and park. About 100 feet ahead on the left, follow a jeep road (heading downhill) and bear left at a fork just ahead which leads to a powerline corridor. Now look immediately to the right for a primitive trail through the blackberries, across a gully and into the forest. (Hip boots may be helpful in winter.) Follow elk trails perpendicular to the powerline toward the river for the first 100 yards. Then bear left (parallel to the no longer–visible power line) until you see the large cottonwoods. Return as you came, or make a loop by watching for elk trails back across the wetland (gully), and follow the powerline corridor or railroad track back to your car. (A pair of hand clippers can help you survive the blackberries.)

6. Whitehorse County Park

Big old cottonwoods, willows, maples and ash along the Rogue River, almost directly across from the mouth of the Applegate River.

Josephine County
USGS 15' GRANTS PASS (1954)

ABOUT THE AREA
This Josephine County Park, with several hundred acres of land, sloughs and backwaters, provides diverse examples of the lowland riparian woodlands that once covered much of western Oregon's lower river valleys. With agricultural development, this type of habitat has been eliminated in all but a few such exceptional spots. It is an outstanding bird and wildlife area. Beaver workings are abundant. The Siskiyou Audubon Society deserves everyone's thanks for their efforts to maintain this park's natural values.

GETTING THERE
In downtown Grants Pass, by the "It's the Climate" sign, turn west on G Street. In one mile drive west on either Upper or Lower River Road (the roads rejoin in about five miles). Continue two miles further west on Lower River Road to Whitehorse Park on the left.

RECOMMENDED
On the west end of the grassy area, an unmarked trail leads along the edge of a wooded pond. Another option is to follow a sign for the river and then bear right into a grove of tall cottonwoods.

Mature and old growth cottonwood riparian zones, which once criss-crossed Oregon's river valleys, are perhaps the most endangered ancient forest community in the state.

Douglas-fir, Oregon's state tree. (Photo by US Forest Service)

Checklist: Oregon's Trees

Most of the trees native to Oregon, including all species noted in this book. Nomenclature generally follows Randall, Warren R., et al. *Manual of Oregon Trees and Shrubs*. Corvallis: Oregon State University Press, 1988.

Conifers

Pacific silver fir	*Abies amabilis*
white fir	*Abies concolor*
grand fir	*Abies grandis*
subalpine fir	*Abies lasiocarpa*
Shasta red fir	*Abies magnifica shastensis*
noble fir	*Abies procera*
incense-cedar	*Calocedrus decurrens*
Port-Orford-cedar	*Chamaecyparis lawsoniana*
Alaska yellow-cedar	*Chamaecyparis nootkatensis*
Siskiyou (Matthews') cypress	*Cupressus bakori matthewsii*
common (dwarf) juniper	*Juniperus communis*
western juniper	*Juniperus occidentalis*
Rocky Mountain juniper	*Juniperus scopulorum*
western larch	*Larix occidentalis*
Brewer (weeping) spruce	*Picea brewerana*
Engelmann spruce	*Picea engelmannii*
Sitka spruce	*Picea sitchensis*
whitebark pine	*Pinus albicaulis*
Jeffrey pine	*Pinus jeffreyi*
lodgepole pine	*Pinus contorta*
sugar pine	*Pinus lambertiana*
western white pine	*Pinus monticola*
ponderosa pine	*Pinus ponderosa*
Douglas-fir	*Pseudotsuga menziesii*
coast redwood	*Sequoia sempervirens*
Pacific (western) yew	*Taxus brevifolia*
western red-cedar	*Thuja plicata*
western hemlock	*Tsuga heterophylla*
mountain hemlock	*Tsuga mertensiana*

Broadleaf Species

vine maple	*Acer circinatum*
Douglas maple	*Acer glabrum*
bigleaf maple	*Acer macrophyllum*
red alder	*Alnus rubra*
Sitka alder	*Alnus sinuata*
madrone	*Arbutus menziesii*
golden chinquapin	*Castanopsis chrysophylla*
mountain-mahogany	*Cercocarpus spp.*
Pacific dogwood	*Cornus nuttallii*
red-osier dogwood	*Cornus stolonifera*
Oregon ash	*Fraxinus latifolia*
tanoak	*Lithocarpus densiflorus*
quaking aspen	*Populus tremuloides*
black cottonwood	*Populus trichocarpa*
canyon live oak	*Quercus chrysolepis*
Oregon white oak	*Quercus garryana*
California black oak	*Quercus kelloggii*
Scouler willow	*Salix scouleriana*
Oregon-myrtle	*Umbellularia californica*

About the Author

Wendell Wood grew up in southern California, where he discovered the outdoors in chaparral-covered arroyos near his home. He became enamored with the Sierra Nevada Range during summer vacations. Wendell attended Humboldt State College in Arcata, California, where he received Bachelors degrees in Biology and Wildlife Management. With his wife Kathy he then moved to Myrtle Creek, Oregon, where he taught high school biology for several years.

In 1981 Wendell was discovered by ONRC. He had been active in local conservation issues in Douglas County, and soon was recruited by the Council's Board of Directors. He served as its President for two years. In 1986 Wendell joined the ONRC staff, and today serves as Conservation Coordinator, the senior staff position in the Western Regional Office in Eugene. Although much of his immediate focus is western Oregon, he has statewide responsibilities for many issues and coordinates field staff involvement with the Council's headquarters in Portland. Wendell and Kathy live in Eugene.

Photo by John Bauguess

About ONRC

The Oregon Natural Resources Council is a nonprofit association of more than fifty local and statewide conservation, educational, sporting and outdoor recreation organizations, and of businesses and others concerned with the protection and conservation of Oregon's natural resources. With over seven thousand individual members, ONRC is the largest independent statewide conservation organization in the American West, and is regularly described, by admirers and detractors alike, as among the most effective environmental groups in the country. In the words of one member, "ONRC is a statewide organization with regional presence and national impact." The Council's mission is "to protect Oregon's natural heritage through education, advocacy and grassroots empowerment."

ONRC was founded in 1972 as the Oregon Wilderness Coalition, with a dozen charter groups and about 150 individual members. For the past nineteen years the Council has made the protection of Oregon's remaining ancient forests its top priority. But old growth forests are only the most obviously threatened part of the state's tremendous endowment of natural wealth. From its inception, the Council has worked to protect Oregon's forest wilderness, free-flowing streams and rivers, high desert wilderness, air, coast and ocean resources, and has been involved in resource management in many forums. In 1982, the Oregon Wilderness Coalition formally changed its name to the Oregon Natural Resources Council, to more accurately reflect the full range of its conservation responsibilities.

ONRC is an educational, scientific and charitable corporation, recognized as 501(c)(3) tax-exempt by the IRS. The Council is committed to working in the legislative, legal and agency planning arenas as an advocacy organization, and emphasizes those activities in conjunction with a multitude of educational endeavors.

Notable accomplishments in which ONRC has participated include:
- Passage of four landmarks bills in Congress to protect Oregon Wilderness Areas, in 1975, 1978, 1979 and 1984;
- Filing of a 1983 lawsuit which delayed construction of the Bald Mountain Road into the North Kalmiopsis roadless area of the Siskiyou National Forest, the most diverse forest in North America;
- The historic 1984 lawsuit which broke the national logjam over the Forest Service's inadequate review of roadless (undesignated wilderness) lands (called RARE II), catalyzing a veritable cascade of statewide Wilderness bills which followed Oregon's;
- Successful coordination of citizen efforts to protect Oregon's free-flowing rivers, including both the 1988 Oregon Rivers Initiative and Congressional Wild and Scenic Rivers legislation for Oregon in 1975, 1984 and 1988;
- Efforts to protect wild rivers and salmon runs by preventing construction of Elk Creek Dam on the Rogue River System, Salt Caves Dam on the Klamath

River, Walker Creek Dam on the Nestucca River System, and Asotin Dam on the Snake River, among many others;

- Working with local organizations to designate new State Scenic Waterways in the State Legislature, such as the North Fork of the Middle Fork Willamette River and Waldo Lake;
- Enactment of the 1981 Oregon Riparian Protection Act in the State Legislature, a voluntary tax-incentive program designed to protect riparian values and enhance streamside management on private lands statewide; and
- Nationalizing the ancient forests issue, moving it to the top of the national environmental movement's agenda of priorities.

Despite these successes, and notwithstanding notable signs of recovery in a few instances, the condition of Oregon's natural resources continues to decline. ONRC's chief priorities for the next decade include:

- Securing protection for Northwest ancient forest ecosystems, by enactment of protective legislation; by litigation, to enforce existing environmental laws routinely violated by federal forest agencies; by working to enlighten public land-managing agencies; and by expanding public education efforts;
- Protecting Oregon's remaining free-flowing rivers and streams, by pursuing state and federal legislative designations as well as appropriate management plans from government agencies;
- Ensuring comprehensive protection for all of Oregon's threatened and endangered species and associated ecosystems, including wild salmon and steelhead of the Columbia River Basin and Coast Range;
- Gaining protection for some of the largest and most intact wild areas left in Oregon, by expanding Crater Lake National Park and establishing new National Parks or Preserves in the Siskiyou-Klamath Mountains, Hells Canyon, and other deserving areas;
- Protecting and restoring the flora and fauna of portions of Oregon's Great Basin High Desert, threatened today by the old scourge of livestock grazing and the new assault of cyanide heap leach gold mining, both encouraged by the Bureau of Land Management (BLM); and
- Working to protect both Oregon's world-famous coast and ocean and adjacent wildlands from the threat of unsustainable, environmentally damaging mining practices, including offshore oil and gas drilling.

The Council needs your support and assistance in its efforts to protect Oregon's natural resources. Please become an ONRC member today, and consider working with the local conservation group of your choice as well. Please contact us at:

Western Regional Office	**Main Office**	**Eastern Regional Office**
1161 Lincoln Street	522 SW Fifth Avenue	1005 NW Newport
Eugene, Oregon 97401	Suite 1050	Bend, Oregon 97701
503-344-0675	Portland, Oregon 97204	503-385-6908
	503-223-9001	

Selected Agency Addresses & Phone Numbers

(all Oregon area codes 503)

National Offices

US Forest Service, Washington (Chief's) Office. Department of Agriculture (USDA), 201 14th Street SW, Washington DC 20250. 202-447-3760.

US Bureau of Land Management (BLM), Director's Office. Department of Interior (USDI), 18th and C Streets NW, Washington DC 20240. 202-208-3801.

National Park Service, Director's Office. Department of Interior (USDI), PO Box 37127, Washington DC 20013. 202-343-4621.

US Fish and Wildlife Service, Director's Office. Department of Interior (USDI), 1849 C Street NW, Washington DC 20240. 202-208-4717.

Regional Offices

US Forest Service, Pacific Northwest Regional Office (Region Six). PO Box 3623, Portland 97208. 326-2877.

US Bureau of Land Management (BLM), Oregon State Office. 825 NE Multnomah Street, Portland 97208. 280-7027.

National Park Service, Pacific Northwest Regional Office. 83 South King Street, Suite 212, Seattle, Washington 98104. 206-553-0170.

US Fish and Wildlife Service, Pacific Regional Office (Region One). 911 NE 11th Avenue, Portland 97232. 231-6828.

National Forests and Ranger Districts

Deschutes National Forest. Supervisor's Office, 1645 Highway 20 East, Bend 97701. 388-2715.

  Sisters Ranger District. PO Box 248, Sisters 97759. 549-2111.

  Bend Ranger District. 1645 Highway 20 East, Bend 97701. 388-5664.

  Fort Rock Ranger District. 1645 Highway 20 East, Bend 97701. 388-5664.

  Crescent Ranger District. PO Box 208, Crescent 97733. 433-2234.

Fremont National Forest. 524 North G Street, Lakeview 97630. 947-2151.
   Silver Lake Ranger District. Silver Lake 97638. 576-2107.
   Paisley Ranger District. Paisley 97636. 943-3114.
   Bly Ranger District. Bly 97622. 353-2427.
   Lakeview Ranger District. HC-64, Box 60, Lakeview 97630. 947-3334.

Klamath National Forest. 1312 Fairlane Road, Yreka, California 96097. 916-842-1631.
   Oak Knoll Ranger District. 22541 Highway 96, Klamath River, California 96050. 916-465-2241.

Malheur National Forest. 139 NE Dayton Street, John Day 97845. 575-1731.
   Long Creek Ranger District. 528 East Main Street, John Day 97845. 575-2110.
   Prairie City Ranger District. 327 SW Front Street, Prairie City 97869. 820-3311.
   Bear Valley Ranger District. 528 East Main Street, John Day 97845. 575-2110.
   Burns Ranger District. Star Route 4 - 12870 Highway 20, Hines 97738. 573-7292.

Mount Hood National Forest. 2955 NW Division Street, Gresham 97030. 666-0700.
   Columbia Gorge Ranger District. 31520 SE Woodard Road, Troutdale 97060. 695-2276.
   Hood River Ranger District. 6780 Highway 35, Mount Hood-Parkdale 97041. 666-0701.
   Barlow Ranger District. PO Box 67, Dufur 97021. 467-2291.
   Bear Springs Ranger District. Route 1, Box 222, Maupin 97037. 328-6211.
   Zigzag Ranger District. 70220 Highway 26 East, Zigzag 97049. 666-0704.
   Estacada Ranger District. 595 NW Industrial Way, Estacada 97023. 630-6861.
   Clackamas (Ripplebrook) Ranger District. 61431 Highway 224 East, Estacada 97023. 630-4256.

Ochoco National Forest. 155 North Court Street, Prineville 97754. 447-6247.
   Prineville Ranger District. 2321 East 3rd Street, Prineville 97754. 447-3825.
   Big Summit Ranger District. Box 255, Mitchell Star Route, Prineville 97754. 447-9645.
   Paulina Ranger District. 6015 Paulina Star Route, Paulina 97751. 447-3713.
   Snow Mountain Ranger District. HC-74, Box 12870, Hines 97738. 573-7292.
   Crooked River National Grassland. 2321 East 3rd Street, Prineville 97754. 447-9640.

Rogue River National Forest. Federal Building, 333 West 8th Street, Medford 97501. 776-3600.
   Prospect Ranger District. Prospect 97536. 560-3623.
   Butte Falls Ranger District. PO Box 227, Butte Falls 97522. 865-3581.

Ashland Ranger District. 645 Washington Street, Ashland 97520. 482-3333.

Applegate (Star) Ranger District. 6941 Upper Applegate Road, Jacksonville 97530. 899-1812.

Siskiyou National Forest. 200 NE Greenfield Road, Grants Pass 97526. 479-5301.

Powers Ranger District. Powers 97466. 439-3011.

Gold Beach Ranger District. 1225 South Ellensburg, Gold Beach 97444. 247-6651.

Galice Ranger District. 1465 NE 7th Street, Grants Pass 97526. 476-3830.

Chetco Ranger District. 555 5th Street, Brookings 97415. 469-2196.

Illinois Valley Ranger District. 26568 Redwood Highway, Cave Junction 97523. 592-2166.

Siuslaw National Forest. 4077 Research Way, Corvallis 97333. 750-7000.

Hebo Ranger District. Hebo 97122. 392-3161.

Alsea Ranger District. 18591 Alsea Highway, Alsea 97324. 487-5811.

Waldport Ranger District. Waldport 97394. 563-3211.

Mapleton Ranger District. Mapleton 97453. 268-4473.

Oregon Dunes National Recreation Area (NRA). 855 Highway Avenue, Reedsport 97467. 271-3611.

Umatilla National Forest. 2517 SW Hailey Avenue, Pendleton 97801. 276-3811.

Pomeroy Ranger District. Route 1, Box 53-F, Pomeroy, Washington 99347. 509-843-1891.

Walla Walla Ranger District. 1415 West Rose, Walla Walla, Washington 99362. 509-522-6290.

North Fork John Day Ranger District. PO Box 158, Ukiah 97880. 427-3231.

Heppner Ranger District. PO Box 7, Heppner 97836. 676-9187.

Umpqua National Forest. 2900 NW Stewart Parkway, Roseburg 97470. 672-6601.

Cottage Grove Ranger District. 78405 Cedar Parks Road, Cottage Grove 97424. 942-5591.

North Umpqua Ranger District. 18772 North Umpqua Highway, Glide 97443. 496-3532.

Diamond Lake Ranger District. HC-60, Box 101, Idleyld Park 97447. 498-2531.

Tiller Ranger District. 27812 Tiller-Trail Highway, Tiller 97484. 825-3201.

Wallowa-Whitman National Forest. 1550 Dewey Avenue, Baker 97814. 523-6391.

Wallowa Valley Ranger District. Route 1, Box 83, Joseph 97846. 432-2171.

Eagle Cap Ranger District. PO Box M, Enterprise 97828. 426-3104.

Pine Ranger District. General Delivery, Halfway 97834. 742-7511.

La Grande Ranger District. 3502 Highway 30, La Grande 97850. 963-7186.

Baker Ranger District. Route 1, Box 1, Pocahontas Road, Baker 97814. 523-4476.

Unity Ranger District. PO Box 38, Unity 97884. 446-3351.

Hells Canyon National Recreation Area (NRA). PO Box 490, Enterprise 97828. 426-3151.

Willamette National Forest. 211 East 7th Avenue, Eugene 97401. 465-6561.

Detroit Ranger District. HC-60, Box 320, Mill City 97360. 854-3366.

Sweet Home Ranger District. 3225 Highway 20, Sweet Home 97386. 367-5168.

McKenzie Ranger District. McKenzie Bridge 97413. 822-3381.

Blue River Ranger District. Blue River 97413. 822-3317.

Lowell Ranger District. Lowell 97452. 937-2129.

Oakridge Ranger District. Westfir 97492. 782-2291.

Rigdon Ranger District. Oakridge 97463. 782-2283.

Winema National Forest. 2819 Dahlia Street, Klamath Falls 97601. 883-6714.

Chemult Ranger District. PO Box 150, Chemult 97731. 365-2229.

Chiloquin Ranger District. PO Box 357, Chiloquin 97624. 783-2221.

Klamath Ranger District. 1936 California Avenue, Klamath Falls 97601. 882-7761.

BLM Districts and Resource Areas *

Burns District BLM. HC-74, 12533 Highway 20 West, Hines 97738. 573-5241.

Coos Bay District BLM. 1300 Airport Lane, North Bend 97459. 756-0100.

Eugene District BLM. 1255 Pearl Street, Eugene 97401. 683-6600.

Lakeview District BLM. 1000 South 9th Street, Lakeview 97630. 947-2177.

Klamath Falls Resource Area. 2795 Anderson Avenue, Building 25, Klamath Falls 97603. 883-6916.

Medford District BLM. 3040 Biddle Road, Medford 97504. 770-2200.

Prineville District BLM. 185 East 4th Street, Prineville 97754. 447-4115.

Roseburg District BLM. 777 NW Garden Valley Boulevard, Roseburg 97470. 672-4491.

Salem District BLM, District Manager's Office. 1717 Fabry Road SE, Salem 97306. 375-5646.

Tillamook Resource Area. 6615 Officer's Row, Tillamook 97141. 842-7546.

Vale District BLM. 100 Oregon Street, Vale 97918. 473-3144.

Baker Resource Area. Federal Building, Baker 97814. 523-6391.

*where Resource Areas have separate offices.

National Park Service Agencies

Crater Lake National Park, Superintendent's Office. PO Box 7, Crater Lake 97604. 594-2211.

Oregon Caves National Monument. 19000 Caves Highway, Cave Junction 97523. 592-2100.

John Day Fossil Beds National Monument. 420 West Main Street, John Day 97845. 575-0721.

Fort Clatsop National Memorial. Route 3, Box 604-FC, Astoria 97103. 861-2471.

US Geological Survey Offices

USGS Western Mapping Center. 345 Middlefield Road, Menlo Park, California 94025. 415-853-8300.

USGS Rocky Mountain Mapping Center. Map Sales, PO Box 25286, Denver Federal Center, Building 810, Denver, Colorado 80225. 303-236-7477.

State Agencies

Oregon State Parks and Recreation Division (Oregon Department of Transportation). 525 Trade Street SE, Salem 97310. 378-6305 or 1-800-233-3306 (in Oregon) or 1-800-547-7842 (outside Oregon). Also: 238-7491 (Portland) and 343-7812 (Eugene).

Oregon Division of State Lands. 1445 State Street, Salem 97310. 378-3805.

Oregon Department of Fish and Wildlife. 2501 SW 1st Avenue, Portland 97201. 229-5403.

Oregon Department of Environmental Quality (DEQ). 811 SW 6th Avenue, Portland 97204. 229-5696.

Oregon Department of Water Resources. 3850 Portland Road NE, Salem 97310. 378-3739.

Oregon Department of Forestry. 2600 State Street, Salem 97310. 378-2560.

Oregon Department of Land Conservation and Development. 1175 Court Street NE, Salem 97310. 373-0050.

Suggested Reading

Guidebooks

Ambler, Julie, and John Patt, editors. *Guide to the Middle Santiam and Old Cascades*. Corvallis: Marys Peak Group Sierra Club, 1981.*

Anderson, H. Michael. *Umpqua Wilderness Trails*. Roseburg: Umpqua Wilderness Defenders, 1978.*

Conley, Frank, editor. *Hiking the High Wallowas and Hells Canyon*. Enterprise: Wallowa Resource Council/Pika Press, 1988.

Bucy, David E.M., and Mary C. McCauley. *A Hiker's Guide to the Oregon Coast Trail*. Salem: Oregon State Department of Transportation, Parks and Recreation Division, 1977.

Dittmar, Ann, et al. *Visitors' Guide to Ancient Forests of Western Washington*. Washington, DC: The Wilderness Society, 1989.

Dodge, Nicholas A. *A Climbing Guide to Oregon*. Beaverton: Touchstone Press, 1975.*

George, Tony. *The Mount Jefferson Wilderness Guidebook*. Solo Press, 1983.

George, Tony. *The Olallie Scenic Area Guidebook*. Solo Press, 1983.

George, Tony, editor. *Oregon's Hidden Wilderness*. Salem: Central Cascades Conservation Council, 1978.*

Hart, John. *Hiking the Bigfoot Country*. San Francisco: Sierra Club Books, 1975.

Henrie, Charis, editor. *Old Growth Forests: A Casual Hikers' Guide*. Portland: USDA-Forest Service/USDI-BLM/World Forestry Center, 1990.

Houle, Mary. *One City's Wilderness: Portland's Forest Park*. Portland: Oregon Historical Society Press, 1988.

Love, Ken and Ruth. *A Guide to the Trails of Badger Creek*. Signpost Books, 1979.

Morton, Kenneth, et al., editors. *Hiking the Hardesty Wilderness*. Eugene: Hardesty Mountain Study Group/Northwest Working Press, 1981.*

Newman, Doug, and Sally Sharrard. *Oregon Ski Tours*. Beaverton: Touchstone Press, 1973.

Schaffer, Jeffrey P. *Crater Lake National Park and Vicinity*. Wilderness Press, 1983.

Schaffer, Jeffrey P., and Bev and Fred Hartline. *The Pacific Crest Trail, Volume 2: Oregon and Washington*. Wilderness Press, 1986.

Stoltmann, Randy. *Hiking Guide to the Big Trees of Southwestern British Columbia*. Vancouver, British Columbia: Western Canada Wilderness Committee, 1987.

out of print, although copies for loan are usually not difficult to locate.

Sullivan, William L. *Exploring Oregon's Wild Areas*. Seattle: The Mountaineers, 1988.

Vielbig, Klindt. *Cross-Country Ski Routes of Oregon's Cascades*. Seattle: The Mountaineers, 1984.

Wellborn, Sherry, editor. *Oregon Coast Range Wilderness*. Corvallis: Siuslaw Task Force, 1980.*

Willamette National Forest. *Willamette Trails*. Eugene, 1979.*

Williams, Jerold. *McKenzie Trails*. Calapooya Books, 1979.*

Williams, Paul M. *Oregon Coast Hikes*. Seattle: The Mountaineers, 1985.

Articles and Periodicals

Baker, Dean. "Virgin Forests Under Fire." *National Wildlife*, Feb.-March 1986.

Carey, John. "The Roads Less Traveled." *National Wildlife*, Apr.-May 1988.

Caufield, Catherine. "The Ancient Forest." *The New Yorker*, May 14, 1990.

Daniel, John. "The Long Dance of the Trees." *Wilderness*, Spring 1988.

Durbin, Kathie, Paul Koberstein, et al. "A Special Report: Forests in Distress." *The Oregonian*, Portland, Sept. 16-21, 1990.

Findley, Rowe. "Will We Save Our Own?" *National Geographic*, September 1990.

Ford, Pat, editor. "The Northwest Rediscovers Its Ancient Forests." *High Country News, vol.* 22 no. 22, November 19, 1990.

Greacen, Scott, editor. Special issues of the quarterly journal *Wild Oregon* including: vol. 16 no. 1, Fall-Winter 1989-90; vol. 16 no. 3, Fall 1990; and vol. 17 no. 1, to be available March 1991. Published by Oregon Natural Resources Council (ONRC), Portland.

Gup, Ted. "Owl vs. Man." *Time*, June 25, 1990.

Kelly, David, and Gary Braasch. "The Decadent Forest." *Audubon*, March 1986.

Laycock, George. "Trashing the Tongass." *Audubon*, November 1987.

McKee, Russell, and Carl R. Sams. "Tombstones of a Lost Forest." *Audubon*, March 1988.

"Of Trees and Hope in the National Forests." *Wilderness*, Summer 1987.

Pochnau, William. "Last Stand for the Old Woods." *Life*, May 1990.

St. Clair, Jeffrey, editor. Many issues of the monthly journal *Forest Watch* address ancient forest topics. Published by Cascade Holistic Economic Consultants (CHEC), Portland.

Wilcove, David S. "What I Saw When I Went to the Forest." *Wilderness*, Spring 1988.

Williams, Ted. "The Spotted Fish Under the Spotted Owl." *Fly Rod and Reel*, January-February 1990.

*out of print, although copies for loan are usually not difficult to locate.

306

Books and Documents: "Classics"

Eagan, Timothy. *The Good Rain: Across Time and Terrain in the Pacific Northwest.* New York: Alfred A. Knopf, 1990.

Ervin, Keith. *Fragile Majesty, The Battle for America's Last Great Forests.* Seattle: The Mountaineers, 1989.

Franklin, Jerry F., and C. T. Dyrness. *Natural Vegetation of Oregon and Washington.* USDA-Forest Service General Technical Report PNW-8. Portland: Pacific Northwest Forest and Range Experiment Station, 1973.

Franklin, J. F., et al. *Ecological Characteristics of Old Growth Douglas-Fir Forests,* USDA-Forest Service General Technical Report PNW-118. Portland: Pacific Northwest Forest and Range Experiment Station, 1981.

Harris, Larry D. *The Fragmented Forest.* Chicago: University of Chicago Press, 1984.

Kelly, David, and Gary Braasch. *Secrets of the Old Growth Forest.* Salt Lake City: Peregrine Smith Books, 1988.

Maser, Chris. *Forest Primeval: The Natural History of An Ancient Forest.* San Francisco: Sierra Club Books, 1989.

Maser, C. *The Redesigned Forest.* San Pedro, California: R. & E. Miles, 1988.

Maser, C., R. F. Tarrant, James M. Trappe and J. F. Franklin, editors. *From the Forest to the Sea: A Story of Fallen Trees.* USDA-Forest Service General Technical Report PNW-GTR-229. Portland: Pacific Northwest Forest and Range Experiment Station, 1988.

Maser, C., and J. M. Trappe, editors. *The Seen and Unseen World of the Fallen Tree,* USDA-Forest Service General Technical Report PNW-164. Portland: Pacific Northwest Forest and Range Experiment Station, 1984.

Mathews, Daniel. *Cascade-Olympic Natural History.* Portland: Portland Audubon Society/Raven Editions, 1988.

Norse, Elliott A. *Ancient Forests of the Pacific Northwest.* Washington, DC: Island Press, 1989.

Pyle, Robert Michael. *Wintergreen.* Houghton Mifflin, 1986.

Stafford, Kim R., and Gary Braasch. *Entering the Grove.* Salt Lake City: Peregrine Smith Books, 1990.

Wallace, David Raines. *The Klamath Knot.* San Francisco: Sierra Club Books, 1983.

Wuerthner, George. *Oregon Mountain Ranges.* American Geographic Publications, 1987.

Semi-Technical Papers and Articles

Cline, S.P., et al. "Snag Characteristics in Douglas-Fir Forests, Western Oregon." *Journal of Wildlife Management*, 44: 773-786, 1980.

Franklin, Jerry F., and Richard T.T. Forman. "Creating Landscape Patterns by Forest Cutting: Ecological Consequences and Principles." *Landscape Ecology*, vol. 1 no. 1, pp. 5-18, 1987.

Franklin, J.F., and Richard H. Waring. "Distinctive Features of the Northwestern Coniferous Forest." *Forests: Fresh Perspectives from Ecosystem Analysis*, Corvallis: Oregon State University Press, 1979.

Franklin, J.F., et al. "Importance of Ecological Diversity in Maintaining Long-Term Site Productivity." *Maintaining the Long-Term Productivity of Pacific Northwest Forest Ecosystems*, edited by David Perry, et al. Portland: Timber Press.

Franklin, J.F., et al. "Old Growth Definitions Task Group: Interim Definitions for Old Growth Douglas-Fir and Mixed-Conifer Forests in the Pacific Northwest and California," USDA-Forest Service Research Note PNW-447. Portland: Pacific Northwest Forest and Range Experiment Station, 1986.

Franklin, J.F., et al. "Effects of Global Climatic Changes on Forests in Northwestern North America." *The Consequences of the Greenhouse Effect for Biological Diversity*, to be published by Yale University Press, New Haven.

Friedman, Mitch, editor. *Forever Wild: Conserving the Greater North Cascades Ecosystem*. Bellingham, Washington: Mountain Hemlock Press, September 1988.

Harmon, Mark E., William K. Ferrell and Jerry F. Franklin. "Effects of Carbon Storage on Conversion of Old Growth Forests to Young Forests." *Science, vol.* 247, Feb. 9, 1990.

Harris, Larry D. "Landscape Linkages: The Dispersal Corridor Approach to Wildlife Conservation." *Transactions of the North American Wildlife and Natural Resources Conference*, 53: 595-607, 1988.

Harris, L.D., and Patrick Kangas. "Reconsideration of the Habitat Concept." *Transactions of the North American Wildlife and Natural Resources Conference*, 53: 137-144, 1988.

Harris, L.D., Chris Maser and Art McKee. "Patterns of Old Growth Harvest and Implications for Cascades Wildlife." *Transactions of the North American Wildlife and Natural Resources Conference*, 47: 374-392, 1982.

Haynes, Richard W. "Inventory and Value of Old Growth in the Douglas-Fir Region," USDA-Forest Service Research Note PNW-437. Portland: Pacific Northwest Forest and Range Experiment Station, 1986.

Mannan, R.W., et al. "Use of Snags by Birds in Douglas-Fir Forests, Western Oregon." *Journal of Wildlife Management*, 44: 787-97, 1980.

Meslow, E. Charles. "The Relationship of Birds to Habitat Structure — Plant Communities and Successional Stages." *Proceedings of the Workshop on Nongame Bird Habitat Management in the Coniferous Forests of the Western*

United States, edited by R. DeGraff, USDA-Forest Service General Technical Report PNW-64. Portland: Pacific Northwest Forest and Range Experiment Station, 1978.

Meslow, E.C., Chris Maser and Jared Verner. "Old Growth Forests as Wildlife Habitat." *Transactions of the North American Wildlife and Natural Resources Conference*, 46: 329-335, 1981.

Moldenke, Andrew R., et al. *A Key to Arboreal Spiders of Douglas-Fir and True Fir Forests of the Pacific Northwest*, USDA-Forest Service General Technical Report PNW-GTR-207. Portland: Pacific Northwest Forest and Range Experiment Station, 1987.

Olsen, Jeffrey. "Pacific Northwest Lumber and Wood Products: An Industry in Transition." *National Forests Policies for the Future*, vol. 4. Washington, DC: The Wilderness Society/National Wildlife Federation, 1988.

Perry, David A. "An Overview of Sustainable Forestry." *Journal of Pesticide Reform*, vol. 8 no. 3, Fall 1988.

Perry, D.A., and Jumanne Maghembe. "Ecosystem Concepts and Current Trends in Forest Management: Time for Reappraisal." *Forest Ecology and Management*, 26: 123-140, 1989.

Ruggiero, Leonard F., et al. "Ecological Dependency: The Concept and Its Implications for Research and Management." *Transactions of the North American Wildlife and Natural Resources Conference*, 53: 115-126, 1988.

Spies, Thomas A., and Jerry F. Franklin. "Old Growth and Forest Dynamics in the Douglas-Fir Region of Western Oregon and Washington." *Natural Areas Journal*, vol. 8 no. 3, pp. 190-201, July 1988.

Thomas, Jack Ward, editor. *Wildlife Habitats in Managed Forests of the Blue Mountains of Oregon and Washington*, Forest Service Handbook No. 553. Washington, DC: USDA Forest Service/USDI Bureau of Land Management/ Wildlife Management Institute, 1979.

Thomas, J.W., et al. "Management and Conservation of Old Growth Forests in the United States." *Wildlife Society Bulletin*, 16: 252-262, 1988.

Background References

Alt, David D., and Donald W. Hyndman. *Roadside Geology of Oregon*. Mountain Press Publishing, 1978.

Arno, Stephen F., and Ramona P. Hammerly. *Northwest Trees*. Seattle: The Mountaineers, 1977.

Ashworth, William. *Hells Canyon: The Deepest Gorge on Earth*. New York: Hawthorne Books, 1977.

Baldwin, Ewart M. *Geology of Oregon*. Eugene: University of Oregon Press, 1964.

Barney, D. *The Last Stand*. New York: Grossman, 1974.

Beckham, Stephen Dow. *The Indians of Western Oregon*. Coos Bay: Arago Books, 1977.

Brockman, C. Frank. *Trees of North America*. New York: Golden Press, 1968.

Brown, Vinson, Charles Yocum and Aldene Starbuck. *Wildlife of the Inter-Mountain West*. San Martin, California: Naturegraph, 1958.

Clawson, Marion. *Forests For Whom and For What?* Baltimore: Resources For the Future/Johns Hopkins University Press, 1975.

Clawson, M., editor. *Forest Policy for the Future*. Baltimore: Resources For the Future/Johns Hopkins University Press, 1974.

Dana, Samuel Trask, and Sally K. Fairfax. *Forest and Range Policy: Its Development in the United States*, second edition. New York: McGraw Hill, 1980.

Douglas, William O. *My Wilderness*. Garden City, New York: Doubleday, 1960.

Douglas, W. 0. *Of Men and Mountains*. Seattle: Seattle Book Co., by arrangement with Harper & Row, 1981.

Freeman, Orville L., and Michael Frome. *The National Forests of America*. New York: Putnam's, 1968.

Fritz, Edward C. *Clearcutting: A Crime Against Nature*. Dallas, Texas: Forest Reform Network/Ekin Press, 1989.

Frome, Michael. *The Forest Service*, 2nd edition. Boulder, Colorado: Westview Press, 1984.

Frome, M. *Whose Woods These Are: The Story of the National Forests*. Garden City, New York: Doubleday, 1962.

Gabrielson, Ira N., and Stanley G. Jewett. *Birds of the Pacific Northwest*. New York: Dover Publications, Inc., 1970.

Gilkey, Helen M., and La Rea J. Dennis. *Handbook of Northwestern Plants*. Corvallis: Oregon State University Press, 1980.

Hansen, Arne, editor. *Carmanah: Artistic Visions of an Ancient Rainforest*. Vancouver, British Columbia: Western Canada Wilderness Committee, 1989.

Hitchcock, C. Leo, and Arthur Cronquist. *Flora of the Pacific Northwest*. Seattle: University of Washington Press, 1978.

Horwitz, Eleanor. *Clearcutting: A View From The Top*. Washington, DC: Acropolis Books, Ltd., 1974.

Ingles, Lloyd G. *Mammals of the Pacific States*. Stanford: Stanford University Press, 1965.

Islands Protection Society. *Islands at the Edge*. Vancouver, British Columbia: Douglas and McIntyre, 1984.

Kaufman, Herbert. *The Forest Ranger*. Baltimore: Johns Hopkins University Press, 1967.

Ketchum, Glenn and Carey. *The Tongass, Alaska's Vanishing Rainforest*. New York: Aperture, 1987.

Leopold, Aldo. *Sand County Almanac and Essays from the Round River*. New York: Ballantine/Oxford University Press, 1966.

Lewis, M., and W. Clark. *The Lewis and Clark Expedition*, vol. 3, edited by Nicholas Biddle. New York, 1961.

Loy, William G. *Atlas of Oregon*. Eugene: University of Oregon Press, 1975.

Maddan, Robert W., editor and photographer. *America's Spectacular Northwest*. Washington, DC: National Geographic Society, 1982.

Marshall, Robert. *The People's Forests*. New York: Smith and Haas, 1933.

Maser, Chris, and Bruce Mate. *Natural History of Oregon Coast Range Mammals*, USDA-Forest Service General Technical Report PNW-113. Portland: Pacific Northwest Forest and Range Experiment Station, 1981.

McArthur, Lewis A. *Oregon Geographic Names*, 5th edition, revised by Lewis L. McArthur. Portland: Oregon Historical Society/Western Imprints, 1982.

Norse, Elliott A., editor. *Conserving Biological Diversity in our National Forests*. Washington DC: The Wilderness Society/Ecological Society of America, 1986.

O'Toole, Randal. *Reforming the Forest Service*. Covelo, California: Island Press, 1988.

The Principal Laws Relating to Forest Service Activities. Forest Service Handbook No. 453. Washington, DC: Government Printing Office, revised 1983.

Public Land Law Review Commission. *One-Third of the Nation's Land: A Report to the President and Congress*. Washington, DC: Government Printing Office, 1970.

Randall, Warren R., et al. *Manual of Oregon Trees and Shrubs*. Corvallis: Oregon State University Press, 1988.

Ross, Charles R. *Trees to Know in Oregon*. OSU Extension Bulletin #697. Corvallis: Oregon State University Extension Service/Oregon State Department of Forestry, 1978.

Schrepfer, Susan. *The Fight to Save the Redwoods*. Madison: University of Wisconsin Press, 1983.

Shands, William F., and Robert C. Healy. *The Lands Nobody Wanted*. Washington, DC: Conservation Foundation, 1977.

Spurr, S. H., and Burton Barnes. *Forest Ecology*, 3rd edition. New York: John Wiley and Sons, Inc., 1980.

Whitney, Stephen. *The Audubon Society Nature Guides: Western Forests*. New York: Alfred A. Knopf, 1985.

Williams, Chuck. *Bridge of the Gods, Mountains of Fire: A Return to the Columbia Gorge*. Seattle: The Mountaineers, 1980.

Wood, Nancy. *Clearcut: The Deforestation of America*. San Francisco: Sierra Club Books, 1971.

Yocum, Charles, and Vinson Brown. *Wildlife and Plants of the Cascades*. San Martin, California: Naturegraph, 1971.

Yocum, C., and Ray Dasmann. *The Pacific Coastal Wildlife Region*. San Martin, California: Naturegraph, 1965.

Young, Cameron, et al. *Forests of British Columbia*. Vancouver, British Columbia: Whitecap, 1985.

Credits

Conceptualized and written by Wendell Wood.

Edited by James Monteith and Scott Greacen.

Design and maps by Diane Valantine.

Cover photograph by Phillip Renault.

Photographs by the author except as noted.

Photographers:

Diane Kelsay	Sandy Lonsdale
Gary Braasch	Ed Meyerowitz
Phillip Renault	Eric Forsman
John Bauguess	Ray Fillon
Bob Harvey	Chris Maser
Frank Isaacs	Chuck Swanson
Michael Williams	Don DeFazio

Published by Oregon Natural Resources Council (ONRC), Portland, Oregon (copyright 1991).

Printed by Oregon Lithoprint, Portland, Oregon.

Distributed by The Mountaineers, Seattle, Washington.

Typeset by Grapheon Design and Type
Portland, Oregon

Index to Walks

A

Abert Rim Wilderness Study Area 257
Acker Divide Trail 166
Applegate Wilderness (proposed) 95

B

Babyfoot Lake, Kalmiopsis Wilderness 119
Badger Creek Wilderness 83
Bagby Hot Springs, Bull-of-the-Woods Wilderness 76
Baker Canyon, Huckleberry Mountain Additions to Eagle Cap Wilderness (proposed) 177
Barlow Pass 81
Bear Creek Trail, Hellhole Wilderness (proposed) 149
Benham Falls 28
Bennett Ridge Connector Cross-Country Ski Tour 81
Big Bottom 75
Big Draw 107
Black Butte 16
Blue Jay Springs Research Natural Area 233
Boulder Creek to Boulder Lake 78
Breitenbush Spotted Owl Trail 197
Brice Creek 155
Browder Ridge Unit, Old Cascades Wilderness (proposed) 208
Brown Mountain Wilderness (proposed) 238
Browns Mountain, Deschutes River 20
Buck Creek, Yamsay Mountain Wilderness (proposed) 31
Bull Run Creek Additions to Monument Rock Wilderness (proposed) 193

C

Camp Comfort 165
Canton Creek Roadless Area 157
Cape Creek 135
Cape Lookout State Park 275
Cape Meares State Park 273
Cascade Head 127
Cascadia State Park 278
Catherine Creek Additions to Eagle Cap Wilderness (proposed) 179
Cherry Creek Research Natural Area and Vaughns Creek 247
Chinquapin Mountain Grove, Pacific Crest Trail 251
City of Ashland Watershed 97
City of Astoria, Urban Forest City Park (proposed) 267
Clackamas River Trail 73
Coleman Rim Wilderness (proposed) 39
Coquille River Falls Research Natural Area 111
Cottonwood Meadows Lake 43
Cougar Butte Trail 168

Cow Creek Trail 47
Crabtree Valley 243
Crane Mountain Wilderness (proposed) 45
Crane Prairie Osprey Management Area 18
Crater Lake National Park 263
Crescent Lake, Diamond Peak Wilderness 21
Cultus River, Benchmark Butte 17
Cummins Creek Wilderness 136

D

Davis Lake 23
Dead Horse Rim Wilderness (proposed) 34
Delta Grove 216
Drift Creek 130
Drift Creek Wilderness 131
Dutch Flat Creek Additions to the Elkhorns Unit,
    North Fork John Day Wilderness (proposed) 189

E

Eagle Creek 179
Eagle Creek, Salmon-Huckleberry Wilderness 70
Echo Mountain - Iron Mountain Unit, Old Cascades Wilderness (proposed) 206
Ecola State Park 271
Eightdollar Mountain Botanical Area 118
Elk Lake, Bull-of-the-Woods Wilderness 77

F

Fairview Peak Wilderness (proposed) 156
Fall Creek Corridor 221
Fish Lake (Rogue River NF) 106
Fish Lake (Umpqua NF) 166
Fish Lake (Willamette NF) 210
Fremont Point 32
French Pete Creek, Three Sisters Wilderness 217

G

Gearhart Mountain Wilderness 39
Gold and Silver Falls State Park 278
Gold Lake Bog Engelmann Spruce 229
Gordey Creek 129
Gordon Peak Trail 201
Grande Ronde Canyon Wilderness (proposed) 146
Gwynn Creek 135

H

H.J. Andrews Experimental Forest 215
Hackleman Creek Ancient Forest Grove 208
Hardesty Mountain Wilderness (proposed) 222
Hash Brown Loop Ski Tour 214
Hells Canyon National Recreation Area 172
Herman Creek Ancient Cedar Grove 64
Hobart Bluff Grove, Pacific Crest Trail 252

House Rock Loop 204
Humbug Mountain State Park 279

I

Illinois River Trail 115
Imnaha River 180
Incense-Cedar Grove 164

J

Jackson Creek, Yamsay Mountain Wilderness (proposed) 231
Jefferson Lake Trail, Candle Creek 14
Johnson Creek Trail 110

K

Kentucky Falls 138
King Spruce Trail, Sky Lakes Wilderness 103

L

La Grande Watershed 188
Lake Fork Additions to Hells Canyon Wilderness (proposed) 182
Lake of the Woods 237
Larch Mountain Unit, Multnomah Basin Additions to Columbia Wilderness (proposed) 66
Larison Creek and Larison Rock Trails 223
Lillian Falls, Waldo Wilderness 226
Lobster Creek Botanical Area 112
London Peak 250
Lookout Mountain Wilderness (proposed) 87
Lost Creek Grove 217
Lost Lake (Mount Hood NF) 69
Lost Lake (Willamette NF) 213
Lower Rogue River Trail 113
Luckiamute River 287

M

Magone Lake, Nipple Butte Wilderness (proposed) 51
Malheur River Canyon Wilderness (proposed) 56
Malone Springs and Pelican Butte Additions to Sky Lakes Wilderness (proposed) 235
Marys Peak Watershed 133
McKenzie Pass Ski Tour 16
Memaloose Lake 74
Metolius Breaks Wilderness (proposed) 11
Metolius River Trail 15
Middle Fork Applegate River Trail 92
Middle Fork Willamette River Old Growth Riparian Area 290
Middle Santiam Wilderness and Pyramid Creek 202
Mill Creek Wilderness and Green Mountain 85
Millennium Grove, Gordon Lakes Unit, Old Cascades Wilderness (proposed) 205
Miller Lake 91
Minam River, Eagle Cap Wilderness 176
Mohawk Research Natural Area and McGowen Creek Outdoor Education Area 244
Monument Rock Wilderness 59
Mount Emily Lookout and Wilderness (proposed) 185

Mount Ray - Fuji Mountain Additions to Waldo Wilderness (proposed) 227
Muir Creek 98
Munson Creek Falls County Park 274
Murderers Creek Wilderness (proposed) 53
Myrtle Park Meadows 55
Myrtle-Silvies Wilderness (proposed) 55

N

North Fork Burnt River 192
North Fork Crooked River 89
North Fork Malheur River Wilderness (proposed) 58
North Fork Umatilla Wilderness 147
North Fork Wilderness Study Area 259
North Lake 63
North Umpqua River Trail, Tioga Segment 248
North Umpqua River Trail, Upper Segments 158

O

Ochoco Summit and Bandit Springs Rest Area 86
Onion Creek Trail 117
Opal Creek Additions to Bull-of-the-Woods Wilderness (proposed) 196
Oregon Caves National Monument 265
Oregon's Ancient Redwoods 123
Oregon's Biggest Ponderosa Pine 26
Oswald West State Park (North) 271
Oswald West State Park (South) 273
Oxbow Park, Sandy River Gorge 276

P

Page Mountain Ancient Forest Grove 122
Pamelia Lake Trail, Mount Jefferson Wilderness 199
Pine Bench, Boulder Creek Wilderness 160
Pine Grove Trail 114
Pine Mountain 29
President Taft Grove 161
Pyramids Unit, Old Cascades Wilderness (proposed) 203

R

Red Blanket Creek, Sky Lakes Wilderness 102
Red Buttes Wilderness 93
Redwood Tree Nature Trail 125
Reynolds Creek, Wildcat Backcountry (proposed) 61
Riverside Trail 75
Roaring River Wilderness (proposed) 72
Rock Creek Additions to the Elkhorns Unit, North Fork John Day Wilderness (proposed) . . . 190
Rosary Lakes Trail, Maiden Peak Wilderness (proposed) 21
Rye Spring 105

S

Salmon River Trail 71
Sauvie Island Wildlife Management Area 281
Seven Mile Ridge, Red Mountain Special Interest Area 95

Shale Ridge Trail 225
Silver Falls State Park 277
Soda Mountain Wilderness (proposed) 253
South Fork Desolation Creek 152
South Fork Rogue River Trail 104
South Fork Umatilla River, Hellhole Wilderness (proposed) 148
Spring Creek and Glacier Mountain Wilderness (proposed) 60
Strawberry Mountain Wilderness 54
Sucker Creek, Red Buttes Wilderness 121
Surveyor Campground 256
Sycan River Gorge 234

T

Thomason Meadows, Chesnimnus Creek 174
Tillamook Head 270
Tongue Point 269
Towering Trees Ancient Forest Grove 220
Triangle Lake, Cripple Camp 167
Twin Lakes, Calf Creek Wilderness (proposed) 162

U

Umatilla Ancient Forest Auto Tours, Bridge Creek Wildlife Management Area 150
Union Creek 99
Upper Briggs Creek 116
Upper Cow Creek Trail 169
Upper Deschutes River Floats 23
Upper Deschutes River, Pringle Falls Research Natural Area 25
Upper McKenzie River Trail (North) 210
Upper McKenzie River Trail (South) 212
Upper Rogue River Trail and Scenic Drive 100

V

Valley of the Giants 242
Van Duzer State Park 275

W

Wahtum Lake, Columbia Wilderness 67
Walla Walla Watershed Wilderness (proposed) 143
Warm Springs 224
Wassen Creek Wilderness (proposed) 140
Wassen Lake 246
Wauna Viewpoint Trail 65
White River 79
Whitehorse County Park 291
Willamette Mission State Park 284
William L. Finley National Wildlife Refuge 289
Wolf Creek Falls 249
World's Largest Port-Orford-Cedar 109

Y

Yellow Jacket Glade Loop Trail 163